CULTURE BEYOND COUNTRY

# Culture Beyond Country

*Strategies of Inclusion in the
Global Iranian Diaspora*

Amy Malek

NEW YORK UNIVERSITY PRESS
New York

NEW YORK UNIVERSITY PRESS
New York
www.nyupress.org

© 2025 by New York University
All rights reserved

Please contact the Library of Congress for Cataloging-in-Publication data.
ISBN: 9781479831739 (hardback)
ISBN: 9781479831753 (paperback)
ISBN: 9781479831777 (library ebook)
ISBN: 9781479831760 (consumer ebook)

This book is printed on acid-free paper, and its binding materials are chosen for strength and durability. We strive to use environmentally responsible suppliers and materials to the greatest extent possible in publishing our books.

The manufacturer's authorized representative in the EU for product safety is Mare Nostrum Group B.V., Mauritskade 21D, 1091 GC Amsterdam, The Netherlands.
Email: gpsr@mare-nostrum.co.uk.

Manufactured in the United States of America

10 9 8 7 6 5 4 3 2 1

Also available as an ebook

*For my parents, Iranian and American*

CONTENTS

*List of Figures and Tables*   ix

*A Note on Transliteration*   xi

Introduction   1

1. Departures and Arrivals   35
2. Asserting "Freedom, Dignity, and Wealth" in Los Angeles   89
3. Contesting Cultural Belonging(s) in Stockholm   136
4. Navigating Multiculturalism in Toronto   179
5. Comparing Iranian Diasporic Strategies in Multicultural Societies   228

Conclusion: Belonging, Like Homes, Must Be Built   265

*Acknowledgments*   279

*Notes*   285

*References*   311

*Index*   331

*About the Author*   351

LIST OF FIGURES AND TABLES

Figure I.1 Taking control of representation at the 2007 Persian Parade in New York City.    6
Table I.1 Comparing three contexts.    25
Table 1.1 Immigrants by percentage of population in the United States, Sweden, and Canada, 1971 and 2021.    47
Figure 1.1 Anti-Iran Protest, December 4, 1979, Los Angeles Coliseum.    48
Figure 1.2 Mickey Mouse flipping off Iran on a bumper sticker, c. 1980.    49
Figure 1.3 Iranians Obtaining Lawful Permanent Resident Status in the United States by year, 1971–2021.    51
Figure 1.4 Number of asylum applications from Iranians to Sweden by year, 1984–2023.    61
Figure 1.5 Iranian immigration to Sweden by Grounds for Settlement, 2004–2023.    66
Figure 1.6 Iranian Immigration to Canada by Admission Type and Period of Immigration, 1980–2021.    70
Figure 1.7 Iranian businesses in North York, Toronto.    76
Figure 2.1 Press photo from Washington, DC, stop of the 2013 Cyrus Cylinder tour.    93
Figure 2.2 Bumper sticker advertising the Cyrus Cylinder exhibition at The Getty Villa, Los Angeles.    95
Figure 2.3 Front page of the newspaper of the Imperial Celebrations of Iran, November 21, 1971.    99
Figure 2.4 Larger-than-life Cyrus Cylinder at Los Angeles City Hall, 2015.    102
Figure 2.5 The commodification of the Cyrus Cylinder and Cyrus the Great on- and offline.    103
Figure 2.6 The Freedom Sculpture, Los Angeles.    108

Figure 2.7 Advertising frames a stage decorated by ancient Persian architecture and artifacts at a 2016 Nowruz block party in Los Angeles. 115
Figure 2.8 American symbolisms joined with nostalgic Iranian ones at the 2017 Freedom Festival in Los Angeles. 127
Figure 2.9 2017 Freedom Festival Photo booth slideshow. 128
Figure 2.10 The Freedom Sculpture activated as a site of protest in 2022. 133
Figure 3.1 Fire-jumping at Eldfesten in Stockholm, Sweden, 2012. 138
Figure 3.2 Mana Neyestani, "Banning Chaharshanbeh Suri." 138
Figure 3.3 Advertisement for Eldfesten 2014: free and for everyone. 140
Figure 3.4 Screenshot of Eldfesten 2018 stream via Swedish national television (SVT). 142
Figure 3.5 "Eldfest went up in smoke," *Dagens Nyheter*, March 17, 2009. 164
Figure 4.1 Large crowds at Tirgan 2013 and 2017 at the Harbourfront Centre, Toronto. 188
Figure 4.2 Arash the Archer advertising for Tirgan 2011. 193
Figure 4.3 Photo-ops as nostalgic place-making at Tirgan 2015 and 2017. 196
Figure 4.4 Tirgan Festival posters, 2013 and 2017. 199
Figure 4.5 Volunteers celebrate at Tirgan 2013. 208
Figure C.1 Statue of Cyrus the Great in downtown Atlanta, 2023 and 2024. 266

A NOTE ON TRANSLITERATION

Throughout the text, I have used conventional spellings of Persian words as they appear in English whenever possible. Otherwise, I have employed a transliteration system commonly used in English by lay Persian-speakers with the standardized Tehrani dialect, and removed diacritical marks that would be present in more formal transliteration. For example, for the ease of the reader, I have opted for *Chaharshanbeh Suri* instead of *Chahārshanbeh Sūrī* and *Shahr-e Ghesseh* instead of *Shahr-i Qiṣṣah*.

# Introduction

The opening day of the 2011 Tirgan Festival was the hottest day of the year in Toronto. As the heat index soared to 46°C (114°F) that sweltering July afternoon, the nearly three hundred volunteers I had worked with for the last several months were abuzz with activity, making final preparations for the largest biennial festival of Iranian arts and culture in the world. As the overtaxed HVAC system strained impossibly to keep the invited politicians and VIP guests at the indoor opening reception from sweating through their suits and summer dresses, members of the operations team were hard at work outside. They were hustling to finish setting up key areas of the grounds, like Persianissimo, an outdoor exhibition of contemporary Iranian poster art, and the Tehran Tea House, which would serve hot tea and saffron ice cream to a lucky few among the estimated 130,000 guests who would attend that weekend.

As one of the volunteers for the festival that year, I was tasked with photographing the operations team at work, making note of areas for the team's improvement, especially the hours-long line ups of Iranian families, young newcomers, and non-Iranian Torontonians seeking entry into the free concerts, film screenings, poetry readings, and dance performances that populated the four-day schedule. We tried everything to keep cool that weekend: Several of us rolled up the short sleeves of our Tirgan-issued volunteer T-shirts; others dipped their sandaled feet into a shallow pool at the Lake Ontario–adjacent venue for quick relief. We all took turns dashing inside for water breaks.

After four packed days that had brought out a record-breaking crowd, on the closing evening, as festivalgoers lingered on the water's edge boardwalk, I came upon *Nooshin and *Ashkan, two volunteers who were busy packing a large van with materials that had decorated the tea house.[1] Their sweat-drenched Tirgan-logo T-shirts revealed the long day they'd had. As they transferred boxes filled with garlands, a brass samovar, and tablecloths, Nooshin told me about the intense days and nights they had worked over the last several weeks. She and others on her team had taken off work and missed shifts to prioritize their Tirgan duties, devoting long hours that had been challenging but also exhilarating. Ashkan added that the logistics subcommittee had been giving rides nonstop to invited artists and guests from the airport and to and from hotels; he estimated that they had made seventy such trips in just three days.

That night, as a handful of volunteers worked a closing gala for invited artists and dignitaries at a swanky hotel up the street, their exhausted but exuberant colleagues could be found on the festival grounds occasionally pausing their clean-up duties to take selfies together. Though tired, they shared a collective enthusiasm and sense of satisfaction: The festival had been an undeniable success thanks to their months of hard work. As I took photos of *Fereshteh and her hospitality team packing up the information booth they had spent the better part of four days working, she looked at me with tears welling in her eyes and said, "I can't believe it's almost over. I wish it could last forever."

Tirgan had clearly become a passion project for hundreds of Iranian Canadians, mostly young professionals and graduate students who did not even get to watch much of the performances and lectures they had worked so hard to make possible. By 2023, an estimated three thousand Iranian Canadians had served as Tirgan volunteers. Why had so many Iranian Canadians committed so much of their free time—and even taken time off from their studies and full-time jobs as attorneys, tech professionals, architects, and sales reps—to plan and run a biennial arts and culture festival?

When I put this question to Maria, the festival's artistic director in 2011, she answered by recalling the beginning of her cultural work in the early 2000s, before she had completed her PhD in Theoretical Chemistry at the University of Toronto. She referred specifically to 2003, when Zahra Kazemi, a Canadian Iranian photojournalist, had been killed in an Iranian prison. The news had led to a media maelstrom in Canada. "The papers were full of 'IRAN KILLS JOURNALIST,'" she said. "Iran, Iran, Iran—and it was always continued by something negative. And I wrote this email [to a newsgroup of Iranians in Toronto], and said, 'You know, the name Iran, itself—not necessarily [just] the government—is usually mentioned with something really negative, very ugly. Let's do something cultural. Let's put a face to this name, to this word, Iran. Because people can relate to culture quite easily. Let's just show another face of Iran.'"[2]

In over 125 interviews conducted over the course of sixteen years (2007–23) and in fieldwork among cultural organizers and community members in the Iranian diaspora in three countries, I repeatedly heard that countering negative stereotypes and taking the reins of representation (e.g., "show[ing] another face of Iran") had motivated their participation in cultural organizing. Immigrants from diverse political, ethnic, and professional backgrounds across the diaspora have worked to insert their own cultural representations in mainstream publics not only to evangelize about a homeland, but specifically to correct what they view as misrepresentations that have resulted from and led to the misrecognition of Iranians in their diasporic homes. They especially have sought to reassert the dignity of Iranian identity in the face of over four decades of geopolitical tensions between governments in Iran and the West that have contributed to their personal experiences of stigmatization, prejudice, and discrimination. To fight these exclusions and misrecognitions, diasporic Iranians have purposefully turned to culture as a strategy of inclusion in their multicultural societies.

This book examines how Iranian immigrants in Los Angeles, Stockholm, and Toronto mobilize cultural production—festivals, exhibitions, parades, and public art—to counter exclusion, shape public perceptions, and build new forms of belonging. By tracing how Iranians engage with multicultural policies, media representations, and intracommunity debates over authenticity, I show that culture serves as a critical strategy for negotiating inclusion in diaspora. While often framed as apolitical, these cultural projects are often deeply political in their efforts to reclaim representation, resist misrecognition, and navigate the racial, social, and economic hierarchies of their adopted societies.

Hearing diasporic Iranians express these motivations during fieldwork did not surprise me. I grew up as a second-generation Iranian American[3] in the 1980s US south; my family and I had collected similar experiences and frustrations. And, like many other children of immigrant families who were moving into our suburban Atlanta neighborhood, my father's homeland was nowhere to be found in my public elementary school's textbooks. Iran only entered these halls of learning when classmates repeated their parents' reactions to the nightly news in menacing tones, or when my family was called upon by my teachers to represent it at "multicultural nights" hosted by the school's parent-teacher association. Through performances on the cafeteria stage, in makeshift displays featuring items grabbed from our living room, or in homemade Iranian food served as samples on cafeteria tables, my family and I quickly learned that these forms of multicultural representation were created primarily for consumption by our white American neighbors and classmates. My family had understood this and participated hoping our American friends might remember us and the alluring aroma of my grandma's stuffed eggplants or the intricate designs of the painted ceramics (*minakari*) on our display when they saw the next fearful barrage of negative representations of Iranians on their televisions. Like so many of the diaspora organizers I would later meet, my father and our extended family sought to represent themselves and assert their Iranian culture as an antidote to the pains of migration and experiences of exclusion that had so deeply impacted their lives. Though young, I too was internalizing these messages, and became socialized in an American assimilative atmosphere in which trying to fit in—to be accepted, to belong—meant asserting a mainstream American identity in public settings like my elementary school, momentary exceptional spaces of multicultural celebration aside.

In the same period that Maria and her friends were embarking on cultural organizing in Toronto, Iranians in New York were organizing the first Persian Parade, one of 180 ethnic parades to march down Manhattan's avenues each year, making it a key form of ethnic visibility in a multicultural city.[4] Explaining their motivations for volunteering substantial time and resources for such an endeavor since 2004, Zohreh, a lead organizer of the parade, echoed Maria as she described to me in 2009 the hypervisibility of a view of Iran in the media that had led to feelings of invisibility for Iranians in her community:

> We want to *show* the Iranian community [and] that as a community we are very powerful and really should take pride in our achievement in this country.... And also for our American friends to see us in a different light. *To see us*, that we are a peaceful nation, that we come from a long heritage of civilization.... That we are not the images that they see on

TV. We really are not. And we are their friends. We are their neighbors. We are their doctors, their lawyers, their accountants. . . . And they really, really should look at us in that light. Not the way that the media has portrayed us in the last few years.[5]

While the post-9/11 atmosphere in the United States formed the context of Zohreh's reference to "the last few years," concerns among diasporic Iranians in Europe and North America about the impacts of media (mis)representations on their communities—including how their neighbors see them or misrecognize them—have been well documented since at least the 1980s. The narrow depiction of Iranians as hostage takers, religious extremists, and terrorists in newspapers and on the nightly news in these societies have directly contributed to experiences of discrimination and targeted violence.[6] The most recited example has surely been the melodramatic depiction of one Iranian American family's experience of domestic violence in the 1987 bestselling book and 1991 film *Not Without My Daughter*, which enjoyed decades of TV screenings around the world and even in some US schools long after it left theaters. The film especially contributed to the negative gendered stereotyping of both Iranian men and women that played out in jobs, social settings, divorce settlements, and child custody battles across the diaspora.[7] Later, building on years of geopolitical animosity and negative media depictions, the representation of ancient Persians as savage nonhuman monsters in the 2006 Hollywood blockbuster film *300* brought together Orientalist stereotypes with ahistorical storytelling, triggering an already fed-up diaspora to fight back (fig. I.1). As geopolitics and domestic politics in North America and Europe continued to frame Iranians as eternal enemies well into the 2010s, and as Iranians became the target of toughened sanctions, migration bans, and "extreme vetting," the need for community action became even more pressing.

In addition to chipping away at media stereotypes, in many of our conversations, Iranian diaspora organizers also framed arts and cultural events as an ideal format for building unity and democratic practices in their communities, a step deemed necessary to achieve their political goals both in diaspora and in Iran.[8] Implicit in these conversations—and sometimes made explicit—was a sense that Iranian culture was above politics and therefore the best tool not only

Figure 1.1. Taking control of representation at the 2007 Persian Parade in New York City. A banner (above) condemns the film *300* as racist next to artistic renderings of the Immortal Guard of the Achaemenid Empire, insisting "Hollywood: This is the image of Persians!" A second banner called on Hollywood to "STOP Persian Phobia." Later, a float (below) carried a dozen Iranian American men costumed as the ancient Immortal Guard. (Credit: Amy Malek, 2007)

to demonstrate "another face of Iran" and restore a stolen dignity, but also to build stronger, more unified communities. The deep internal fragmentations of Iranian diaspora communities that created the need for such a strategy have been well documented: Whether in Los Angeles,[9] Texas,[10] London,[11] Stockholm,[12] Dubai,[13] or Malaysia,[14] Iranians living in diaspora represent a diverse population with distinct ethnic, class, linguistic, religious, political, and generational differences that have led to conflicts and a general sentiment that Iranians do not work well together. To these fragmentations add the very different experiences of first-generation Iranians who left Iran in the 1960s and 1970s as students to those of later first-generation cohorts who had lived through revolution and war and ongoing repressions, whether of political opposition groups, ethnic and religious minorities, women, and/or LGBTQ+ identities, all of which have been compounded by the debilitating effects of economic sanctions. The result is a set of communities with overlapping age and cohort effects that have created deep challenges for community-building and teamwork. With these challenges in mind, Mehrdad, a software engineer and cofounder of the Tirgan Festival, had explained to me in 2011 his own turn to cultural organizing: "Cultural work is the only thing that the Iranian people—everyone, without exception—will not argue over."[15]

In the first two decades of the twenty-first century, meeting these dual inward-facing community goals and outward-facing didactic goals not just by *telling* non-Iranians about Iranian culture, but by *showing* them through experiential and sensorial displays at public-oriented sites and events became increasingly common across the global diaspora. Coinciding with a flourishing of multiculturalist discourses and policies in Europe and North America in this period, large annual and biennial Iranian arts and culture festivals especially began to proliferate. Festivals established earlier, like the Mehregan Festival of Autumn in Orange County, California (est. 1994), were joined by new events like the Persian Arts Festival in New York in 2005; the Tirgan Festival in Toronto, Canada, in 2008; the Strass'Iran Festival in Strasbourg, France, in 2009; the Eldfesten festival in Stockholm, Sweden, in 2010; the Edinburgh Iranian Festival in Scotland in 2010; the New Sounds of Iran festival in Hamburg, Germany, in 2013; and many others.

In the late twentieth century, activism in Western societies demanding the recognition and representation of social groups—such as women, racial and ethnic minorities, LGBTQ+ communities, Indigenous groups, and others—sparked theoretical debates surrounding the politics of recognition and politics of representation, including the role of identity in advocating for social and cultural rights vis-à-vis other forms of social injustice such as economic inequalities. These debates centered around questions of power, justice, and inclusion, especially in multicultural societies.[16] Renewed debates in the first decades of the twenty-first century recentered the politics of identity and the approach of identity politics, especially highlighting its limits. Nevertheless, the interdependent nature of representation and recognition is evident: Representation shapes the possibilities for recognition and access to rights, while misrecognition can be compounded my misrepresentation or a lack of representation, leading to greater inequities. For Iranians in the diaspora, being misrecognized by colleagues, neighbors, and government officials as extremists, religious zealots, or terrorists has been both a consequence of and been reinforced by the misrepresentations of Iranians in Western media, politics, and culture, which have often relied upon stereotypes and a lack of positive or self-representations. Building a sense of belonging and social inclusion has required fighting back against misrepresentations while fighting for positive cultural representations, and thus "correcting" what they view as a pervasive misrecognition of their Iranian identity.

Among the many communities in the Iranian diaspora, Iranian Americans have been especially prolific in these didactic approaches of *showing*, due in part to the larger population in the United States and in part to the greater ubiquity of negative representations stemming from the intense antagonism between the governments of Iran and the United States since the 1979 Iranian Revolution and Hostage Crisis (1979–81). But this relative prevalence is also reflective of a long history of public performances of ethnic identity by immigrant groups in the United States. Seeking to counter "Persian Phobia"[17] and to "shape how the world views Persians,"[18] since the early 2000s, Iranians have devoted extensive resources, time, and energy to follow other immigrant groups' lead in displaying their vision of Iranian culture and history in large public spaces before non-Iranian audiences. I have observed these efforts not only in street parades in New York City and downtown Los Angeles but also at permanent multicultural displays like the House of Iran at San Diego's famed Balboa Park Cultural Cottages since 2003 and in the halls of power in American cities, such as Nowruz (new year) celebrations organized each March in the City Halls of Los Angeles since 2005, San Francisco since 2006, and, thanks to the election of second-generation Iranian American officials, Seattle since 2017, Atlanta since 2017, and Orlando since 2019. Promotion of the Seattle City Hall Nowruz event in 2017 beckoned its audience: "Bring the whole family, learn new fun facts, expand your horizon, bust some myths and walk away with a better understanding of 300 million more people!"[19]

Taking control of representation can of course take any number of forms, including filing legal claims against irresponsible journalism, creating organizations to increase civic representation and political participation, funding artists and cultural workers to produce their own media, and encouraging Iranians to be included in writers' rooms, newsrooms, and boardrooms. While these efforts also have been underway, for many in communities in the global Iranian diaspora, the more accessible and frequently attempted method has been to organize their own representations through public performances of Iranian art and culture.

Taken together, the growing global proliferation of festivals, parades, galas, exhibitions, public art, and street celebrations in the Iranian diaspora is a widespread phenomenon of strategically countering experiences of *exclusion* by turning to public performances of art and culture as arguments for *inclusion*. These cultural approaches of what I collectively term *strategies of inclusion* mark frustrated but determined responses to events both "here" in diaspora and "there" in Iran that have led, in part, to the stigmatization of Iranians in popular media and everyday life in their diasporic homes.

Through a comparative transnational ethnography of Iranian cultural citizenship in Los Angeles, Stockholm, and Toronto, in this book, I examine how processes of representing Iranian culture in the diaspora generates not only competing views on what it means to be Iranian, but also competing modes of belonging that variously subvert and reinforce existing power relations across local, national, and transnational scales. That Iranians increasingly have sought to represent themselves in their various diasporic homes is clear; *how* they have done so reveals that variations in lived experiences, state structures, and social contexts have direct impacts not only on strategies of inclusion within nation-states, but across them—on diasporic identity itself. Even when they draw on similar repertoires of histories, cultural forms, and traditions (though they do not always do so), the processes that Iranians have undertaken in different locations demonstrates important strategic decisions related to the governments (national, state/provincial, and municipal), civil society institutions, and social and cultural relations through which they must negotiate diasporic belonging.

## Belonging, Inclusion, and Cultural Citizenship

Belonging—feeling that you are a part—is both an individual affective state and a social designation of being recognized by others through inclusion. Creating an "us" distinguishable from "them" allows groups to create feelings of shared identity upon which to build a coconstructed solidarity.[20] For immigrants, these inclusions and exclusions are rarely made uniformly, nor do they necessarily align with legal citizenship. They also do not singularly constitute an individual's feelings of emotional attachment to their social surroundings, though both may strongly impact it. Inclusions and exclusions are subject to fluctuating power dynamics, such that notions like national identity, diasporic identity, and other forms of belonging become, in the words of Nira Yuval-Davis, simply "a naturalized construction of a particular hegemonic form of power relations."[21]

Numerous forms of power, including those influencing political, legal, economic, cultural, and social conditions, shape processes of belonging among immigrants.[22] That diasporic Iranians have sought to put forward cultural arguments for belonging attests to the role of culture in processes of everyday forms of recognition and misrecognition, inclusion and exclusion. Meanwhile, at a state level, cultural policies in systems developed by governments for "managing diversity" aim to bring about these feelings of belonging and inclusion through what is variously termed assimilation, integration, and incorporation.[23] In countries where philosophies of multiculturalism have been used to formulate policy, tools such as instrumental support and symbolic messages from institutions of power like government programs, schools, and media have been used to encourage both immigrants and, importantly, nonimmigrants to incorporate diverse cultural practices and ethnic identities into mainstream public life.[24]

The presence or absence of these instrumental policies can have deep impacts on immigrant belonging and inclusion.[25] But they cannot alone guarantee either, and immigrants do not necessarily experience these processes in similar ways, to similar degrees, or with similar outcomes as one another, especially given intersecting differences in class, religion, gender, and racial, ethnic, and (multi)national identities. Both of these points were made especially evident during my fieldwork in Stockholm. Unlike their family and friends in the United States, Iranians who arrived in Sweden had been the beneficiaries of migration and multiculturalism policies that encouraged the maintenance of Iranian cultural and linguistic practices and offered significant instrumental support toward fostering belonging, such as free Swedish-language instruction (and as refugees or asylum seekers, housing and income support while in classes) but also access to Persian-language public media like radio programs, budgets to facilitate cultural associations, and state-funded afterschool language classes that educated Iranian youth in their parents' "mother tongue" (i.e., *modersmålsundervisning*). Yet in interviews, I repeatedly heard recollections of experiences of prejudice and exclusions, from Iranians who had been assailed with racial slurs that have commonly been used against immigrants in Sweden (literally "black skulls," referring to dark hair color) to more group-level exclusions, like the housing policies that had kept them and other immigrants segregated to the outer suburbs, the targeted surveillance they experienced through securitization measures, or the closed occupational networks and educational pathways that had led to a relative absence of immigrants in cultural institutions like the national theater, the media, and the arts until the 2000s.

Among those in Stockholm sharing this perspective, I came to know *Gelareh, whose family arrived in Sweden in 1986 when she was just six years old. Her experience confirmed that multiculturalism policies alone cannot guarantee inclusion or belonging, but that a threatened future without them was also worth fighting against. Gelareh was educated entirely in Sweden, where she had learned a perfect standard Swedish accent and how to navigate Swedish social institutions and interactions. Yet in seeking to establish herself as an artist, she had experienced exclusionary racialization in all sectors of Swedish society, and especially in ways that required her to fight to make spaces for herself and other immigrants among Stockholm's notoriously homogenous cultural elite. She described these experiences as not only having negatively impacted her and her generation but, significantly, having done so in different ways than her first-generation parents and their peers had experienced. Where her parents at least had a strong Iranian identity and sense of belonging as Iranians—an emotional attachment to which they could cling in the face of exclusions in Sweden—her generation, she argued, found themselves no longer feeling nor being seen as primarily or exclusively Iranian and, despite their fluency and their engagement with Swedish culture and society, also barred from being included and *seen* as Swedish.

When multicultural societies condition full inclusion along parameters of social constructions of race and class (including through individual markers like visible appearance, language or accent, and comportment), it is unsurprising that immigrant communities develop responses focused on representations of their identity, asserting what it means to be—or even that one *can* be—Iranian *and* Swedish, American, or Canadian. These anxieties motivated many of my interlocutors to strategically use Iranian culture as a means to resist exclusion, build more united communities, and navigate exclusive societies undergoing multicultural change.

In Sweden, perhaps the most prominent example of the mobilization of Iranian cultural strategies has been Eldfesten, an annual public festival celebrating Chaharshanbeh Suri in the center of Stockholm and a number of other Swedish cities since 2010. Eldfesten not only draws tens of thousands of spectators in often below-freezing temperatures to an outdoor festival in March, it has also been broadcast on national Swedish TV and radio and livestreamed via Persian-language satellite and digital media platforms, reaching thousands and potentially millions of additional viewers. In 2014, during these national and international broadcasts and in news segments on digital platforms, Mansour, the Iranian producer of Eldfesten, was interviewed about his goals for the festival. An employee of the national touring theater of Sweden (Riksteatern), which had fully funded the 2014 festival, Mansour was explicit about wanting this large event to not only offer a space for Iranians to celebrate and have Iranian cultural traditions publicly celebrated by Swedes but also for it to become so common in Sweden as to become counted as a *Swedish* national holiday: the ultimate recognition of national inclusion.[26] Just three years later, in 2017, the CEO of Riksteatern declared it as such when he announced from the festival stage: "[Eldfesten] is nowadays a Swedish tradition."[27]

*Becoming Cultural Citizens*

I examine these kinds of cultural strategies of inclusion as part of larger debates surrounding immigrant integration, cultural difference, and belonging, all key elements of *cultural citizenship*. Defined as the ability for minoritized groups to belong as full members of society without having to diminish their ethnic or cultural practices and identities,[28] cultural citizenship is a process that involves "self-making" by immigrants—for example by advocating for their right to representation through public cultural displays (e.g., Eldfesten)—but also their "being made" as citizen subjects within and through hegemonic power structures (e.g., the Swedish state) and their institutional intermediaries (e.g., Riksteatern).[29]

To avoid exclusion and, better, be accepted as full members of their societies, first-generation Iranians have attempted both individual and collective strategies. Like many immigrants in North American and European societies, Iranians have changed their names, dyed their hair, removed body hair, undergone cosmetic surgeries like rhinoplasty, and chosen to identify themselves through "safe" regional or ethnic markers like "Mediterranean" or "Persian" rather than stigmatized and racialized national markers like "Iranian."[30] Changing one's physical appearance to "appear white," known as *passing*, or downplaying markers of difference like choosing ethnic markers that conjure images of Persian cats or rugs rather than extremism and terrorists, known as *covering*, are among the strategies immigrants have used in an effort to be recognized as full citizens and to feel included.[31] But these strategies can only go so far: Where passing and covering could prevent everyday exclusions for clean-shaven Jim, like avoiding profiling and unwarranted scrutiny by law enforcement or getting him past the résumé stage of a job search, he will nevertheless be seen and heard as accented-English speaking Jamshid in a job interview.[32] Covering with the ethnic marker "Persian" could help Shirin smoothly navigate everyday interactions like being asked by a neighbor about her background, but her Iranian citizenship nevertheless could be a limiting factor when opening a bank account or in attempts to secure a visa—leading to other possible exclusions.[33]

These strategies, as personal choices, are not without controversy or criticism from within the community, nor do they have consistent effects, especially across the diaspora.[34] The national category of Iranians includes members of dozens of ethnicities and a variety of visible appearances, many of whom, like Black or Afro-Iranians, might only selectively attempt some of these strategies, if at all. Moreover, whatever advantages covering practices may have offered some Iranians seeking to prevent everyday exclusion in the United States, these measures were never an option for Gelareh and her family in Sweden. Swedish national identity has been so rooted in ethnic and racial exclusion that, at best, people with dark hair are identified by default as non-Swedes; at worst, they are targeted with slurs and violence.[35] As a 1.5-generation immigrant,[36] Gelareh's Swedish passport, education, and linguistic fluency were no match for her dark hair and visible appearance that already marked her social location as outside of accepted Swedishness.

Being denied belonging in these ways was also a denial of cultural citizenship.[37] The persistence of exclusion based on racial ascriptions and ethnic classifications, despite individual and collective efforts, like those of Gelareh or Mansour, by immigrants to assert full membership through unfettered cultural and social expression, confirms that processes of cultural citizenship must be considered as ongoing and dialectically determined by state institutional power and its subjects.[38]

Drawing on Michel Foucault's notion of subjectification (described by Aihwa Ong as "self-making and being-made by power relations that produce consent through schemes of surveillance, discipline, control, and administration"), the concept of cultural citizenship acknowledges the impact of these everyday cultural processes, practices, and beliefs that constitute the bases for negotiations of belonging that occurs between subjects, states, and, critically, civil institutions and social groups who, as Ong shows, also become "disciplinary forces in the making of cultural citizens."[39] In settings like state agencies, nonprofit organizations, and neighborhood councils, civil society institutions instill normative behaviors and identities as cultural processes of subjectification.

Here, notions of "civilized conduct," for example as professionalism or social etiquette, intersect with class, race, and gender as criteria of belonging within a given nation. These cultural processes of determining full citizenship (as belonging) depends on "how one is constituted as a subject who exercises or submits to power relations."[40]

In the twenty-first century, these power relations in Western societies are increasingly influenced by neoliberal principles and reforms. As Wendy Brown and others have shown, the rise of neoliberalism has brought about state disinvestment in the public and withdrawal from society more generally.[41] Neoliberal reasoning renders all aspects of life, including culture, in economic terms and places value primarily in individualism, freedom, and self-regulation. Neoliberal subject formation therefore requires that immigrant subjects vying for inclusion fill the voids left by absent or defunded government programs by acting as "entrepreneurs of themselves."[42] Revising Adam Smith's concept, Brown describes "today's *homo economicus*" as "an intensely constructed and governed bit of human capital tasked with improving and leveraging its competitive positioning and with enhancing its (monetary and non-monetary) portfolio value across all of its endeavors and venues."[43] As a hegemonic ideology of states, then, neoliberalism also sets "the normative standards of good citizenship in practice" where deservingness is ascribed to those deemed capable of "pulling themselves up by their bootstraps," Horatio Alger–style, rather than those who draw upon the state for their welfare. As a result, hegemonic understandings of belonging and nonbelonging, often coded as *deserving* and *undeserving*, frame immigrants and minorities in "implicit terms of productivity and consumption."[44]

Everyday practices like struggles over representation are part of the "ideological work of citizen-making" in the United States and in Western democracies more generally.[45] The growth of neoliberal ideologies globally in the intervening decades has led to the development of similar understandings of a one-to-one relationship between class status and "good" citizenship (as opposed to "bad" immigrants who burden the state), even in welfare states like Sweden, dwindling though that welfare structure may be.[46] Gaining success in the form of class status, according to Ong, also has a racializing effect: "Because human capital, self-discipline, and consumer power are associated with whiteness, these attributes are important criteria of nonwhite citizenship in Western democracies."[47] States not only regulate political, economic, and legal identities, they also normalize certain cultural and social identities. Inequalities in society, then, are rendered not only along economic or class lines, but also along intersecting cultural lines, where *culture* can gloss categories like race, ethnicity, religion, gender, sexuality, and (dis)ability.

A cultural citizenship framework allows us to see the impacts of these global shifts on immigrant belonging while attending to intersections of race and class.[48] As a measure of inclusion, cultural citizenship involves "the right to symbolic presence and visibility (vs. marginalization); the right to dignifying representation (vs. stigmatization); and the right to propagation of identity and maintenance (vs. assimilation)."[49] This is the aim of much of the arts and culture organizing that has proliferated in the Iranian diaspora.

In community-produced public demonstrations of Iranian culture like festivals, exhibitions, and public art, the relationship between increasing neoliberal disinvestment in multiculturalism and the resulting strategies employed by immigrants are revealed in at least two lines of negotiation over access to resources that are evident throughout the book: (1) competition with and across immigrant groups for resources and symbolic inclusion from the state and institutions of power and (2) contestations among community members over who receives these resources and recognition, and thus holds the rights to cultural ownership, representation, and, ultimately, Iranian diasporic identity. Across both, Iranians are navigating webs of power within social structures through developing and mobilizing assets that facilitate access to social mobility and inclusion. These extend beyond financial assets to include networks and relationships as forms of *social capital*, education and language proficiency as forms of *cultural capital*, and prestige and recognition as forms of *symbolic capital*.[50] The strategic investment in and use of these forms of capital form important tools for immigrant groups navigating social inclusion.

## Who Are "We"?: Identity and Belonging in Multicultural Societies

Because they seek to combat exclusions on economic, political, social, and cultural levels, strategies of inclusion used by immigrant communities must address each of these, and therefore are varied and multiple. In this book, I focus attention on cultural events and representations that highlight how the cultural is always intertwined with the economic, political, and social. While using cultural strategies of "representing ourselves" that seek to correct misrecognitions by showing "who we really are," *how* and *what* Iranians choose to represent as Iranian culture, identity, and values also demonstrates the interplay between economic, political, and social lines of inclusion.

Since the late twentieth century, when states have attempted to create possibilities for inclusion by correcting histories of exclusion, many have done so through policies of official multiculturalism. *Multiculturalism* has come to be a polysemic term meaning different things to different people in different times and places. It simultaneously refers to a demographic reality of multiple cultural, religious, ethnic, and national groups living in the same polity; a philosophy that puts forth principles of equality and the protection of cultural diversity in pluralistic societies; and a set of policies and discourses for governments and institutions to realize principles of equality in conditions of demographic diversity.[51] The breadth of usages for the term is so wide that Stuart Hall had already decried it in 2001 as "a maddeningly spongy and imprecise discursive field: a train of false trails and misleading universals."[52]

Common to most official multiculturalisms (e.g., as a set of policies) is an understanding that in pluralistic nation-states home to Indigenous groups, national minorities, and/or immigrants and their descendants, liberal emphasis on individualism can actually prevent equality and increase inequality. Assuming differences between individuals have no impact on their belonging as full members of society denies minoritized communities' full citizenship.[53] Addressing this inequality, some multiculturalism policies have sought to ensure rights and enable full participation for immigrants and minoritized groups without having to fully forgo aspects of their identities in favor of a majority language, culture, or practice. In other words, these policies seek to ensure cultural citizenship.

Whether multicultural policies have been successful in doing so or not has been the subject of intense debates in the last several decades. Though there are critics on all sides, the loudest voices of late have been among right-wing political parties across Europe and North America. Whether based on gender, sexual, racial, ethnic, or national characteristics, the question of "who we are" as a nation has ignited a renewed set of culture wars, especially promoted among the far-right, whose rise in the late 2010s and early 2020s across Europe and the United States has heavily relied on anti-immigrant and xenophobic rhetoric. Indeed, many countries find themselves—still and again—in heated struggles over unity and difference that pivots on the identities of their citizen subjects. In the face of demographic changes that have produced increasingly multicultural societies, far-right politicians have asserted conspiracy fantasies like replacement theory while asserting white nativist identities through slogans like Donald Trump's "America First," the Sweden Democrats' "Keep Sweden Swedish" (*Bevara Sverige Svenskt*), Alternative for Germany's "Germany. But Normal" (*Deutschland. Aber normal*), and the League's "Italy First" (*Prima l'Italia*).[54] Diversity, and especially immigrant-driven diversity, has been a mainstay in these heated debates across liberal democracies where the rhetoric of the multiculturalism debates of previous decades has returned to public discourse through fiery populist screeds against immigrants accused of being unwilling or unable to integrate or assimilate, thereby eroding "social cohesion" by living "parallel lives" in isolation.[55]

While some scholars insist that official multiculturalism is needed to address the persistent disadvantages that can be masked in the notion of universal citizenship and formal equality, others have argued that multiculturalism policies can result in a strong overemphasis on representation among immigrant groups facing multiple forms of oppression.[56] In what has been criticized as "shallow multiculturalism," pressures to conform to particular norms and logics can produce easy-to-swallow, essentializing cultural performances for majority audiences to consume without actually addressing inequalities.[57] In efforts to show "who we really are," immigrants respond to the affordances and limitations of the societies in which they live. Multiculturalism, in these cases, risks becoming another mode of assimilation disguised as difference.[58]

## "We Are Iranian:" Iranian Identity, Representation, and Recognition in Diaspora

At the heart of so much of the literature on Iranian and Western encounters is a question of identity formation: Through whose representations, eyes, and power dynamics have we come to recognize ourselves? In her

2001 excavation of Persian identity, *Missing Persians*, Nasrin Rahimieh described how identity is a coconstruction that relies on recognition: "The fictions of identity I and other Persians have created for ourselves may not have always replicated a spirit of mutual understanding and syncretism, but, in all their complex and varied manifestations, they tell us much about our ways of seeing and comprehending ourselves vis-a-vis others."[59] Fictions of identity rely on the repetition of narratives, stories, myths, and symbols that both create and reflect meaning, telling us who we are, again and again. As Clifford Geertz famously put it, this assemblage of "stories they tell themselves about themselves" constitutes culture.[60] What are the narratives that Iranians tell themselves—and others—about themselves? What constitutes Iranian culture? And what does it mean to be Iranian beyond the borders of Iran?

Belonging in diaspora involves emotional attachments to the country of origin as much as to the new country of residence and to those who share the name "Iranian," wherever they may reside. Cultural representation in Iranian communities in diaspora have relied on interpretations of Iranian national identity rooted in twentieth-century Iranian nationalism. Nationalism and its bearing on Iranian cultural identity has been the source of much historical and social scientific analysis about Iran in English since at least the 1990s,[61] yet more rarely has it been examined through its cultural uses and abuses in diasporic contexts.[62] When multiculturalist policies and social imperatives impel immigrant communities to mine their historical, linguistic, and cultural repertoires for representational material adequate for narrowly defined goals of mainstream inclusion, nationalist depictions often result in problematic representations ripe for internal contestation. When multiculturalist policies and the societies they influence instead encourage engagement with contemporary forms, experimentation, admixture, and innovation, the impulse to draw on ready-made nationalist tropes may be diminished, but these innovations can similarly result in contestations, this time over who owns and has the right to experiment with a national culture and identity. Often at issue are questions of authenticity, such that asserting "who we really are" becomes framed as a question of what constitutes authentic "Iranianness."

As various scholars have detailed, Iranian identity has been formed over many centuries by pre-Islamic, Islamic, and European influences.[63]

However, while each of these are discernable, political and intellectual movements in multiple periods have attempted to shape Iranian identity based on the marginalization of one or two of these three confluent influences. For example, while twentieth-century nationalist discourses promoted by Iran's Pahlavi monarchy (1925–79) had emphasized pre-Islamic Persian and European influences while seeking to marginalize Islamic ones, the early leaders of the Islamic Republic of Iran (1979–) responded by emphasizing the reverse and diminishing the pre-Islamic past. In examining these competing claims to Iranian culture and identity at the level of diaspora, and across transnational landscapes with different migration patterns, cultural policies, and social contexts, I show how contestations over Iranian identity reach well beyond nation-state borders and reveal fractures in what it means to be "of" or "from" a homeland.

To better understand these efforts, I take festivals, exhibitions, and public art as starting points for an analysis that examines Iranian diasporic cultural citizenship. The contests and negotiations described in this book are, at one level, about how Iranians seek to engage with fellow Iranians and, as Rahimieh emphasized, ultimately, how they come to recognize themselves vis-à-vis others. Furthermore, how Iranian immigrants seek to be seen by their Swedish, American, or Canadian colleagues, neighbors, or elected representatives is also a reflection of how Americans, Swedes, and Canadians wish to see themselves. A common concern about belonging across immigrant groups and across Iranian communities in diaspora involves questions of cultural ownership (*To whom does Iranian culture belong?*), control over the representation (e.g., of Iran and Iranianness), and whether those representations challenge or reinforce hegemonic structures, norms, and ideologies.[64] The answer to these questions centers on who has power and access to power in a global diaspora.

In debates about belonging and inclusion, one question is often repeated: "Inclusion into what"? While there is not one satisfying short answer (*Society? The mainstream? Positions of power? Elite status?*), the question itself reveals the multiple and layered strategies that diasporic communities undertake. Into what are immigrants seeking inclusion, and how does the specificity of that answer in different locations then impact how they navigate—or innovate—pathways to achieve it? Because

Iranian diasporic communities are not homogenous, the answer to this question in any given location is also likely to vary and be contested. A comparative view of these contestations provides a window into the ways belonging, like identity, is negotiated, rather than given or taken, and can either reproduce hegemonic structures of power and social relations or resist them.

## Three Cities in the Global Iranian Diaspora

Diasporas are transnationally networked communities of immigrants and their descendants who share a common homeland, real or imagined, and who maintain social relations here, there, and elsewhere.[65] As multiple scholars have argued, diaspora is not simply a description, but also a practice: "a way of being in the world and a way in which the world comes to be."[66]

Although focused on a networked global diaspora of five to eight million people, in this comparative ethnography I focus on three cities where Iranian populations have grown following late twentieth- and early twenty-first-century migrations from Iran to North America and Europe. Los Angeles, Stockholm, and Toronto and the states they lie within each experienced different periods of peak Iranian migration, due not only to political, economic, and social changes in Iran, but also to varying migration policies and state approaches to immigrants in the rest of the world, including the development or absence of official multiculturalism. These cities are therefore well-suited for tracing the impacts of different approaches to immigrant integration and specifically the differing variables that have contributed to variations in Iranian cultural representation and diasporic identity.

While collectively home to well over a million Iranians, these cities should not be taken as exemplary of the experiences of all Iranians in diaspora, whether in the same country or in other large cities like Paris, London, Hamburg, Sydney, or Tokyo.[67] As Iranian diaspora studies grows as a field that endeavors to study the global Iranian diaspora expansively and comparatively,[68] I seek to emphasize the impacts of local social norms, policies, and histories on immigrant belonging, and the continued importance of recognizing scales of power and place in diasporic lives, communities, and identities.

The departures and arrivals of Iranians over the course of more than four decades has overlapped with global shifts in attitudes and policies surrounding immigration, refugees and asylum, integration, and multiculturalism. As liberal democracies in the late twentieth century reacted to changing global norms surrounding human and civil rights in the postwar period, policy changes removing cultural and ethnic discrimination in immigration policies resulted in the development of more demographically multicultural societies. When the impacts of the 1979 Revolution and Iran-Iraq War (1980–88) led Iranians to depart in great numbers, new immigration laws and the growing international refugee regime had an enormous impact on their (im)mobility, including how, when, and where they arrived, how they would be treated, and what rights they would be afforded, including what their educational, employment, and community prospects would be in their new homes.

The diasporic Iranian communities of Los Angeles, Stockholm, and Toronto represent successive, if overlapping, periods of heightened Iranian migration, each with multiple and overlapping cohorts of immigrants with similar motivations for emigration, experiences of Iran, and socioeconomic characteristics. The United States had already become a choice destination for Iranian university students in the 1960s–1970s; by 1975, they had grown to be the largest foreign student population in the country's colleges and universities. In the politically turbulent years surrounding the 1979 Revolution, the United States also became a key site of refuge for Pahlavi elites, ethnic and religious minorities such as Jews and Baha'is, and students whose plans were interrupted by political turmoil—all while the Hostage Crisis led to targeted animus against Iranians in the United States. After 1986, changes to US immigration law and refugee priorities made it more difficult for Iranians to initiate immigration but opened greater possibilities for family reunification with refugees and immigrants who had already arrived. This led to a rapid growth and diversification of the Iranian American population, as older parents, siblings, and spouses joined loved ones in the United States. An early active enclave in Los Angeles (later known as "Tehrangeles" or "Irangeles") and Southern California would soon become the largest community of Iranians in the world outside of Iran, followed by large concentrations in the San Francisco Bay Area and the Washington, DC, Maryland, and Northern Virginia (DMV) area.

As the Iran-Iraq War presented opportunities for the Islamic Republic to consolidate its power through increased repression, Iranians experiencing or fearing persecution by the new state fled to neighboring Pakistan and Türkiye seeking refugee protections, for example through the United Nations and third-country resettlement programs. They did so just as Sweden's migration priorities were shifting from labor recruitment to humanitarian protection, leading a sizeable Iranian refugee population to be resettled across Sweden, eventually congregating in the immigrant suburbs of Stockholm, Gothenburg, and Malmö. These communities include former and current political activists, cultural workers, and other educated middle-class Iranians who arrived with cultural capital but little else to a country that was still in the early years of its experiment with multicultural policymaking. In the midst of sharp demographic shifts that social programs struggled to accommodate, many Iranians seeking to continue their professional lives in Sweden faced challenges learning Swedish, finding housing, and gaining employment matching their educations, due in part to discrimination.

By the end of the war, Sweden's refugee resettlement priorities had shifted to other parts of the world. Meanwhile, Iran experienced both economic stagnation and high unemployment in the 1990s, especially in scientific fields; Iranians seeking postgraduate education and employment opportunities found a pathway for both in Canada. Making use of the country's recently increased student permits, its points system that favored skilled migration, and investor categories that offered eventual permanent residency, a mix of students, highly educated job seekers, investors, refugees, and family members of all these would create large and vibrant communities in Canadian cities, especially Toronto (nicknamed "Tehranto"), Vancouver, and Montréal. Because Canada had not only been an innovator of official multiculturalism but had committed to it as a cornerstone of Canadian national identity, policies supporting immigrants and their integration benefitted these Iranian newcomers.

The repression of the Green Movement in Iran in 2009–10[69] and difficult economic conditions in the 2010s—significantly worsened by the return of broad economic sanctions following the 2018 US withdrawal from the 2015 "nuclear deal"[70]—led to continued migration from Iran to each of these three diasporic cities and beyond. Despite increased securitization measures like the US Muslim Ban (which targeted the mobility of citizens of seven Muslim-majority countries, including Iran), Iranian students, refugees, and economic migrants have continued to arrive to the United States, as well as to Canada and Sweden, into the 2020s. Like the flows of immigrants and refugees before them, these ongoing departures and arrivals require Iranians to work creatively to navigate the migration pathways and laws available—and unavailable—to them, often relying heavily on social and cultural capital.[71]

Attention to emigration flows and the political and social environments to which Iranians arrived in North America and Europe offers important context for understanding the ways Iranian immigrants have negotiated identity and belonging and developed strategies for inclusion.[72] Iranians in all three countries have been active in economic, political, and cultural arenas, if to varying degrees and with varying levels of support from the state. Comparison of these contexts, summarized in table I.1, demonstrates not only similarities and differences in terms of migration histories, multicultural policies, and social expectations and attitudes toward immigrants, but also how the intersections of race, religion, and class impacted strategies of inclusion and opportunities for participation in American, Swedish, and Canadian societies. The comparisons in this book demonstrate the ways that diasporic identity, citizenship, and belonging are configured dialectically between states, intermediaries, and subjects in a global diaspora.

## Methodology

This book offers an up-close comparative ethnography of immigrant and diasporic cultural citizenship through the lens of cultural production. Comparative ethnographies propose a greater focus on analyses across and between sites than traditional ethnographic attention on one fieldsite. In his influential survey of the emergence of multisited ethnography in 1995, George Marcus noted that as globalization enables greater interconnectivity and mobility, and as humans migrate across greater distances more frequently and rapidly than ever before, so too shall ethnographers be required to innovate methods with greater mobility, and beyond the single fieldsite model of research.[73] However, as Ghassan Hage and others have suggested, studies of diasporas that in part motivated Marcus's observation also trouble this approach: For

TABLE 1.1. Comparing three contexts.

| | United States | Sweden | Canada |
|---|---|---|---|
| Migration policy histories | Restrictive immigration based on race and/or country of origin until 1965; Refugee Act (1980) defined refugee policy; IRCA (1986) created pathways for lawful permanent residency & family reunification | Emigration country through nineteenth century; postwar focus on labor migration from S. Europe shifted in 1970s toward global refugee & humanitarian priorities; Aliens Act (1980) established asylum policy | Restrictive immigration based on race and/or country of origin until 1962; 1967 regulation established points system to prioritize "skilled" labor; Immigration Act (1976) defined refugee policy |
| Sources of demographic multiculturalism | Indigenous groups; descendants of European settler colonialism; descendants of forced migration of enslaved peoples; immigration flows, which diversified post-1965 | Indigenous and national minorities; immigration flows, diversified from 1970s policy shift to humanitarian migration priorities | Indigenous groups; descendants of European settler colonialism; descendants of forced migration of enslaved peoples; immigration flows, which diversified post-1967 |
| Integration policies, expectations, and attitudes | No official multiculturalism as federal policy; unofficial neoliberal multiculturalism; "laissez-faire" with regard to integration; social expectation of immigrants to assimilate | Official multiculturalism established in 1975 with focus on freedom of choice; policy shift to interculturalism in 2010; policies and budgets that support immigrant integration facing cuts | Official multiculturalism introduced in 1971, formalized in Canadian Multiculturalism Act (1988), and remains a cornerstone of Canadian national identity; policies and budgets support immigrant integration |
| Role of race in society vis-à-vis immigrants | Race considered a "master status" along a Black-white continuum; nonwhite ascription of immigrants and their descendants aligns with white supremacist prejudice and discrimination* | Anti-racism seen as baked into Swedish national identity; "race" scrubbed from all legislation in 2014, yet racial scandals, segregation, and discrimination persists; nonwhite ascription overlaps with immigrant background† | Nonwhite citizens counted as "visible minorities" in government data until 2021; shift to "racialized groups" acknowledges persistence of systemic racial discrimination, including barriers to immigrant integration |
| Percentage foreign born population in 2021 | 13.6%‡ | 20%§ | 23%¶ |
| Year: Iranian population according to official estimates (% of total pop.) | 2021: 504,927 (0.11%)** | 2020: 121,019 (1.1%) †† | 2021: 200,465 (2.2%) ‡‡ |

TABLE I.1. (cont.)

|  | United States | Sweden | Canada |
|---|---|---|---|
| Key periods and trends of Iranian migration | Primarily students prior to 1979; joined by refugees & family reunification post-Revolution; choice destination for onward migrations; high heterogeneity in terms of age, ethnicity, religion, and class | Mid- and late-1980s political refugees, largely from educated urban classes resettled through UN, with little financial capital but high cultural capital; joined by large flows of students and economic immigrants, especially post-2009 and again in 2015–16 | A top destination from 1990s to present for economic immigrants, students, and refugees; high cultural capital and diverse mix of class positions, including extremely wealthy "nouveau riche", middle, and working classes |
| Common Iranian racialization experiences | Racial paradox: many self-identify as white *de facto*, but are nonwhite *de jure*; covering as a common strategy in 1980s and post-9/11 in response to exclusion§§ | Racialized as nonwhite, and thus presumed non-Swede; covering seen as ineffective; inclusion limited by ascription | Racialized as non-white in everyday encounters; counted as "racialized population" in government statistics |
| Common strategies of inclusion among Iranian cultural organizations | Contributionism, emphasizing education and class status, and narratives of shared values like freedom and diversity through invocations of imperial nostalgia | Creating state-supported cultural associations, radios, and events; activism and arguments for shared values and expansion of Swedish national symbols and identity, though contested within the community | State-community partnerships, federal- and provincial-grant-supported cultural events; emphasis on community-building through arts-and-culture organizing and alignment with Canadian multiculturalism |

\* Bloemraad 2006.
† Hübinette 2023.
‡ US Census Bureau, 2021, *Place of Birth by Nativity and Citizenship Status*, 2021 American Community Survey 1-year estimates, table B05002.
§ Statistics Sweden, 2022, *Foreign Born by County, Municipality, Sex and Country of Birth December 31 2021*, table be0101 (Stockholm: Statistikmyndigheten SCB), https://www.scb.se/.
¶ Statistics Canada, 2022, "Immigrants Make Up Largest Share of Canada's Population in Over 150 Years," *The Daily*, October 26, 2022. https://www150.statcan.gc.ca/.
\*\* Estimate of population coded by Ancestry as "Iranian." US Census Bureau, 2021, *Selected Population Profile in the United States: Iranian*, 2021 American Community Survey 1-Year Estimates, Table S0201, https://data.census.gov.
†† Count of individuals born in Iran or born in Sweden to one or more parent born in Iran. Statistics Sweden, 2020, *Foreign-Born and Persons Born in Sweden with One or Two Foreign-Born Parents by Country of Birth/Country of Origin 31 December 2019, total*, Table be0101 (Stockholm: Statistikmyndigheten SCB), https://www.scb.se/.
‡‡ Estimate of population coded by "Ethnic or cultural origin" as "Iranian." Statistics Canada, 2023, "Census Profile, 2021 Census of Population," Statistics Canada Catalogue no. 98–316-X2021001. Released November 15, 2023. https://www.statcan.gc.ca/.
§§ Maghbouleh 2017; Tehranian 2009.

Hage, a global diaspora is a milieu, a single "site" through which we might trace networks and attachments that cross national borders and other geographies. Doing so as an individual researcher, he noted, is a tall order.[74]

Rather than distinguishing a slate of separate variables across sites for comparison, I draw together participant observation, interviews, and ethnographic description from long-term fieldwork conducted in three countries, presenting each one holistically in extended case study chapters before considering them relationally in the final chapter.[75] Tracing the networks and flows of Iranian immigrants led me to three key cities in the Iranian diaspora—Los Angeles, Stockholm, and Toronto. While the common "variable" across these cities was the presence of sizeable Iranian communities, they each varied in their state's approaches to immigration, the role of immigrants in national founding mythologies, the racial hierarchies and norms in each society, the geopolitical engagement with Iran by each government, and the role of multicultural policies in their approaches to immigrant integration (table 1.1). Beginning with an initial comparison between Stockholm and Toronto that offered the similarity of having established official multiculturalism around the same time (the mid-1970s), the case of Los Angeles presents a "negative case" or a confounding variable in its lack of an official multicultural policy at the federal level. But even between Sweden and Canada, varying logics and historical roles of immigration offered differences with important impacts for the communities studied in this book. Moreover, while the presence of large Iranian communities in these three cities may appear as a controlled variable, the diverse periods of migration, motivations of emigration, and pathways of immigration for Iranians in each of these locations have created important distinctions in both composition and identity formation between and within these communities. As a result, rather than attempt to fully disaggregate each of these variables, I have sought instead to consider them holistically and relationally to gain greater insights into the roles of states, intermediaries, and Iranian diaspora communities in navigating belonging and inclusion.[76]

Over the course of sixteen years, I engaged directly with community members in Los Angeles, Stockholm, and Toronto through various forms of participant observation. In all three cities, I observed dozens of cultural events like festivals, exhibitions, concerts, performances, screenings, and lectures. I closely observed community organizations' planning meetings, volunteered in Persian- and English-language classes for youth, participated in Iranian university and community groups, and joined Iranian musicians on national tour. I also volunteered with two large Iranian cultural festivals in Toronto and Stockholm that would become key locations for the book. There, I worked alongside volunteers and professionals engaged in the everyday practices of community organizing to understand more closely the production side of these events in relation to the social, political, and economic affordances or obstacles that organizers, artists, and community members encountered in conducting their work.

Implicit in many studies of multiculturalism are dismissals of cultural events like festivals or exhibitions as shallow representations feeding a multiculturalism-fueled consumerist approach to immigrant integration. But as this book demonstrates, festivals also can be lenses through which the role of culture becomes visible as a source for strategizing inclusion and gaining access to power. For example, disputes within a community and between communities in diaspora over who holds the power of representation, what is deemed (in)authentic, and which cultural forms should be represented reveal fault lines in community identity as well as the power of regulating structures in host societies and the state and intermediary groups through which immigrants must navigate belonging in multicultural societies.

Examining the everyday experiences of multicultural life—coined "everyday multiculturalism"[77] and "multiculturalism from below" as opposed to "multiculturalism from above"[78]—is critical to understanding how state cultural policies produce experiences of inclusion and exclusion. I offer this micro-level perspective through ethnographic attention to everyday interactions, interviews, and participant observation in community events and local spaces across three cities of the Iranian diaspora. But, as important, I also attend to the meso-level, where state intermediaries and community members interact. My comparative ethnographic approach and focus on culture seeks to disrupt narratives of immigrant incorporation and integration that are either solely state-centric and presume the most important impacts remain at the level of the state or municipality or solely community-centered and presume the most important outcomes through which to gauge inclusion are socioeconomic status factors.

To do this, alongside participant observation, I conducted more than 125 semistructured interviews with Iranians engaged in cultural and community work at a variety of levels, including artists, musicians, actors, dancers, writers, filmmakers, producers, theater directors, playwrights, comedians, authors, television personalities, radio DJs, journalists, educators, politicians, nonprofit leaders, community activists, audience members, gallery owners, festival organizers, volunteers, language teachers, and social service providers. Selected using purposive and snowball sampling, the individuals I interviewed represent a highly diverse diaspora. They held a variety of ethnic, religious, class, and political identities as well as legal and social statuses vis-à-vis migration. They included those who migrated prior to or directly after the 1979 Revolution, those who migrated just months before our interview, and those in between—as well as their children born in diaspora. My interlocutors thus included members of the first, 1.5, and second immigrant generations, who were between twenty and seventy-five years of age at the time of our interview(s). Interviews were conducted in Persian and English based on the preferences of the interviewee. I also interviewed non-Iranians engaged with multiculturalism policy and/or the events under study, for example through their work at state intermediaries and cultural nonprofit organizations. Seeking to cast a wide net, I also interviewed non-Iranian friends, fellow band members, artistic collaborators, and audience members.

In these interviews and in informal conversations over dinner, tea, and *fika* (Swedish afternoon coffee), I heard stories of refugees' navigation of the United Nations resettlement system, of the jarring displacement of immigration, of the uncomfortable realizations of cultural difference in elementary school classrooms, of the isolation of sudden exile, and of the struggle to find employment while learning a third foreign language as an adult. I also heard of achieving personal triumphs, of breaking glass ceilings for ethnic minorities among the cultural elite, of successfully sponsoring family members' migrations during times of war, of recreating support networks through friends rather than kin, of recording albums while holding down two jobs, of being selected by a major party as the first Iranian to hold public office, of defying parents by taking artistic (read: risky) career paths rather than traditionally prestigious ones. While the content of some of these conversations appears directly in the pages of this book, they all greatly informed my research and understanding of these communities in diaspora.

Complementing these ethnographic methods, this book also analyzes secondary data in the form of policy and legal documents, demographic analyses of national population data, newspaper and magazine publications, opinion pieces, social media interactions, and pieces of ephemera I have collected over the last two decades.

While there is little doubt that my longer-term presence in the United States and identity as an Iranian American has influenced this book, it has been my goal to widen the scholarly view on the Iranian diaspora, with networks and identities that defy nation-state borders. I entered the Los Angeles, Stockholm, and Toronto communities as an adult without previous experience in these cities, nor extended familial networks to guide me. The observations and analyses that I offer here reflect the practices and thoughts of Iranians in diaspora in multiple locations and periods between 2007 and 2023. One of the challenges and benefits of long-term anthropological research is the ability to observe changes and their effects over time. Much has changed in the societies, governments, and communities and for the individuals with whom I have worked. Many of those shifts and changing circumstances are reflected in this book. Similarly, the views of my interlocutors also are liable to change over time; as such, when quoting directly, I have endeavored to indicate the year in which individuals stated their thoughts in an effort to remain true to the context in which I conducted the fieldwork.

This book cannot be, nor is intended to be, a comprehensive study of the entire global Iranian diaspora, nor does it offer a summary of every organization, position, approach, or event in the cities of focus. Instead, it offers an up-close look at everyday processes of cultural citizenship through the lens of a prominent cultural production in each city, chosen as much for its suitability for the study as by serendipitous circumstance. My aim in this project has not been to judge whether the decisions or approaches described have been good or bad, or right or wrong, nor to prescribe alternatives. Rather, I aim to take seriously the deep investments of time, finances, emotions, and labor that my interlocutors and the communities of which they are a part have devoted to certain strategies, narratives, ideas, and symbols during this period and in these locations of the diaspora. I do so aiming to understand the meanings these have had for Iranians in diaspora, and especially the impacts they have had when mobilized as strategies for inclusion in multicultural societies.

## Chapter Overview

The argument of this book is presented in five chapters. Chapter 1, "Departures and Arrivals," draws on interviews, national statistical data, and archival material to trace the global trajectory of Iranian emigration and immigration since the second half of the twentieth century. The following three chapters focus on each of the three cities under study and, through the lens of Iranian community-produced public art, exhibitions, and festivals, they examine the strategies of inclusion that result from different approaches to and negotiations with multiculturalism. Chapter 2, "Asserting 'Freedom, Dignity, and Wealth,' in Los Angeles," focuses attention on the 2013 US tour of the Cyrus Cylinder and the 2017 Freedom Sculpture and Freedom Festival it inspired in Los Angeles. Iranians, like other immigrants in the United States, are navigating neoliberal multiculturalism as an alternative pathway to power, centering notions of immigrant success and contribution alongside nostalgic and nationalist renderings of Iranian culture to demonstrate "good citizenship" and thus deservingness for belonging. Given this context, I examine how and why certain forms of imperial nostalgia have permeated so many Iranian American representations of culture and history.

Unlike American neoliberal multiculturalism, Sweden's rapidly changing demographics and new approaches to official multiculturalism in the 1970s were reformed by the 2010s to prioritize cultural policies that tied financial and symbolic support to specific integration efforts. Chapter 3, "Contesting Cultural Belonging(s) in Stockholm," examines how Swedish discourses of *interculturalism* animated the efforts of Iranians in Stockholm's cultural industries to produce Eldfesten, the largest celebration of the Iranian holiday of Chaharshanbeh Suri in the world. The chapter demonstrates how state intermediaries enacting cultural policies of Swedish interculturalism challenged fellow Iranians to break away from nationalist and essentialist claims on culture, including imperial nostalgia, but also to practice—to rehearse as much as enact—Swedish ideals of democracy, inclusion, and transparency and institutionalized norms of behavior, like professionalism. The debates and controversies presented here pivot on questions of (in)authenticity and the dual meanings of *belonging*: Does cultural belonging (as in inclusion) in multicultural Sweden require immigrants to give up their "cultural belongings" (as in ownership of Iranian culture)?

Chapter 4, "Navigating Multiculturalism in Toronto," turns to the large and growing communities of Iranians in Toronto, home to the biennial Tirgan Festival. Produced through a community partnership model, this large public representation of contemporary Iranian culture was inspired by and benefits from Canadian multiculturalism. By mobilizing art and culture (cultural capital) as a resource for building symbolic and social capital for the community, Tirgan's leaders created an avenue for inclusion and integration for young Iranian newcomers who have come to see the "Tirgan Family" as one of the most effective pathways for building belonging in Canada. But while relying on nonpartisanship and "the Canadian Way" proved successful in developing these forms of capital in a fragmented community for over a decade, how should these freshly acquired community assets be used amid calls for political and social change in both Canada and Iran? What new forms of belonging can emerge when resistance is not only permitted but enabled?

These three extended case study chapters are followed by a final chapter that draws together their insights and examples to offer a relational comparison of strategies of inclusion and their implications. Chapter 5, "Comparing Iranian Diasporic Strategies in Multicultural Societies," identifies different approaches to multiculturalism and immigrant inclusion in each location that have produced variation in approaches to representing and, in many ways, negotiating Iranian diaspora identity and inclusion. Acknowledging the many overlapping lines of belonging, the chapter highlights lines of class, religion, and race, both within communities and in relation to their countries of reception. These comparative discussions ultimately demonstrate that across diasporic locations, those who work within and reinforce hegemonic forms have been best positioned to prevail, but that contestations and local variation can also present openings for change.

The concluding chapter considers how strategies of inclusion and belonging ultimately are acts of home-building. As the examples in this book attest, cultural strategies of inclusion operate in conjunction with political, economic, and social strategies in multicultural societies. As Iranian communities build ever greater attachments to their homes, they also experience ongoing migrations, react to shifting geopolitical circumstances, and navigate belonging in creative ways. The book concludes with a reflection on how these ongoing processes have opened conversations and challenged attitudes about race, class, and religion not only in the mainstreams these public events seek to enter but within their own communities.

*　*　*

The tireless efforts of volunteers like Nooshin, Ashkan, Fereshteh, Zohreh, Maria, Mansour, and their colleagues exemplify the commitments of time, energy, and resources to Iranian arts and cultural organizing that are described throughout this book. Their dedication, driven by a desire to reclaim and celebrate Iranian identity, mirrors the strategic cultural mobilizations of Iranian diaspora communities globally. By weaving together the experiences of Iranians across Los Angeles, Stockholm, and Toronto, this book reveals how these public events are more than mere celebrations—they can also be powerful acts of resistance and inclusion. Through these cultural endeavors, Iranians in diaspora seek to not only counter negative stereotypes but also carve out spaces of belonging in their multicultural societies, ultimately redefining what it means to be Iranian beyond Iran.

1

Departures and Arrivals

The Iranian diaspora today is a globally dispersed but highly networked population of between five and eight million people worldwide. This wide estimate points to the difficulty of measuring a dispersed population; the common understanding that the diaspora is large and growing is not always borne out in national census figures or scholarly estimates, which are limited by a number of methodological challenges.[1] Nevertheless, Iranians today live on nearly every continent, and the diaspora reflects the multicultural diversity of Iran, including an array of ethnic, religious, and linguistic identities. The communities they have created in diaspora have emerged through a variety of overlapping migration flows. Early arrivals of Iranian students to universities abroad in the mid-twentieth century were joined by subsequent waves of emigration during overlapping political, social, and economic crises: the turmoil of the 1978–79 Revolution, violence and repression during the 1980–88 Iran-Iraq War, high inflation and unemployment in the 1990s, and ongoing political oppression, economic sanctions, and restricted life choices for a young, highly educated, and ambitious Iranian population from the 2000s to the present. Refugee flows and family reunifications during and following each of these periods have been enabled, limited, or made more challenging by immigration policies in receiving countries holding the levers on student, tourist, and work visas.

Despite potentially similar motivations for emigration, the societies to which Iranian immigrants have arrived in the last six decades have directly influenced how they have negotiated their identities and developed their communities in these new homes. To better understand migration flows, motivations, and conditions of reception and life in an emerging global diaspora, this chapter outlines the immigration histories of three of the countries to which large populations of Iranians arrived and that have become key nodes of the Iranian diaspora: the United States, Sweden, and Canada. After mapping out the general timelines and motivations for departure from Iran, the chapter offers an overview of the correlated trends in Iranian arrivals to each country, highlighting the historical and political context, demographic particularities, and immigration experiences of these emerging communities across the final decades of the twentieth century and into the twenty-first. The chapter concludes with an analysis of how these newly multicultural societies pursued policymaking in ways that led Iranians to prioritize culture and representation, often as catalysts for community organizing across the Iranian diaspora.

## Departing Iran

Homa Sarshar was born in Shiraz in 1946 to a Jewish Iranian family. While earning her BA in French literature at Tehran University, she became a working wife and mother, joining the inaugural editorial board of a new publication: *Zan-e-Ruz* women's magazine. There she reported on issues like the status of women in the job market and family planning among low-income families. She also became a columnist for the *Kayhan* daily newspaper and, in 1972, she was invited to bring her pathbreaking work on women's and family issues to Iran's National Iranian Radio and Television (NIRT). She continued this work with passion until 1978, when she was abruptly fired from both posts. In December of that year, in what she described as "a state of utter turmoil," she left Iran with her husband and two children, just weeks before the fall of the monarchy:

> The ten to twelve years before the revolution was really an era of prosperity [for our family]. All of these opportunities were available, and the country was rapidly moving towards progress and modernization and development. Anyone could pursue anything they dreamed and succeed at it. By then, travel to Europe and summer holidays in Paris or London had become routine and we were part of it all. I have very fond memories of those last ten years before the Revolution, from our married life with children. We travelled a lot inside Iran, and we also worked very hard. When the riots and uprising started, within one week they fired all religious minorities from [National Iranian Radio and] Television [where I worked]. They thought that, given the tone of the impending revolution,

most of the opposition was targeted at religious minorities and that they might be able to stop the revolution this way—which, of course, did not happen. They also fired me from *Kayhan* [newspaper] at that same time. So within two weeks, I was fired from both the [NIRT] and *Kayhan*. And the reasons were very, very obvious: because I am a woman and because I am Jewish, both of which counted as minority categories. And those who were leading the revolution in Iran—meaning followers of Khomeini—even now, forty years later, they are anti-woman and anti-other minorities. Back then, some thought that it was [political] posturing and they needed to respond in-kind. But in reality it wasn't a political game, rather it was a bitter reality that very quickly all of us who were oppressed and the first to be fired—what they called "*paak-saazi*" [purged].... We felt with every fiber of our being what was actually happening. My husband was also purged from the Ministry of Energy. [NIRT] gave no letter or reason—just that initial note that said I was fired. And *Kayhan* only informed me verbally. They said: "Don't come back tomorrow." And so my entire career in journalism and television was terminated in those first months before the Revolution, unfortunately. In a very sad and unexpected circumstance, in a state of utter turmoil, my husband and I decided to leave Iran—not permanently, but temporarily.... We decided to get out of Iran and wait and see when the situation would calm down and then return.[2]

In the second half of the twentieth century, Sarshar's family was part of an increasingly affluent segment of society in Iran, earning handsome incomes by working in sectors like engineering, industrial development and real estate that afforded them the latest European fashions, cutting-edge technologies, and leisure activities like trips to Europe and North America. There, they established networks and sometimes even second homes in these abroad locations that would unexpectedly become sanctuaries when political upheaval beset the country in 1978–79. But just as the economic development underway in Iran was of an uneven nature, this high level of affluence was neither evenly distributed across Iranian society nor reached far beyond circles loyal to the Pahlavi monarchy.[3]

Development and modernization initiatives led by the Pahlavi government in the mid-twentieth century also led to a sizeable trend in foreign education, sending the children of Iran's growing urban middle class abroad for university. The same economic development and industrialization that had afforded an emerging cosmopolitan lifestyle for some required a professional skilled labor force that the country's insufficient higher education institutions struggled to meet.[4] While Sarshar was accepted for one of the limited spots in Iran's universities at the time, many others looked to state scholarships, technical apprenticeships, international exchange programs through foreign embassies, and international education agencies that sent young, promising Iranians—mostly, but not exclusively, single men—to universities in Europe and the United States with the hope that they would return as professionals with foreign degrees and expertise, especially in engineering and other technical fields.[5]

As a result, from the 1950s through the 1970s, the number of Iranians—whether tourists, students, or immigrants—in Europe and the United States steadily increased year by year. An estimated four thousand Iranians were studying abroad in 1957; just five years later, by 1962, that number had increased nearly fivefold, with an estimated thirteen thousand in Europe, especially France, England, and West Germany, and six thousand in the United States.[6] By 1968, the number of Iranians at foreign universities had outgrown the number attending institutions of higher education in Iran itself.[7] The desirable prestige of European universities began to give way to the accessibility of US ones, and, by 1977, Iranians accounted for the largest number of foreign students in the United States, constituting around half of the one hundred thousand Iranian students abroad that year.[8] At the time of the 1979 Revolution, Iranians accounted for 18 percent of all foreign students in the United States and could be found at colleges and universities across the country.[9]

These students may have shared a goal to seek higher education abroad, but their trajectories and experiences were not uniform. Some Iranian students at foreign universities prior to the 1979 Revolution enjoyed scholarships from the Pahlavi state; others were abroad thanks to their wealthy parents' funds and networks; and still others were self-funded overachievers seeking the social and class mobility that evaded them in Iran.[10] Many were active on campus, whether by dedicating themselves to 1960s campus politics with other minority groups or by leading their own activism organizations seeking to garner global attention for growing political struggles back home.¹¹ Once their studies were complete, many of these students returned to Iran as planned and contributed to the ongoing development of dams, oil refineries, industrial construction, and irrigation projects or took the lead on urban planning, education, media, and housing projects. Other graduates remained abroad to begin new jobs or to begin their lives with American or European romantic partners. Still others stayed abroad primarily to remain active in Iranian politics in ways that they could not do freely at home, for example as members of groups agitating for the overthrow of then-Shah Mohammed Reza Pahlavi from their positions in Paris, London, Washington, DC, or Los Angeles.¹² These student groups sought to gain international attention on campuses in Europe and the United States in solidarity with a growing opposition movement in Iran, centered especially at Iran's university campuses.

The Pahlavi government's modernization efforts led to economic growth, but its fruits were not distributed evenly across the country. Urban centers like Tehran experienced mass urban migration as the landless left rural areas plagued by poverty, unemployment, and lack of access to basic services.¹³ Discontent spread widely as economic disparity, demographic shifts, and cultural changes joined with one-party rule, political repression, and authoritarian methods of the Shah's government, including censorship, imprisonment, and torture of political dissenters at the hands of the secret police (SAVAK). This, alongside perceptions of large-scale corruption, galvanized public resentment. Student groups, trade unions, multiple leftist political parties and guerilla groups, and Muslim clerics and their followers found themselves in a broad-based movement that would lead to national strikes and recurring protests that dominated the country in 1977–78. In January 1979, the Shah left Iran for the last time and, on February 1st, Ayatollah Ruhollah Khomeini—an influential high-ranking cleric whose oppositional lectures distributed on cassette tape had gained wide audiences and mass support—returned from fourteen years in exile to assume leadership. A December 1979 referendum established the new Constitution of the Islamic Republic of Iran, furthering rapid economic, social, and political change.¹⁴

Iranian students abroad faced the news of each of these events with a mix of excitement, shock, hope, and fear and were confronted with difficult decisions for their future. Having agitated for revolution from positions in the West, many activists and patriotic hopefuls returned home with goals of influencing the direction of the new government, fulfilling a duty to put their education to work for their country. Others remained in their country of study to wait out what they hoped was a short period of uncertainty; still others left with their European or American partners and children to live in Iran. But for former members of the Shah's government, Pahlavi elites (e.g., investors, bankers), and ethnic and religious minorities (especially Baha'i and Jewish Iranians), the increasingly authoritarian and Islamic fundamentalist direction of the country made the decision of whether to stay or go for them: Those in Iran felt forced to leave for their safety (as Sarshar described), while those already abroad felt forced to stay abroad, becoming exiles for fear of the persecution that befell their comrades, coreligionists, and coethnics in Iran.

Immediately following the 1979 Revolution, Khomeini's new government and ensuing "Cultural Revolution" consolidated power through a series of repressive, coercive, and violent measures, including the increasing curtailment of personal liberties, especially for women and minorities; confiscation of property; imprisonment and repression of former military and Pahlavi government officials and a wide swathe of political opposition groups; targeted oppression of religious minorities; strict censorship of media, journalism, and the arts; restriction of academic freedom and occupational access; and, following the Iraqi invasion of Iran in September 1980, the forced conscription of men and boys who were sent to an increasingly devastating war front. Iranians who had been abroad on student or tourist visas as the Revolution unfolded often were encouraged by family members in Iran to wait out this period of upheaval, a choice that sometimes required overstays of visas that expired amid political turmoil and war.

As a result of this confluence of impacts and untold other uncertainties of revolution and war, those students who had remained abroad were soon joined by hundreds of thousands who fled Iran from 1978 into the early 1980s, whether quickly via flights to Europe, North America, and Australia or, when official border crossings were not possible (for example, due to being marked by the state as *mamnu' al-khuruj*, barred from exit), in clandestine, harried, difficult, and dangerous journeys across Turkish or Pakistani border areas that required the aid of smugglers. As both groups—those already abroad at the time of the Revolution and those who fled Iran after 1979—came to be included as members of protected categories under international refugee law, by the end of the 1980s, an estimated one million Iranians had dispersed to nearly every continent.

As Iran's economy struggled to recover from an eight-year war and concurrent baby boom, job prospects remained limited. Graduates from Iran's best universities found themselves frustrated in a domestic job market with high unemployment and limited prospects for postgraduate advancement, leading them to join what came to be described as a brain drain of Iran's top talent in the 1980s and 1990s. Continuing and intensifying in the 2000s, academically promising Iranians increasingly emigrated to complete their undergraduate and postgraduate degrees abroad, especially in countries like the United States, the United Kingdom, Germany, Sweden, and Canada.[15] The economic impact of this outflow of Iran's "top minds" was noticed by successive government leaders and reported on in the Iranian media. An Iranian newspaper reported in 2013 that all ten of the top scorers on the 2007 *konkur* (university entrance exam) had since moved abroad to Europe, the United States, or Canada to seek postgraduate education and job opportunities.[16] Another 2012 report in *Shargh* newspaper found that over 62 percent of Iran's medal-winners in international math and science competitions between 1993 and 2007 had since left the country and were enrolled in or had graduated from top universities in the United States or Canada.[17]

While political and social repression ebbed and flowed in the 2000s, the election crisis and protests that became known as the 2009 Green Movement led to a period of intense repression by the Islamic Republic that created a new flow of out-migration of Iranians, whether as refugees, students, or economic migrants. During the early and mid-2010s, Sweden, Canada, and the United States each experienced renewed spikes in the arrivals of Iranians, especially during the 2015–16 "refugee crisis" in Europe. But in the United States, a halt to refugee admissions and a complete ban targeting Iranian citizens (and those from six other countries) in 2017 became the most aggressive and directed US policy against Iranian arrivals since 1980. The tightening of immigration restrictions like these and the related rise of populist politics in North America and Europe into the 2020s have had deep impacts on Iranians in Iran and in the global diaspora.

## Contextualizing Migration to North America and Europe

The departure of hundreds of thousands of citizens from Iran in the late twentieth century occurred in the same period that fundamental shifts in national immigration policies took shape in many European and North American countries. These late twentieth century policy reorientations responded to trends in global population flows heightened during decolonization processes and global struggles for human and civil rights.

With shared histories of settler colonialism and the displacement, elimination, and forced assimilation of Indigenous populations, both the United States and Canada had established immigration policies in the decades prior to World War II that were founded upon racially discriminatory legislation. In the United States, the Chinese Exclusion Act of 1882 had banned the immigration of Chinese laborers and was broadened to exclude most of Asia in the Immigration Act of 1917. Racial prerequisite laws in the United States further ensured that nonwhite immigrants would not be able to naturalize and thereby codified scientific racism into US citizenship law.[18] To further stem the flow of migration to the United States from southern and Eastern Europe, federal legislation in 1921 and 1924 created a quota system that restricted permanent immigration through limits determined proportionally by the national origin of immigrants already present in the United States, as counted by the 1890 Census.[19] This effectively limited new immigration during the mid-twentieth century to northern and western Europeans, primarily from the United Kingdom, Ireland, and Germany. Over the course of several decades, the foreign-born population of the United States thus declined from 14.7 percent in 1910 to an all-time low of 4.7 percent in 1970.[20]

Similarly, in Canada, the Chinese Exclusion Act of 1923 banned most Chinese immigration outright, and restrictions on Chinese, Japanese, and South Asian migrants already in Canada denied them voting and electoral rights and restricted their rights to employment in law, pharmacy, public works, education, and civil service sectors. As in the United

States, immigration to Canada dropped to fewer than one immigrant per one thousand population in the early 1940s,[21] and as of 1966, 75 percent of all Canadian immigrants were European.[22] These restrictive policies not only constrained immigration in terms of national origins or race, they also discriminated against would-be immigrants based on literacy, mental and physical health, political activities and ideologies, and sexuality. These exclusionary measures in twentieth-century US and Canadian law were exacerbated by unofficial forms of discrimination practiced by immigration officials as much as by other legal arms.[23]

These official and unofficial structures were rooted in a mix of scientific racism and nationalism that effectively maintained the domination of both countries' white European populations well into the first half of the century. During World War II, as Nazis systematically persecuted and murdered Jews, Roma, and others in Europe, the United States and Canada incarcerated Japanese, Italian, and German people, including their own citizens. But in the postwar period, the discrediting of scientific racism and eugenics and the subsequent rise of human rights discourses alongside postcolonial liberation movements led to challenges to discriminatory immigration and citizenship policies like those in the United States and Canada.[24] Amid Cold War pressures and growing domestic civil rights movements, maintaining an immigration system that effectively barred migration from Asia, Africa, and Latin America presented a glaring example of racial and ethnic discrimination at the federal level.[25]

The Immigration and Nationality Act of 1965 fundamentally altered the US immigration system and the demographic composition of the country's population. The act abolished the national origin quota system and thereby opened migration pathways that had blocked much of the world from the United States in the same period as rapid decolonization and emigration were occurring in much of Africa, Latin America, and Asia.[26] In its place, the act created a quota preference for skilled immigrants and family reunification. The Refugee Act of 1980 brought the country's immigration law in line with United Nations definitions and separated refugees out from this preference system. Importantly, the act expanded the annual numbers of refugees that could be admitted annually, creating an important pathway for refugees, including Iranians, in the following decade.

In the case of Canada, global norms mixed with domestic political opportunities that enabled it to bring liberalizing changes "quickly and quietly" in comparison with other countries.[27] The major shift in Canadian immigration policy came in 1967, when the Canadian government adopted a universal admissions policy that was codified in the Immigration Act of 1976. More commonly referred to as "the points system," this reform shifted the country's immigration policy away from openly racial or cultural discrimination while prioritizing the potential economic benefits of immigration. It did this by giving priority to applicants with higher education, official language fluency, and the ability to fill needs in the Canadian labor market. This meant that Canada, too, admitted a much higher number of immigrants post-1967 and, within that flow, greater numbers of non-European immigrants than ever before.

These shifts in immigration policy brought greater diversity of racial and ethnic identities to both the United States and Canada. While Europeans accounted for 74.5 percent of all immigrants in the United States in 1960, by 2021, they only accounted for 10.7 percent; the majority hailed from the Americas (51.9 percent) and Asia (31 percent).[28] In terms of ethnic and racial diversity, the 2020 US Census showed a decline in the percentage of the population that was white alone (61.6 percent), meaning 38.4 percent of Americans were either nonwhite or of mixed race.[29] In Canada, while immigration from Asia, Africa, Latin America, and the Caribbean had been but a trickle in 1966, by 1977, these groups constituted over 50 percent of annual arrivals,[30] and by 2010, only 16 percent of immigrants had migrated to Canada from European countries.[31] Between 1981 and 2001, the population of "visible minorities" in Canada (the Canadian government's term until 2021 for "persons, other than aboriginal peoples, who are non-Canadian in race or non-white in color"[32]) nearly quadrupled, growing from 5 percent to 13 percent of the total Canadian population in just two decades.[33] Between 2001 and 2021, the overall number of racialized people in Canada increased 130 percent, such that, by 2021, 26 percent of the Canadian population self-identified as a "racialized person" (the government's term that replaced "visible minorities").[34] This shift accompanied an incredible diversification of the population, as well as increased understanding of the diversity of both Indigenous and immigrant populations by the state: Where the

1901 Canadian Census had listed roughly 25 ethnic groups, by 2021, the Census reported over 450 ethnic or cultural origins.[35]

Sweden presents a different migration history and national ethos, albeit with its own histories of colonialism, embedded racial ideologies, and exclusionary practices.[36] There are multiple Indigenous communities in Sweden, for example the Sami, an official national minority who were subjected to forced assimilation, removals, and discriminatory policies.[37] Unlike the United States or Canada, Sweden's nineteenth-century migration history is a story of mass emigration rather than immigration. For centuries, Sweden had only experienced small-scale immigration from neighboring areas like Finland and what is now northern Germany, but between 1850 and 1930, famines sent over one million Swedes abroad, primarily to the United States and Denmark. Thus, unlike the United States and Canada, Sweden only became a country of net immigration flows in the mid-twentieth century. Nevertheless, like other countries, Sweden's first immigration law, the 1927 Aliens Act, was rooted in theories of racial exclusion, seeking to "control immigration of peoples that do not to our benefit allow themselves to meld with our population."[38]

In the 1930s, the Swedish Model was introduced, bringing together universal state welfare, labor protections, and a liberal market economy—a system called by American onlookers during the Cold War as the "Middle Way" between American-style capitalism and Soviet-style socialism. The emerging welfare state needed a large tax base from which to build the public sector, which required immigrant labor.[39] Between 1950 and 1970, immigration to Sweden tripled and was primarily constituted by labor migrants from Nordic countries (mainly Finland) and southern and eastern Europe (Yugoslavia, Greece, Türkiye, Hungary, Austria, Italy).[40] But unlike other European countries post-WWII (e.g., Germany and Switzerland), Sweden did not create an official guest worker program wherein foreign workers were recruited through temporary contracts with the promise of returning home. To the contrary, while labor immigrants to Sweden were seen as temporary, they were eligible for the same social benefits as Swedish-born citizens. Sweden's strong labor unions ensured this: To protect the Swedish labor force, they guaranteed that labor immigrants would be paid the same wages, offered the same employment rights, and given access to the same unemployment benefits as Swedish citizens.⁴¹ As a result, the experience of many of these laborers differed significantly from those in Germany and elsewhere, and they chose to remain in Sweden.

The period of heavy labor migration begun in the late 1950s peaked at eighty thousand people arriving in 1970 alone, which accounted for just under 1 percent of the Swedish population at the time.⁴² To stem this trend and protect a slowing labor sector experiencing an economic downturn, regulations were changed in 1972 to forbid non-Nordic laborers, such as southern and eastern Europeans. Simultaneously, Sweden continued to accept refugees, the number of which grew steadily in the 1970s and 1980s. Thus, from 1972 to 1989, Swedish immigration shifted from mostly white, Christian, European labor migrants to humanitarian asylum seekers, refugees, and their family members from countries like Uganda, Chile, Argentina, Türkiye, Iran, and Iraq.

The result, much like in Canada and the United States, was a rapid increase in the presence of non-European immigrants in Sweden. The share of non-European immigrants jumped from less than 10 percent during 1945–72 to an average of 40 percent in the following decades, excepting the large number of refugees and migrants from the Balkan war in the 1990s.⁴³ As in Canada and the United States, family reunification became a key pathway, and, by 2021, over one-third of Sweden's population was either foreign-born (20 percent) or born in Sweden to at least one foreign-born parent (14 percent).⁴⁴

As this brief sketch shows, despite variations in historical trajectories and internal politics, the United States, Sweden, and Canada each shifted their immigration policies in the late twentieth century in ways that led to rapid rates of growth for immigrants and their descendants (table 1.1) as well as rapid diversification of the geographic, ethnic, and racial composition of immigrant flows. These policy changes and their effects created opportunities and limitations for the Iranian citizens who found themselves experiencing an extended period of political, social, and economic upheaval that would lead them to migrate.

### Arriving to the United States

Between October 1981 and February 1985, more Iranians (11,055) were granted asylum in the United States than any other nationality.⁴⁵ The

TABLE 1.1. Immigrants by percentage of population in the United States, Sweden, and Canada, 1971 and 2021.

|  | Foreign-born as percentage of total population in 1971 | Foreign-born as percentage of total population in 2021 |
|---|---|---|
| United States * | 4.7% (record low) | 13.6% |
| Sweden †·‡ | 6.6% | 20% |
| Canada §·** | 15.3% | 23% (record high) |

\* "U.S. Immigrant Population and Share over Time, 1850–Present," Migration Policy Institute, www.migrationpolicy.org.
† Statistics Sweden, "Immigration and Emigration 1970–2022 and Projection 2023–2070," Graph 1.2, be0401_2023i70, last updated April 25, 2024, https://www.scb.se.
‡ Statistics Sweden, 2024, *Foreign Born by County, Municipality, Sex and Country of Birth December 31 2021*, Table be0101, February 22, 2024, https://www.scb.se/.
§ Statistics Canada, 2009, "Number and Share of the Foreign-Born Population in Canada, 1901–2006," November 20, 2009, https://www12.statcan.gc.ca/.
\*\* Statistics Canada, 2022, "Immigrants Make Up Largest Share of Canada's Population in Over 150 Years," *The Daily*, October 26, 2022. https://www150.statcan.gc.ca/.

United States that these Iranians arrived to, however, was not the same society in which hundreds of thousands of Iranian students had lived during the 1970s. Amid the upheavals of the Revolution, a geopolitical whiplash rocked Iranians in the United States in November 1979, when Iranian student activists occupied the US embassy in Tehran and held fifty-two Americans hostage. In what became known as the Iran Hostage Crisis, then-President Jimmy Carter quickly retaliated by cutting nearly all trade with Iran and limiting the entry of Iranians with nonimmigrant visas (e.g., students, tourists) through Executive Order 12172. Over a third of the estimated 150,000 Iranian visa holders present in the United States at the time were students; the order required them to appear before the Immigration and Naturalization Service (INS) within one month, by December 31, 1979, at the risk of deportation. In April 1980, amid growing domestic pressure, Carter broke diplomatic ties with Iran, imposed sanctions, froze Iranian assets, and canceled all valid visas issued to Iranians who were outside of the United States, suddenly leaving traveling students stranded in European airports or at the Canadian border.[46]

One of America's closest allies in the Middle East had become its most fearsome enemy almost overnight, a shift that was experienced by Iranians in the United States in nearly every aspect of their lives. Campuses across the country, especially in the south, held protests using slurs against their Iranian classmates and calling for their deportation;

Figure 1.1. "Anti-Iran Protest," December 4, 1979, Los Angeles Coliseum. (Credit: Bromberger Hoover Photography/Getty Images)

one South Carolina campus's student board voted to ban Iranian students from classes altogether.[47] State universities like those in Louisiana and New Mexico banned all Iranian student enrollment,[48] while the state legislature of Mississippi doubled the tuition for Iranian students enrolled in public universities.[49] Close friends became silent former-friends; lovers pulled away; professors grew hostile; neighbors turned suspicious, if not outright violent; and employers turned into antagonistic managers who passed over Iranians for jobs or promotions.[50]

These overlapping forms of interpersonal turmoil and targeted legal action occurred alongside demonstrations by and between Iranians about the future of their country, as well as protests against Iranians that sparked violent reactions in the streets (fig. 1.1). Ron Kelley, a photographer and writer who laboriously documented this period in Los Angeles, summed up the situation a decade later:

> In 1979–80, during the so-called "hostage crisis," any and all Iranian demonstrators were subjected to vile expletives and other verbal abuse

by passing motorists who had no basis by which to make distinctions between Iranian political factions. To some degree, this hostility against the generic Iranian (narrowly defined as an irrational, fanatical, uncivilized terrorist/Khomeini worshipper) persists to this day. Shouted epithets against the Ayatollah Khomeini by passing American motorists and curses to "Go home!" occur during even recent demonstrations, directed—incredibly—to *Anti-Khomeini* demonstrators![51]

These experiences both heightened and reflected the growing acrimony of anti-Iranian rhetoric across US culture and media. The message from the US government, newspapers, television, radio, film, music, and ephemera like T-shirts, posters, pins, and bumper stickers was clear: Iranians were not welcome in the United States.[52] As a 1.5-generation immigrant who arrived to Texas in 1980 as a child recalled to me in an interview, the ubiquity of these messages was not limited to the media, but seemed to be everywhere, including on the bumper of his neighbor's car. He shook his head, recalling his childhood shock: "Even Mickey Mouse hated us" (fig. 1.2).

In response to these messages and to direct experiences of discrimination, and regardless of ethnic background, Iranians in Los Angeles and many other parts of the United States adopted covering strategies (defined by Kenji Yoshino as strategies used "to tone down a disfavored identity to fit into the mainstream"[53]) to protect themselves, such as self-identifying as "Persian" rather than Iranian and changing names (e.g., Zahra to Sarah, Mohammad to Mike), hair color (e.g., brunette to

Figure 1.2. Mickey Mouse depicted as flipping off Iran on a bumper sticker popular in the United States, ca. 1980. (Author's collection.)

blonde), and facial features (e.g., rhinoplasty).[54] These strategies were most commonly initiated during tumultuous periods of the 1980s, and reemerged in the post-9/11 period.

Despite this antagonistic atmosphere, INS data demonstrates that thousands of Iranians still considered the United States their top destination through the 1980s. Along with ongoing asylum and refugee applications, the 1986 Immigration Reform and Control Act (IRCA) created an opportunity for individuals without valid documentation (e.g., students who had overstayed visas during political turmoil) who had entered the United States prior to January 1, 1982, and remained continuously, to adjust their status and apply for legal permanent residency. Iranians took advantage of this opportunity alongside nearly three million other immigrants, leading to a sharp spike in permanent residencies granted between 1987 and 1991 (fig. 1.3).[55] Once legalized, these lawful permanent residents (LPR) could then take advantage of a new family-sponsored preference category enabled by the act that allowed for LPRs to sponsor spouses and children and for citizens to sponsor siblings and parents.

These new pathways allowed Iranian Americans to sponsor new emigrants from Iran, help family members with new asylum applications and apply for reunification with spouses, children, parents, and siblings who had temporarily landed in cities of Europe—Hamburg, Paris, Madrid, Vienna—where they had found immediate refuge as they awaited US visas. These onward migrations were common, usually following extended but temporary stays (whether one to two months or two to three years) in countries that had made quick departures possible through tourist visas, family and hometown networks, and asylum pathways. Family reunifications in the late 1980s also led to an important demographic shift: For the first time, Iranian immigrant women now outnumbered men, and a large number of elderly Iranians entered the United States.[56] This confluence of pathways, as well as events in Iran—like the ongoing Iraqi bombardments of Iranian cities (1984, 1985, 1987, 1988) and the 1988 extrajudicial mass executions of tens of thousands of political prisoners—worked in tandem to motivate Iranian immigrants in the United States to apply for permanent residency in large numbers in the late 1980s (fig. 1.3).

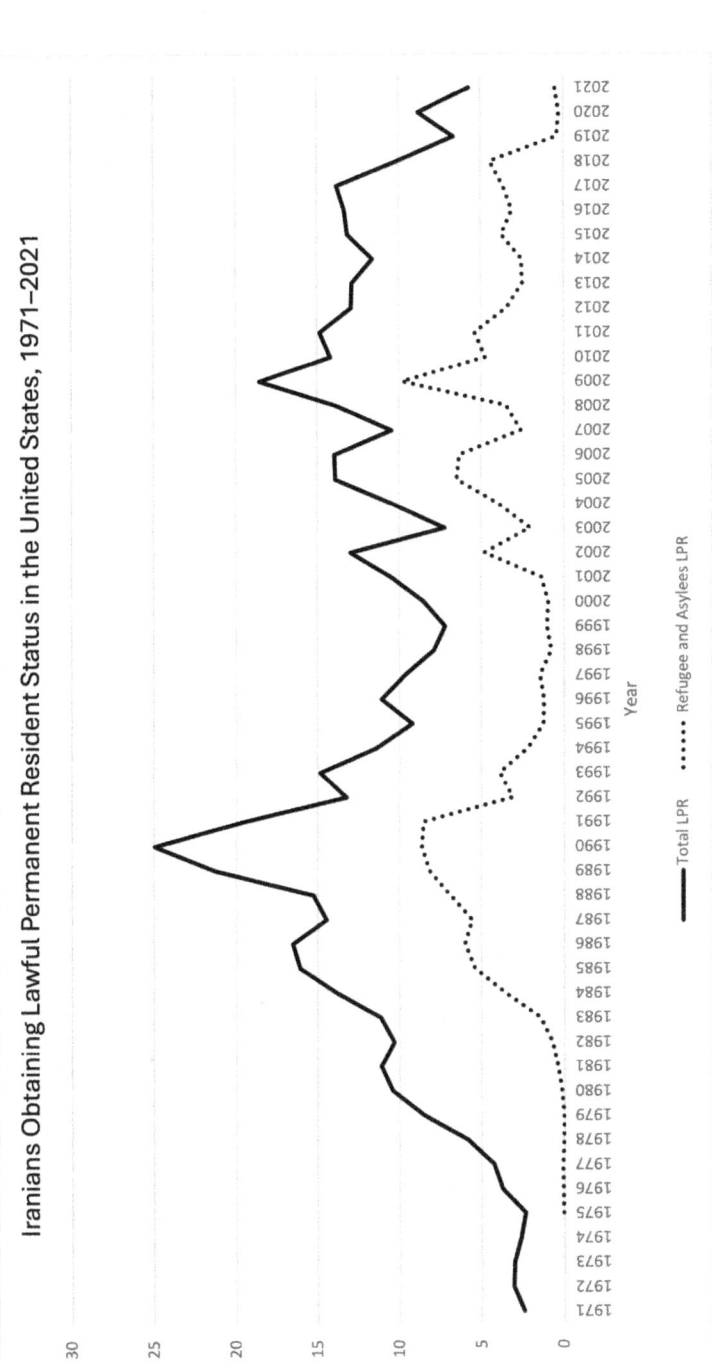

Figure 1.3. Iranians Obtaining Lawful Permanent Resident Status in the United States by year, 1971–2021. This table does not indicate year of arrival, but rather year of status approval, and thus includes a count of those who entered on nonimmigrant visas (e.g., students, tourists) and later adjusted their status. This accounts in part for the 1990 LPR peak. Source: US Department of Homeland Security, *Yearbooks of Immigration Statistics*, Table 3D, "Persons Obtaining Lawful Permanent Resident Status by Region and Country of Birth," Washington, DC: US Department of Homeland Security.

## Building Tehrangeles

In addition to transnational onward migrations, Iranian Americans working to reunite with family and friends who had settled in cities across the United States created an internal migratory flow to growing Iranian communities in California. The state of California had already drawn one-half of all Iranian immigrants to the United States in the second half of the 1970s.[57] Los Angeles's large universities, including the University of California, Los Angeles, and the University of Southern California, along with its familiar warm weather and Hollywood appeal, had attracted twice as many Iranians as San Francisco, the US city with the second largest Iranian population at the time.[58] This already sizeable Iranian population could therefore serve as a haven for those who had faced targeted discrimination and hostility, to say nothing of loneliness and isolation, as the only Iranian(s) in their small towns in Middle America. Having arrived to a country that did not provide immigrants with resources like housing, language training, or employment support unless they were resettled refugees, the presence of family and coethnic networks was pivotal for Iranians in the United States. Los Angeles could provide not only a sense of safety in numbers but also job opportunities and cultural familiarity, making it a choice destination for internal migration of Iranian Americans as much as for onward migration from other global locations.

Even prior to the Revolution, Iranian Americans in Los Angeles began to cluster in areas like North Hollywood, Westwood (just south of UCLA, and where the first Iranian business is said to have opened in 1974), and Beverly Hills.[59] In the 1980s, Iranian shops and restaurants in Westwood became key nodes of a small but emerging entrepreneurial ethnic enclave, with bookstores, travel agencies, hair salons, insurance and loan agents, and attorney's offices soon to follow. This already sizeable concentration was active in responding to geopolitical crises emerging from the Revolution and Hostage Crisis. LA newspapers at the time documented revolutionary groups' protests at the Beverly Hills homes of the Shah's family members and, later, against the Islamic Republic at the Wilshire Federal Building. These demonstrations drew anti-Iranian pushback, but also included fights between Iranians of differing persuasions, reflecting the internal diversity among Iranians in Los Angeles across a wide array of political views (e.g., monarchists, leftists, supporters of the dissident organization Mujaheddin-e Khalq [MEK]),[60] ethnoreligious identities (e.g., Jewish, Armenian Christian, Baha'i, Muslim),[61] and class positions (from whose who managed to bring their extensive wealth out of Iran just prior to the Revolution to those who arrived as refugees with less than $100 USD to their name) that made for an early fragmented Iranian population in Los Angeles that has endured.

As Iranian families spread across west Los Angeles, north to the San Fernando Valley, northeast to Glendale, and south to Palos Verdes and Orange County, Angelenos became increasingly familiar with Iranian traditions, foods, and holidays. A growing young 1.5 and second generation (some one-third of the Iranian American population as of 2000[62]) attended area schools, sometimes in large concentrations: By 1991, Iranian students, most of them Jewish, accounted for 19 percent of the population of Beverly Hills High School, leading in part to their caricature as a wealthy "Persian Mafia" in 1995's coming-of-age comedy *Clueless*.[63] By 2012, that school's Iranian heritage student population had grown to nearly 40 percent.

From the 1980s onward, Iranian presence in Los Angeles has been marked visually by Persian-language shop signs and event posters advertising concerts, plays, and poetry nights, especially in the ethnic enclave of Westwood and in West Los Angeles more generally but also in large billboards harkening the Iranian New Year and in public art across the city. As Homa Sarshar's story exemplified, among the Iranians who migrated to Los Angeles in the 1980s (the decade during which its Iranian population quadrupled) was a disproportionately high number of Iran's journalists, filmmakers, television and radio producers, and musicians, who, like Sarshar, resettled in Los Angeles seeking to develop new strategies for continuing their careers in exile. These individuals were prolific, beginning with print publications, short radio, and TV programs on public access airwaves and eventually innovating ethnic satellite television programming in an effort not only to reach dispersed diasporic audiences but especially to reach audiences in Iran itself.[64] The advent of satellite and digital networks assured that opposition figures could spread their political messages across borders, but also that whatever style was in vogue among the Iranian cultural elite in Los Angeles, including whatever image of wealth (real or imagined) they chose to portray and whatever symbolic and cultural repertoires they chose to employ, became the representation of a particular *Los Anjelesi* style for Iranians across the diaspora and in Iran itself.[65]

Whatever tentative acceptance of their new homes Iranians felt in the United States by 2000, just as their exilic suitcases were being replaced by a more permanent diasporic condition, the terrorist attacks of September 11, 2001, led to renewed suspicion, discrimination, and exclusion. The Enhanced Border Security and Visa Reform Act of 2002 marked Iran as a "state sponsor of terrorism" by the US Department of State and thus halted nonimmigrant visas for all Iranians and sharply reduced immigrant and refugee approvals in 2003 (fig. 1.3). In what felt to many Iranian Americans as a terrifying callback to the targeting of Iranians in 1979–80, in 2002, the US government announced the National Security Entry/Exit Registration System (NSEERS) that required nonimmigrant male nationals over sixteen years of age from twenty-five countries, including Iran, to report to INS offices to be registered, questioned, photographed, and fingerprinted and to provide additional information about themselves.[66] When approximately one thousand Iranian men in southern California arrived to comply, hundreds were handcuffed, arrested, and detained for days without the ability to notify loved ones of their whereabouts nor to access their attorneys or physicians.[67] While a small number were deported for visa infractions, others were detained for simply awaiting the outcome of their pending permanent residency applications.[68] Perhaps unsurprisingly, the number of Iranians who were actually granted that status the following year was the lowest since 1978 (fig. 1.3).

On a national scale, anti-Iranian rhetoric and actions not only were renewed but reached new heights during the War on Terror, as then-President George W. Bush named Iran as part of an "Axis of Evil," falsely suggesting a connection between the 9/11 attacks and Iran, Iraq, and North Korea. This led to heightened and targeted discrimination, prejudice, sanctioned profiling, and violence against Iranian Americans and other Middle Eastern and Muslim (or Muslim-perceived) individuals. The surveillance of Muslims, including Iranians, by the Federal Bureau of Investigation; interrogations by the Transportation Security Administration (TSA) or Customs and Border Patrol; denials of visas and security clearances; and the continued stigmatization and negative representations in media led Iranians in the United States to organize in the 2000s. First-generation Iranian Americans had established local associations in the 1980s and 1990s focused on maintaining Iranian cultural identity, practicing religion, or debating homeland politics; this new burst in the 2000s and 2010s included national Iranian American organizations such as media watch groups, civic responsibility and know-your-rights campaigns, and advocacy coalitions, often led by 1.5- and second-generation Iranians who had grown up in the diaspora. They sought to defend civil rights, promote civic participation, increase the representation of Iranian Americans in American politics, and insert positive representations of their communities in mainstream culture and media.

In line with these national-level efforts to organize Iranian Americans, Southern California Iranians had also become more active in political organizing in this period. The city of Glendale elected Armenian Iranian Bob Yousefian to the Glendale City Council in 2001; he then became mayor in 2004. Beverly Hills meanwhile elected an Iranian Jewish businessman, Jimmy Delshad, to Beverly Hills City Council, leading to his two turns as the mayor of Beverly Hills (2007–8, 2010–11).[69] More Iranian American candidates ran for local offices in southern California, but with few electoral successes. Indeed, relative to Iranians in countries like Sweden, Canada, or Germany, Iranian Americans have had remarkably few successes in electoral politics across the United States, despite a larger population size, and despite standing for municipal, state, and federal elections, reflecting the ways electoral systems and geopolitics can deeply impact immigrant participation and inclusion.[70]

Through transnational cultural productions, a common sense developed among Iranians globally about Los Angeles, including that it was not only home to the largest number of Iranians outside of Iran, but also that Tehrangeles constituted the diaspora's capital. As a result, and in contrast to Western-news-media- and Hollywood-driven stereotypes of Iranians as terrorists and religious extremists, competing stereotypes of "LA Persians" also emerged—and in many ways, were encouraged by some community members—that promoted conspicuous consumption, materialism, and extreme wealth.[71] While this latter set of stereotypes was preferred to the former by many, others loudly contested it as portraying Iranians as shallow consumers while problematically homogenizing the ethnic and class diversity of Iranian communities in Los Angeles. These competing sets of narratives offer a glimpse at the "common sense" that has been cultivated in the US mainstream, the diaspora, and in Iran about Iranians in Los Angeles.

*Demographics: Iranians in the United States Today*

Despite the various limitations placed upon Iranian migration to the United States following the 1980s, Iranians continued to arrive through family reunification, onward migration from other diasporic locations, the Diversity Immigrant Visa program (known as the "green card lottery"), and especially student visas. As in other parts of the diaspora, the increased out-migration of Iranians following the 2009 Green Movement and subsequent repression by the Islamic Republic also contributed to a spike of Iranian student and immigrant arrivals to the United States in 2009 and into the 2010s (fig. 1.3). Whereas a vast majority of Iranian students who had arrived in the 1970s (90 percent in 1979) indicated an intention to return to Iran upon graduation, just 8 percent of Iranian doctoral students in the United States in 2017 reported the same intention.[72]

Given the large number of students in the United States at the time of the Revolution and a common set of beliefs across generations that education is a pathway for social mobility, it is unsurprising that Iranian Americans as a group since the 1980s have held a high level of educational attainment and remain among the most educated ethnic groups in the United States.[73] As of 2014, over two-thirds of Iranian immigrant men and half of Iranian immigrant women in the United States held bachelor's degrees; second-generation educational attainment is even higher.[74] Relatedly, labor force participation is relatively high as well, especially in high-skilled professions. As in other parts of the diaspora, entrepreneurship is a common avenue for Iranian American economic vitality,[75] and in a 2000 study, Iranian Americans ranked just third (behind Greeks and Koreans) in self-employment rates.[76] However, while these oft-repeated socioeconomic trends certainly offer a picture of the lives of many Iranian Americans, the overemphasis on educational attainment and labor force participation also risks masking a clear class heterogeneity that is also indicated by official estimates. For example, the 2022 American Community Survey estimated a significantly higher poverty rate among Iranian American elders aged sixty-five years and older (17.8 percent) than among non-Iranians in the same age group (10.6 percent).[77] A similar disparity appeared among Iranian American single mothers (women heads of households who are living with their minor children without a spouse), where the estimated poverty rate (30%, ±13.2) again is significantly higher than their white, non-Hispanic (28.4%, ±0.4) and Asian (22.0%, ±1.4) counterparts.[78]

Although US Census data placed the population of Iranian Americans in 2022 at over half a million (519,658),[79] scholars and community leaders have repeatedly suggested that Census data represents an undercount, with the actual population at between 1 and 1.5 million.[80] Nevertheless, this data shows that Iranians are the largest Middle East and North African (MENA) group in the United States to self-identify as MENA alone,[81] and that nearly half (45 percent) of all individuals who self-identify as having Iranian ancestry in the United States still live in California. Furthermore, over half (57 percent) of Iranians in California live in adjacent Los Angeles and Orange Counties.[82] Beyond California, large and active Iranian communities live in the DC-Maryland-Virginia (DMV) area, the New York–New Jersey–Connecticut (Tri-State) area, and Texas, with smaller but growing communities in Georgia and Washington.

Just over half of Iranians in the United States in 2017 (56.46 percent) were immigrants, with an average age of fifty-four; the second and subsequent generations composed 34.25 percent (and growing) of the Iranian American population, with an average age of twenty-one.[83] These figures indicate that the second generation had come of age and numerically grown steadily, as expected, while the first generation was both aging and not being replenished with new immigrants as quickly in the 2010s as they had in the previous decade. Deepening this gap, the 2017 Executive Orders and Presidential Proclamations that came to be known as the "Muslim Ban" were implemented in 2018, effectively barring Iranian nationals from entering the United States, and thus all but halting immigrant replenishment for the first and 1.5 generations during the years the ban was implemented.[84] The first Donald Trump administration (2017–21) also effectively ended refugee resettlement in fiscal year 2018, leading to a sharp drop in Iranian refugee arrivals, from 2,575 in 2017 to just 41 individuals in 2018.⁸⁵ As a result, after a relatively steady, if modest, number of green cards were issued annually to Iranians in the early 2010s, during the first Trump administration these too declined for Iranians, dropping in 2019 (e.g., even prior to pandemic-related delays or restrictions on migration) to levels not seen since 1979 (fig. 1.3).

Iranian American organizations took leading roles alongside other advocacy groups in combatting the Muslim Ban, including through filing lawsuits against the United States government. The organizations established in the 2000s to advocate for a community that had no national representation prior to 9/11 were better-prepared to respond collectively for the first time, and the coalitions and networks they had built in the intervening decade became instrumental in opposing discriminatory policies and the specifically anti-Iranian rhetoric that emerged during the first Trump presidency, albeit with mixed results. These efforts were joined by those undertaken by cultural organizations seeking to represent Iranian culture and history as strategies for inclusion.

Though immigration to the United States became more difficult in several periods of the last fifty years, as evidenced in the sharp dips and peaks in the flow of Iranian arrivals, Iranian migration globally did not halt in those periods. Iranians who could not or did not seek to reach the United States sought refuge elsewhere—in the 1980s, that often meant through third-country refugee resettlement programs that led them to countries like Sweden.

## Arriving to Sweden

Susan Taslimi has one of the most recognizable faces in Iranian cinema history. Active in Iranian cultural industries both prior to and directly after the Iranian Revolution, her résumé includes performances that transformed Iranian theater and film in the late 1970s and early 1980s. She had stayed in Iran through the Revolution and early years of the Islamic Republic and was poised to reach a high point in her acting career when postrevolutionary government-enforced changes in Iran's cultural sector finally forced her and other prominent artists, especially women, out of the industry. Rendered unable to work without fearing for her safety, Taslimi fled Tehran in

1987, at the age of thirty-seven. She didn't tell anyone of her plans to seek asylum, fearing what would happen to her family if word got out:

> I had two [asylum] interviews; first at the airport and then the next day at the detention center. I tried to be very focused in my interview, to really emphasize the main issue and not go into the margins. I told the officers what the problem had been; I said, "I wasn't at all political, not a member of any party." Because the best thing to do is to tell the truth. But that, "Due to the cultural problems that we have [in Iran], well, naturally in any dictatorial regime anyone who does cultural work is truly at the front lines.... I mean, you don't need to have a gun in your hands; people who do cultural work are more exposed to attacks and assaults. [Because] cultural work is related to opening minds." So when I told them that, and explained the conditions in Iran, I think that had a proper effect.[86]

After her asylum interviews, Taslimi was placed in a remote camp in the north of Sweden where she and other asylum seekers—mostly political asylees from Chile and Iran—awaited adjudication of their cases: "I arrived on 2 November.... Those days were actually okay at first, but then it got cold and the lake froze. I had never seen a frozen lake before. People said you could drive across it, but they were lying—no one ever drove across it. But it froze, it was amazing, I had never seen ice like that."[87] She was there for a difficult two months, though her wait was relatively short in comparison with others, some of whom spent years waiting in these camps.

Significant numbers of Iranians began to arrive in Sweden in the second half of the 1980s, peaking in 1986, primarily as asylum seekers and refugees who had stayed in Iran through the Revolution (fig. 1.4). Unlike the students, religious minorities, and monarchists who composed much of the initial Los Angeles immigrant and refugee population of the late 1970s and early 1980s, Iranian refugees who claimed asylum in or were resettled to Sweden in the late 1980s were more often secular, Leftist, and/or ethnic minority opponents (e.g., Kurds) of the Islamic Republic. Many had been activists, civil servants, intellectuals, or cultural workers like Taslimi who had stayed in Iran through the early 1980s seeking to continue their work and, in the case of activists, to ensure the direction of the new government and Iranian society would meet their revolutionary expectations. When those expectations were not met, and especially when these individuals faced targeted harassment, imprisonment, and/or violence in Iran, they fled to neighboring Türkiye and Pakistan with little to no assets, often through incredibly difficult journeys on foot or pack animals, requiring the help of smugglers. Once in neighboring countries, they sought refuge and resettlement through the United Nations. Key among the countries accepting quota refugees in this period was Sweden, where immigration priorities had shifted only recently to focus on humanitarian categories. Other Iranians, like Taslimi, found their way to Sweden by plane, through smugglers or social networks aware that Sweden's refugee system and asylum policies had grown favorable to Iranians.

Once her residency papers arrived, Taslimi was moved to a second "camp," this time a residential building in a more populated area in the south of the country. Where the first camp was situated so that refugees lived apart from the community, here she was given a one-room apartment where her neighbors were Swedish. She lived there with her daughter for over a year, waiting their turn in a new refugee reception system established in 1985 that relied on government quotas and budgetary incentives to encourage Swedish municipalities to place refugees.[88] As the number of refugees entering Sweden increased, municipalities in points-of-entry (e.g., Stockholm, Malmö) with higher numbers of immigrants carried the majority of the burden of support for refugees waiting for decisions on their asylum cases. To remedy this, Sweden implemented an active "Sweden-wide" program of refugee dispersal from 1985 to 1994, during which nearly all municipalities across Sweden held agreements with the state for refugee placement. After asylum was granted, refugees were permitted to move, but wait times were often long and moving was difficult for some. When the policy was reformed in 1994 to allow refugees to arrange their own accommodation upon arrival, the program already had created demographically multicultural municipalities across Sweden.

Unlike the first camp, free Swedish-language classes were offered to refugees in this second location, and Taslimi noticed that many refugees there attended the classes. She knew language would be the key to her survival, and yet, she also knew she could not attend:

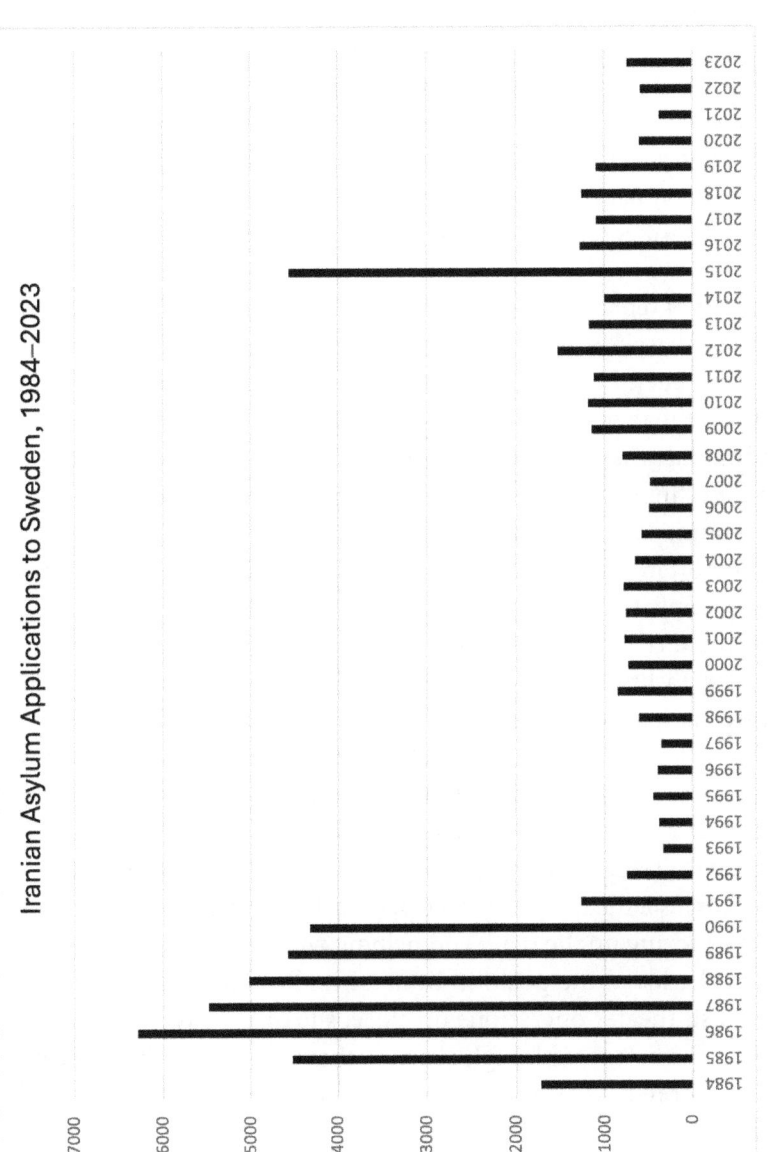

Figure 1.4. Number of asylum applications from Iranians to Sweden by year, 1984–2023. Sources: Swedish Migration Agency, "Applications for asylum received 1984–1999" www.migrationsverket.se. Statistics Sweden, "Asylum-Seekers by Country of Citizenship and Sex," table 00003WL, www.statistikdatabasen.scb.se.

In the second camp there were more [Iranians], so I thought it was better that, rather than [intermingling with their families], I should be a bit quieter. Because they had already interrogated my mother and father in Iran. They asked, "Where's your daughter?" And [my parents] had answered, "We don't have any information. Maybe she went to study? Maybe she went abroad for vacation? I have no idea." They asked, "Did she go to stay? Is she trying to get asylum?" They had said, "No, it's nothing." For the safety of my family, I wanted to stay on the sidelines. And that necessitated that I was forced to learn Swedish on my own.[89]

The long arm of repression of the Islamic Republic of Iran (IRI) extended to countries of asylum, putting in the regime's crosshairs not only family members back home but also fellow exiles and refugees abroad. Especially in the 1980s and early 1990s, Iranian dissidents were targeted and in some cases assassinated in European cities of refuge like London, Paris, and Berlin. For these and other reasons, Iranians often were wary of fellow countrymen in refugee camps and other exilic settings, among whom they often found themselves forced to live as roommates and neighbors simply because they spoke the same language.

When the city of Gothenburg finally sent her acceptance thirteen months later, Taslimi finally was able to enroll in Swedish for Immigrants (SFI), a free language course provided by the Swedish government for both refugees and new immigrants. Because she was an actor by profession, Taslimi needed language skills to continue in her work, but she also sought to learn more about Swedish theater, in particular. A job placement officer for refugees, also provided by the Swedish state, helped find her a position as a theater producer's personal assistant, making her coffee and tea, picking up the mail, and helping with show tickets.

Though she loved the position because it allowed her to finally observe Swedish theater operations up close, she didn't have much interaction with the actors; although she saw them as equals, they saw her as merely a foreign assistant. Around the same time, a film in which Taslimi had starred as a lead actor prior to her departure screened at the 1989 Gothenburg International Film Festival. The experience of silently making coffee for her employer in the morning and riding a public bus to take center stage at a buzzy film festival screening of *Maybe Some Other Time* in the evening threw into relief the major changes that had so rapidly transformed her life: "For two hours I was a big star at Gothenburg Film Festival; at the opening, speaking before the screening—it was like returning to what I was. And then returning here . . . it was like time travel, really."[90]

## Iranian Community-Building in Sweden

That Sweden had begun focusing its migration policy on humanitarian refugees in the same period that Iranians were seeking asylum in large numbers is a coincidence that led to the growth of a large and active Iranian community in the country. Sweden's policy of refugee dispersal between 1985 and 1994 resulted in the distribution of Iranians across the country, often to remote towns in need of the financial benefit that came with taking in refugees. During my fieldwork in Stockholm, nearly all the Iranians with whom I spoke who had arrived during the 1980s as refugees related tales of the challenges they faced having fled bustling cities like Tehran only to arrive to camps in tiny, snowy villages with no money, no family, and no prior knowledge of Swedish language or culture.

These reception camps and resettlement structures were part of a developing refugee system that required newcomers to adapt not only to the frigid weather but to a society and culture that had not caught up with the migration policies that had enabled their arrival. When Iranians were resettled into immigrant suburbs in areas surrounding Stockholm, for example, the process of integration was slow and, in many cases, lopsided. While some described to me positive experiences with their neighbors, especially fellow refugees, others recalled the frightening presence of neo-Nazis and threats of violence against immigrants in these changing suburban neighborhoods of the 1990s. As one 1.5-generation Iranian in Stockholm told me, "In the '90s, I got harassed or hit on the streets all the time by skinheads, by Nazis. And people didn't do anything [about it] because they were so afraid of these Nazis themselves."[91] This was the setting of the early 1990s during which the Sweden Democrats emerged as a xenophobic and anti-Muslim fringe party; three decades later, it became the second-largest party in Swedish Parliament.

Though the majority of Iranians arriving in Sweden in the 1980s carried little to no financial assets with them, what they did arrive with was a relative abundance of cultural capital.[92] Iranians were then and remain now one of the most highly educated immigrant groups in Sweden, with more than 25 percent of both men and women having attained at least three years of postsecondary education—6 percent higher than the Swedish average.[93] Although framed by some conservative analysts as exceptional immigrants,[94] the case of Iranians in Sweden is nevertheless demonstrative that high or even simply equal education rates do not guarantee success against the high under- and unemployment rates suffered by immigrant groups.[95] Despite having achieved educational attainment at a higher average rate than nonimmigrant Swedes, only 54.4 percent of Iranians in Sweden were employed in 2011, compared to 81.6 percent of Swedes.[96]

Despite Sweden's reputation for progressive immigration policies, labor market integration remains a significant challenge for immigrants due to structural discrimination, credential barriers, and implicit biases that have led to persistent underemployment.[97] According to a 2012 Swedish labor force survey, nearly 80 percent of native-born men and women in Sweden with postsecondary education held jobs that required their level of education, while the same applied to less than 50 percent of foreign-born men and women.[98] In other words, many educated immigrants in Sweden, including Iranians, have been doing jobs that are beneath their skill level and at a far greater rate than educated native-born persons. Indeed, out of all the Nordic countries, Sweden has had the highest unemployment gap between foreign-born and native persons of working age.[99] By the end of 2021, the immigrant unemployment rate was a staggering 16.2 percent, 4.7 times the nonimmigrant unemployment rate of just 3.4 percent.[100]

The intersecting causes of these inequalities are debated among scholars, politicians, and journalists, including within immigrant communities. When I asked Maryam, a member of Swedish Parliament, in 2012 about the high levels of unemployment among immigrants in Sweden, she told me, "That's because of discrimination, I would say, and racism. My father who is a PhD, it took him four years after his PhD to get a job. People say, 'Well it's because you are not educated,'—Swedes always say that—and I say, 'Okay, do you want me to show you an engineer working at a 7/11? Do you want me to show you a doctor who speaks *perfect* Swedish but who's driving a cab?'"[101] Even among 1.5-generation Iranians with high education and fluent Swedish like Maryam, "foreign-sounding" names can still prevent their employment opportunities: "I never got a job by applying. Never, ever. During my first twenty-six years not being in the Parliament, I always got [employment] by personal contacts. Because I don't have a 'good Swedish name.'"[102]

Beyond employment, as might be expected given their activities in Iran prior to migration, Iranian communities in Stockholm and Gothenburg have remained very active in political and cultural realms.[103] Many political refugees told me of their continued activism once they arrived in Sweden, which some continue to engage in today. Though later waves of migration have resulted in a politically mixed population, activists of various persuasions nevertheless maintain public resistance to the Islamic Republic in Sweden's major cities, primarily in struggles for human rights, women's rights, and religious freedom in Iran. But Iranians also have been active in Swedish politics, especially the 1.5 and second generations, the latter of which has recently started to come of age. Unlike in the United States, Iranians in Sweden have become leaders in each of Sweden's major political parties, through which they have held municipal positions, served in Swedish Parliament, and been appointed to Ministerial positions in government (e.g., Ardalan Shekarabi, Minister for Public Administration [2014–19] and Minister for Social Security [2019–22], and Romina Pourmokhtari, Minister for the Environment [2022–], a second-generation Iranian Swede and the youngest-ever cabinet minister in Swedish history). That Iranian MPs have represented nearly all Swedish parties in Parliament (e.g., as the leader of the Left party and as MPs from the Swedish Social Democratic party, the Liberals party, the Moderate party, Center party, and, as of 2022, the far-right Sweden Democrats) hints at the wide diversity of political opinion among Iranians in Sweden.

Iranians who had been professional artists in theater, film, media, and music in Iran have worked to continue their careers once in Sweden. They have done so within the community through Sweden's corporatist model of community organizing, leading to dozens of Iranian cultural associations (over one hundred in 2011), small-scale productions of Persian-language theater, ethnic media like Iranian talk-radio programs (over twenty in 2018), and Persian-language book stores and publishing firms.[104] Many of these radio programs, associations, and Persian mother-tongue language schools (*modersmålsundervisning*) are

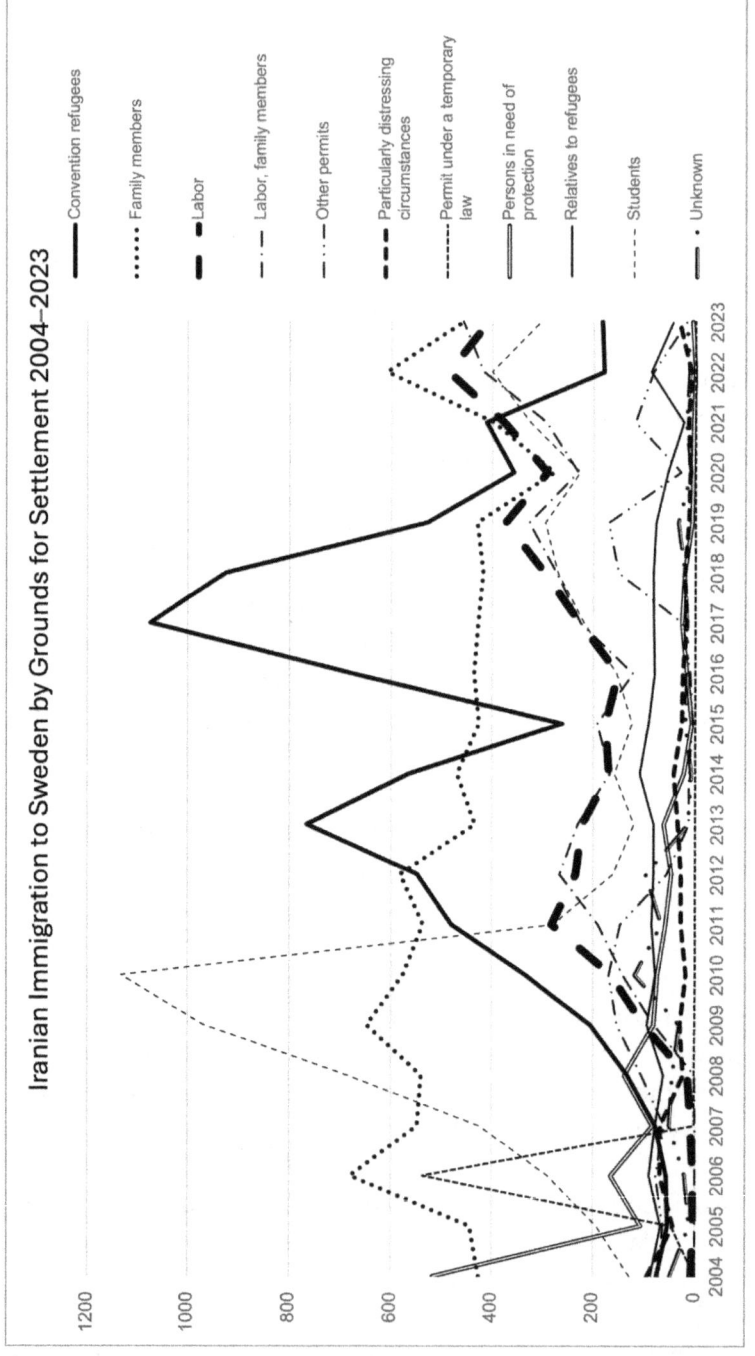

Figure 1.5. Iranian immigration to Sweden by grounds for settlement (2004–2023); categories with fewer than five hundred total immigrants excluded. Source: Statistics Sweden, "Immigrations (except citizens from Nordic countries) by grounds of settlement, country of citizenship and sex. Year 2004–2023." Table BE0101AP. March 22, 2024. www.statistikdatabasen.scb.se.

operated by Iranians through financial support from Swedish state multiculturalism policies.

Some artists like Taslimi were eventually—and with varying levels of success—able to break into Swedish media, theater, and film. In the 2010s, Iranian Swedish musicians and dancers were performing on public stages across the country, including in Melodifestivalen, Sweden's immensely popular annual competition for representation in the Eurovision Song Contest, considered something of a barometer of European pop culture. They served on arts councils and worked in leading organizations that determined funding of city and provincial programming. The 1.5 generation has been especially active in Swedish cultural industries, directing and appearing in the casts of award-winning Swedish films, on popular Swedish TV series, and serving as news anchors on Swedish TV. In Swedish theater, they have increasingly gained lead roles and positions of authority among the notoriously homogeneous cultural elite that has run Stockholm's prestigious theaters. Recognizing the imbalances in the country's arts and cultural fields, young Iranian Swedes have used these hard-won positions to diversify casting and to develop productions that consider questions of Swedish identity and immigrant exclusion.

## Demographics: Iranians in Sweden Today

Beyond the early wave of asylum seekers in the mid-1980s and early 1990s, between 2000 and 2011, Iranians accounted for 3 percent of all immigrants arriving in Sweden.[105] While Iranians continued to arrive as refugees (e.g., on the grounds of politics, religion, ethnicity, sexuality), especially following the 2009 Green Movement and crackdowns in Iran, other motivations like family reunification, jobs, and education also were more frequent than in the previous period (fig. 1.5). In the 2000s especially, young Iranians sought out Sweden's free postsecondary education in rapidly growing numbers; students quickly became the largest flow of Iranians to Sweden. But this flow sharply dropped when the government withdrew this form of support for immigrants from beyond the European Union and European Economic Area in 2011 (fig. 1.5).[106] The 2000s also saw shifts in Swedish migration policy favoring skilled labor, and Iranians arriving in this category sharply rose at the end of the decade and again at end of the 2010s, when, in 2019, skilled workers became the largest category of Iranian immigration, partially due to the restriction of asylum policies that year (fig. 1.5). While other countries took priority in Sweden's asylum and refugee admissions for most of the 2010s, Iranians nevertheless joined Syrians, Kurds, and Afghans in the record-breaking flow of asylum seekers who arrived in 2015–16—known in the media as the "Migrant Crisis." These flows, including Iranians, declined sharply following the 2019 shift in asylum policies.

Some 133,189 individuals of Iranian origin were registered as living in Sweden in 2023, making up 3.6 percent of the total foreign-background population and nearly 1.3 percent of the total Swedish population of approximately 10.55 million.[107] Geographically, although Iranian immigrants live across the country, they are most concentrated in the cities of Stockholm, Gothenburg, Malmö, and Uppsala. The largest of these concentrations (nearly 38 percent of all foreign-born Iranians in Sweden) is in Stockholm County, including both the city of Stockholm and its populous suburbs, where individuals born in Iran constituted 4.8 percent of the total foreign-born population there in 2024.[108]

In Stockholm county districts and municipalities like Solna, Sollentuna, Järfälla, and Upplands Väsby, Iranians often have lived in estates built as part of the Millions Program, a state-led 1960s housing scheme to build one million dwellings in just ten years for Sweden's growing urban populations.[109] Within the municipality of Stockholm, at the end of 2013, over one-third of the city's residents were immigrants and their children, but, unlike Los Angeles, Toronto, or other multicultural cities, there are no named ethnic enclaves in Stockholm. But there is extreme urban segregation: The sharp rise in refugee and nonwhite migration of the 1980s and 1990s saw the demographics of the suburbs where rental housing was newly available shift dramatically, as immigrants moved in while the number of nonimmigrant Swedish residents in the same areas declined.[110] Meanwhile, large-scale tenure conversion starting in the 1990s has meant the waiting list for a rent-controlled apartment in central Stockholm is decades-long, and immigrants are at a distinct temporal disadvantage. Due to a mix of the liberalization of the housing market, a sharp decline in the number of available rental units, historic refugee resettlement restrictions, economic constraints, discrimination, and personal choice, it has been most common for Iranians and other immigrants in Stockholm to live among an array of other immigrants in the suburbs rather than solely among fellow coethnics.[111] Thus, although over 12,600 Iranians lived in the city of Stockholm in 2023, they resided across all eleven districts.[112] The largest numbers lived in the highly diverse districts of Kista, Akalla, Rinkeby, and Husby, all located in the district area of Järva, where 75.6 percent of the population had a foreign background in 2023.[113]

As the end of the Iran-Iraq War and the atrocities of 1988 ended, the number of Iranian refugees being resettled in Sweden also declined in the 1990s (fig. 1.5). A new trend in Iranian migration emerged in its place: a wave of students and economic migrants seeking educational and employment opportunities in Sweden, but also—and increasingly—in multicultural Canada.

## Arriving to Canada

Born just after the 1979 Revolution, Behrouz arrived in Toronto in 2002 for his undergraduate education in computer science at York University. With his eyes set on a new life in Canada, and especially on getting into law school, he avoided the growing number of Iranians in his new city as a language-learning strategy:

> I came to Toronto [in 2002]. And in the beginning, I tried to sort of stay away from the Iranian community so I could work on my English. During my undergrad years, I was pretty much focused on studying only. I wasn't doing anything [else]. So, I didn't really hang out with the Iranian community, didn't know any of them, didn't know what was going on in Toronto. I just knew there was a big Iranian community here. I stayed away because I just knew that I have a goal here, and I need to focus on that, and I need to go to law school.

In contrast, when Nima arrived in Toronto the next year at the age of twenty to attend Toronto Metropolitan University (TMU, formerly Ryerson University) for a degree in architecture, he did just the opposite. He sought out Iranians right away, finding comfort in fellow Persian-speakers:

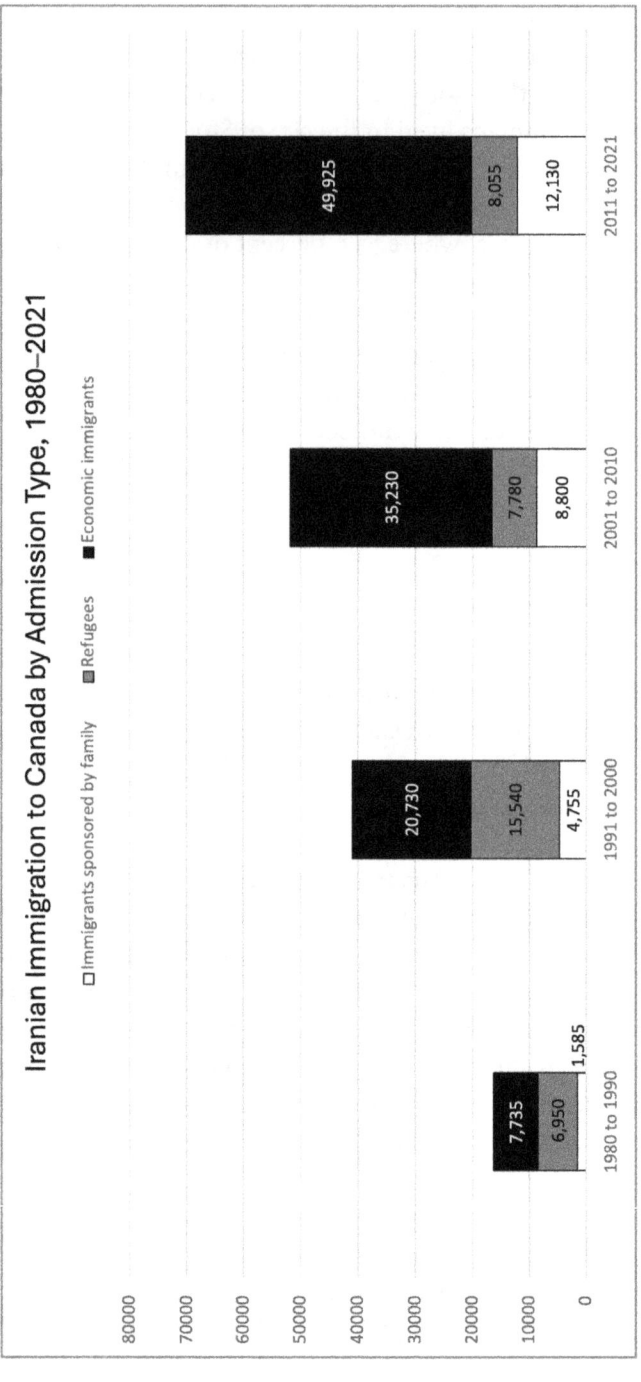

Figure 1.6. Iranian Immigration to Canada by Admission Type and Period of first obtaining landed immigrant or permanent resident status, 1980–2021. Ten-year counts through May 11, 2021. Source: Statistics Canada, "Period of immigration by admission category and place of birth: Canada, provinces and territories, census metropolitan areas and census agglomerations with parts," Table 98-10-0317-01, October 26, 2022.

I came to Canada in 2003. I didn't have any family here. So when I got to university, I started to create my own group of friends. And personally, I always feel more comfortable doing things in a group. So when I got to [TMU], my English was not that good, so I gravitated towards my own community. And when I searched for my community in [TMU], there was a group of people, but scattered. So I put together a group to create a website and we started posting announcements that we want to gather, play backgammon, and so on. And eventually that became the Iranian Students' Association of Ryerson University. In 2003, we registered the association, and we went through the procedures, wrote the constitution, and eventually I became one of the players.

Though they took different approaches, Behrouz's and Nima's experiences were exemplary of the large flow of promising young Iranian students arriving alone to Canada in the late 1990s and 2000s. Upon graduation, they found jobs in Canada and became permanent residents, building their careers and families in Toronto, and joining the growing "Tehranto" community.

A relatively small number of Iranians had been present in Canada prior to the 1979 Revolution, but it was not until 1984 that Iranians began arriving in large numbers. This growing flow of migration surged in the 1990s, again in the 2000s, and yet again in the 2010s (fig. 1.6). A new refugee determination system implemented by the Immigration and Refugee Board of Canada on January 1, 1989, enabled Iranian refugee admissions to peak in the 1990s, first in 1991–92 and then again in 1995–97. In both the 1980s and 1990s, refugees and other protected persons (e.g., designated classes, such as Baha'is as of 1982) constituted over a third of all Iranian immigrant arrivals.[114]

Despite these high proportions of refugee admissions, and consistent with shifts in Canadian immigration more broadly, economic immigrants have represented the largest portion of Iranian immigration to Canada. While in 1981 most Iranians arriving in Canada had been protected persons, twenty years later the number of Iranian immigrants had grown more than five times and were more likely to be admitted as economic immigrants, even if economic, political, familial, and social reasons often intersected as motivations for migration.[115] Although the political situation in Iran began to stabilize postwar, the economic outlook remained bleak. Meanwhile, access to legal migration to the United States became more challenging without family sponsors in the late 1980s and 1990s, and Sweden's humanitarian priorities had shifted toward admitting refugees from the Balkans. Thus, whereas revolution and war were critical impetuses for the large flows of Iranians to the US and Sweden, the lack of employment and economic prospects felt by an educated generation of Iranians during the postwar economic restructuring of the 1990s ended up greatly benefitting Canada.

Canada's points system favored this flow of Iran's brain drain migration: highly skilled, educated, linguistically capable, young, and often single Iranians were particularly successful in a system that calculated entry based on these characteristics. By 1996, Iranians already represented 2.6 percent of all immigrants arriving in Canada and Iran was among the top ten sending countries for all landed immigrants admitted to Canada.[116]

In 1990s Iran, top graduates from the country's best universities entered a domestic job market with high unemployment and few prospects for postgraduate advancement, a situation that has intensified in the following decades. Frustrated, academically promising Iranians increasingly have left Iran to continue their undergraduate and postgraduate education abroad. In the same period, Canada had developed strategies to attract postgraduate international students from which they then would have a pool of talent for permanent residency applications. The approach was effective: 48 percent of immigrants who had arrived to Canada between 2000 and 2004 as international students then applied for permanent residency in the economic class, many Iranian immigrants among them.[117] Iranians who had first arrived with student visas in the 1990s joined job seekers and others in acquiring permanent residency in Canada at a rate 2.5 times higher than they had in the 1980s, and these numbers continued to grow through the 2010s (fig. 1.6).

Joining these entrants, a new stratum of Iranian immigrants also arrived in significant numbers in this period: the investor immigrant class. In this scheme (ended in 2015), immigrants to Canada who invested a minimum dollar amount in land or business ventures were entitled to landing papers that enabled them to live in Canada legally and acquire eligibility to apply for citizenship within just three years.[118] One group described by one of my interlocutors as the "nouveau riche of the

Islamic Republic" especially took advantage of this new pathway, practicing what Aihwa Ong has termed *flexible citizenship*: "the cultural logics of capitalist accumulation, travel, and displacement that induce subjects to respond fluidly and opportunistically to changing political-economic conditions."[119] In Ong's formulation, entrepreneurs and other elite citizens "collect" passports that enable them to travel without need for additional visas (thereby guaranteeing mobility) and to "flexibly" take advantage of social welfare, tax benefits, and other advantages not offered in their home countries. These additional citizenships enabled wealthy Iranians to flexibly move money and sponsor family members who would benefit from the education and social capital gained from a North American foothold.

In 2000s and 2010s Toronto and Vancouver, for example, Iranian investor immigrants purchased condos or mansions in the northern suburbs where their children (sometimes arriving alone as "parachute kids" and cared for by nannies) attended local schools, while they themselves remained in Iran or traveled back and forth, spending time in Canada for medical treatments (thanks to Canada's provincially funded universal healthcare) or maintaining businesses and other investments.[120] It is well known that the children of Iran's government-affiliated elite are regularly sent abroad for education, a practice openly criticized as evidence of hypocrisy. One 2013 Facebook commenter responded in exasperation to seeing a photo of the Canadian university graduation ceremony of the great-granddaughter of Khomeini himself: "Honestly, is there anyone among you [who are tied to the regime] who educates your children in Iran? *Mashallah!* All of you, reformist or conservative, educate your children in either Europe or America. The West and America are only bad and dirty for the rest of us, but for you all they're heaven."[121]

Though still a less common case in the Iranian context compared to larger immigrant communities in Canada, this phenomenon is nonetheless resonant in the Iranian diaspora and one that was mentioned to me multiple times during fieldwork. It also marked one of a number of stratifications in the community, leading to whispers (especially by middle-aged Iranians who had lived and worked in Toronto since the late 1990s) that the financial sources of newly arrived investor immigrants were suspicious, asking "off whose backs" their wealth had been accumulated after the Revolution and in exchange for what political gains and losses for the people of the country. These suspicions only intensified with a series of highly publicized, transnational embezzlement and fraud cases in the early 2010s,[122] and again in the 2020s when the Woman, Life, Freedom protests led to a barrage of diaspora accusations and demands for Canadian officials to investigate.[123] The internal diversity of Toronto's Iranian community includes a wide array of political, religious, and economic positions that has made for a particularly active and vibrant, if volatile, environment for community organizing.

## Building Tehranto

The province of Ontario is home to more than half of the Iranian population in Canada, and, although significant numbers of Iranians have concentrated in cities like Vancouver and Montréal, and near large universities in cities like Edmonton, the largest population growth has been primarily in Toronto, or "Tehranto."[124] The city itself is home to a highly diverse populace where, in 2021, over 46 percent of the metro area's residents were immigrants and 57 percent were counted as "visible minorities," including Iranians.[125] Since the 1990s, the University of Toronto, York University, and TMU have attracted top Iranian students who have found work in Toronto and other areas of the province, including at firms like IBM and, later, RIM (Blackberry), Mozilla Firefox, and Google. The city has grown into not only the largest Iranian community in Canada, but, should its pace of growth continue, it may soon overtake Los Angeles as the largest community of Iranians outside of Iran.

As students, refugees, and economic immigrants settled in Canada, family reunification became another key pathway of migration for parents, children, and siblings. While the number of Iranian-born refugees admitted to Canada halved between 1991–2000 and 2001–10, family sponsorships grew steadily each decade: Admissions doubled from the 1980s to the 1990s, nearly doubled again in the 2000s, and continued to grow by over a third in the 2010s (fig. 1.6). This large flow of families with children and older parents brought the need for targeted services and programming in municipalities like Toronto. Programs such as Persian StoryTime at public libraries and care services for elderly Persian-speakers answered the call, as did a growing number of Persian-language radio and TV programs for kids and adults on public access channels.

These audiovisual programs would soon develop into a thriving Persian-language media, especially in the Toronto community, which had produced small-scale Persian-language publications as early as 1979.

Among those that have been most successful, *Shahrvand* newspaper was established in 1991 as a free biweekly newspaper reporting on local, national, and international news.[126] At its height, *Shahrvand* was published three times a week and circulated not only in Toronto but also Ottawa, Montréal, Edmonton, and Calgary, and even in some US cities, leading it to boast its status as "the biggest weekly magazine in North America."[127] As Sima Sahar Zerehi, the daughter of cofounding editor Hassan Zerehi, would reflect later in its English pages, locally produced Persian-language media like *Shahrvand* became a key feature of everyday life and community-building in 1990s and 2000s Toronto: "When we would arrive at Yonge just south of Finch there would be a line-up of eager community members awaiting the weekly publication, people would rush to get their copy of *Shahrvand* and immediately flip through the pages. Within a few minutes, full-fledged debates over the articles would ensue and the street corner by the grocery store would become a makeshift town hall."[128]

While some families were reunited by immigration, others remained divided by oceans in search of higher education, job opportunities, or neoliberal flexibility. These divisions became mapped onto the city's landscape: Young, single, well-educated technocrats and graduate students have tended to live cosmopolitan lifestyles in downtown Toronto, while a mix of well-heeled families and working- and middle-class refugees and immigrants live in the mixed-class uptown and outer suburbs. Whereas Toronto's downtown core is home to bustling ethnic enclaves in neighborhoods like Chinatown, Little Italy, Little Korea, and Little Portugal, suburban northern Toronto neighborhoods—where Iranians live in large numbers—are better characterized by overlapping ethnic clusters, reflective of the city's ever-expanding superdiversity. The suburban neighborhoods of Richmond Hill, North York, and Thornhill are composed of large numbers of Iranians and their flourishing supermarkets, restaurants, and service-oriented businesses, whether in well-known strip malls such as Iranian Plaza, or sandwiched between Korean schools, South Asian salons, and Chinese restaurants along Yonge Street (fig. 1.7).[129] Korean,

Figure 1.7. Left: The businesses of multiple immigrant communities mingle on Yonge Street in North York, Toronto. Right: Iranian Plaza, North York. (Credit: Amy Malek, 2015, 2011)

Jamaican, Chinese, Iranian, and South Asian people live and work side by side in northern suburbs like North York, where Mel Lastman Square—the site of community events like the Latin Arts Festival or the Korean Harvest Festival—provides the go-to public venue for Toronto Iranians' protests, festivals, and promenading. In recent decades, large suburban real estate developments—including condominiums, subdivisions, and apartments—have been built by Iranian developers and mark exceptional sites where the Iranian residents may outnumber their neighbors.

In addition to businesses, from as early as 1973, when the Iranian Student Association was established at the University of Toronto, Iranian Torontonians have developed a wide array of cultural, social, professional, political, religious, sporting, and children's organizations for the city's residents.[130] Toronto's Iranian community has been notable for its prolific cultural productions created through community-based institutions, including theater companies, art galleries, and festivals. It has also been a leader in the diaspora in Iranian LGBTQ+ advocacy and representation through multiple organizations founded by queer Iranians in Toronto, such as the Iranian Railroad for Queer Refugees (now International Railroad for Queer Refugees), founded in 2008 in Toronto as the first nongovernmental organization working on behalf of Iranian LGBTQ+ people in the world. The organization registered the first official Iranian contingent in the Toronto Pride parade in 2011 and Iranians have participated every year since, with a reported three hundred Iranians marching in 2023 Toronto Pride.

In Tehranto, there is significant community participation in both social and political spheres and in both homeland and Canadian politics. Unlike their counterparts in the United States, but similar to those in Sweden, Iranian Canadians have found electoral successes and representation at provincial and federal levels. The first two Iranian Canadian members of Parliament in Canada were both elected in 2015 from suburban Toronto area ridings (Ali Ehsassi, MP for Willowdale; Majid Jowhari, MP for Richmond Hill). But the Toronto Iranian community has been especially active when Iranian and Canadian politics cross. For example, in 2012, when Canada severed diplomatic ties with the IRI, Iranians in Canada not only were left without consular services, but experienced similar discriminations in business and financial transactions as compatriots in the United States did when companies refused services for fear of violating sanctions regulations.[131] For example, Canadian multinational financial services corporation TD Bank gained notoriety in 2012 for having summarily closed dozens of Iranian Canadians' personal and business accounts and lines of credit without explanation or recourse. Iranian Canadians responded by calling for a boycott, holding protests in Toronto, and spreading the news on both traditional and social media, leading to what was described by *Maclean's* editors at the time as "a public relations nightmare."[132]

Community activism directed at the Canadian government reignited again in 2014 when a bill was passed that would have effectively made Iranian Canadians and other dual citizens into second-class citizens, and again in 2020 when dozens of Iranian Canadians on a passenger aircraft were killed by surface-to-air missiles launched by the IRI, leading to widespread calls from the community for the Canadian government to more aggressively pursue justice.[133] As part of these campaigns, and especially during the 2022 Woman, Life, Freedom protests, many Iranian Canadians called on officials to investigate the presence of individuals affiliated with the IRI in Canada, leading the prime minister to publicly respond: "We know that there are people today in Canada who have benefited from this horrible and corrupt regime and who are hiding in the middle of the community enjoying the opportunities that Canada offers. They are using the wealth they stole from the Iranians. We say: enough is enough."[134] These efforts of community activists also contributed to Canada's listing of the Islamic Revolutionary Guard Corps as a terrorist entity in June 2024.[135]

### *Demographics: Iranians in Canada Today*

According to the 2021 Canadian Census, 200,465 individuals in Canada identified as "Iranian" in "ethnic or cultural origin," constituting 2.2 percent of the total Canadian population, while some 182,940 individuals listed Iran as their place of birth.[136] This data, though imperfect,[137] helps to confirm observations that the second generation in Canada is as yet a small proportion of its Iranian population. Iranians in Canada are dispersed across multiple provinces, but the largest concentrations are in Ontario (Toronto), British Columbia (Vancouver), and Quebec (Montréal). In 2021, nearly half of Iranians (an estimated 90,000) lived in the Toronto metro area alone.[138]

During the 2010s and into the 2020s, students, job seekers, and investor immigrants continued to arrive to Canada, as did refugees and those seeking asylum based on political activities, religious persecution, and sexual orientation. As in the United States and Sweden, journalists, activists, students, and other politically active young professionals who had participated in the 2009 Green Movement fled to Canada following arrests, prison torture, and repression. While some arrived in Canada as refugees, many came as economic immigrants, contributing to a sharp uptick between 2010 and 2011 (fig. 1.6). The 2010s brought a significant surge of young Iranians to Canada: The number of immigrants from Iran admitted to Canada rose from eighth to fourth place among all Asian sending countries in 2011.[139]

Any of these newcomers arriving in Canada, regardless of immigrant category, could seek out free services provided by state-funded agencies. For example, Toronto's Welcome Centre Immigration Services employed Persian-speaking professionals to provide free assistance with finding housing, job referrals, résumé prep, accreditation, education and training workshops, legal and social assistance, and English-languages classes. Volunteering in these classes in 2012, I observed as Iranian Canadian educators taught recently arrived Iranian adults and children language skills and lessons in Canadian history and culture, and also linguistic and behavioral norms.

While nationwide statistics suggest that the unemployment rate among immigrants remains close to that of those born in Canada (in 2022, 5.7 percent and 5.0 percent respectively),[140] scholars have shown that immigrant underemployment has been a pervasive problem. For example, one study found that "only 40 per cent of skilled principal applicants who arrived in 2000–2001 were working in the occupation or profession for which they were trained" ten years later.[141] In what has become known as "the foreign-trained-professionals problem," immigrants who arrived to Canada through the points system as skilled laborers often found after arrival that their credentials were either misrecognized or not recognized at all, forcing them to either seek reeducation or accept jobs well below their skill level, what scholars have called "survival jobs."[142] While the Canadian government technically ended the points system in 2015 through a Conservative-led change intended to mark a shift of focus to economic immigrants (coinciding with neoliberal reforms across the government's platform), it continues to assign applicants to the Express Entry program (an online application system for "skilled workers") a score based on their human capital, ranking them in a pool of would-be immigrants and thus effectively maintaining a system of preference based on education, linguistic ability, skills, and work experience.[143]

Due to ongoing flows ensuring immigrant replenishment, the first generation of Iranians in Canada includes community leaders who have lived in Canada for over forty years, but also those who continue to arrive daily and have begun to outnumber the earlier cohort(s). This newer mix includes activists and refugees fleeing the government of the Islamic Republic as well as those who have been active in and maintain ties to that same government. Perhaps to a greater degree than in some other diasporic locations, the milieu in Canada therefore mixes widely differing orientations to Iran. Despite the severing of diplomatic relations between Canada and Iran as of 2012, given the large proportion of recent immigrants among Iranian Canadians compared to the United States or Swedish cases (and the different restrictions on mobility in each, such as single-entry US visas), it is unsurprising that Iranian Canadians are also more likely to travel and maintain close connections to family, friends, and acquaintances in Iran. It was this active transnationalism that became tragically highlighted in January 2020 with the loss of so many Iranian Canadians returning home from trips to Iran on Ukraine International Airlines Flight 752.[144]

The second generation in Canada has only recently begun to come of age, later than their American second-generation counterparts. Second-generation Iranian Canadian adults thus relate stories of growing up in the "Canadian mosaic" prior to the growth of the Iranian community, and feeling their difference acutely in elementary school classrooms where they were pressured to fit in. Indeed, second-generation racialized persons have reported feeling less attachment to Canada, with one study reporting "feelings of alienation and disenfranchisement."[145] Yet while some feel disenfranchised, other second-generation Iranians in Canada—like in the United States—describe themselves as "assimilated" and are not as active in the day-to-day life of the Iranian community, marking another line of stratification along generational as well as cohort lines. For leaders and activists in the 1.5 or second generation, the perceived cultural difference between Iran and their diasporic homes is keenly felt in intergenerational contexts and can be a further source of tension in the large and diverse Toronto Iranian community.

## Arriving to Multicultural Societies in Transition

Shifting policies and migration trends in the late twentieth century meant that Iranians arrived to the United States, Sweden, and Canada in the midst of deep, and often contentious, societal changes. These countries were rapidly becoming demographically multicultural while they and other liberal democracies were still experimenting with policies and practices that could ensure equity. Debates about assimilation, integration, and multiculturalism grew into national conversations, albeit at varying rates and intensities.

Studies of nineteenth-century North American assimilation among mostly white European immigrants had theorized a "straight-line" assimilation model wherein immigrants and successive generations conform to a majority (white) culture over time. But a theory of eventual conformity to a white US majority culture could not explain the decades of exclusions experienced by immigrants from Latin America, Asia (including the Middle East), and Africa.[146] For Canadians, with their French, British, and Indigenous communities vying for power or autonomy, the question over whether a majority culture existed uniformly across the country was itself a matter of lengthy debates even before surges of non-European immigrants and refugees arrived in the late twentieth century.

As Asian American, Chicano/a American, and African American civil rights movements blossomed in the 1960s and 1970s, the question of what it meant to be American and how equal rights and belonging would be protected for all citizens—not just legally but as practiced in everyday life—was a topic of increasing debate. But while these groups agitated for reforms with measured success, the governments of Sweden and Canada were instituting legislation and policy directives to address the inequities experienced by racialized citizens through codified legal channels.

Multiculturalism as a concept and as a policy was in many ways born in Canada.[147] After nearly a decade of debates and government commissions on the subject, in 1971, then–Prime Minister Pierre Trudeau announced that the Canadian government would adopt a multiculturalism policy: "Although there are two official languages [in Canada], there is no official culture, nor does any ethnic group take precedence over any other. No citizen or group of citizens is other than Canadian, and all should be treated fairly."[148] Acknowledging the maintenance of two official languages of English and French, Trudeau described the new policy as "a policy of multiculturalism within a bilingual framework" and emphasized the dual importance of cultural retention and individual freedom, the latter of which would be "hampered if [individuals] were locked for life within a particular cultural compartment by the accident of birth or language."[149]

Canada's reputation as a country of pluralistic tolerance was built on a recognition of difference that historians suggest was necessitated by its history: The coexistence of political contests between the descendants of the two "founding nations" of France and Britain led many to support *biculturalism*, but the struggles of First Nations communities for equal rights protections and self-governance alongside civil society demands to symbolically recognize the contributions of a growing number of immigrants (first from Europe, as described earlier, and increasingly from non-European homelands) demanded a federal plan for policy that guaranteed rights for multiple national minorities, not just two. Canada's history of colonial settlement, immigration, and violent coercion against Indigenous peoples (e.g., through the residential school system) are therefore integral to understanding the country's role in the development of multiculturalism, both at its establishment and today.

In 1982, the Canadian Charter of Rights and Freedoms was signed, and in 1988, over a decade and a half after Trudeau's announcement, the Canadian government adopted the Canadian Multiculturalism Act. The act provided for ten policy directives committing Canada to recognition and respect for cultural diversity, including the "freedom of all members of Canadian society to preserve, enhance, and share their cultural heritage," "equal treatment and equal protection under the law, while respecting and valuing diversity," and "the full and equitable participation of individuals and communities of all origins in the continuing evolution and shaping of all aspects of Canadian society and [assistance] in the elimination of any barrier to that participation."[150] The government claimed that the dual focus on valuing diversity and ensuring equity "distinguishes the Canadian approach, and moves it beyond a policy that merely tolerates minority groups, to one that actively seeks to build an inclusive Canadian society."[151]

By affirming multiculturalism as a fundamental characteristic of Canadian nationalism, the 1988 act codified a sentiment upon which the government would consistently draw and that provincial governments would take as a model for their own policies. It is also one that remains unique in the Western world.[152] Regardless of its flaws in implementation, rather than merely a descriptor of demographic realities or even a policy recommendation among many others, multiculturalism forms both Canada's normative approach to immigrant integration and the core of its efforts at nation-building; it is now considered a foundational cornerstone of Canadian identity.[153]

In Sweden, similar ideas were under discussion in the 1970s. The decade marked not only a pivotal shift in Swedish immigration but was, relatedly, also the period in which Sweden adopted its first multiculturalism policies. These policies, passed by Parliament and guaranteed in a revision of the Swedish constitution in 1975, were multicultural in the sense that they were specifically aimed at creating equal opportunities for immigrants and improving integration while providing opportunities for immigrants to choose to participate. This was part of the foundation of the Swedish social democratic principles of equality, security, and freedom of choice. Participation was meant to be a real choice: Immigrants could choose to participate in state-funded Swedish-language training while also choosing to maintain their own linguistic and cultural practices—and not just in private, but through publicly funded ethnic associations and "mother-language" education programs provided in Sweden's primary schools. Coherent with the Swedish Model, this interpretation of freedom of choice and equality sought to treat everyone in Sweden with the same fundamental social rights, including rights to culture, which would encourage a sense of belonging and duty to contribute to society.

Just as Canadian multiculturalism continued to be debated through the 1990s, so too was this debate ongoing in Sweden. Despite its policy efforts, immigrants in Sweden were still being considered and treated as outsiders. Some advocates of reform suggested the emphasis on ethnic associations in early Swedish multiculturalism had created a detriment to belonging. As a result, the language of these policies shifted away from targeting immigrant groups and began focusing instead on the individual. In what scholars have argued marked a conceptual shift from "immigrant policy to integration policy," a 1997 bill indicated integration should be understood as a process that concerned all individuals—meaning both Swedish citizens and newcomers—rather than an assimilation process that only required change from immigrants.[154]

Relatedly, it was also in the 1990s that incremental neoliberal policy reforms began in Sweden to move away from the social democratic corporatism model, weakening the labor unions and undermining the welfare state. This happened alongside the growth of immigrant and refugee populations, leading conservative and far-right parties to gain popularity by suggesting that the widening inequality caused by these neoliberal reforms was actually due to the increasing presence of immigrants. In their research on the deterioration of the Swedish Model, Carl-Ulrik Schierup and Simone Scarpa argue that these "neoliberal and austerity-oriented reforms of the welfare state have progressively eroded the integration potential of social policies and have thus been a major factor in shaping the current reality of deepening, and increasingly ethnically tinged, class divisions and long-term social exclusion."[155] This, they suggest, was a harbinger of the end of Swedish exceptionalism.

In 2009, the Swedish Parliament passed a new government bill on cultural policy that acknowledged that "*intercultural* exchange, like international exchange, is extremely important for the development of cultural life."[156] This shift to interculturalism—and away from multiculturalism—has been a strategy in other policy contexts in Europe as well. But interculturalism has been as difficult to define as multiculturalism. While some scholars have argued that there is no substantive difference between the terms, others have insisted that, unlike multiculturalism, interculturalism more explicitly encourages a two-way process of immigrant incorporation, or what is often called *integration*, as opposed to traditional forms of straight-line assimilation. In the idealized form that Swedish cultural policymakers envisioned, interculturalism would result in a shift in identity for both immigrants and nonimmigrants, ultimately changing the commonsense understanding of who belongs as a Swedish citizen.

Back in Canada, a debate between multiculturalism versus interculturalism was also underway, but under different circumstances. In the context of Québécois nationalism, what has been called the "reasonable accommodation crisis" of 2006–8 centered on the rights of religious minorities like Sikh, Muslims, and Hasidic Jews and the "reasonable accommodations" that should or should not be provided to ensure their equal participation in society (e.g., in government employee uniform exceptions or exemptions). This renewed the tensions between Quebec and English Canada that had nearly resulted in secession in 1995. So, too, did related debates surrounding a right-wing proposal for a "Quebec Charter of Values" in 2013–14 that would have forbidden public sector employees from wearing conspicuous religious items or symbols at all. In each case, critics took aim at what they viewed as encroachment by religious minorities, especially Muslims, on Quebec's "values." These frustrated efforts led scholars to pit a Québécois *interculturalism* that permits Quebec to sustain its "majority culture" against a Canadian *multiculturalism* that seeks to remove majority culture altogether in favor of equal respect for all cultural forms in the laws of the land.

While policy makers in Canada and Sweden spent the last decades of the twentieth century defining and experimenting with multiculturalism through policies seeking to ensure equity in cultural pluralism, the United States took a sharply different approach: The federal government neither sought to define multiculturalism nor to implement multiculturalist policies. With its "nation of immigrants" national mythology and a larger, older immigrant population, the issues of equity and equal access may have been raised in the United States earlier than in Canada and Sweden, but these efforts met far greater resistance in late twentieth century American political discourse. By the late 1980s and 1990s, policies and initiatives with multiculturalist aims had been implemented at the state and federal levels (e.g., affirmative action in education and employment), but not through an official multiculturalism that would have required the apportionment of state resources and institutional support, and not without opening new fronts in an already raging set of culture wars. Critics hotly contested what constituted American identity and values through advocating for or condemning programs like affirmative action or curriculum reform in public schools and universities (e.g., seeking to tighten or widen the canon to exclude or include African American, Native American, Asian American, and Chicano/a histories and literatures). Despite (or perhaps because of) a growing politics of difference nationally, at the federal level, the United States never enacted official multiculturalism and thus has not provided federal resources for immigrant-centered programs intended to foster inclusion, as Canada and Sweden have done. Instead, a neoliberal multiculturalism has developed instilling, among other ideas, the commonsense understanding among Americans that assimilation is the responsibility of immigrants, rather than the state-supported bidirectional model that was being explored in other multicultural societies.[157]

While Canada and the United States, as former settler colonies built by immigrants at the expense of Native groups' sovereignty and rights, share some historical trends, the history of the United States and its attitudes toward minorities, immigrants, and Indigenous communities has varied from Canada in important ways. These have included the primary emphases in the United States on racial difference and the American commonsense belief that not only should immigrants pull themselves up by the bootstraps to reach the mythologized American Dream, but that ethno-cultural difference should be relegated to the home and private spaces in favor of an American identity in public. In contrast, while racialization is of course prevalent in Canada and has contributed to persisting inequities, political sociologist Irene Bloemraad has shown that Canadian ideals of multiculturalism nevertheless have included encouraging political incorporation of immigrants by providing instrumental support, like funding resettlement and community programs alongside legal protections, and symbolic inclusion, like creating feelings of inclusion and attachment to the country through government programs but also modeling openness to public difference.[158] Moreover, financial and in-kind support to organizations has enabled ethnic communities to legitimately cultivate "multiple identities while promoting Canadian citizenship" and to publicly present their cultural and artistic talents and heritage across Canada.[159]

That multiculturalism has been a sustained and integral component of Canadian cultural identity makes it exceptional in North America and Europe. That said, life in Canada is not universally experienced as a multicultural utopia where equality is applied deeply and evenly across groups and geographies. Racism and discrimination within the system continue to create problems for immigrants and Indigenous groups, especially in a labor market that continues to underutilize immigrant education and skills.[160] The rise of extremism and xenophobia in political discourse and everyday life also have been marked in Canada since the 2010s, even if they have not yet reached the same levels as in the United States or Sweden.[161] Conservative governments sought to shift policy priorities and remove multicultural funding in the early 2010s; much of the country's multicultural resources now originate from municipalities and provinces rather than coming directly from the federal government. These bodies are also taking on more of the creative multicultural policy work.[162]

In Europe, along with the rise of far-right political movements and neoliberal economic shifts, anti-immigration critics and xenophobic parties railed against multicultural polices in the 2010s. In a number of western and northern European countries—including Sweden—incidents like uprisings or acts of terror were routinely blamed on refugees and immigrants, and consequently also on multiculturalism as a failure of policy. While criticism of multicultural policies in Europe emerged even before they began to take root in the 1980s and 1990s, the 2000s saw the development of fuller and louder criticisms from a wider and more diverse set of critics. By the early 2010s, critiques of multiculturalism became so loud in Europe that many scholars and journalists declared a "backlash" and suggested that multiculturalism had become a "poisoned term," especially in countries like Germany, France, the Netherlands, and Great Britain—despite the fact that several of these countries had never actually implemented official multiculturalism.[163]

In Sweden, multiculturalism was blamed for immigrant "rioting," high unemployment, increasing crime rates, and racial tensions; this political rhetoric gained popular appeal regardless of conflicting or scant sociological evidence to back it. Such rhetorical strategies were led by the Sweden Democrats (SD), a far-right anti-immigration party with neo-Nazi roots, and helped them to win Parliament seats steadily between 2010 and 2018—making it the third largest party in Swedish Parliament (Riksdag) by the end of the decade. In the 2022 general election, SD had their strongest result to date, garnering 20.6 percent of the vote and becoming the second-largest party in Sweden. Immigrants have joined the far-right party in increasing numbers, including Iranians: Two of SD's newly elected members of the Riksdag that year were Iranian-born men, one of whom published a collection of his essays in 2015 titled *Why Multiculturalism is Oppression*.

The politicization of cultural policy by SD and center-right parties has meant funding for key multiculturalism programs like mother-tongue education and immigrant associations has been slashed and a new focus on cultural heritage and "traditional national culture" (defined as distinct from multicultural or cosmopolitan elite culture) has been proposed.[164] Meanwhile, hate crimes against immigrants, and especially young men from Muslim countries, nearly doubled in Sweden between 2011 and 2016.[165] Acts of arson against refugee centers, mosques, and synagogues also rose in the same period, with the Associated Press reporting some 112 fires at Swedish refugee and reception centers in 2016 alone.

The impact of these discourses and violent acts is a sense among many Swedish immigrants, especially people of color, that they will never belong or be seen as Swedish, leading to a crisis of identity especially for the 1.5 and second generation. While covering strategies and claiming a white identity or a proximity to whiteness may have helped some first-generation Iranian Americans prevent discrimination and feel less exclusion in the United States, such strategies have not been feasible, if even desired, in Sweden, where belonging *as Swedish* has been so deeply tied to a narrowly defined whiteness that full inclusion has been denied to Iranians and other non-European immigrants and their descendants.

While migration policies in the United States, Sweden, and Canada each evolved to accommodate new global realities, their approaches produced distinct Iranian diaspora formations. Where the United States enabled broad economic participation but limited political participation, Sweden's strong welfare policies aided early resettlement but failed to address labor market discrimination. Canada's points-based system meanwhile created a skilled migrant class that was also aided in their arrival but is still navigating cultural representation and internal diversity. The multicultural policies mentioned here—or lack thereof in the case of the United States—have shaped how Iranians in each of these diasporic locations have worked to contest negative representations and put forward their version of Iranian culture and identity as one among many strategies of inclusion. But these strategies are not uniform, nor without contestations. Especially for a diaspora that so often describes itself as unable to work well with one other, the process of representing Iranian culture generates competing views on what it means to be Iranian, but also, as we will see, competing modes of belonging that variously subvert and reinforce existing power relations across local, national, and transnational scales.

2

# Asserting "Freedom, Dignity, and Wealth" in Los Angeles

In a 2013 announcement promoting its new exhibition, *The Cyrus Cylinder and Ancient Persia: A New Beginning*, the Smithsonian Institute heralded the arrival of the Cyrus Cylinder to the United States for its first national tour: "Making its U.S. debut is a football-sized, barrel-shaped ancient clay cylinder covered with Babylonian cuneiform, one of the earliest written languages, that announced Cyrus's victory and his intention to allow freedom of worship to communities displaced by the defeated ruler Nabonidus. Under Cyrus (ca. 580–530 BCE), the king of Persia, the Persian empire became the largest and most diverse the world had known to that point. His declarations of tolerance, justice, and religious freedom inspired generations of Philosophers, policymakers, and leaders, including Alexander the Great and Thomas Jefferson."[1] Organized through a partnership between the British Museum (which formally acquired the cylinder in 1880) and London-based diasporic nonprofit organization the Iran Heritage Foundation, the tour exhibited the cylinder in the five US cities with the highest number of Iranian-American residents. To do so, the exhibition relied on close cooperation between local Iranian American community organizations and donors, and highly respected US museums such as The Metropolitan Museum of Art in New York City; the Smithsonian Institute in Washington, DC; and the Getty Villa in Los Angeles.[2]

The exhibition displayed the Cyrus Cylinder alongside clay fragments, gold jewelry, carved seals, and vessels dating back to the Achaemenid Empire (550–330 BCE), the expansion of which was framed as "a new beginning" for the ancient Near East. Related marketing, like that just quoted, especially highlighted the importance of Cyrus II, known as Cyrus the Great, to American history, suggesting a more contemporary "new beginning." Indeed, curators and sponsors stressed that the exemplary leadership of Cyrus the Great had "inspired generations of philosophers, policymakers, and leaders" in the West, including those responsible for America's democracy.³ Exhibition wall text and the display of additional items at certain stops of the tour stressed this interpretation. For example, alongside quotations from the Bible and Machiavelli's *The Prince* that referred to Cyrus, text from a letter Thomas Jefferson penned to his grandson appeared on the exhibition wall: "I would advise you to undertake a regular course of History and Poetry in both languages. In Greek, go first thro' the Cyropaedia, and then read Herodotus, Thucydides, Xenophon's Hellenus and Anabasis."⁴

At the Smithsonian stop of the exhibition, thanks to a loan from the Library of Congress, one of Jefferson's two copies of the *Cyropaedia* was displayed prominently in a glass case opened to a page Jefferson is said to have annotated. Described by scholars as a romanticized and largely fictional biography of Cyrus II of Persia written by Xenophon around 370 BCE, the *Cyropaedia* was a favored text for learning Greek, as Jefferson had recommended to his grandson.⁵ These annotations implied a close reading that suggested how deeply influenced Jefferson must have been by the statecraft and legacy of Cyrus the Great. The book's presence in the libraries of US founding fathers such as Jefferson, John Adams, and Benjamin Franklin was used as supporting evidence for "the importance of Cyrus to those who wrote the Constitution of the United States" and thus made the case for why Cyrus the Great should be regarded as important by elite American institutions and their hundreds of thousands of American visitors.⁶ British Museum director Neil MacGregor argued as much in an article produced by the US State Department about the Smithsonian stop of the tour: "The story of Persia—Iran—is part of the story of the modern United States. . . . Although 18th-century Europeans read and commented on the tenets of religious freedom and tolerance set down by Cyrus, only the United States' founders enshrined them in law."⁷

In concurrent events with the exhibition, British and American scholars and curators described in great detail, with the authority that their credentials provided, assurances of the crucial influence of ancient Persian statesmanship on core American ideals—not only on the notion of human rights, but on the American experiment of democracy itself. Such representations of the cylinder imbued it with contemporary ideological value. But this was not the first time Cyrus or his cylinder were made into symbolic resources for modern purposes. Mohammad

Reza Pahlavi, the former Shah of Iran (1941–79), and the political and intellectual elite in the same period had made Cyrus the Great a symbolic cornerstone of midcentury Pahlavi nationalism. Through their efforts, Cyrus and his cylinder were furnished as representations of Iran's great historical contributions to the world.[8]

This line of reasoning was taken one step further in the 2013 US exhibition tour. Cyrus the Great was presented especially by Iranian American cosponsors, donors, and attendees as the source of American values and liberal ideals, and thus a premodern contribution by contemporary Iranians—as "the heirs of Cyrus"—and especially those now resident in the United States. The then-executive director of the Farhang Foundation, the community cosponsor for the cylinder's Los Angeles stop, made this connection explicitly when she told the *Los Angeles Times* that the Cyrus Cylinder "is important because of the ideals it represents, that say who we really are. . . . Non-Iranians can get to know the Iranian culture and its people in the correct light, rather than the portrayals in the media that we hear every day."[9]

Echoing the sentiments of so many Iranian diaspora community organizers seeking to repair the representation of Iranians in the mainstream, the implication of this and similar statements was that this exhibition would not only demonstrate a global acceptance of the ancient Iranian roots of all the abstract notions attributed to the cylinder in the late twentieth century—including human rights, "tolerance, justice, and religious freedom"—but also a specifically American acceptance of the worthiness of Iranians in the present day, especially those who now live in the United States. Through Cyrus the Great, Iranian Americans put forward an argument that they should no longer be rendered as "enemies within" but as the original ideological donors to the very fabric of American identity.

This presentation of an ancient Persian artifact and its legacy in American history thus also suggested a "new beginning" for the representation of Iranians and Iranian Americans in the United States. Revising an American collective memory that marks the beginning of the US-Iran relationship in twentieth-century political events—whether the Iran Hostage Crisis (1979–81), 1979 Iranian Revolution, or the 1953 overthrow of then–Prime Minister of Iran Mohammad Mossadegh—here a "new beginning" was located in the ancient reign of Cyrus II, allowing for a much earlier and friendlier relationship forged in a perceived shared ideological kinship. That perception relied as much on shared mythologies of benevolent empire as on the willingness to ignore the fundamental contradictions between liberal pronouncements of human rights and the illiberal actions of the leaders who pronounced them.[10]

But there can be no doubt that this approach was successful in garnering attention: Over four hundred news outlets reported on the exhibition, helping to draw in the over 315,000 visitors (including 155,000 in DC and 75,000 in LA) who viewed the cylinder while on its nine-month tour.[11] When the cylinder arrived at its final stop at LA's Getty Villa Museum, Angelenos attended the cylinder exhibition in droves; it was reported at the time as the most well-attended exhibit in the museum's history.[12] Dozens of school groups contributed to the high attendance figures, and Iranian American families especially turned out, some from across the country, lining up for hours with their non-Iranian colleagues and friends to bear witness.

Once inside, many Iranian Americans were moved to tears in front of the small cylinder in its glass case, feeling through it the pride and honor that had been denied them for decades in the United States (fig. 2.1). Though their scholarly legitimations were important, the curators and directors of these British and American museums did not need to convince older first-generation Iranian immigrant audiences of the cylinder's relevance; they had been taught about Cyrus the Great through school lessons, media, and official events in prerevolutionary Iran and had been eager to share them in their diasporic communities. In media interviews reporting on *A New Beginning*, Iranian Americans expressed that their frustrations about feeling misunderstood in the United States were momentarily released by seeing this ancient object revered in a major American museum. The experience was extremely emotional for many; as one attendee told a reporter: "I cried. I got goosebumps. It means a lot. I'm very happy that it came to [the] US."[13] Another shared, "I burst into tears. I got so excited, and something inside me just reacted. I don't know, maybe it's Iranian blood."[14]

Iranian Americans with these deeply emotional responses found in the exhibition confirmation of their identifications with Cyrus but also confirmation of the ideas ascribed to the cylinder during childhoods in Iran long before their migration. If Cyrus—an icon representing

Figure 2.1. Press photo from the Washington, DC, stop of the 2013 Cyrus Cylinder tour. (Credit: Hassan Sarbakhshian / www.easternviewerphotos.com)

the essence of Iranian identity—had influenced Jefferson—an icon representing the founders of American democracy, if not American democracy itself—then in this exhibition, Iranian Americans, their American-born children, and their non-Iranian neighbors all were confronted with evidence not only of the importance of Cyrus but of an ancestral Iranian goodness, one that had contributed to America before these immigrants had arrived at its shores.

For many Iranian Americans who felt othered and excluded, this message became a source of redemption and dignity: They described feeling seen, and symbolically included, in a place where otherwise their persistent invisibility in the mainstream had only been temporarily interrupted by hypervisibility in everyday experiences in airports, immigration offices, and difficult encounters with colleagues and neighbors during particularly tense geopolitical moments.[15] One young daughter described to a reporter seeing her mother's emotional reaction to the cylinder: "All of a sudden I turn around and I see [my mother] has got tears streaming down her face and she's staring at it and was overwhelmed. And I saw another daughter with her mom and she had the same reaction. It was very overwhelming for her.... There's a lot of awe and respect for it. It's a big deal to see something that's part of my heritage that I don't get to see very often."[16] To be associated with something positive, to be recognized as a member of a group being honored, and, as one exhibition-goer stated, to be described as "peace-loving people,"[17] was a salve for members of a group scarred by being defined by their own president as part of an "Axis of Evil."

In my interviews in Los Angeles and other US cities, Iranian community leaders repeatedly listed among their goals a desire to educate an American public woefully unaware of or, worse, misinformed about Iranian culture. This didactic aim was particularly motivated by a goal of rehabilitating Iranian identity and history in the eyes of American friends, colleagues, and neighbors who had only seen negative depictions of Iran thanks to contemporary politics and its representation in mainstream US media. Especially in the 2000s, with a heightened focus on Iran as part of an Axis of Evil, threats of terrorism were consistently featured in Orientalist depictions that presumed violence and oppression were essential dimensions of Iranianness, not a political disposition of particular state actors in a particular political moment.[18] Efforts to rehabilitate Iranian American reputations through knowledge-sharing and awareness-raising, especially against stigmatizing stereotypes, were directly motivated by these experiences of misrecognition and exclusion.

History, ancestry, power, and legacy all swam around this small artifact of cracked clay that had been injected with contemporary ideological meanings. In his critical take on the exhibition tour and focus on the Cyrus Cylinder in the United States, scholar Hamid Dabashi called the object a "floating signifier of meaning and meandering."[19] If its meaning was ever floating, diaspora community leaders and exhibition organizers worked tirelessly to harness it firmly to one set of meanings propagated in twentieth-century Iran and repeated in twenty-first-century American press releases, interviews, public lectures, teacher trainings, school field trips, blog posts, news media, and social media and even in a resolution introduced in Congress (H.Res. 130).[20] This production of meaning has been repeatedly mobilized by scholars, curators, critics, journalists, publicists, artists, donors, organizers, and community members well beyond 2013.

In a phenomenon I call *Cyromania*, a twenty-first-century diasporic field of cultural production has emerged to give twentieth-century

Figure 2.2. Bumper sticker advertising the Cyrus Cylinder exhibition at The Getty Villa, Los Angeles, 2013. A send-up of the famous "Got Milk?" advertising campaign of the 1990s and 2000s, the cylinder here indexes freedom. (Author's collection. Credit: Farhang Foundation)

Pahlavi nationalist significations a new utility in diaspora.[21] Part of a larger strategy of employing Iranian American *imperial nostalgia*—a wistful longing or affection for past empire,[22] in this case, the Achaemenid Empire—Cyromania has become a favored way to introduce "real" Iranian culture and history to American audiences. Along with images of the ruins at Persepolis and Zoroastrian symbols like the *faravahar*, the Cyrus Cylinder has become especially ubiquitous: on bumper stickers (fig. 2.2) and billboards; as commercial goods such as necklaces, cufflinks, broaches, T-shirts, handbags, pens, and paperweights; on advertisements, posters, and invitations for community events; as replicas decorating restaurants and offices; and as a source of discussion in blogs and social media posts that cite it as a demonstration of "who we really are" to non-Iranians as much as to second- and third-generation children and grandchildren.

Cyromania focuses especially on the life and legacy of Cyrus the Great through the proliferation of artifacts, narratives, and symbols originally made popular during the Revivalist period of the Pahlavi era (1925–79).[23] Though different from the phenomenon of nineteenth-century Egyptomania in important ways, Cyromania nevertheless is similar in its implications for politics, identity, and racial ideas.

What do these nationalist histories, symbols, and ideologies do for Iranians in diaspora? Rather than dismiss imperial nostalgia in diaspora as purely nostalgic or purely ideological, I analyze Cyromania primarily as a strategy in competitions for inclusion, particularly, though certainly not exclusively, in the United States. While the US exhibition tour made many Iranian Americans cry just looking at the Cyrus Cylinder, it also prompted non-Iranian museum-goers to reconsider their understanding of the relationship between Iran and the United States and forced the mayors of the first and second most populous cities in the United States to take notice of the immigrant community that lay claim to it—and that had worked so hard to promote it.[24] Drawing on notions of nostalgia and on the historical and aesthetic repertoires of twentieth-century Pahlavi nationalism, in their widespread and sometimes larger-than-life invocations of Cyrus, Iranian Americans have not only or simply parrotted nationalist tropes in response to geopolitical events in Iran. They have also responded specifically to American assimilationist trends that require immigrant groups to render their own histories and cultures within an American neoliberal frame of multiculturalism.

Imperial nostalgia, as a diasporic strategy of inclusion, aligns a view of Iran's historical stature as a benevolent Persian empire with a similar view of the contemporary United States and its empire. It has emerged and operates within neoliberal forms of power: Rather than making a case for inclusion as enactments of equality and basic human rights—the principles attributed in these narratives to Cyrus the Great—these efforts instead traffic in the history of Cyrus to feed American assimilationist demands and to affirm the integrity of the American project, including who belongs as American and why. In other words, community members have "bootstrapped" their own inclusion by putting forward ancient Iranian history and culture as testimony of contemporary Iranian Americans' moral goodness through their contributions to American ideals, mythologies, and hegemonic structures—even if they had not effectively guaranteed Iranian American inclusion from the outset.

This chapter offers a brief history of the development of the field of cultural production that I have termed Cyromania and demonstrates its strategic functions in the neoliberal multicultural United States through the example of the festive unveiling of a public memorial sculpture in Los Angeles, known as the Freedom Sculpture.

## A Brief History of Cyromania

The Pahlavi brand of Iranian nationalism established during the reign of Reza Shah Pahlavi (1925–41) found a focus during the reign of his son, Mohammad Reza Pahlavi, in commemorating Cyrus the Great as a national hero. This focus took form in extravagant events such as the Shah's own coronation in 1967, scholarly conferences and publications (especially in the field of archaeology), and media and cultural productions (e.g., films, books, exhibitions) highlighting the glory of the pre-Islamic Iranian past. These efforts culminated in the large and lavish 2500 Year Celebrations held across four days at the ruins of Persepolis in October 1971, an event so costly, over-the-top, and ultimately criticized that observers have regularly included its excesses as among the tipping points leading to the eventual fall of the Shah less than eight years later.[25] According to documentation at the time, the Shah sought in these festivities "to re-awaken the people of Iran to their past and re-awaken the world to Iran."[26] Despite the suggestion of two key audiences, these lavish invitation-only events were closed to the Iranian general public, attended instead by some six hundred foreign royals, celebrities, and dignitaries. At the opening event at the tomb of Cyrus the Great (fig. 2.3), the Shah famously tied the Pahlavis to the Persian Empire by placing himself as the descendant of a 2,500-year uninterrupted line of Iranian kings, proclaiming: "Cyrus, hero of Iran and the world, rest in peace, for we are awake and will always be awake."[27] In this way, the Shah sought to affirm his legitimacy through establishing a continuity and even parallelism between his reign and that of the founders of the Achaemenid Empire before the eyes of the world.

On the final day of the celebrations, a ceremony opened the newly completed Shahyad Tower (now Azadi Tower) in the center of Tehran, where a new museum of Persian history featured a display of the Cyrus Cylinder (the first time it would appear in Iran) on temporary loan from the British Museum. Dating back to approximately 539 BCE, the cylinder originally served as a foundation deposit, a genre of ancient documentation written by kingly scribes and buried in the foundation of buildings to be found by future generations who would learn of the king's accomplishments. When two small artifacts in the British Museum were discovered in 2010 to detail the same narrative as the cylinder, they were seen as confirming that Cyrus's message was not just intended to be found in the future, but also was likely spread as a public message to the people of Babylon, heralding Cyrus as a benevolent and powerful king.

If the cylinder was indeed intended as a public relations tool, that purpose was renewed when it was made the official symbol of the 2500 Year Celebrations, as commemorated on the official emblem of the event as well as on stamps and coins minted for the occasion (fig. 2.3). The focus on Cyrus continued when, in 1976, the Shah went so far as to change the official Iranian calendar to begin with the accession of Cyrus the Great in 559 BCE rather than the Hijra of Mohammad, shifting the year from 1355 to 2535 overnight.[28]

The long-term impact and collective effect of this field of cultural production on Iranian national identity has been significant. For as ever-present as he seemingly has become in a current period of Cyromania, Cyrus was not regarded by most Iranians as their ancestral national hero prior to these twentieth-century efforts. As Talinn Grigor has shown, while several kings of the Qajar dynasty (1789–1925) had commissioned replicas and friezes of themselves in a style inspired by the Achaemenid period, it actually was during Reza Shah's reign when this revivalism began to thrive, especially through state-commissioned neo-Achaemenid and neo-Sassanian architecture of government buildings and through cultural and education policy. Mohammad Reza Shah heightened this use of archaeological artifacts and ruins—such as Persepolis, the tomb of Cyrus (Pasargadae), and the Cyrus Cylinder itself—as meaningful symbols of ancient Iran for a modern global audience.[29] The Pahlavi efforts were an important departure: Cyrus is absent in key cultural sources such as the epic *Shahnameh* and had been unremarked upon by revered Persian-language poets and historians for centuries.[30] The only texts likely to be known among educated Iranians relating to Cyrus's life and conquests prior to the discovery of the Cyrus Cylinder in 1879 were ancient Greek sources, such as Xenophon's *Cyropaedia*, or the Hebrew Bible, which was likely to be familiar in Iran only among its Jewish and Christian minority communities.[31] So minimal was the role of Cyrus and these related sites and artifacts prior to the opening of the 1971 celebrations that the tomb of Cyrus at Pasargadae was described in official documents at the time as "a lonely, plundered, almost forgotten" place "left to lizards."[32]

Figure 2.3. The front page of *Ruznameh-ye Jashn-e Shahanshahi-e Iran* (Newspaper of the Imperial Celebrations of Iran), a special publication of one hundred issues dedicated to the 2,500 Year anniversary of the Persian Empire in 1971. The masthead featured the official emblem of the Celebrations, centering the Cyrus Cylinder within a stylized lotus motif topped by the Pahlavi coat of arms. (Source: *Ruznameh-ye Jashn-e Shahanshahi-e Iran*, no. 100, 31 Aban 1350/November 21, 1971.)

Scholars have suggested that the impetus for the modern project to fashion Cyrus the Great as a national hero was less likely to have been a desire to recuperate Iranian history (though it undoubtedly involved this) and more a desire among Pahlavi elites to create a politically useful heroic figure familiar and amenable to the modern—and largely Western—values and ideologies they sought to promote. This narrative asserted that Cyrus the Great had enacted the first declaration of human rights and was the first leader to promote ideas such as religious tolerance, diversity, and individual freedoms. Buttressed by accounts from the ancient Greeks and by favorable translations of the Cyrus Cylinder, in this interpretation, the cylinder confirmed the Biblical accounts of Cyrus's freeing of the Jews in the Book of Ezra, even if the cylinder never mentions the Jewish faith or people by name.

The interpretations of key lines of text continue to be debated, especially claims that Cyrus abolished slavery as a practice and that the cylinder should be read as the first charter or declaration of human rights.[33] Citing scholarly accounts and histories from the 1920s, archaeologist John Curtis has shown that while the cylinder was understood upon its nineteenth-century discovery in present-day Iraq to hold historical significance due to its description of Cyrus's taking of Babylon and its outlining of a genealogy, it was not recognized at the time for any connections to contemporary understandings of freedom, human rights, or democracy.[34] That argument only emerged in the mid-twentieth century, through efforts toward consolidating an official ideology by and for the Pahlavi elite. Curtis asserts that it is not clear who first employed the terms "first bill of human rights" or "first declaration of human rights" in describing the Cyrus Cylinder, but the notion that Cyrus was a moral founder who innovated principles of freedom and individual rights was not prominent prior to the 1960s, when it was advocated by Iranian elites, publicists, state officials, and, of course, the Shah himself.[35] These ideas were especially legitimized by Iranian and European scholars, whose academic treatises were promoted by Pahlavi elites in an effort to "reinforce the official state narrative"[36] and to give it a "scientific aura."[37]

The campaign to have Cyrus and his cylinder recognized in this way received its clearest push at the opening of the first United Nations Conference on Human Rights, held in Tehran in 1968. There, the Shah referred to the Cyrus Cylinder as "the precursor to the modern Universal Declaration of Human Rights."[38] He made the same claim again in 1971 during the 2500 Year Celebrations, which were billed as the culmination of Cyrus the Great Year, a year-long commemoration of the ancient king.[39] Concurrent with the Celebrations, a major international conference of Iranian Studies was held in Shiraz, reportedly attended by 275 scholars from thirty-eight countries, many of whom presented papers attesting to the attributes of Cyrus.[40] While these events were taking place in Iran, in New York the Shah's sister, Princess Ashraf, presented an exact replica of the Cyrus Cylinder to then–Secretary General of the United Nations, U Thant, providing a ready interpretation of its significance: "The heritage of Cyrus was the heritage of human understanding, tolerance, courage, compassion, and, above all, human liberty."[41] The presence of this gift in a glass case on the second floor of the United Nations Secretariat continues to be referenced by Iranians in diaspora and by Western politicians to demonstrate Cyrus's founding role—and by extension Iranians' role—in the development of human rights as defined and enshrined by that same international institution.

Experts such as Curtis, however, explicitly rejected these ideas, as he told an audience at the Metropolitan Museum of Art in New York in 2013: "The cylinder is not the first declaration of human rights. It wasn't intended to be anything of that kind. And indeed, the concept of human rights didn't exist at that time. However, . . . taken as a whole, the contents of the cylinder do certainly demonstrate a break with past tradition and the ushering in of a new era."[42] Academic skeptics decades earlier had also questioned the archaeological and historiographic evidence for these claims as they were being popularized, such as British historian Peter Avery, who called it "phoney [sic] history."[43] Meanwhile, vocal anti-Pahlavi activists in the 1960s and 1970s (including at the very same 1968 UN Conference of Human Rights in Tehran) pointed to the hypocrisy of promoting freedom, tolerance, and diversity as Iranian values at the same time that the Shah's secret police (SAVAK) were actively suppressing ethnic minorities and imprisoning and torturing political opponents.[44] Nevertheless, according to historian Menahem Merhavy, the "marketing" of Cyrus, his cylinder, and the Persian Empire to Iranians and the world through these kinds of public relations projects, scholarly books, academic journals, and conferences was to a large degree

Figure 2.4. Revelers dance with flags in front of a larger-than-life Cyrus Cylinder at Los Angeles City Hall during the 2015 Los Angeles Persian Parade. (Credit: Amy Malek)

successful precisely because most Iranians did not know much about this historical period prior to the emergence of this field of cultural production. As a result, he argues, the details of the figure of Cyrus were "flexible and easily imbued with the values held by the agents of memory who propagated his image."[45]

The pervasive repetition of these narratives and symbols through imperial nostalgia in the twenty-first-century Iranian diaspora reveals how powerful twentieth-century nationalist symbolism has remained. It also demonstrates how these significations have been useful in new contexts. From the enormous 3D replicas of the Cyrus Cylinder in parades and festivals in US cities (fig. 2.4), to the innovative celebrations of Cyrus the Great Day on October 29 since the early 2000s, to the marketing of clothing, jewelry, accessories, collectibles, and home décor (fig. 2.5) featuring the Cyrus Cylinder, renewed meanings and new traditions have emerged around nostalgia for enduring symbols of ancient Iranian empire in new geopolitical and cultural contexts.[46]

In just the last decade, Cyrus the Great was repeatedly invoked by an impressively wide array of Iranians: nationalists, secularists, monarchists, democrats, far-right politicians, human rights activists, Zoroastrians, Jews, and Islamists. The draw of Cyrus of course often overlapped these nondistinct categories. To better understand when, how, and why diasporic Iranians have engaged in imperial nostalgia as Cyromania— whether through promoting it, confronting it, contesting it, or mobilizing it—it helps to locate it as a *diasporic* strategy for specifically diasporic ends. For many Iranian Americans, imperial nostalgia offers a form of relief against stigmatization, political stereotyping, and media portrayals that have created a troubling "common sense" about Iranians as Islamic fundamentalists, terrorists, and enemy Others of the United States.[47]

These diasporic mobilizations of Cyromania as political rejoinders are not entirely separate from the political uses of (or against) Cyrus in Iran. For example, as Iranians emigrated in large numbers in the period of the Revolution and through the 1980s, they did so amid comprehensive campaigns by the Islamic Republic of Iran (IRI) to diminish the role of pre-Islamic history and Pahlavi-endorsed symbolism.[48] For some in diaspora, then, reasserting these histories and symbols has served as an act of resistance against not only US stereotyping but also the IRI and

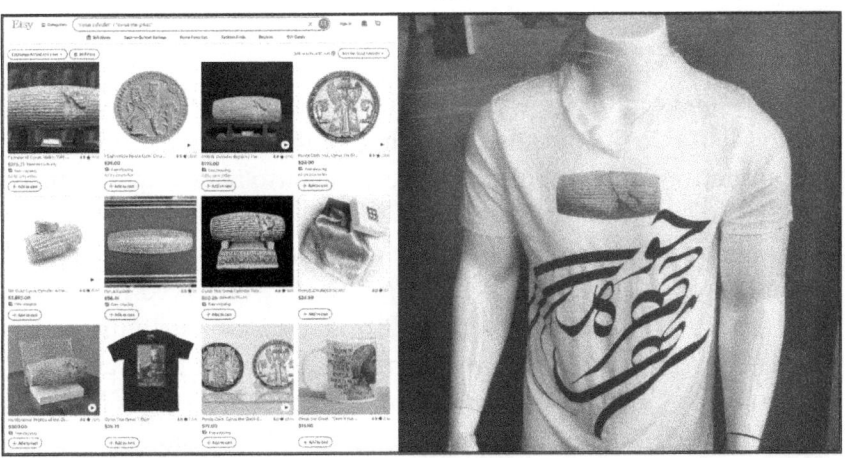

Figure 2.5. The commodification of the Cyrus Cylinder and Cyrus the Great as merchandise online (left: via Etsy) and offline (right: in a shop window in Westwood, Los Angeles). (Credit: Amy Malek)

its weaponization of religion in a political battle over cultural history, collective memory, and Iranian identity.[49]

In these latter uses, imperial nostalgia for a pre-Islamic Iranian past has served simultaneously as an explicit counter to the influence of Islam on Iranian culture and history and as a counter to the racialization of Iranians by Americans as nonwhite and, in many cases, as Muslim. These are neither unrelated goals nor coincidental impulses: As numerous historians have demonstrated, Pahlavi nationalist understandings of Iranian history and racial identity were developed primarily through the outcome of selective readings by Qajar-era intellectuals of European Orientalists who argued that the apparent "decay" of nineteenth-century Iranian society and culture relative to Europe was a result of a rupture caused by seventh-century Islamic invasion.[50] As such, the pre-Islamic period was read as the Golden Age of an uninterrupted 2,500+ years' history and thus the location of an essential Iranianness.[51] This version of Iranian nationalism often mixes stories of the *Shahnameh*—an epic work of mythology—with historical events and figures, aggrandizing both in order to establish a utopian view of the past that is emblematic of essential features of a uniquely Iranian—*Aryan*—racial character. In this narrative, any shortcomings of contemporary Iranians should be blamed on what they describe as the violent coercion of that Islamic invasion, while Aryan racial identity should stand as continued evidence of shared heritage between Iranians and Europeans, rather than with Arabs or other regional neighbors.[52]

Just as nineteenth-century Iranian intellectuals aimed to restore dignity to the Iranian people by embracing, reproducing, and innovating these narratives and symbols that were later consolidated under Pahlavi nationalism, late twentieth-century Iranian migratory flows to a US society no longer welcoming of Iranian newcomers led to the extension of similar pragmatic logics.[53] As Hamid Naficy observed in his 1993 study of exile cultural production, "To many Iranians living in Los Angeles, . . . this official culture looms larger and more truly 'authentic' from a position in exile. To them it represents a fulfillment of an Iranian national aspiration and utopian imagining."[54] Expressions of Iranian Aryan identity in twentieth- and twenty-first-century America not only put forward a proud national ancestry in the face of exclusion, but also staked out a racial position seeking proximity to whiteness in the US racial hierarchy, accomplished in part by distancing Iranians from Islam, and thus from the increasingly virulent post-9/11 discourses against Muslims.⁵⁵ At best, this distancing is a covering strategy; at its worst, it is expressed explicitly by Iranians in diaspora as anti-Muslim racism.⁵⁶

In the first decades of the twenty-first century, officials of the Islamic Republic, too, began to re-embrace pre-Islamic history and nationalist symbols, whether figures such as Cyrus the Great or heroes from the *Shahnameh*.⁵⁷ When the Cyrus Cylinder traveled to Tehran in 2010, it was welcomed with great fanfare, including by unlikely figures (given the early antagonism of the IRI towards Pahlavi nationalism) such as then-President Mahmoud Ahmadinejad. In the intervening years, the increasing popularity of pre-Islamic symbolism in Iran has been evident in many ways, including in state-produced media and in the transnational flow of objects.⁵⁸ It was widely known in the 2000s and early 2010s that the highest-quality nationalist jewelry worn by diasporic Iranians came not from diasporic producers but from Iran itself.⁵⁹ Thus, the presence and growing importance of imperial nostalgia in diaspora should not be read as entirely separate from its growing prevalence in Iran nor from the complex political dance of competing nationalisms. Its persistence in diaspora is important for these reasons, but *also* because it is mobilized for outcomes unique to diaspora, including diasporic belonging.

While the large numbers of attendees, article placements in popular media, and mentions on social media offer basic metrics as to the success of the Cyrus Cylinder's US tour, they only partially reveal the impact of these kinds of projects and the Cyromania that ensued. In 2015, a year after the cylinder's US tour, an enormous Cyrus Cylinder replica was marched past Los Angeles City Hall in that city's first Persian Parade (fig. 2.4). Two years after the tour, in 2016, National Geographic's *History Magazine* featured a full spread photo of the cylinder. In the same year, efforts that had begun just prior to the tour to amend the sixth, seventh, and tenth grade world history curricula in California's public schools to include Cyrus the Great and the Persian Empire were finally successful.⁶⁰ And just three years after the exhibition tour concluded, in 2017, a large public sculpture directly invoking the Cyrus Cylinder and its diasporic significance was unveiled in Los Angeles. Titled *Freedom: A Shared Dream*, or simply, the Freedom Sculpture, the story of this monumental sculpture offers a clear demonstration of Cyromania as a strategy of inclusion, and of all the hopes and future possibilities that many Iranian immigrants place in the American values articulated by a neoliberal form of multiculturalism.

## The Gift of Freedom

On July 4, 2017, less than six months after the first announcement of the United States' Muslim Ban, amid court challenges to the ban's second iteration, and during a particularly heightened anti-immigrant and anti-Muslim national discourse, an estimated seventy-five thousand Iranian Americans gathered in Los Angeles to celebrate a new installation of public art gifted to the city. Described as sitting at "the most prestigious and highly trafficked heart of Los Angeles," the ten-ton, sixteen-foot-tall modernist interpretation of the Cyrus Cylinder sits on a median strip of a ten-lane stretch of Santa Monica Boulevard, just over the tree-lined fence of the notoriously exclusive Los Angeles Country Club golf course and mere blocks from Beverly Hills High School.[61] Lined by multi-million-dollar high-rise condos, offices, and a high end megamall, the large thoroughfare was unprecedentedly closed to vehicle traffic for the Freedom Festival, a free 4th of July celebration and concert to gift the sculpture to the city.

After several hours of performances and speeches, the tens of thousands of Angelenos gathered for the occasion were addressed via video message on large screens by their mayor, Eric Garcetti:

> I'm so proud of all of you tonight and I regret that I couldn't join you on this special occasion as we welcome the Freedom Sculpture to Los Angeles. This beautiful piece of art that celebrates religious freedom, multiculturalism, and inclusiveness—ideals shared by people all around the world and throughout all of history, from Cyrus the Great in Persia to America's founding fathers—that we celebrate today. This Freedom Sculpture embodies universal values and it received more crowdfunding than any project of its kind in the country, with more than 1 million people across America and 50 countries around the world supporting the creation of this project. That's extraordinary. So thank you to everyone who supported the Freedom Sculpture. . . . This is a great gift to the City

of Angels. And what better day to receive it on than Independence Day, a day when we celebrate freedoms that make our country and this city so special. Now, for the moment you all have been patiently waiting for, it is my pleasure to present: the Freedom Sculpture![62]

At this proclamation, the opening notes of an instrumental version of John Lennon's "Let it Be" filled the air while the mayor's video transitioned to a series of quotes around the themes of freedom, equality, happiness, and human rights attributed to Nelson Mandela, Martin Luther King Jr., Thomas Jefferson, Mahatma Gandhi, Shirin Ebadi, John Lennon, and, finally, Cyrus the Great. Quoted from a translation of Xenophon's *Cyropaedia,* "Freedom, dignity, wealth—these three together constitute the greatest happiness of humanity," closed out this sequence, attributed on-screen to Cyrus the Great.

Spotlights and smoke effects engulfed a regal-looking tent of gold and royal blue silk that had hidden the sculpture all afternoon. From my position deep in the crowd, the thousands of camera phones that rose all at once appeared like sequins simultaneously reflecting and recording what was before them. The tempo of the music intensified dramatically and, with each drumbeat, more smoke emerged and dozens of spotlights flashed, heightening the crowd's anticipation. When both sound and light finally reached a crescendo, the enclosing fabric fell to reveal the Freedom Sculpture: two large concentric stainless steel sculptural cylinders—one smaller, gold-colored cylinder encased in a larger silver-colored one (fig. 2.6). Balanced on two metal rings, each of the LED-lit cylinders was composed of a "puzzle-like pattern design . . . based on mathematical equations using universal prime numbers."[63]

The crowd's loud cheers and whistles eventually emerged as a chant: "IRAN! IRAN! IRAN!" As if to remind them that this was still an American Independence Day festival, the chants were interrupted by a sudden burst of red-white-and-blue fireworks erupting in the sky above the sculpture. Music filled the speakers again, but unlike the Persian-language pop that had entertained the lively crowd moments before, and unlike the anthems or patriotic American classics expected at 4th of July events, English-language pop songs were the first songs chosen to accompany the fireworks. As the colorful display lit up the sky, the playlist echoed the messages of the LA politicians who had spoken at length

Figure 2.6. The Freedom Sculpture installed on the median of the intersection of Santa Monica Boulevard and Century Park East in Century City, California. (Credit: Amy Malek, 2017)

on stage about celebrating freedom, multiculturalism, and democracy. When the fireworks turned red, white, and green (the three colors of the Iranian flag), Pharrell Williams's "Freedom" blasted from the speakers:

> Your first name is Free
> Last name is Dom
> We choose to believe
> In where we're from
> Man's red flower
> It's in every living thing
> Mind, use your power
> Spirit, use your wings
> Freedom Freedom Freedom Freedom!"

Both the sculpture and this professionally produced festival were the projects of the Farhang Foundation, a 501(c)3 nonprofit organization based in Los Angeles with a mission to "celebrate and promote Iranian art and culture for the benefit of the community-at-large."[64] Farhang, meaning "culture" in Persian, had also been the local cosponsors of the Los Angeles stop of the 2013 tour *A New Beginning*. Its leaders described the importance of the Freedom Sculpture to the press in the days leading up to its big reveal with reference to the same ideas put forward by that exhibition about the influence of Cyrus and his cylinder: The Freedom

Sculpture "is a precious gift from our community to the most diverse city in the U.S. as a permanent reminder of the ideas of liberty, tolerance and multiculturalism which was espoused by Cyrus the Great over 2500 years ago. The same ideas that were later adopted by the Founding Fathers of the United States and enshrined in our Constitution."[65] Throughout the 4th of July event, these ideas were repeated on stage by politicians and organizers as fundamental to not just Americans, but also—and originally—to Iranians. "These rights are [not only] part of our heritage," a founding trustee of Farhang emphasized in *The Huffington Post*, "they *came* from us!"[66]

Farhang's emphasis on Iranian American contributions as cultural gifts reflects an approach long deployed by other immigrant and minority groups seeking inclusion in US national identity and its attendant racial hierarchy. For example, in the mid-twentieth century, Italian Americans had invoked their ancestor Christopher Columbus as among their many contributions to the United States, ultimately winning his commemoration in statues across the country and in a federally recognized national holiday.[67] As historian Danielle Battisti has shown, Italian Americans effectively mobilized rhetorics of contributionism and immigrant gifts in their efforts to seek dignity and honor in the face of anti-Italian stereotypes and discrimination.[68] They had done so by arguing that Italian immigrants starting with Columbus had "helped transplant 'Western civilization' to the Americas," especially the "republican traditions of ancient Rome, the roots of Christianity and the cultural spirit of the Renaissance," all of which were fundamental to Americanism.[69] This rhetorical strategy was especially prominent in their work toward immigration reform to favor other would-be immigrants from Italy: "Contributionist narratives argued that various immigrant or ethnic groups should be rewarded with greater immigration opportunities for past meritorious behavior that conformed to highly racialized standards of inclusion in the nation."[70] Notably, Italian Americans did not resist the discrimination faced by all immigrants at the time, nor the racialized system that had excluded them as nonwhite. As Battisti highlighted in a 2020 *Washington Post* article arguing for the reconsideration of Columbus Day as a national holiday, Italian Americans instead "used evidence of their group's meritorious contributions to the nation to make the case that it was time to move Italian Americans to the other side of the ledger."[71] In this way, she argued, "Italian Americans used pluralist tactics to write themselves into a narrative of White citizenship and laid claims to its benefits in the process."[72]

Contributionism as a minority discourse has always been informed (and in many cases limited) by racial and class politics. As a strategy for inclusion, contributionist claims have been successful for Ellis Island immigrants (e.g., southern and eastern Europeans who immigrated to the United States in the late nineteenth and early twentieth centuries), while failing to produce equivalent results for others.[73] Despite this, Iranian Americans continue to use contributionism in their responses to government securitization and negative media representations of Iranians over nearly five decades of heightened antagonism between the United States and the Islamic Republic. Like Italians before them, in order to demonstrate deservingness for belonging in the United States, Iranian American leaders historically have appealed less to common cause with other immigrants (even to fellow Middle Eastern Americans, such as Arabs or Afghans, both of whom have instead been historical targets of Iranian racism), or even to legal codes that should protect their rights. Instead, prevailing arguments have highlighted assertions of high socioeconomic class status, immigrant exceptionalism,[74] and, as with *A New Beginning*, shared ideals of tolerance and diversity—with mixed results.

The incorporation of immigrants onto US racial classifications of whiteness historically was adjudicated through equal protection cases that "lumped" Iranians and other Middle Easterners together as white.[75] Yet everyday experiences of racialized discrimination nevertheless continued to exclude Iranian Americans and others, despite efforts to maintain proximity to whiteness.[76] According to sociologist Neda Maghbouleh, it has been only among a subset of second-generation Iranian Americans that solidarity with other Middle Eastern and racialized groups has begun to emerge. These solidarities became more evident in Iranian Americans' reactions to policies such as the 2017 Muslim Ban[77] and the Black Lives Matter protests of 2020, though neither produced widespread demonstrations of Iranian American solidarity with other minority groups. Indeed, the prevailing arguments by Iranian Americans into the 2020s have continued to highlight shared liberal ideals of tolerance and diversity; assertions of high socioeconomic class status and immigrant exceptionalism ("the most acclaimed"; "the most prestigious"), while remaining relatively quiet on questions of racism or discrimination against other groups in the United States, demonstrating instead a continued attachment to Aryan racial identities as whiteness.

*Neoliberal Multiculturalism and Its Exceptional Entrepreneurs*

What drives this continued confidence in the redeeming power of the rhetoric of immigrant contributions? As Wendy Brown has demonstrated, the rise of neoliberalism has brought about state disinvestment in the public but also withdrawal from society more generally. In the privatization, deregulation, and other economic strategies that are traditionally associated with neoliberal reforms, Brown has argued that the aim is actually "to change the soul" through neoliberalizing society itself, diminishing and denigrating dependency on the state and the very idea of society as a source of welfare and security. Instead, citizens are encouraged to become independent "self-investors" who "socially and monetarily invest in themselves to become more valuable;"[78] or, in Aihwa Ong's words, to become "entrepreneurs of themselves."[79] This "entrepreneurializing" of every institution, activity, and service includes of course cultural activities and institutions, for immigrants as much as for other citizens. Relatedly, in her analysis of differentiated and cultural citizenship, Ong describes a "dual process of self-making and being-made" in which subject formation is negotiated between state and subject through state intermediaries such as universities, nonprofit organizations, social service providers, and cultural institutions that work to create self-regulating racialized subjects.[80]

In this context, and in the absence of a set of federal directives organizing national policy and support to encourage the active participation of immigrants, from at least the 1990s forward, the United States has evolved a form of neoliberal multiculturalism wherein municipal and state governments develop and highlight difference, appropriating it rather than seeking to undermine it. As Jodi Melamed has shown, concepts associated with liberal multiculturalism as focused on group rights have been "recycled" into "multicultural rights for individuals and for corporations."[81] In this process, she argues, anti-racism discourses from previous forms of multiculturalism are abstracted to such a degree that "sometimes, as in the ubiquitous discussions of diversity, the racial context is more residual than overt. In place of direct reference to race, neoliberal multiculturalism has more often spoken of difference."[82] As a result, these discourses and the policies that reflect them limit methods of participation for minoritized populations in the public sphere to participation in the neoliberal project, especially through the incorporation of difference in the name of freedom and diversity rather than through the extension of access to rights and equity.

In neoliberal subject formation, then, immigrant subjects vying for inclusion are expected to become self-entrepreneurs not just in the financial, educational, or health aspects of their lives, but also in the social and cultural ones. In this iteration of multiculturalism, immigration policies are mobilized alongside national mythologies of the United States (e.g., as "a nation of immigrants" seeking the American Dream which is accessible simply by "pulling oneself up by one's own bootstraps") to create immigrant citizens whose identities as hyphenated Americans are both rooted in and dependent on the interlocking values of individual responsibility, self-sufficiency, and contributions to society. Iranian communities in the greater Los Angeles area, considered by many to be the capital of the diaspora with its large and diverse population of Iranians, provides an exemplary case. Without the symbolic or instrumental benefits of directed public support provided for immigrant communities in countries such as Sweden or Canada, Iranian Angelenos have sought to develop belonging through promotions of imperial nostalgia, neoliberal interpretations of exceptional entrepreneurial and economic success, and celebrations of their "immigrant gifts" to the United States.[83] The result is an Iranian American cocktail of nationalist interpretations of Iranian history and culture with US assimilationist and neoliberal multiculturalist ideas about diversity, race, and class.

These strategies reveal a belief among many Iranian Americans, sometimes articulated directly by community organizations and political leaders, that immigrants who have successfully attained equal status in American identity (including racial identity) have *earned* this inclusion. In this line of thinking, they have done so not by virtue of their legal rights as humans or citizens, but by contributing to American society, thereby *earning* equal rights and high status. In other words, they believe that the contributions of Iranians haven't been adequately recognized, for if they had—and if through their efforts they can make them so—then Iranian Americans would not continue to be stereotyped as terrorists or extremists; would not continue to be targeted by government agencies such as Homeland Security, the Transportation Security Administration, and Customs and Border Patrol;[84] would not continue to face employment discrimination[85] or have their bank accounts scrutinized and closed without warning based solely on their names;[86] and would not be separated indefinitely from their family members while simply attempting to attend weddings, funerals, and graduations.[87] In short, they would be treated with dignity as equal US citizens.

This approach is reflective of at least two processes: a neoliberal construction of citizenship in the United States that has heightened immigrant contributionism as a strategy for inclusion as full members, and a related contest between and among diasporic leaders and cultural producers over who "owns" culture, who controls representation, and, ultimately, who belongs—and how. Neoliberal language of productivity, personal responsibility, self-regulation, and contribution permeate many immigrants' understandings of US citizenship and processes of US subject formation. Consequently, when the "nation of immigrants" turns against certain immigrants, whether through discrimination, targeted surveillance, or outright bans, the commonsense reaction by many Iranians has not been to see themselves as one among an array of minoritized groups in a common struggle for equal rights but rather to respond through citations of exceptional academic achievement, economic success, and even ancient contributions to American values as markers of their deservingness to belong.

*"Support Our Farhang": Private Patrons and Privatized Participation*

Even in Southern California, with its sizeable and established Iranian communities, efforts to organize large public cultural events have faced numerous difficulties. Challenges common across the diaspora, such as teamwork and community fragmentation, also pose difficulties in LA. But in relying entirely on grassroots fundraising, financial challenges have also been pervasive: reliance on hard-won individual donations, advertising by local businesses, and/or ticket sales has brought down more than one effort. Perhaps the best example is the annual two-day

Mehregan Festival of Autumn in Orange County (1994–2011), which, after eighteen years of grassroots volunteer-driven organizing by the Network of Iranian American Professionals of Orange County (NIPOC), a networking organization for Iranian professionals, finally succumbed in 2012 under the weight of heavy production costs that required raising ticket prices, which ultimately led to low sales. The ticketed festival had drawn upward of twenty thousand spectators at its peak each October and was recognized through multiple proclamations from local government offices and politicians. But a wary, aging first-generation volunteer base proved unable to motivate the second generation to continue, especially in the face of financial difficulties.[88]

Other efforts faced similar organizational challenges: The Los Angeles Persian Parade (fig. 2.4), inspired by the New York Persian Parade that has operated annually since 2004, held multiple fundraisers but managed to process in front of LA City Hall only twice, in 2015 and 2016. A free Nowruz Multicultural Festival had accompanied the first parade in 2015, leveraging the professional networks and financial contribution of its lead organizer, a marketing and events professional who had managed to draw sponsorships from Evian water, Emirates Airlines, Johnny Walker, and a handful of local businesses. But even with this impressive array of sponsors, he was left in heavy personal debt and the event became a one-off.[89]

More successful has been the annual Westwood Nowruz Festival and block party. A mainstay in the area officially recognized by the City as Persian Square, it relies entirely on the local businesses of the enclave to organize and sponsor it outside of their storefronts on Westwood Boulevard, the number of which have significantly declined in the 2020s. Like the large ticketed *Sizdeh Bedar* event in the Valley and smaller, free Mehregan festival in West Los Angeles, marketing dominates the visual field at the Westwood Nowruz block party with large advertisements for attorneys, insurance agents, and mortgage lenders prominently displayed on, over, and around the concert stage and event areas (fig. 2.7).

It was in this milieu that the Farhang Foundation began its work in 2008. Like so many organizations in the diaspora, Farhang, too, began in an effort to counter the misrepresentations of Iranians in US mainstream media. The foundation quickly built a strong reputation among Iranian Americans in Southern California for organizing concerts, exhibitions,

Figure 2.7. Advertising frames the replicas of lamassu Persepolitan columns and gates, and a hanging Cyrus Cylinder on stage at the 2016 Nowruz Festival in Westwood, Los Angeles. (Credit: Amy Malek)

conferences, film festivals, and lectures that were free of sponsor advertising without sacrificing production quality. It has since grown to be the "largest and most successful Iranian cultural organization in the United States," producing more than eighty programs and events in Southern California each year and gaining a global audience once the COVID-19 pandemic required a pivot to virtual programs.[90]

In person, Farhang's events are known for their consistency in producing well-organized and polished affairs, especially relative to other diasporic community events. This approach contributes to its goal of making a positive impression on the publics it seeks to reach. Indeed, in order to promote Iranian arts and culture among Angelenos and "the community at-large" rather than just for Iranians, at least 50 percent of Farhang events have free admission and are held in popular public settings, for which it regularly partners with elite cultural and educational institutions in Southern California. For example, the organization has sponsored the inclusion of Iranian musicians in the popular free Downtown LA Grand Performances concert series; large exhibitions such as the 2013 Cyrus Cylinder exhibition at the Getty Villa or the 2019 Shirin Neshat retrospective at The Broad contemporary art museum; film festivals like the annual Celebration of Iranian Cinema at the Hammer Museum; and their large annual Nowruz (new year) celebrations at the Los Angeles County Museum of Art (LACMA), the Orange County Pacific Symphony, and the University of California, Los Angeles (UCLA). The organization has also financed educational initiatives that draw attention to Iranian language and culture, for example through establishing endowed academic chairs at several California universities, creating an Iranian Studies degree and language program at the University of Southern California ($2.5+ million gift), and funding an Iranian music major at UCLA ($1 million gift). The organization also pioneered an afterschool Persian-language program through the Los Angeles Unified School District, the first of its kind in the nation, that, as of 2020, had enrolled over eight hundred students since its inception in 2015.[91]

The Farhang Foundation built its remarkable résumé thanks to the contributions and fundraising efforts of its board of trustees, dozens of dues-paying council members, and an extensive list of donors (known as "Patrons"), many of whom contribute during attendance at the foundation's annual fundraising gala.[92] According to its annual reports, between 2016 and 2024, annual dues and contributions from Farhang's trustees and council members made up between 44 and 66 percent of the foundation's total reported funds of over $15.8 million USD; donations through its Patron Program (mostly though not exclusively Iranian Americans and corporations) and from the general public contributed the remaining funds in this period.[93] This high level of revenue clearly sets Farhang apart from other Iranian diaspora cultural organizations.[94] Though it is common for community organizations in the United States to have to operate without government financial support, Farhang has operated without this support *and* without private grants, as well as without resort to intrusive advertising from large corporate sponsorships. This method of fundraising has allowed Farhang to maintain control over its own destiny and to produce a wide array of educational and cultural events with high production value, often provided free to the public. Doing so has garnered considerable attention not only in California, but across the diaspora, leading its chairman to describe Farhang in 2020 as "the premiere Iranian cultural organization in the world."[95]

Farhang's programming choices are the result of an internal proposal vetting process through the board of trustees and the foundation's unique council structure. The board of trustees, including founders of the foundation, each pay annual dues ($20,000–28,000 each in 2017) in addition to contributions and are responsible for ensuring both the sustainability of the foundation and the fulfilment of its mission. Farhang's councils are composed of anywhere from five to fifteen volunteer members, as well as trustees. Here, well-established professionals, scholars, and entrepreneurs are responsible for innovating, vetting, and shepherding proposals for the Foundation. Like trustees, council members are also required to pay annual dues ($3,000–$5,000 in 2017) that go toward the council's activities. Council members also make significant contributions to the foundation.[96] Once approved by the board of trustees, projects are then marshalled by the councils who oversee their implementation alongside targeted committees consisting of recruited experts who work on a volunteer basis and do not pay dues. Finally, the foundation's management team, including an executive director and two additional paid staff members, are responsible for day-to-day operations and project management, including contracting with event production companies, venues, and public relations and marketing professionals. Thus, Farhang's programming decisions are made by its dues-paying trustees and council members, who work as unpaid volunteers, but unlike most Iranian diaspora cultural organizations, its operations are generally undertaken by paid professional project managers, event production companies, and public relations experts.[97] This structure has led to Farhang's reputation for consistently high production value and a focused, consistent approach to branding.

As effective as this operational workflow has been, it also has raised some questions in the community. The professionals contracted by Farhang ensured consistent and clean productions, and that the organization's name, logo, and brand were prominently displayed at every event. This led to some criticism that a preoccupation with image, prestige, and elite class status guided not only fundraising efforts but the organization's program choices and representations of "Iranianness." For example, a local artist with mixed feelings about the organization described Farhang to me in 2015 as a "*community* organization in name only," because, in her eyes, the foundation represented a wealthy elite who favored a "slick, shiny, and *chichi*" image over, for example, encouraging community involvement in its programs.

Given the difficulty for other cultural events or organizations to compete with Farhang's strong fundraising, elite networks, and impressive social capital, the foundation's trustees and council and committee members have collectively determined what the representation of Iranian art and culture has been for mainstream audiences in Southern California since the early 2010s. Apart from these individuals, and unlike large volunteer-run arts and culture organizations and events elsewhere in the global diaspora, Farhang does not ask community members for extended contributions of time, ideas, input, or feedback. Participation at most Farhang events, then, is generally limited to serving as donors, audiences, or as one of a limited number of day-of volunteers.

*From Cracked Clay to Public Monument*

Having cosponsored *A New Beginning* at the Getty Villa, Farhang's leaders recognized the potential for the Cyrus Cylinder and the figure of Cyrus the Great to serve a more permanent representational role in Los Angeles. That said, the source of the original idea of a sculpture of Cyrus or his cylinder in Los Angeles depends on who you ask. There certainly were a number of precedents: In 1994, Iranians in Australia worked to install a bas-relief monument to Cyrus and his cylinder in Sydney's Bicentennial Park.[98] A decade later, in 2004, a monument to the Cyrus Cylinder was unveiled outside of the House of Iran in San Diego's Balboa Park, described as a "replica of the First Declaration of Human Rights of Cyrus the Great cylinder."[99] In 2010, an LA City Hall committee voted to "move forward on an offer by downtown property owner Ezat Delijani to pay for and maintain" a bronze sculpture of Cyrus the Great that would join statues of Beethoven, the Doughboy (a monument to LA's WWI soldiers), and a Spanish-American War monument in Pershing Square, in the heart of downtown LA.[100] That project never came to fruition, but the idea of a Cyrus sculpture clearly had been swirling in the community's leadership circles for years. The idea to place a large replica of the Cyrus Cylinder in Westwood—considered the heart of Tehrangeles and officially designated by the City as Persian Square in 2010 through the community's efforts—was described to me in the 2010s by more than one respected business leader in the community. One suggested to me that it had been usurped by Farhang's project, which, he added, in the end didn't even look much like the Cyrus Cylinder.

Regardless of the source of the idea, it seems only Farhang had the financial, political, and social capital to see it realized. In 2014, their Fine Arts Council announced an open competition for the design of a public art piece that would serve as "a permanent landmark . . . an ongoing and permanent testament to the humanitarian ideals of Cyrus the Great, that inspired the Founding Fathers of this great nation."[101] A July 2014 press release announced a detailed timeline for the project as well as the international jury of experts who would select the winner: three non-Iranians representing four LA art institutions (the Los Angeles Contemporary Museum of Art, the Museum of Contemporary Art, the J. Paul Getty Museum, and the Century City Chamber of Commerce Art Council) and two Iranians, Paris-based Kamran Diba, former architect and first director of the Tehran Museum of Contemporary Art (1976–1978), and Shazad Ghanvari, an architect and Farhang Foundation trustee.[102] From the more than three hundred submissions received, five finalists were chosen, and in November 2015, the jury selected the design of internationally recognized architect Cecil Balmond. A sixteen-member Freedom Sculpture Committee—populated with several trustees, members of the foundation's Fine Arts Council, and volunteers who brought experience working in and with city government—extended their social networks, made crucial introductions, and consulted on key steps of the process. The construction of the monument itself was facilitated by Arya Group, a design firm owned by committee member and trustee Ardie Tavangar, a developer and "starchitect" known for his multimillion-dollar mansions for LA's superrich. Finally, in 2017, at the cost of $2.6 million, the project was completed, the sculpture was installed in Century City, and it was successfully unveiled on July 4th at the Freedom Festival.

Gifting the sculpture in a large public festival on Independence Day, rather than in a small dedication ceremony, was not part of the original plan. With only four months to coordinate such a large event, the foundation contracted with an events production company, but multiple logistical challenges remained. Acquiring notoriously limited permits, for example to close Santa Monica Boulevard for two days and to allow for fireworks, would require mobilizing networks in LA city government. But this date held multiple layers of significance that made this heavy lift worth the effort in the eyes of Farhang's leadership. First, it built on a model common in diaspora of looking to create a public celebration during a popular holiday in the host society. Whereas other community organizations had sought to reanimate ancient Iranian holidays near American ones (e.g., Mehregan near Thanksgiving; Sepandarmazgan near Valentine's Day), the Freedom Festival instead reimagined an American holiday to put forward the idea that Iranians were intimately tied to the very birth of America. Here, Iranian American leaders in Los Angeles sought to connect the promise of multiculturalism found in an ancient Persian artifact to its fulfillment in superdiverse Los Angeles. Along the way, they would submit an argument that Iranian Americans should be included in multicultural America because they were ideologically more American than Americans (e.g., "It *came* from us!").

Second, a large festival on this date could mean the reputational and political rewards of the project would be multiplied. A community leader and member of the Sculpture Committee told me in the days following the event that the Freedom Festival helped to establish Iranian American presence in the city: "The [Freedom] Festival is a way [to] say to people that we exist and we are part of this community. There are symbols of our being here forty years: the Cyrus Cylinder [exhibition] is also a byproduct that we live here, we got the Persian Square [official designation], etc. These are signs that we exist and we are part of this community. This is home; so if it's home, you put a mark on it. You own it; we are owners." Iranians in Los Angeles thus sought to put their stamp on their city—to claim ownership—and followed the example of other immigrant communities in doing so.[103] Whereas some 180 ethnic parades serve this purpose for immigrant communities in New York City, sculptures, festivals, block parties, and official street signs marking City recognition of ethnic neighborhoods are ways to achieve this goal in traffic-locked Los Angeles.

Third, alongside the US flag, the Statue of Liberty, and the Declaration of Independence, the leaders of Farhang sought to contribute a new ideologically imbued symbol to US Independence Day. Describing the Freedom Sculpture in press materials and media interviews as a "Statue of Liberty for the West Coast," Farhang sought to present this gift as a modern interpretation of the Cyrus Cylinder that shared with Lady Liberty the symbolism of immigrants' dreams of freedom and democracy, but also the value of diversity.

The organization also sought to connect the Freedom Sculpture with the Statue of Liberty due to its lesser-known history of having been crowdfunded. An animated video used for fundraising explained this connection: After introducing the historical figure of Cyrus and his cylinder as the "first declaration of human rights, religious tolerance, and individual freedom" that had inspired the US Founding Fathers, the narrator then described the Statue of Liberty as the first major crowdfunded campaign. "Over 100,000 people led by the French helped create the Statue of Liberty, a symbolic gift that recognized America as the leading light for these ideals and of freedom around the world."[104] Farhang, the video asserted, had therefore set up its own crowdfunding campaign, with a goal "to inspire over 100,000 people to support the creation of this monument so we become just the second example in history where this many people got together to create a gift—a monumental symbol to freedom as a shared cultural value."[105]

Rather than using one of the several existing crowdfunding platforms (e.g., Kickstarter, which charged fees and required the entire campaign goal be met) for this purpose, Farhang hired equity agency Arora Project to create and run its crowdfunding campaign and media promotion. Arora launched the project's Facebook page in November 2016, which it grew "to over 1 million likes," and, once the crowdfunding campaign was launched in May 2017,[106] it eventually raised a reported $2,103,576 USD.[107]

In exchange for a donation of any amount, individuals would be added to a permanent virtual Donor Wall that included a list of wealthy donors and "notable supporters," including politicians (e.g., LA Mayor Eric Garcetti, California Governor Jerry Brown), famous investors (e.g., Elon Musk of Tesla, Lynda Resnick of POM and Fiji Water), and prominent Iranian Americans (e.g., Firouz Naderi of the Jet Propulsion Lab and NASA, Salar Kamangar of Google and YouTube).[108] While the bulk of early fundraising for the Freedom Sculpture was guaranteed through private fundraisers in 2015, where several individuals had committed donations between $5,000 to $100,000 each, the crowdfunding campaign offered several benefits. In addition to providing funds that would make the festival and upkeep of the sculpture possible, it also offered a pathway for participation. Farhang executive director Alireza Ardekani explained to me that the foundation created the campaign as way for anyone, anywhere in the world to be able to feel a part of the project: "We wanted this to be something not just funded by several handful of very wealthy individuals. We wanted something that everyone can participate and lend their name. And we thought, how cool would it be to have somebody who just donates $10 add their name to the project? It's a perfect crowdfunding project."[109]

Over one thousand individuals agreed, as they added their names and the names of their loved ones, including memorials, to the virtual donor wall. Most crowdfunded donations listed on the wall were under $50 USD and, in combination with private fundraisers, the foundation reportedly raised over $2.6 million USD in total.[110] But as one Iranian Angeleno put it to me, some saw the campaign as being invited "to paste our name on the project." Farhang had not sought community input or involvement in the conceptual stage, nor the art selection stage, nor in the location selection stage, nor later, in the condensed Freedom Festival planning stage. Indeed, despite positioning the sculpture and festival as a gift from Iranian Americans to the city of LA, the foundation had offered no public opportunities for idea-sharing or consultation by that community during the years-long process. Attending as a spectator, signaling support by "liking" the Facebook campaign, and donating to the crowdfunding project were the only methods for community participation in the development of the Freedom Sculpture.

In addition to raising money and offering a form of community participation, in our interview, Ardekani described an important third benefit of the crowdfunding campaign: garnering attention, especially from non-Iranians. "We invested a lot of money in Facebook [advertising] and brought a whole social media team that worked with us and started a whole messaging campaign. And we really focused it on everyone, not just the Iranians. . . . [T]he messaging [on our Facebook page] was very geared towards the general audience; it wasn't very Iranian-centric, because we knew that Iranians were the low-hanging fruit and they get it. So the people that we need to educate and reach out to were people who are not familiar with Cyrus." In this way, a key goal of the project—and that of so many Iranian diaspora organizers' public-facing work—was one that the crowdfunding and social media campaigns could uniquely achieve: messaging. The choice of location of the sculpture reinforced the primacy of this goal: "We wanted to get as many eyes on [the sculpture] as possible and we didn't want it necessarily to be in an Iranian community where only Iranians are going to see it."[111]

By adding thousands of additional names to the project, Farhang strategically positioned the sculpture as a gift from a global community, over a million strong, who not only supported the ideals of freedom and diversity, but also endorsed the narrative of Cyrus the Great as the founder of these concepts and the sculpture as a monument to the Iranian American contribution of both to the United States. Their statements were thus made easy for politicians to support and repeat—as Garcetti had done in his recorded speech at the festival.

While many Iranian diaspora organizations list informing the host society about Iranian culture and history as a key goal, Farhang's approach was particularly successful thanks in part to its adherence to principles of the US form of neoliberal multiculturalism. But where building immigrant community participation through promoting arts and culture, such as by developing practices of teamwork, leadership, volunteerism, democratic debate, and cultural, civic, and political activism, is a feature of other large diasporic festivals (e.g., in Stockholm and Toronto), this was not among Farhang's primary aims. Unlike in these other locations, in the United States, where there is no official state multiculturalism and therefore no dedicated resources for immigrant groups, meaningful inclusion relies on participation in capitalism, particularly through entrepreneurship, self-regulation, and individualism. It follows that, for an organization with tremendous financial capital, public relations and financial contributions would then be prioritized over other forms of community participation and development. In other words, *messages* of democracy as a shared ideal were prioritized by the Freedom Sculpture project over *practices* of democracy themselves.

Despite not having sought their input, community members offered it anyway in the form of social media comments, gossip, and informal conversations. When Sri Lankan-British artist Cecil Balmond was announced as the winner of the open design competition, some local artists wondered aloud why Farhang's jury had not selected one of the many talented Iranian artists—two of whom had been among the top five finalists, one of whom made it to the top three—to create this Iranian American gift.¹¹² Perhaps, one art professional wondered aloud to me, had the jury included more experts in Iranian American art rather than representatives from prestigious cultural institutions in LA, the outcome would have more closely reflected the inspiration and the community from which the gift was to be given. Indeed, new voices joined these critiques when Balmond's winning design renderings were first made public: For a sculpture marketed as having been inspired by the Cyrus Cylinder, it not only was not a faithful replica, it did not even look very much like the artifact. The artist's "large-scale, modern-day sculptural interpretation of the Cyrus Cylinder" led some Iranian Americans, motivated in large part by imperial nostalgia, to argue that the sculpture should have been a more faithful mimic, if larger than life. One Iranian American elder who had been active in the early stages of the project but who ultimately felt some disappointment in its outcome sighed to me a week after the festival, "How will anyone learn about Cyrus the Great from this thing?"

Creatives less concerned with nostalgia and more with aesthetics and representation debated both: A Facebook commenter described its silver and gold coating as "trashy and flashy," while another responded that this would just be seen as the fulfillment of the derogatory stereotypes of LA Iranians as materialistic show-offs. Still other individuals simply felt the piece was ugly: In response to online news reports about the festival, unidentified commenters compared the Freedom Sculpture to "a bundle of chain link fencing on a forklift"¹¹³ and "that thing that spins the lottery balls."¹¹⁴ As if to confirm the worry of "trashy and flashy" stereotypes, another user commented: "Cyrus the great of Persia . . . that would explain all the gold . . ."¹¹⁵

When the $2.6 million price tag of the sculpture project was revealed, some community members (including journalists) asked if the foundation and its donors had not considered more pressing community needs for such a large sum, especially in the face of the recently announced travel ban that was directly targeting Iranians and their families.¹¹⁶ And finally, the location of the sculpture, on a median in the middle of Santa Monica Blvd, drew questions: Why not place it in Westwood, the heart of Tehrangeles, where Iranian business owners, shoppers, and neighbors could see it regularly and enjoy it? According to Farhang, the median location was considered ideal for the LA-traffic lifestyle, but also for finding the eyes of those they sought to influence: The median was situated in "one of the busiest and most expensive locations in the world, with up to 100,000 cars driving by it on a daily basis, on the way to and from Beverly Hills, CA."[117] Indeed, the open call for artists had encouraged designs that would be viewed at thirty miles per hour. Critics wondered, would anyone ever see, let alone read, the inlaid plaque at the base of the sculpture between ten lanes of traffic to learn about the Cyrus Cylinder and that the sculpture was an Iranian American gift? To some, what this location really meant was that the sculpture would be seen as just a shiny blur in traffic—a metal sculpture without signification.

These criticisms aside, positive reactions to the project were also abundant. Online, hundreds of messages were posted to the organizers' Facebook pages, many expressing pride and describing their emotional responses to seeing the sculpture, reminiscent of the reactions many had had to seeing the Cyrus Cylinder itself: "[Passing by the sculpture] brings tears to my eyes every time! Could not be more proud of our native land and the City of Angels that we now call home. Thank you Farhang... for giving our Iranian community an incredible sense of pride and joy. The legacy of Cyrus the Great lives on!"[118] Six months later, another commenter echoed this sentiment: "It melts my heart every time I see The Freedom Sculpture . . . breath taking!! Proud of it!! Thank you Farhang Foundation!!"[119] A donor to Farhang connected seeing the physical sculpture to her sense of belonging in the United States, commenting: "Every time I am in that area, I would choose my route to pass by The Freedom Sculpture. It gives me a sense of joy and belonging... as if I am visiting home. Now here is my home, my place of birth that I have been longing to visit. Now it seems not too far, it's here, where my family and friends live. Where I can feel the peace and unity. Isn't that amazing?? Thank you Farhang, and thanks for the vision!"[120]

*Feeling Iranian American: Imperial Nostalgia at the Freedom Festival*

In person, over seventy-five thousand people, mostly Iranian Americans, attended the Freedom Festival. They, too, took to Facebook to express their emotional responses to the evening: "I wish I could go back in time and experience that magical evening again. Felt so proud to be Iranian."¹²¹ Pride and memory became common themes in these comments; as one put it, "Thank you for a great memory and mak[ing] history for all of us, proud to be Persian / American."¹²² Across the event space, design choices had sought to draw out these reactions by mixing nostalgic Iranian culture with patriotic American symbolism: While US and California state flags (the only flags present) hung from the stage, multiple rows of fairy lights were strung along the light posts all the way down Santa Monica Boulevard, reminiscent of the *cheraghnavari* of festive outdoor spaces in Iran. Large, staged areas featured nostalgic Iranian scenes: fruit and flower displays evoked *bazaar* stalls; Persian-carpet-draped *nimkats* offered respite; and 3D replicas of Persepolis and the Cyrus Cylinder, displays of handicrafts, and even a yellow Paykan, the first Iranian made car, all sparked nostalgic reactions while a larger-than-life costumed Lady Liberty roamed among the crowd on stilts, posing for photos with amused festivalgoers (fig. 2.8).

The blending of times and places on the festival grounds was assisted by visual, olfactory, and gustatory prompts. Long lines of attendees in red-white-and-blue hats and shirts waited for Persian kabobs, *pashmak* (cotton candy), and *faloodeh* (an iced noodle dessert), as well as hot dogs, Mexican tacos, kale bowls, and Chinese bao from Los Angeles's trendiest food trucks. On light poles and LA Metro bus stop signs along the boulevard's median, replicas of Iranian street signs in Persian script indicated popular Tehran squares and streets, often using their prerevolution names (e.g., Abbasabad Avenue rather than Shahid Beheshti Avenue; Shahyad Square rather than Azadi Square) (fig. 2.8). This evocation of the nostalgia for prerevolution place names on postrevolution-era street signs joined with the wide repertoire of symbols and scenes at the Freedom Festival to emplace nostalgic memories of Tehran in contemporary Los Angeles. The result was reminiscent of how anthropologist Halleh Ghorashi had described the Orange County Mehregan Festivals of years past: "an attempt to create an imaginary space in America for Iranians" by "bringing the Iranian past closer to the American present."¹²³

On stage, in between Iranian pop musical performances and standup comedy, speeches from Farhang's leaders and numerous local politicians drew connections (through the Cyrus Cylinder) between Iranians' and Americans' "shared dream" of freedom, human rights, diversity, and multiculturalism. Indeed, multiculturalism and diversity were named

Figure 2.8. American symbolisms joined with nostalgic Iranian ones: a Statue of Liberty on stilts, Farhang Foundation's large griffin logo, and Tehran street signs, often with prerevolution names (in the design of postrevolution signs) all became photo ops at the Freedom Festival, July 4, 2017. (Credit: Amy Malek)

repeatedly as key features of Los Angeles that had allowed the Iranian community there to thrive. To reinforce this message, a photo booth encouraged the crowd to take photos with patriotic props and large signs with keywords that summed up the speeches delivered on stage: FREEDOM, UNITY, PERSIAN, IRANIAN, MULTICULTURALISM, ACCEPTANCE (fig. 2.9). It perhaps was telling, too, that of all the possible quotes attributed to Cyrus the Great in the *Cyropaedia*, the Festival had highlighted "Freedom, dignity, and wealth." These appeals, in form and function, are emblematic of American forms of multiculturalism, where freedom and dignity are deeply intertwined with wealth, which then fosters certain kinds of claims over others. Neoliberal appeals to diversity and tolerance bring favor to those who have the resources to espouse it, but without requiring the policies to provide support for meaningful equity under the trappings of inclusion.

Figure 2.9. Photos from an on-site photo booth with props were projected on large LED screens for the crowd during breaks between performances during the 2017 Freedom Festival. (Credit: Amy Malek)

## *Mediating Human Rights: From Monument to Memorial*

Farhang's investment in professional firms to handle the event's campaign and promotion paid off in the form of a slew of local, national, and diasporic media coverage. According to the foundation, "News crews and photographers from Associated Press, ABC, NBC, KTLA, BBC, CBS, UNIVISION, KIRN, NPR, KNX, KPCC among others reported on the festival," and it was featured on the front page of *The LA Times* California section on July 5.[124] If a key aim of the crowdfunding campaign was to garner this national and international attention and greater engagement, this goal was clearly met.

The political environment at the time, and especially an increasingly hostile anti-immigration rhetoric and specifically anti-Iranian policy, likely spurred both Iranian and non-Iranian donors to give to a project that promoted their opposite. While Farhang's representatives were careful to clarify in media interviews that the Muslim Ban had not inspired the sculpture project (it had begun long before Donald Trump even announced his candidacy in 2015), they nevertheless acknowledged that the political atmosphere of 2016–17 had likely contributed to their project succeeding so phenomenally. It also very likely had encouraged many of the seventy-five thousand attendees to show up to the festival itself. In this way, the Freedom Sculpture's virtual donor wall also became a badge of not just economic, ethnic, or nationalist pride, but of political honor. Facebook comments and donor statements referred to current politics and the deep need for messages of freedom, multiculturalism, and inclusivity in such a politically charged moment. The sculpture had come to be seen as a powerful rejoinder to Trump's boldly divisive, racist, and xenophobic statements. Although the sculpture's critics suggested symbolic projects were not as needed in these moments as legal funds, scholarships for Iranian students whose bank accounts had been unjustly frozen, or advocacy for those whose family members were stuck at borders or suffering in Iran under sanctions, for others, the value of messaging "who we really are" and putting a stamp of Iranian American belonging in their cities was deemed especially powerful in this period of political volatility.

And the message was heard: Politicians across California and even the country took notice of the sculpture. Notably, the same presidential administration whose anti-immigration and xenophobic policies had motivated increased support for the organization's crowdfunding campaign later invoked the Freedom Sculpture—co-opting its message—in its own effort to reach Iranians and Iranian Americans. Beginning in 2019, Trump administration officials such as Secretary of State Mike Pompeo connected the dots between the claims made in *A New Beginning*, the Freedom Sculpture, and the Biblical relevance of Cyrus the Great. On October 29, Pompeo tweeted: "Today in 539 BC, Cyrus the Great entered Babylon and freed the Jewish people from captivity. His respect for human rights and religious freedom inspired America's founding fathers. The U.S. stands with the Iranian people, who are blocked by the regime from celebrating his legacy."[125] Despite being an unofficial holiday that only emerged in the mid-aughts, US government officials on Twitter treated Cyrus the Great Day as though it were an ancient holiday with global adherents, and framed it in light of IRI attempts to prevent its celebration in Iran.[126]

One year later, in a 2020 video message posted in both Persian and English on US State Department Twitter accounts just two weeks before the US presidential election, then–Special Representative for Iran Elliott Abrams made these connections even more explicitly. Standing before a backdrop of the official seal of the United States, he began his speech, which also was translated in Persian subtitles: "On behalf of the United States, I want to wish Iranians around the world a happy Cyrus the Great Day. Cyrus left an enduring legacy of religious tolerance and human rights that inspired many of our presidents, including Thomas Jefferson, the author of the Declaration of Independence and the Virginia Statute of Religious Freedom. We continue to honor Cyrus in America. Recently, the city of Los Angeles was inspired by the Cyrus Cylinder and built a Freedom Sculpture in its likeness. Tens of thousands of Iranian Americans came out to celebrate its unveiling."[127] As images of both appeared, Abrams directly invoked the LA festival and Freedom Sculpture—giving credit to the city for its existence and erasing Farhang's role altogether—as evidence of the freedoms in the United States that are absent in Iran. Abrams emphasized that Americans celebrate this Iranian history before arguing that the IRI does not allow Iranians to do the same "because the Islamic Republic represents the antithesis of Cyrus's legacy." After enumerating oppressions and violations of human rights, Abrams continued: "This regime doesn't want Iranians to remember the wisdom and tolerance of Cyrus, because as they do, the people are reminded just how much this regime has harmed their great nation."[128] While some users thanked Abrams for acknowledging the holiday, others quickly highlighted the extreme hypocrisy of the video: as assistant secretary of state in the Reagan administration (1981–89), Abrams had not only supported authoritarian regimes while they committed devastatingly brutal human rights violations in multiple Central American countries, he had also been complicit in the Iran-Contra Affair, drawing a direct line between his actions and the ability for the Islamic Republic and its oppressive practices to continue to "harm their great nation."[129]

The video echoed Abrams's strategy during his role in the Reagan administration of co-opting human rights discourses to achieve other foreign policy priorities.[130] He had delivered a message in support of upholding human rights using an interpretation of an ancient Persian empire to combat the current Islamic Republic in a way that ignored both the United States' role and his own in the perpetuation of that very entity, presenting a reminder of the relationship between the distinct but related concepts of imperial nostalgia and imperial*ist* nostalgia. Renato Rosaldo coined *imperialist nostalgia* to describe an individual's longing for a lost time, place, or set of behaviors "that they themselves have transformed."[131] The neoliberal multiculturalist description of the Freedom Sculpture and other immigrant gifts in platitudes about diversity, human rights, justice, and freedom as abstract values derived from an ancient ruler of empire, rather than in real terms for Iranians today, had been among the criticisms of the sculpture from community members. But in making that connection to present-day Iranians, Abrams's video also laid bare that imperial nostalgia rests on an argument for benevolent empire, casting both Persian and US empires as just, moral, and protective of human rights, when the records of both reflect otherwise.

Around the same time as Abrams's 2020 video message, an LA-based Iranian American artist and activist, Kurosh Valanejad, "defaced" the Freedom Sculpture to point out the lip service that had been paid to human rights without actual advocacy for Iranian victims of human rights abuses. Valanejad, whose name is also included as a donor on the virtual Donor Wall, described his actions as "activating" the Freedom Sculpture, converting it into a Freedom Memorial by adding to its structure the names of political prisoners such as human rights advocates (e.g., Nasrin Sotoudeh) and those who had already been executed (e.g., Navid Afkari) (fig. 2.10). Naming his intervention "The Freedom Sculpture, Revisited (2020–21)," in his activations Valanejad sought to realize "the potential of a public monument about freedom to combat the lack of freedom in Iran."[132] Valanejad posted a video of his intervention on Facebook with a comment reflecting on the symbols of kinship it invoked: "Like an ornate setting on a pair of matching wedding rings, the Freedom Sculpture may also represent a proposition of fidelity of diasporic Iranians to our adopted home. But with no mention of Iran and the serial human-rights violations to its own people, have we also divorced ourselves of any concern for our birth country? The gold and silver powder-coated steel of the sculpture may be stainless but its ideals are tarnished by the seemingly endless tragic stories of Iranians terrorized by a pseudo-Islamic regime."[133] Here Valanejad refocused Farhang's message, utilizing the "dormant" sculpture's highly-trafficked location as an effective tool in calling attention to the very current human rights concerns of Iranians in the 2020s.

In October 2022, when the Woman, Life, Freedom protests erupted in Iran following the death of Jina Mahsa Amini, Valanejad's proposal gained renewed urgency as well as attention. When he posted a photo of his latest decal addition to the sculpture, reading "Say my name—Mahsa Amini—Be my voice," other Iranian American artists joined his activations. Opposing the mandatory hijab among a raft of other oppressive practices of the IRI, Iranian American artist Nushin Sabet tied her headscarf to the sculpture: "I had been forced to wear this veil in Iran, due to the compulsory hijab laws over there. So, tying it to the Freedom Sculpture and seeing my veil blowing freely in the wind was a way of sending my hopes and wishes to the courageous women and people of Iran as they fight for these basic freedoms that we take for granted here in America."[134] Dozens of other Iranians followed suit, tying headscarves, ribbons, and flags to the activated monument. As stewards of the sculpture, Farhang did not remove these interventions or view them as vandalism—instead, they were promoted on Farhang's social media, on two large billboards in west LA, and in interviews to local and international media (fig. 2.10).

### At the Limits of Freedom, Dignity, and Wealth

Taken together, the 2013 *A New Beginning* exhibition tour of the Cyrus Cylinder and the 2017 Freedom Festival and Freedom Sculpture demonstrate how a growing Cyromania and larger Iranian imperial nostalgia in the United States has combined with contributionism as strategies for Iranian American leaders to assert belonging and seek inclusion in multicultural America. Many Iranian Americans view Farhang's programming as a source of pride for the community—an especially valued outcome in the face of simplistic and negative media representations, xenophobic rhetoric, and political antagonisms. The ways Farhang has positioned the Iranian community in line with discourses of neoliberal multiculturalism before City Hall officials, the mayor, the state governor, and the general population of Southern California and beyond contributes to and reflects the hegemonic norms of US assimilationism. Class

Figure 2.10. The Freedom Sculpture was activated as a site of protest in October 2022 (top); a Farhang Foundation billboard in West Los Angeles promoted the sculpture as site of protest hashtagged with #WomanLifeFreedom and *zan zendegi azadi* (bottom). (Credit: Vafa Khatami)

status as marked by entrepreneurial success, conspicuous wealth and consumption, and access to elite institutions have been mobilized alongside and through imperial nostalgia as evidence of Iranian American contribution and worthiness for belonging.

Farhang of course is not alone in these efforts of Iranian American contributionism. But because Farhang has become the dominant player in the arena of culture in this diasporic capital, that success presents opportunities to examine the ways power, class, and identity operate in Iranian Los Angeles and articulate with (and are sustained and constrained by) the neoliberalist forms of multiculturalism in the United States. In this brand of multiculturalism, immigrant communities are to be applauded for having contributed diversity to the American cultural fabric while taking full responsibility for their own cultural welfare. The subjectification and socialization of immigrants in the United States thus includes being taught that they must earn their belonging, "bootstrapping" not just their economic lives but their social and cultural lives as well. One way to do so has been through representations to the general public not just of upholding American ideals but of being "more American than the Americans" in order to prevent discrimination and gain inclusion. In other words, immigrant groups should nurture their cultural and linguistic roots that benefit American society without relying on state support to do so, symbolically or financially, and without contesting the status quo of power hierarchies.

Where Italian Americans in midcentury America presented Christopher Columbus and their community's laborers and war veterans as significant contributions to the benefit of American society, in the 2010s and 2020s, Iranian Americans presented Cyrus the Great and their community's entrepreneurial successes as their contributions to America. In both cases, immigrants in the United States have used contributionism to argue for inclusion in a raced and classed privileged status and to challenge targeted immigration policies. For Italian Americans, the outcome was that the immigration law that had limited Italian migration was changed, and Italians have been included in the US racial hierarchy as white. But their efforts did not fundamentally change the racial hierarchy itself nor how other immigrants across the country have been treated. Perhaps a more widely felt outcome, then, was the co-optation of this contributionist rationale and rhetoric by US politicians, which then made it appear integral to the "nation of immigrants" myth, leading future immigrants—such as Iranians—to repeat and internalize it as fact. For Iranian Americans navigating belonging more than half a century later, highly choreographed performances of inclusion seeking to reinforce the narrative that Iranian Americans are not outsiders but historic contributors to U.S. democracy have not yet assured similar outcomes from their compatriots. While the Freedom Sculpture was being unveiled as a monument to Iranian contributions, countless Iranian families remained separated by immigration policies that cast them as security threats. This contradiction underscores the limits of contributionism and neoliberal multiculturalism: even as Iranian Americans mobilized their cultural, social, and financial capital as a strategy of inclusion that led their message to be heard by the halls of power, their inclusion nevertheless remained contingent, conditional, and precarious.

# 3

## Contesting Cultural Belonging(s) in Stockholm

Located at the top of a hill in trendy Södermalm, Södra Teatern is the oldest theater in Stockholm, known as much for its modern concerts as for its spectacular views of Saltsjön bay and historic Gamla Stan (Old Town). On a cold Monday afternoon in February, representatives from over a dozen of Stockholm's Iranian cultural associations, language schools, retiree organizations, political associations, student groups, and media outlets gathered in the theater's conference room for a weekly meeting. Most of these individuals had traveled to central Stockholm from suburbs like Kista and Husby, where many Iranians and other immigrants reside. The group was gathering to plan the 2012 Eldfesten, a large annual festival coproduced by this committee, Iranian arts association Farhang Förening (Farhang Association—unrelated to Farhang Foundation in California), and Riksteatern, the national touring theater of Sweden. It marks Chaharshanbeh Suri, a tradition that is celebrated on the eve of the last Wednesday before the spring equinox, marked as the new year, or Nowruz.

As the bells of a nearby church rang out at 5:00 p.m., twenty committee members brought their teas and snacks to the large conference table, greeting one another and settling in. Massood, then a fifty-one-year-old employee of Sweden's prominent Workers' Education Association (Arbetarnas Bildningsförbund; ABF) presided over these meetings. His tall build and warm humor were as useful as his ABF training in democracy promotion for keeping the sometimes contentious proceedings amiable, equitable, and productive. Massood began each meeting with a recap of goals and their progress before presenting the meeting agenda and the process for joining the speakers' list.

Today's meeting was no different. Rapping his knuckles on the table to get everyone's attention, he began in Persian: "Dear friends! Welcome! We'll continue our work today and go over how things have progressed." After offering a detailed introduction of the committee and summary of its activities for the committee's newcomers, he set the tone for the group's work: "Less than two weeks remain [until the festival], and our goal in these remaining two weeks is to have two or three more meetings to complete the program in a high-quality fashion, and also to hold this national-homeland celebration [*marasem-e melli-mihani*] in a good and smooth way so that the people who attend, whether Swedish, Iranian, or any other nationalities, can enjoy it."[1] Massood giving a somewhat clunky description of the event as a "national-homeland celebration" (*marasem-e melli-mihani*) before stating the goal of holding it in "a good and smooth way" (*khub o aram*) for the diverse crowd ("Swedish, Iranian, or any other nationalities") who will attend was a subtle indicator of the main tensions surrounding this event that had reverberated through Stockholm's Iranian community.[2] While Eldfesten's organizers sought to create a professionally produced festival inspired by Iranian traditions for a wide national and even international audience, critical members of the community had decried what they viewed as a loss of "Iranianness" in the resulting event that they framed as betrayal. Here, the awkward construction of "*melli-mihani*" captured the difficulty of translating and representing Iranianness in a multicultural society, while also demonstrating Massood's effort to create consensus among a community at odds over cultural appropriation, authenticity, and mainstream representations of their culture.

Although the practices associated with the celebration of Chaharshanbeh Suri have varied over time and in different areas, a ritual of fire-jumping forms the core of contemporary festivities in Iran and its diaspora (fig. 3.1).[3] Celebrants symbolically give the fire the ills of the previous year with hopes of attracting good fortune in the new one.[4] This fire-jumping ritual in backyards and alleyways is often accompanied by setting off fireworks, eating traditional foods, and dancing with friends and family. Although Iranians consider it a national festivity, as Massood had described it, Chaharshanbeh Suri is not recognized by the Islamic Republic of Iran (IRI), which banned the event outright in the first two years after the 1979 Revolution. When Iranians continued to celebrate anyway, Chaharshanbeh Suri joined other Nowruz rituals that were begrudgingly tolerated by officials, though IRI leaders have specifically discouraged these outdoor celebrations, calling them un-Islamic, superstitious, and a threat to public order (fig. 3.2).[5] As a result, for some

Figure 3.1. Fire-jumping at Eldfesten 2012 in Kungsträdgården Stockholm, Sweden. (Credit: Amy Malek)

Figure 3.2. Mana Neyestani, "Banning Chaharshanbeh Suri," *IranWire*, March 17, 2015. (Credit: Mana Neyestani)

in Iran, celebrating Chaharshanbeh Suri has also become a form of public, if symbolic, resistance to the IRI.[6]

In the Iranian diaspora, it is not uncommon for holidays like Nowruz and its associated festivities to be celebrated in ways that more closely resemble large public festivals, fairs, parades, and carnivals common to their North American or European settings. While Chaharshanbeh Suri had been celebrated in large community gatherings in Stockholm's immigrant suburbs since the 1980s, as of 2010, this Iranian holiday has also been celebrated as Eldfesten in two highly prominent locations in central Stockholm. For its first eight years, Eldfesten was organized in Kungsträdgården, one of Stockholm's most popular and recognizable city parks that hosts free concerts and festivals throughout the year. In 2019, Eldfesten moved to another Swedish landmark, Skansen, the world's oldest open-air museum displaying five centuries of Swedish traditions and crafts and a popular venue for Swedish holidays such as Valborg, Midsummer, and Sweden's National Day. Indeed, the name "Eldfesten"—*fire festival* in Swedish—was selected by its organizers to draw out the connection between the spring rituals celebrated in Iran and those of Swedish Valborg, an annual spring festival celebrated with bonfires each April. In its new location, Eldfesten became the first and only immigrant-origin holiday to grace the festive Skansen calendar, as noted proudly in social media promotions by its Iranian immigrant organizers.[7]

Eldfesten quickly became the largest celebration of Chaharshanbeh Suri in the world, and at its height was co-organized in five large Swedish cities on the same night.[8] In these central Swedish locations, Chaharshanbeh Suri as Eldfesten has been showcased for a larger, more diverse population. To entertain these diverse crowds, the three-hour stage line-up has included traditional Persian, Kurdish, and Azeri musicians and dance numbers; contemporary Iranian, Afghan, and Turkish pop artists and DJ sets; as well as rappers, Latin bands, Afro-Swedish music groups, a Swedish fire circus, and, at Skansen's rink, even Swedish ice dancers.

The diversity of these acts has been intentionally—if controversially—curated to offer something for everyone: From its very first iteration, the colorful print and digital marketing for Eldfesten in Swedish, English, and Persian has consistently advertised that Eldfesten is free, welcoming,

Figure 3.3. Social media advertisement for Eldfesten 2014: free and for everyone. (Source: Eldfesten 2014)

and for everyone (fig. 3.3). And by many accounts, that approach has worked. According to police estimates, in its first year in 2010, Eldfesten drew twelve to fifteen thousand attendees; by 2016, Eldfesten in Stockholm drew an estimated audience of over twenty-seven thousand. Given these sizeable crowds, it is clear that the event drew a significant portion of the Iranian, Afghan, and Kurdish (e.g., non-Iranian Kurds from Iraq or Türkiye) communities of Stockholm to a snowy outdoor festival in March, but also non-immigrant Swedes and those whom Massood had glossed as "other nationalities."

For many of these latter attendees, this cultural event was not simply an opportunity to learn about Iranian culture; for them, Eldfesten confirmed the openness of Swedish society.[9] That message was echoed by Swedish officials and politicians who appeared on stage, underlining the opposition between Swedish democratic and multicultural principles, on the one hand, and the reported repression of Chaharshanbeh Suri in Iran and elsewhere, on the other.[10]

The free and "for everyone" approach to an Iranian holiday has been crucial for Eldfesten's main organizers, who also viewed the festival as an opportunity for bidirectional interculturalism. Although Sweden has experimented with its own forms of multiculturalism since the early 1970s, as we have seen, *interculturalism* became the directive of Swedish cultural policy in a 2009 reform—less than a year prior to the first Eldfesten—encouraging a two-way process of integration through "a mixture of expressions and experiences, both at the individual level and that of society."[11] In contrast to traditional understandings of assimilation that require immigrants to accept and eventually conform to the majority, interculturalism was presented in Swedish cultural policy as a bidirectional process that creates change for both newcomers and the Swedish society at large.

Interculturalism has been portrayed by scholars and policymakers as a foil to multiculturalism, even if they appear synonymous in practice: Where multiculturalism is focused on group-differentiated rights, they argue, interculturalism focuses on individuals as "agents deserving policies";[12] where multiculturalism policy is maligned for having created "parallel lives" and encouraged ethnic separatism, interculturalism is said to create synthesis, interaction, and dialogue, especially in its emphasis on interpersonal cultural encounters and everyday interaction.[13] Despite critics who suggest that the difference between these concepts is only semantic, interculturalism became a powerful discourse in Europe in the late 2000s and emerged in my interviews with Eldfesten's organizers in 2012 as a guiding principle for the event. They interpreted interculturalism in this context to mean that their work should create greater inclusion for Iranians in the Swedish public sphere. They could do this, for example, by presenting an Iranian holiday in prestigious public venues in central Stockholm for a national audience, with a long-term goal of earning the holiday's inclusion on the Swedish national calendar. But also, in order to be bidirectional, they felt that the festival must include non-Iranians, and especially native-born Swedes. They have tried to do this by including both English and Swedish languages on stage for non-Persian-speaking audience members, by presenting a diverse range of performers and musical genres for a wide range of tastes, and by inviting (mostly non-Iranian) national politicians to speak from the Eldfesten stage each year—drawing high-ranking officials such as the Swedish minister of culture, the minister for foreign affairs, and even the prime minister.

The festival's interculturalist approach was encouraged by cultural policy that enabled financial support from the Swedish government, which, through the intermediary of the national touring theater, provided some 90 percent of the costs of the professionally produced Eldfesten. That model has brought the event success, measured by its funders through large and diverse audiences, widespread media coverage, and the strong artistic merit of the event. This success led to the

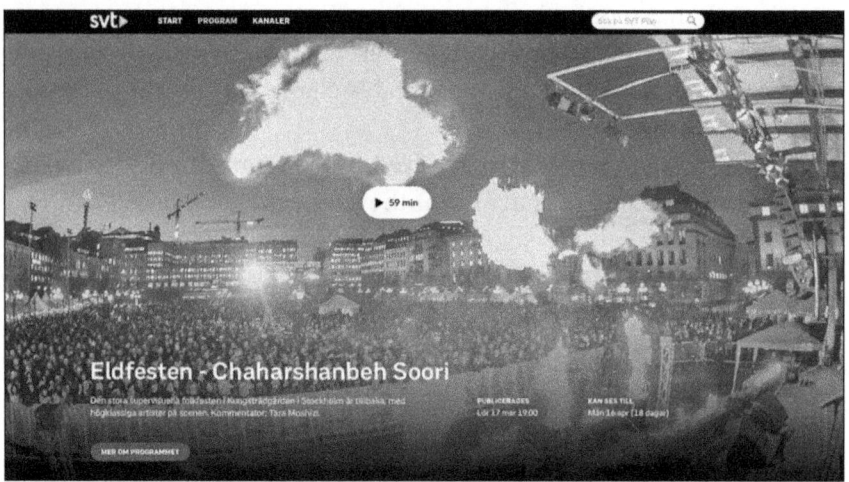

Figure 3.4. Screenshot of the view from the stage during Eldfesten 2018, demonstrating the impressive use of pyrotechnics to creatively incorporate fire into the performances. As streamed on SVT Play (Swedish national television).

expansion of Eldfesten to simultaneous celebrations in multiple Swedish cities and, starting in 2017, its live broadcasts on Swedish national radio (Sveriges Radio) and television (SVT), both of which streamed online (fig. 3.4). But the audience of Eldfesten extends well beyond Sweden: As of 2013 Eldfesten has also been seen by global audiences through Persian-language satellite and digital channels such as US-government-funded Voice of America Farsi, London-based Manoto, and Emirati-based MBC Persia. Due to COVID-19 restrictions, in 2021, the event also streamed live online via YouTube, bringing it to an even larger global audience in diaspora. According to one producer's estimate, through these various outlets each year, Eldfesten is potentially viewed by thirty-five million people worldwide.[14]

Through these efforts, Chaharshanbeh Suri has entered Swedish popular culture and Eldfesten has become a household name in Sweden. By 2017, the Riksteatern CEO could announce to the crowd: "This is nowadays a Swedish tradition."[15] Despite this growth and success in achieving the organizers' goals, not everyone has been a fan of Eldfesten.[16] The openness that is a point of pride for its organizers and the basis of continued funding from Swedish cultural institutions has been the source of contestations in the Iranian immigrant communities of Stockholm. The complaints and rumors circulating in 2012, for example, centered around cultural representation, authenticity, and power—common concerns in diasporic contexts. In these contestations, culture was repeatedly described as needing protection from forces of assimilation and appropriation, stemming from concerns that this state-supported festival had both "stolen" an Iranian tradition (as Swedish appropriation seen most readily in naming it "Eldfesten") and, worse, watered it down with so many "foreign" (e.g., non-Iranian in origin and in familiarity) elements that it was no longer even recognizable as Chaharshanbeh Suri. A frustrated elder expressed this sentiment succinctly in an Eldfesten Committee meeting, exclaiming, "Is there even any sign of *Iran* at this celebration?!"[17] It was this concern that Massood had likely sought to assuage in his clumsy description of Eldfesten as a "*marasem-e melli-mihani.*"

In analyzing Eldfesten 2012 as a site of contestation for the Iranian immigrant community in Stockholm, I seek to highlight a paradox of interculturalist approaches: The Swedish state's goals of integration as inclusion sparked anxieties among community members fearful of what they viewed as erasures that this inclusion required. I demonstrate how some Iranian Swedes, especially those working toward interculturalism for large Swedish cultural institutions, sought to vie for state funding and opportunities to insert Iranians into the mainstream Swedish public sphere and vice versa. With this funding, they aimed to present professionally produced public performances of Iranian culture, seeking greater public exposure, recognition, and, ultimately, inclusion for this large immigrant community in mainstream Swedish society. Encouraged by policies centered on interculturalism and democracy, Iranians working within Swedish cultural institutions served as intermediaries who, as professionals with experience navigating Swedish bureaucracy, could enable the community to make claims on the state—a feat previous organizers had failed to accomplish. But greater public exposure and recognition were not shared goals for everyone in the community, nor were the bidirectional principles of interculturalism that would necessitate what some viewed as theft and manipulation of Iranian culture. The ways this "manipulation" was viewed by different constituencies is also telling of bifurcations within the diaspora: Where one side complained of cultural theft and removing the authenticity or "Iranianness" of the event, the other sought to prevent it from becoming exclusionary, overtly nationalist, or even racist against Arabs and other minorities.

Through ethnographic attention to the discourses in play during Eldfesten Committee planning meetings and in community contestations surrounding 2012 Eldfesten,[18] I also offer micro-level attention to how macro-level Swedish cultural policies and the meso-level institutions tasked with implementing them have created avenues for interaction between immigrants and state intermediaries intended to prepare newcomers for participation in Swedish public life—in this case, through disciplinary discourses of professionalism and democratic practices. These, too, encouraged reconsiderations of cultural attitudes among Iranian immigrants by engaging long-standing predicaments in translating invented traditions in contexts of (trans)national politics.

Furthermore, in making claims on the state, these leaders not only heightened competition *within* the community over the power of representation and access to resources, they also were conscious of being in competition with other immigrant communities vying for the same state support and recognition. Neoliberal reforms to Swedish cultural policy have been incremental and, in its earliest iterations, less tangible than those in other parts of Europe and in North America. Nevertheless, policy reforms and budget cuts have reconfigured cultural policy to target individuals rather than groups and have emphasized that culture is an arena through which the state may inculcate in immigrants democratic practices and Swedish norms. As such, the interplay of culture and democracy has become increasingly pronounced and, in the case of the Eldfesten Committee, individuals' democratic practices—as in, behaviors but also *rehearsals* of those behaviors—became a stated goal of organizers. And, as they told fellow committee members repeatedly, the more that groups such as the Eldfesten Committee could demonstrate their implementation of these kinds of practices and norms, the greater their chances of being awarded the increasingly limited funds in the future.

While the primary work of the 2012 Eldfesten Committee was the production of a cultural festival, the concurrent goals of the Iranians representing Swedish state intermediaries were larger: to model, encourage, and rehearse successful collaboration among Iranians in Sweden and thus demonstrate their deservingness of social inclusion in a multicultural society. Doing so, they argued, involved efforts to influence not only the democratic practices of Iranians in Sweden, but also the democratic nature of a future Iran. This larger political goal was not just a personal one for committee members; it is also how the celebration of this festival became framed within public media and political discourses as evidence of the affordances of Swedish liberal multiculturalism in the face of Islamic Republic repression.

## "For Everyone, Everywhere": Producing Interculturalism

Over the course of six months of interviews and participant observation, I found myself at Riksteatern's large suburban headquarters in Norsborg (Botkyrka), southwest of central Stockholm, on multiple occasions. Founded in 1933 amid the rise of Swedish social democracy, Riksteatern's mission has been to bring theater to all the people of Sweden, wherever they may reside. Major productions tour nationwide, traveling well beyond Sweden's largest cities to even the smallest and most remote towns in the Arctic Circle. Largely state subsidized, Riksteatern's funding is determined annually by the Swedish Parliament, but it is not state-run: Riksteatern is owned and partially financed by more than 230 local theater associations across Sweden (established as Riksteaterförening, or National Theater Associations), with a combined total of over forty thousand members.

Referring to itself as a "democratic movement," this cultural organization aims to produce theater "for everyone, everywhere" (*för alla överallt*). Its 2011 mission statement proclaimed that "Riksteatern should be a pioneer in the exercise and development of new forms of participation, involvement, and influence to create tomorrow's democracy (*morgondagens demokrati*)."[19] Although the state's goal in subsidizing Riksteatern was always "to bring living theatre to the greatest number of people, in the most efficient and just manner available," it was only when a 2007 Ministry of Culture directive ordered cultural institutions to internationalize that the theater began touring productions in multiple non-European languages, producing work on themes of migration and identity, and seeking international performances, performers, and producers.[20] Following increased immigration to Sweden in the late twentieth century, Riksteatern's mission required retooling to bring theater not only to all *places* in Sweden, but to all *people* in Sweden, including immigrants in cities and suburbs.

Toward this effort, the theater established an International Department and hired Rani Kasapi, a producer with experience in intercultural and international nonprofit organizations, as its head.[21] As Rani told me, what Riksteatern had been producing before the establishment of the International Department was "the easy way": creating international programs that would appeal to the audiences the theater was already reaching. Instead of only including French, German, or Canadian performers or collaborating with other European or North American cultural institutions, she sought to reach Sweden's growing immigrant communities, whom she argued had been neglected and were therefore "non-existent" at Swedish theaters, whether in the audience or on stage.

Building on this policy directive, the newly established International Department created a strategy that targeted the inclusion of immigrants (whether from Finland, the Balkans, Chile, the Middle East, or Africa) by hiring individuals who were familiar with these communities. Soon she had gathered a diverse team of employees including Mansour, an Iranian immigrant with experience as a theater performer, director, and producer. Having worked from the ground up by starting his own theater company in Gothenburg after migrating to Sweden in 1985, Mansour had accumulated extensive experience in Swedish theater production. Since 2006, through his position at Riksteatern, he has produced concerts, plays, and television and radio programs in support of human rights, especially highlighting humanitarian struggles in Iran, India, and Africa.

As employees of Riksteatern, Rani, Mansour, and their colleagues were intermediaries of the Swedish state, and their work reflected the vision of Kulturrådet, the Swedish Arts Council. A government body tasked to implement national cultural policy as determined by Parliament, Kulturrådet at the time viewed culture and integration as intimately linked. Among the council's cultural policy objectives in 2012 was the "promot[ion of] international and intercultural exchange and cooperation in the cultural sphere," which it argued "is extremely important for the development of cultural life" in an intercultural society.[22] But the International Department worked differently from other Riksteatern departments: Rather than create new productions to tour, and in order to build networks and introduce the theater to immigrant communities, Rani and her team produced highly subsidized concerts featuring already popular musicians from Türkiye, Bosnia, and the Iranian diaspora that sold out large venues. They considered these costly events as investments; by keeping ticket prices low they encouraged audience turnout, especially among communities otherwise unfamiliar with Riksteatern or theater in Sweden more generally. This investment paid off, she told me, when local associations from these communities, appreciative of the attention the Swedish national theater was paying to their cultural identities, would partner with Riksteatern on future events.

These new partnerships then had two critical outcomes for the cultural integration mission. First, in their role as partners with Riksteatern, local immigrant associations were required to work with their municipalities to raise funding and build networks to successfully produce their events, gaining hands-on experience with local government and long-term benefits for both the municipalities and their communities. Where these communities had previously been either underrepresented in local government or living apart from it, these partnerships, as Rani put it, "placed [communities] in their local context." Second, these partnerships and the performances that were produced through them garnered mainstream Swedish press coverage and increasing attention from nonimmigrant audience members, leading to greater public visibility and recognition for immigrant communities' cultural identities. Rani described the intended impact of this visibility: "It's saying, 'You are important.' I felt that in all the years [I worked on this] that people suddenly feel that they have been *seen*. And [seen] from their cultural side. . . . [Cultural identity] is something that means a lot to people. I think it's a really important gesture from Sweden and Swedish institutions: to show that we're interested in you. You mean something. You are important here."[23]

These symbolic and instrumental overtures from the national theater built goodwill among community members who participated in these partnerships, creating opportunities for collaboration and enabling artistic productions that would have been more difficult or even impossible without state support. Indeed, the events produced by and for Iranian and other Southwest Asian communities in Sweden through the work of the International Department marked a clear shift in production quality, reach, and content from preexisting community events. But these partnerships also created a sense of competition in immigrant communities that manifested in heated debates and anxieties over authenticity and the ownership of culture. These anxieties were spurred by the competition created by state intermediaries in the name of democratic inclusion.

## Cultural Belonging(s): Ownership, Authenticity, and Memory

Criticisms leading up to and directly after the 2012 Eldfesten circulated widely in Persian-language media, such as radio programs, and were expressed in numerous letters of complaint officially addressed to Riksteatern. A local concert producer who had been active in the letter campaign against Eldfesten summarized for me the core of their complaints as a lack of "Iranianness": "Unfortunately, since 2010 when [Eldfesten] began, the celebration's Iranianness has deteriorated [*un halat-i Irani-i jashn be ham khurdeh*]. For that reason, last year [2011], that celebration—it was very well organized, but unfortunately it was not the Chaharshanbeh Suri celebration that Iranians had always celebrated, with all its traditions. It was something different, something new, like a festival instead of a celebration. You know? It wasn't Chaharshanbeh Suri."[24]

This sentiment about the 2011 event had led to competition and contestations in the lead-up to Eldfesten 2012. By *"halat-i Irani,"* which I have translated as "Iranianness," this producer and those who agreed with him referred to an adherence to a particular set of ideas, traditions, and symbols that have come to stand in for Iranian culture. Among these, with regard to Eldfesten, critics insisted on things like speaking or singing in Persian on stage (i.e., rather than in Swedish, English, or other European languages, but also rather than languages of Iran's ethnic minorities, such as Azeri or Kurdish) and playing only classical or *dambooli* pop music (i.e., rather than hybrid genres such as the Persian rap performed by Hichkas in 2011, the reggae with Persian lyrics performed by the Abjeez at several years of Eldfesten, or the pop music with Swedish or English lyrics that Iranian and non-Iranian artists have performed). The critics also insisted that the festival should more prominently feature traditions that Iranians associate with Iran (e.g., Haji Firuz, jumping fire, eating *ash-e reshteh* noodle soup) and display symbols that directly connects to Iran (e.g., the Iranian flag, though which flag is another source of contention).

On several of the numerous local Iranian radio programs, hosts and callers attacked the festival's organizers, criticized its selection of artists and host, suggested impropriety and corruption through an inflated budget, spread rumors about the pocketing of public funding, and misled the public about the nature of the event and its intended audiences, encouraging the community to attend a competing event in the suburbs—assumed to be more authentic and presumably overflowing with *halat-i Irani*—instead.

The question of money—including the size of Eldfesten's budget, what it was spent on, and how much was given to whom—was a source of much debate and gossip during and after Eldfesten 2012 and has continued, if less voraciously, ever since. While these financial accusations swirled, it was differing visions of cultural representation that received the most attention in the community, leading to numerous heated discussions both on- and off-air. The critiques that the organizers faced were most frequently (though not always) delivered by older first-generation community members who saw the event as misrepresenting or underrepresenting Iranian culture, as catering to Swedish tastes before Iranian ones, and as unnecessarily competing with their suburban community event. In cases beyond Eldfesten and across the diaspora, concerns about "Iranianness" are frequently framed as being about authenticity. Proponents of this view share a belief that the traditions and symbols they recognize as being Iranian are timeless, rather than representative of their lived experiences and memories of Iranian culture within their own lifetimes.[25]

Even individuals attending the Eldfesten Committee meetings questioned the leaders of the group over how "Iranian" it was or was not perceived to be. For example, an elder representing a retiree association described passionately what he had seen at the 2011 event:

> When I enter Kungsträdgården holding my [grand]child's hand, we are going to Chaharshanbeh Suri! We are not going to hear so-and-so singer's song—they can go put on a concert [instead].... Last year, I saw a couple of things that left me thinking there must be no leadership here. (Forgive

me, I didn't know . . .) Everyone was gathered in front of the stage, there was no room to dance. And the majority of people there were Swedes! Then, Iranians, hand in hand, were pushing to get to that side of the fire or to this side. It was just a bizarre gathering! And that woman up there [onstage] was singing in Spanish! And then, we Iranians who were off to the side—a guy who couldn't get to the center was saying, "What kind of Chaharshanbeh Suri is this?! I don't understand her language and can't even see where the fire is!" And he was right.[26]

Committee members such as this retiree who sought to remedy the situation by urging the Eldfesten Committee to bring the event more in line with what they considered to be authentic openly shared concerns over the reputation costs they were suffering just by being associated with the festival committee. They expressed feeling targeted by friends and neighbors alike. The tension was so high among organizers during the days leading up to the festival that, in response to anonymous threats received by Riksteatern, Mansour quietly ordered security details for himself and the Kungsträdgården stage for the twenty-four hours prior to show time.

In my interviews with festivalgoers, organizers, performers, and critics, one middle-aged Iranian Swedish concert producer, *Ehsan,[27] stood out as especially adamant in his protests against Eldfesten. Despite speaking with me several months after the event in 2012, time had not softened his resolve and, over the course of an extended lunch at a quiet Persian restaurant in the northern Stockholm suburbs, Ehsan spoke passionately about his charges against Eldfesten's organizers, whom he felt were guilty of "cultural theft," "cultural distortion," and "cultural manipulation." After over an hour of describing to me his position on the matter, and perhaps feeling I had not agreed with him enough, he changed approach by asking, "Have you ever heard of *Shahr-e Ghesseh*?"

*Shahr-e Ghesseh*, City of Tales, is an allegorical play that became immensely popular in prerevolutionary Iran. Although its dialogue is rendered in children's rhymes and themes, the 1968 play was widely understood as satire about the political realities of late twentieth-century Iran. Its film and radio adaptations became cultural touchstones for a generation.[28] In the City of Tales, Ehsan told me, the citizens are all animals, and the travails of characters like Donkey the worker, Mule the blacksmith, and Bear the bureaucrat were meant to represent Iranian society through musical satire. Ehsan emphasized his interpretation of the play's characters as being motivated by trickery, hypocrisy, and deception. He then relayed his recollection of a scene that occurs late in the play:

> One day, a newcomer elephant comes to town, the likes of which none of the animals had ever seen. They questioned everything about him: "Who are you? What are those big teeth? What is that long thing hanging from your face? And, what kind of name is Elephant [*Fil*]?" After ridiculing the elephant and remarking on how strange his appearance and name were, they decided to help him: They cut off his trunk, tore out his tusks and fashioned them as horns on his head, and took him to the registration office to get a new birth certificate, changing his name from Elephant to [the more common] Manuchehr.[29]

Ehsan and other diasporic Iranians have reinterpreted the treatment of the elephant in City of Tales as a critical commentary on traditional assimilation and its expectation that immigrants will conform to the majority in their new societies, leaving their values, languages, behaviors, and sometimes names, at national borders. For Ehsan, invoking *Shahr-e Ghesseh* was a way of expressing to me his frustration with what he called the betrayal of Iranian culture at the hands of Swedish cultural organizations and their Iranian Swedish collaborators:

> What [the organizers of Eldfesten] are doing with Chaharshanbeh Suri is the same thing [as in *Shahr-e Ghesseh*]. They have taken Chaharshanbeh Suri and made its name Eldfest; the ceremony, the things that they put on stage, many of them have nothing to do with Iran, but they want to say that, since *everyone* is coming, then . . . ! [But] you can't change the celebration just because there are *khareji* [foreigners, i.e., non-Iranians] in the audience! It's as if I would go to Swedish Julbord, which is a Christmas feast that Swedes love, and . . . say this Julbord is Iranian! Put a *chelo kabab* there and then also call it "Julbord for everyone!" We wrote this as an example for Riksteatern so that maybe they'd understand. But unfortunately what these people are doing with Chaharshanbeh Suri is the same thing.[30]

Although these kinds of culturally hybrid forms, such as a Julbord including non-Swedish food, are increasingly common (several Persian restaurants in Stockholm serve what they call "Persian Julbord"[31]) Ehsan found such a suggestion absurd and instead described it, and Eldfesten, as cultural manipulation and, ultimately, fraud: "This is something on the level of fraud, a scam [*kula bardari*] . . . Yes, it's to that extent! Do you know what '*tahrif-e tarikhi*' [historical distortion] is? It's to change culture [*sic*]. *Tahrif-e farhang* [distortion of culture]: cultural manipulation. When they say that Chaharshanbeh Suri isn't Iranians'—doesn't *belong* to Iranians—then it begs to be questioned!"[32]

Rather than seeing Eldfesten's "for everyone, everywhere" (*för alla överallt*) approach as an invitation for bidirectional inclusion, as Riksteatern and the Committee leaders had intended, Ehsan viewed Eldfesten as an affront to his understanding of and, importantly, his *ownership* of Iranian culture. That fellow Iranians had produced this festival in collaboration with Swedes using state funds led to his charge of cultural betrayal and fraud.

While some members of the community who had accused Eldfesten Committee members of financial fraud had misunderstood the way government funding structures worked (e.g., assuming the committee was given cash or direct control over this funding and therefore easily could manipulate budgets to line their pockets undetected), those who most rigorously protested the cultural representation of Chaharshanbeh Suri as Eldfesten had read the situation more accurately: They were protesting precisely the innovation and mixing that interculturalism policies encouraged and funded. Though Eldfesten's main organizers disagreed with the protectionist approach to Iranian culture, they repeatedly expressed frustration that their critics would not just take a live-and-let-live approach: "They couldn't just say that, okay, you do your own program the way you like it, and we'll do our own?" Yet for critics whose authority relied on control over authentication, the festival hastened the larger problem of cultural loss in diaspora and, for them, succumbing to a live-and-let-live approach would have signaled defeat.

To Ehsan, and to many immigrants like him, Iranian celebrations are owned by Iranians and thus reserved for specific linguistic and artistic traditions that encompass a bounded, authentic Iranian culture that should be protected from encroachment. The authority over the authenticity of Iranian cultural forms, in this line of thinking, clearly rests with Iranians. But they take offense and protest when other Iranian immigrants or their descendants disagree with their view, and seek to create new forms that challenge this idea of authenticity and their authority to determine what is and is not Iranian. For Ehsan and those like him, a shared understanding of "Iranianness" is rooted both in their own experiences in late Pahlavi Iran, and also in the produced common sense of that time-space that was naturalized for a generation that would later scatter in diaspora. That Iranian culture *in Iran* has changed since individuals such as Ehsan lived in the country is rarely considered in these diasporic outcries over authenticity; the oppositional stance of many in diaspora against the Islamic Republic often forecloses any consideration of these changes as worthy of attention, to say nothing of "authentic."

Rather than dismiss such rigid claims to authenticity or timelessness, anthropologists have sought to understand the utility of the binary logic of (in)authenticity for interlocutors in their everyday lives. Dimitrios Theodossopoulos has shown, for example, that attention to the "meaningfulness and purpose" of authenticity as employed by interlocutors can be an "invitation to change perspectives, . . . compare [views] of tradition, . . . and unpack the local meaningfulness and tactical rhetoric" of singular visions of tradition.[33] In diasporic settings where individuals or small groups of immigrants become representatives for their cultural group and heritage, authenticity takes on a particular "meaningfulness and purpose." In other words, when the power of authentication is felt to be a currency for immigrants to exchange for social inclusion in multicultural societies, a shift toward interculturalism and its processual view of culture not only threatens a key source of identity, but also of power, as it demotes notions of "the authentic" in favor of the hybrid, the innovative, or the cosmopolitan.

In her study of two Iranian celebrations in 1990s Southern California, anthropologist Halleh Ghorashi noted the relationship between memory and authenticity as it played out in community critiques of a commercialized Nowruz event. There, she suggested that, although change is inevitable, because diasporic settings necessitate that individuals rely on memory to authenticate ceremonies and traditions, "a memorized past serves to shape the way that an 'authentic' ritual is reclaimed."³⁴ Furthermore, when the memories of a given tradition are strong enough, she argued, *obvious* changes to those traditions in new contexts are "likely to be rejected."³⁵ Indeed, memory as the prime source of authentication was a powerful influence on critics of Eldfesten, who saw the changes to Chaharshanbeh Suri rituals as too obvious and too numerous.

Negotiations around authentication via memory played out repeatedly in Committee meetings. In one, *Farhad, an elder, described specific traditions he insisted were necessary to celebrate Chaharshanbeh Suri in an authentic way, especially the presence of Haji Firuz, a minstrel figure whom he was adamant should circulate in the crowd rather than just appear on stage.³⁶ While he acknowledged that Haji Firuz was not actually an age-old symbol of Nowruz that had been celebrated for centuries as many people thought, he nevertheless concluded emphatically, "This is what the people want! And this is the tradition of Chaharshanbeh Suri! Not in the form of theater. If [Haji Firuz and musicians] circulate in the crowd, all this [critical] talk will become meaningless."³⁷ Farhad's insistence on a shared "singular vision" of the tradition of Chaharshanbeh Suri through Haji Firuz as a circulating troubadour as the only accurate or authentic one prompted the next committee member on the speaker list, *Kayvan, to challenge this memory-based authentication. Kayvan asserted his own, different, memories of Chaharshanbeh Suri and Haji Firuz in Iran:

> I'm Shirazi, from Bandar Abbas, then came to Sweden. Across Iran, it is celebrated differently! It's not definitively one way across Iran. For example, in Bandar Abbas, the person who is Haji Firuz is clearly *on stage* and he acts, does theater. He doesn't go into the crowd at all. Or in Kurdistan, for example . . . he goes on stage and sings [*balatekhooni mikoneh*]. In Kerman, he goes around the alleys. There are different things Haji Firuz did. On stage, in streets. If it's a tradition, then we need to increase its artistry. Iranian art [*honar-e Irani*] means you are making old tradition modern and in a first-rate form.³⁸

Here Kayvan both challenged a static view of a tradition while referring to a binary of tradition and modernity, mapping intercultural representation as modern and, further, as necessary for artistic work. In these instances, committee members came face to face with fellow countrymen (and they were predominantly men around the table) who were not only from different ethnic groups and regions of Iran but who also had conflicting experiences and memories of the same traditions, leading to arguments over what would constitute authentic representation. These kinds of debates, articulated through meeting procedures emphasizing democratic process, revealed deeply felt philosophies about culture and tradition, maintained even in the face of sure failure to "protect" a traditional or authentic idea of Iranian culture from change. As an anthropologist observing these meetings, I marveled at the fact that no one in the room seemed to have sought out the expertise of historians, folklorists, anthropologists, artisans, or others who may have had useful insights; or, if they had, they hadn't dared challenge the ideas presented in the meeting through reference to those sources. Instead, the more valuable expertise regarding cultural traditions was recognized as that rooted in personal experience.

The ensuing confusion over contested authenticity frustrated 1.5-generation immigrant *Mahnaz, who, after listening to the debate between these men, finally got her turn on the speakers' list. She addressed Farhad directly as she sought a middle ground through reference to Swedish culture:

> Here is the issue: Among us Iranians, we either have a set of traditions or we don't. I'm saying, since I arrived in Sweden as a kid and grew up, Swedes know what *Midsommar* is, what time they are supposed to go around the [Midsummer] pole, when they're supposed to drink schnapps, these kinds of things. We Iranians still don't know—as you said—if Haji Firuz began in 1336 or whatever year you said, . . . or was a person who blackened his face as he came out of the mines—basically, these details are uncertainties. But since they are uncertain and we don't want to embarrass ourselves [*aberurizi*] in front of Swedes, since we ourselves don't really know, and no documents exist to determine if you are right, or Mr. So-and-so is right, . . . or history teachers in Iran [are right], we have to make it symbolic. [And] . . . tell people [about Chaharshanbeh Suri] in a symbolic way.[39]

Here the unresolved—and in Mahnaz's view, unresolvable—question of authenticity, which she framed as requiring a commonly agreed upon set of traditions, met a commonly held concern about presenting Iranian culture before Swedish and other non-Iranian audiences. *Shahin, a representative of the university student group in his twenties who had come to Sweden from Iran in 2009, emphasized this representational dynamic as well. After the contentious debate regarding Haji Firuz, he explained to me (unprompted) his take on the multicultural representation of culture: "In Iran, everyone celebrates Chaharshanbeh Suri in their own places. But we can't really do that here. My Master's degree is in Tourism, so I've worked in that area. You have to create a showcase [*vitrin*]. Bring things in, the beautiful things usually, whatever is more beautiful [*ghashangtar*]—bring them from your culture and arrange them for the eyes of—yes, its correct that ten thousand or twenty thousand Iranians will come, but you're doing this in front of the eyes of Swedes. This is very important."[40]

That Swedes—understood here to mean white, nonimmigrants—were watching was of great concern to Shahin and others. The goals of inclusion necessitated that these "Swedish eyes" would see not only "the beautiful things" of Iranian culture, but also Iranians performing democracy, professionalism, and cool comportment.

## "Like a Swede": Practicing Democracy with Cool Comportment

Despite several weeks of working to inform the public about the upcoming festival through Persian-language radio ads, Swedish-language print media, and a trilingual website (in Persian, Swedish, English), the final planning meeting of the 2012 Eldfesten Committee was repeatedly interrupted with members' concerns over rumored attempts to sabotage their efforts. They were especially worried about misinformation campaigns, such as fraudulent emails and SMS messages claiming the event had been cancelled, or Persian-language radio hosts and callers who had willfully misinterpreted quotes from committee members, attacked them by name, or ran ads for the competing event in the suburbs that again included lies about Eldfesten having been cancelled. In addressing these concerns alongside fears that this sabotage effort would extend to the festival grounds itself, Mansour emphasized that volunteers should defer to security guards and police during the event, but also directly referred to principles of democracy that required the group to allow for freedom of speech, within certain bounds. "Sweden is a free country," he said. "If someone comes [to Eldfesten] to demonstrate or protest, we cannot engage them in any way: Democracy does not allow us to say, 'don't do this,' but on the other side, democracy also says, you can't disturb our professional work, either. This is really important."[41]

Next on the speaker's list was *Behrang, a producer of a local Persian-language radio program based in the suburb of Husby. He described hearing an ad on a competitor's program claiming that Chaharshanbeh Suri was not allowed back at Kungsträdgården, so would be taking place in the suburb of Kista instead (where the competing Chaharshanbeh Suri event was slated to be held). In response, Mansour again invoked democratic principles (and this time, also the limits of Swedish law), framing the larger mission of their work as fundamentally different from the goals of the suburban celebration and of the individuals who saw them as rivals. "Friends, look. There's a law, an advertising law [about] dirty ads . . . but there's not much one can do about it. . . . As we've said from the beginning, this festival is inclusive [*hamishomool*]. We don't want to be racist [*rasist*]. We don't want to say only Iranians should come. We want everyone. We live in a society that has been . . ."[42] As Mansour paused, searching for the right word in Persian to make his point, Massood suggested, "Democratic?" Mansour nodded, "Democratic—*and* multicultural [*hamehrang*]." He explained by citing Swedish history and proverbs:

> We can't say only Iranians [should] come here; if we say this then we will isolate our own kids and grandkids in the future! Because if we open that door then Swedes can say, "Then *this* festival is ours, and only Swedes can come!" I remember someone asked Prime Minister [Olof] Palme why racists are free. He answers, "This is the price that must be paid for democracy." This is for the future of our children—if we say, "Only Iranians should come [to our event]," Swedes will come and say, "Only Swedes should come [to *our* event], *your* children shouldn't

come." Then there's only Swedes in that one, and none in [the other] one. *So everything has to be for everyone.* There's an old expression in Sweden that says, "Celebrations are for those who participate in them" [*jashn maal-e una ke sherkat mikonand*].⁴³

Democracy was invoked as a guiding principle in every meeting of the 2012 Eldfesten Committee. In this exchange, Mansour referred to both democracy and inclusion as foundations of Swedish society, emphasized through a citation to the former Prime Minister Olof Palme (1969–76, 1982–86), who is credited with pushing forward internationalism and social democracy in Sweden. Palme's global stature as a Swedish statesman was well-recognized and well-respected around the world, including by Iranian leftists of the 1970s and 1980s, several of whom now sat around the committee table. Though a cultural festival may appear minor in relation to the political work of Palme, Mansour and his fellow organizers drew explicit connections between their work and his, incorporating lessons of Swedish ideals of democracy and anti-racism into these meetings and in everyday life. Notably, the online call for committee collaborations specifically had included these among the values the group sought to promote: "The committee is open to all organizations that have a democratic and open structure, who have no profit interest in the event and who stand up for the basic values of anti-violence, gender equality, democracy and anti-racism that the event wants to promote."⁴⁴

In another example drawn from committee meetings, Mansour responded to group members' concerns about criticisms by reminding them that disagreements are both unavoidable and a part of democratic practice: "Of course, work that hasn't been done is the only work that won't be criticized! Let me tell you now, anything that we do [will be criticized]—even among ourselves, because our tastes are different, and that's a good thing! We have varying tastes, and a part of democratic work is [compromise]: If there's one thing we have to sacrifice it is our own opinions."⁴⁵ This repeated emphasis on democracy also resonated with Mansour's employment at Riksteatern and Massood's employment at ABF, two Swedish institutions driven by a democracy-promotion mission that aligned with that of the political leanings of many around the table.

Given his decades of professional production experience and the well-established resources of Riksteatern, Mansour could easily have managed the production of the three-hour Eldfesten celebration on his own. In light of the scrutiny, criticism, and threats he faced from community members critical of his work, as well as the intense time commitment he and others had made for these weekly committee meetings, in our interview, I wondered aloud why he and his colleagues had chosen to form a committee at all. He answered matter-of-factly:

> If I want to make a show, it's my job every day. . . . It's what we do, we produce theater here. And I've done it for twenty-seven years. It's nothing strange for me. But the good thing [to do] is to involve the civil society. Of course, I could choose [the artists] and it would have been much easier. But to just discuss with [the committee], to respect them. . . . You know, democracy is not something you just bring overnight. . . . Democracy should be built up. . . . I think it's [important] just to listen to each other—*and culture is the best [way] to rehearse democracy*. It's also a kind of export of democracy. If we [teach] a new generation, they know democracy.[46]

Mansour was clear that he and his partners saw an opportunity to create a coproduction with various Iranian leaders and community members—many of whom would not and did not collaborate with one another in any other capacity. Here they would be tasked with a common goal and guided to engage under the rubric of inclusion and democratic principles. He deemed equality and transparency as critical to this project and culture as the best arena in which to teach, practice, and spread these values. Indeed, Mansour felt that for Eldfesten to be a success in collaboration, the team especially needed to engage with those who had been vocal critics against the previous year's festival. In other words, he sought to demonstrate collaboration and model democratic practice in a multicultural society.

Bringing together Iranian community leaders to collaborate first required that Mansour gather like-minded partners who had well-established and positive reputations in the Iranian community. Massood was one such partner. After arriving in Sweden in 1985 as a twenty-four-year-old political refugee, Massood had started his own publishing house distributing Persian literature for the diaspora. By 2012, he also had worked with Arbetarnas Bildningsförbund (ABF) for over a decade.

As he told me in our interview, ABF is financed almost entirely by the Swedish government, and its focus on liberal adult education is applied through workshops, symposia, and the guided study circle. The study circle is the organization's major pedagogical tool, through which it strives to bring together Swedes of all backgrounds to learn democratic processes and encourage adult education.

In 2012, Massood was based in ABF's Rinkeby location. Consistently maligned by foreign media such as *The New York Times* as one of Sweden's several "immigrant ghettos,"[47] Rinkeby is one of several suburbs north of Stockholm that was part of Sweden's Millions Program, a state housing development program begun in the 1960s seeking to produce one million high-quality, affordable dwellings for the growing population. Today, Rinkeby is known for its dense concentration of immigrants from Africa and Southwest Asia, including Iranians, and particularly for its large Muslim population. As an employee of ABF since 2000, Massood had organized numerous seminars, workshops, film screenings, training sessions, and targeted social programs for Rinkeby's youth, its unemployed, and its majority immigrant population. All these activities, along with Massood's warm demeanor, had made him a well-known and well-liked figure in the community.

Though I would come to expect to see him at a wide array of community events in Stockholm, I first met Massood early in my fieldwork as the leader of the weekly meetings of the Eldfesten Committee. I quickly understood that Massood's insistence on a democratic process at these meetings—including speaker lists, timekeeping, minutes-taking, voting systems, and open debates—was a direct reflection of his experiences in ABF. In our interview, he articulated these principles through reference to the behavioral adaptations required for democratic subject formation, with echoes of Mansour's insistence on "building up" democracy:

> In these years [in Sweden], we learned how to behave, how to act, etc. Because democracy—you don't become democratic in one night. It's a way of life. Democracy is not something where you fly here from Tehran on a plane and in one night become democratic because the country is democratic. You have to learn. You have to learn the process and show how you can coordinate. These societies—Swedish society, European

society, or American—it took years of struggle to be able to reach this level [of democracy]. They set the foundations for expansion. It's possible that in Iran we *spoke* about democracy, but we didn't *live* with democracy. Here living and experiencing [democracy] is difficult. In the meetings, you saw, one would say—they thought they were democratic—they'd say, "Do it this way!" And when you disagreed with it, they'd get upset. The experience of speaking democracy and doing it differ.[48]

Massood's emphasis on the importance of learning "how to behave, how to act" in Sweden were reflected in how he conducted Eldfesten Committee meetings. He reminded meeting attendees that they should feel welcome to speak their mind: "Whether it's a suggestion, an opinion, an agreement, a disagreement, anything—you can say it."[49] Yet he also was careful to model preferred ways of doing so. When agitated committee members jumped the speaker list or ranted, Massood was quick to interrupt with a *"Mersi, mersi!"* ("Thanks, thanks!") to regain control of the floor. When debates escalated, he and Mansour took advantage of these as teaching moments to cite the open, democratic nature of the meetings that required all members' rights to speak be respected. For example, after a heated exchange between two committee members, Mansour waited his turn on the speakers' list to address the group: "Let me say something here—thankfully, up to today, we've been able to have a friendly and intimate tone in the meetings. Please, try to keep this intimate tone. In the same way that you have opinions, you should feel safe to express your opinion—because that is the foundation of democracy, that we should be able to criticize each other and express our opinions."[50]

Among the norms practiced in these meetings, transparency was repeated by numerous members as a common value and the group intended to compete with rumors through adherence to transparency. Meetings were considered open and public: Meeting minutes, documents circulated at meetings, and the summary of the postfestival evaluation meeting were all published on the festival's website or social media for the public to view. After the festival's annual books were closed, Mansour circulated a report in Swedish and Persian that covered everything from audience size, budget, and media coverage to the gender breakdown of artists and areas for improvement.

Despite these efforts, rumors persisted and were amplified on local radio, especially call-in shows where gossip could go unchecked. Where transparency couldn't prevent rumor or innuendo, committee members turned to other Swedish norms, whether principles such as freedom of speech or behaviors such as reacting coolly to insults. For example, in response to a heated debate at a committee meeting regarding how transparent the group should be in response to gossip about the event's finances and direct accusations against Mansour in particular, Mahnaz asked the room flatly, "If Mansour was not Iranian, if he was Swedish and had come from Riksteatern and wanted to put on Chaharshanbeh Suri—would we ask so much of him?"[51] Later in the same meeting, *Afshin, a middle-aged artist and arts association leader, urged the group to see their project as "Swedish work" that therefore required Swedish steadfastness and calm: "Yes, we are an Iranian group but we have to look at this as Swedish work. If this was a Swedish event, these discussions wouldn't happen. . . . The situation has to be seen in this way. The work needs to be done. There's a lot of enemies, lots of talk, but we can't let it get in the way."[52]

This suggestion of "Swedish calm" in response to incitements was also taken up by Mansour in the last meeting before the festival, where he and Massood both urged volunteers not to allow anyone to get a rise out of them, to maintain their composure "like a Swede," and only respond with cool comportment (*khoonsardi*, literally "cold blood"):

> This is very important for us to discuss. There's a series of sabotage happening. For example, Nasser got an SMS, I got an email, [as though] from Riksteatern, saying "Eldfesten at Kungsträdgården is cancelled." Some people are sending these SMS. It is the duty of all of us to say, "No sir, Eldfesten is happening, and it's happening [at Kungsträdgården]." Second thing: It's very common anywhere in the world that those who seek to sabotage create fights [*da'avaa miandazand*], they provoke. . . . It's possible for example, that someone comes [up to you at Eldfesten] to instigate something by making vulgar insults, [or] by calling you a spy. The best thing to do, like a Swede, is just smile. This is the reality. . . . Just stay calm. Just stay calm.[53]

## Professionalism as the Antidote to Exclusion: The Birth of Eldfesten

To better understand this emphasis on remaining calm in the face of possible saboteurs it is helpful to go back to Eldfesten's beginnings. In Sweden, beginning in 1994, a local Chaharshanbeh Suri event was organized annually by an Iranian association (part of a national umbrella organization of Iranian associations known as IRIS) on a soccer field in Rissne, another Stockholm suburb with a large immigrant population. In 2009, a commercial concert producer moved to bring this suburban Iranian celebration to Kungsträdgården, where it could be showcased for a larger population. Mainstream newspaper articles later claimed that the producer had gathered over two hundred people to work on the event over several months, and that they expected upward of twenty thousand attendees.[54] However, the 2009 event never happened. Just after midnight on the night before the scheduled celebration, the stage of Kungsträdgården caught fire. The blaze took three hours to extinguish and resulted in severe damage to one of Sweden's most famous public venues. Upon investigation, the detective inspector of the Stockholm police told the *Svenska Dagbladet* newspaper that he had no doubt that the fire at Kungsträdgården was a case of arson, started with a liquid accelerant (fig. 3.5).[55]

The unfortunate (and perhaps intentional?) irony of arson the night before a fire festival was not lost on observers. According to recollections of Iranian organizers, the attempt to bring Chaharshanbeh Suri out of the suburbs by holding a separate event on the same night (as it is a date-fixed holiday) had sparked rivalries between various Iranian parties who grew suspicious of one another. Theories abounded in the community as to who may have been responsible, but given the national news coverage, speculation about the incident extended well beyond Iranian communities. Swedish online message boards debated and speculated, including ill-informed guesses and negative appraisals about immigrants and "clan wars": "Is it a coincidence that the place where Eldfesten was to be celebrated is burned during the night? Can Global intifada be involved? Or has it been due to an opaque religious conflict between religious minorities? Or is it indeed a work of racist Nazis opposed to the Persian New Year being celebrated here?"[56] Comments responding to

Figure 3.5. "Eldfest went up in smoke"—screenshot of a report in Sweden's largest daily newspaper. "Eldfest gick upp i rök," *Dagens Nyheter*, March 17, 2009.

this Ubuntu Forum post included an array of opinions, including misinformation about Zoroastrianism and Islam alongside anti-Muslim racism and anti-Iranian racism, but also defenses of Iranians in Sweden as "intellectual democrats who have fled Islamist oppression." These public debates, and the reference to "opaque religious conflict" in the original post, are particularly telling about the ways some viewed their Iranian neighbors as "unknowable" others.

Tomaj, a young 1.5-generation community organizer, told me about this incident on two separate occasions, insisting that it did not really matter who committed the arson and why; the result for the Iranian community was the same: disgrace. He explained:

So the day before we're gonna have the biggest Iranian party in Sweden, somebody sets it on fire and it's on the front page of the [national Swedish] newspapers, on the radios—and it was so depressing. I know so many people among my friends, who, for the first time, I've seen that they didn't want to say, "I'm Iranian," because it was so embarrassing for them.[57]

It was a *huge, huge, huge* disgrace for us as Iranians in Sweden. . . . I remember myself that it was a big disgrace for us. . . . And then you get all of these stereotypes back—they are cannibals, they are savages, barbarians, terrorists, whatever. Burning flags, burning stages.[58]

This feeling of disgrace and a fear of exclusion were motivations for Tomaj and a group of fellow young, 1.5-generation Iranians in Stockholm to organize an event in Kungsträdgården the following year (2010), this time as a nonprofit effort involving the cooperation of major national Swedish organizations in collaboration with a committee of local Iranian associations. This 2010 event would become the first Eldfesten. The founding organization, known as Initiativ Iran, was started as a human rights association by three young Iranians living in Stockholm who had been active during the 2009 Iranian election crisis, having planned a large public concert and rally in the center of the Swedish capital. This motivating concern with politics in Iran extended to the group's organization of Eldfesten in 2010, as Tomaj told *Svenska Dagbladet* at the time: "[The festival] is clearly political, the opposition in Iran will take to the streets tonight and demonstrate for human rights, exactly at the same time our celebration starts. We want to show our friends in Iran that we stand up for them."[59]

In the wake of that summer's activism and with the shame of the arson on their minds, Initiativ Iran was particularly interested in repairing Iranians' reputations by showing to mainstream Swedish society that this crime did not define them; that Iranians were not only honorable, but also an open and inclusive group capable of professionalism. To demonstrate this, they approached Iranian colleagues employed in Swedish institutions whom they knew also prioritized cooperation, democracy, and human rights. Tomaj, now as a representative of Farhang Förening, described in our 2012 interview that organization's decision to collaborate:

[Initiativ Iran] approached us and they said that you should do something about this [fire] because this is not good for us. Because now in the whole of Sweden people are saying that, "Oh these Iranians, they can't do anything, they just fight with each other, they burn down the stage, and they do this and do that." So they came to Farhang and to Riksteatern and they said, "We should do something to erase that bad memory. To show that we can cooperate." *That's* why we took this up and arranged Chaharshanbeh Suri. And we also were very insistent of inclusion. That's why we went to [Iranska Riksförbundet i Sverige (IRIS)] and included them. . . . It's only out of respect that we wanted them to be a part of it . . . because we wanted to make this event that is about inclusion, that is about reaching out to *everybody*.⁶⁰

The inclusion of IRIS, a large umbrella organization uniting dozens of Iranian associations in Sweden, was important to Initiativ Iran and its partners precisely because IRIS had been responsible for organizing Chaharshanbeh Suri in the suburbs for over a decade and, later, because their leaders were especially critical of Eldfesten. Seeking to include them in the Eldfesten Committee in 2012 was an effort at living up to the principle of inclusion that the organizers espoused; it was thus also an effort to prevent exclusion of those critical of their vision who could become marginalized in the wake of this state-sponsored event.

But these efforts ultimately failed. After initially meeting together to lay out the terms of participation, IRIS withdrew from the 2012 Eldfesten Committee when their demand that votes be allocated according to organization size was denied, and after balking that they would only be considered a "member organization" alongside a dozen other associations rather than an "institutional partner" (alongside ABF, Riksteatern, and Farhang Förening) without making the required financial contribution of partner organizations (100,000 SEK, roughly $15,000 USD). Nevertheless, the effort at inclusion did pull together over a dozen Iranian associations as member organizations who sent representatives to the Committee, each with one vote. This fulfilled one of the original goals of Initiativ Iran in bringing the event to the center of the capital: They sought not only to broaden the audience of an Iranian event but also to demonstrate to that broad audience the capabilities of the Iranian community to work together for an inclusive, professional cultural production in collaboration with Swedish organizations.

This history suggests one reason why, alongside *inclusive*, the descriptor "professional" (*herfeh-i*) was used repeatedly by Eldfesten's organizers, whether stated as a need to "conduct ourselves professionally," or to "put on a professional production." By "professional," my interlocutors meant adhering to Swedish behavioral norms, such as having "cool comportment," but also being organized, punctual, transparent, and prepared; putting on high-quality events with consistent follow-through; doing precisely what they said they would do from start to finish. These norms were positioned in opposition to a shared impression of Iranian preferences for improvisation and to act at the last minute, putting on amateur events with a warm, if spontaneous and fly-by-the-seat-of-your-pants, energy. An analog might be the preference for musical improvisation, a hallmark of Persian classical music traditions, over fully planned and repeated performances that, while prompt and reliable, can lack uniqueness or room for spontaneous creativity.

Eldfesten organizers expressed to me—and demonstrated in planning meetings—an imperative to perform professionalism through these Swedish behavioral norms with the belief that doing so not only would result in a better event but also would be rewarded by building a positive reputation for the community and securing continued government support in the form of intermediary partnerships and renewed funding.

## Interculturalism Funding and Competition

Thanks to their experiences working in intermediary institutions, whether as grant recipients or as members of granting agencies such as local arts councils, several of these organizers were familiar with how Swedish agencies gauged success, exemplified by a need to demonstrate adherence to Swedish ideals of professionalism, democratic practices, and equality in their applications and productions. They were also aware that other immigrant groups were their competition for increasingly scarce resources. Funding for these kinds of multiculturalism programs has deteriorated as the government of Sweden has moved to the right and especially with the electoral success of the far-right Sweden Democrats (SD). Even in 2012, when SD had only won Parliamentary representation two years prior (twenty seats) and not yet become the second-largest party in Parliament (as it did in 2022), the committee was keenly aware of this threat, as Mansour noted in a meeting: "It must be understood that we are doing this [Eldfesten] two-hundred meters from Swedish Parliament, where the cultural racists, the Sweden Democrats, are sitting, and they say that culture and art are only Swedish folk music! By showing the cultures of others, or different cultures (this time it's Iranian culture we are showing or Iranian music we're showing, with Iranian artists), we can at least demonstrate that Sweden is a multinational [*chand-mellati*] country and other people and ethnicities also have this right to show their traditions."

At several Eldfesten Committee meetings, Tomaj (of Farhang Förening) reminded attendees that if they didn't work well together and put on a good program, next year the funding would go to others: "We fight with so many Swedish organizations to get money for Iranian culture. Remember this—we are in competition with so many others for this money. Rest assured that if we don't do well, next year it will go to Turks or some other groups."[61] This concern was a result of his experience working for Farhang Förening, which he told me was where he learned that Swedish bureaucratic process is "all about transparency, consistency, and doing exactly what you said you were going to do in the grant application."[62]

In our one-on-one interview, Tomaj was clear about why he had felt compelled to remind the meeting participants of the need for professionalism: "Several times [in Eldfesten meetings] I told them (and really it's the truth, it's nothing that I just made up) if we don't handle our funds—Chaharshanbeh Suri funds—in a good way, then they will very easily give it to Serbs [or] they will give it to Somalis. They have plenty of applications, so that's why we have to be very careful not to compromise with our principles and always do what we have applied for."[63]

Tomaj's previous experience in the Swedish military had prepared him for managing the bureaucratic details of the operations of his employer, Farhang Förening. The third institutional partner of Eldfesten,

Farhang provided the remaining 10 percent of the 2012 event's budget not covered by Riksteatern. Farhang was established as a volunteer organization in 1995 by several Iranian cultural workers, including its artistic director Rostam Mirlashari, a Baluchi musician from Iran who arrived in Sweden as a political refugee in 1991. Farhang was officially recognized by the Stockholm municipality as a professional organization in 2000 and began receiving state funding for its operational costs. By the time I visited Farhang's offices in 2012, the organization had grown into a state-grant-supported nonprofit organization based in Stockholm with a handful of salaried employees who produced a full calendar of folk and world music concerts, dance performances, workshops, and festivals.

Farhang's operational budget was composed of a combination of grants from the Kulturrådet, the Stockholm County Council, and the City of Stockholm, for which the organization was required to reapply annually or biannually. It therefore unsurprisingly enlisted the keywords of Swedish cultural policy in articulating its intercultural mission "to inform and spread knowledge about folk and world music to a greater audience" while "building bridges between individuals with different cultural backgrounds."[64] According to Rostam, the funding Farhang had won was nevertheless contingent upon Swedish cultural policy and to the larger political discourse in Sweden: "[Funding bodies] know that it is one of our goals to show the positive face of multicultural society. A multicultural society has the possibility to create new productions. The Right here, in politics, try to say that well, *they* [i.e., immigrants] came so it has become crowded, it's this, it's that, and we try to say that it is not that way at all! We immigrants, both from our working [in society] with the everyday things that everyone does, and from our positive cultural things, we can help this society. And we have!"[65] While acknowledging the importance of adhering to state multiculturalism and its goals, here Rostam framed Iranian immigrant gifts to Sweden as the "positive cultural things," labor, and "everyday things that everyone does" in society, as an answer to anti-immigrant discourses. This list stands in telling contrast to the ways Los Angeles Iranians have framed their contributions to the United States as exceptional grounds for belonging.

## Racial Anxieties of Representation

In the next-to-last Eldfesten Committee meeting prior to the 2012 festival, agenda items included the order of artistic performances, the timing of fire-jumping, and the best way for the group to respond to critics. Two new associations had joined the committee in the previous days, and so the meeting was attended by a larger group than previous meetings. Nearing the last few agenda items, Shahin (the student group representative) raised a new issue, a concern over the costumes of a scheduled dance group. Citing a well-known male Iranian dancer's dictum about costume selection, he said: "The navel is not supposed to be seen in actual *Iranian* dance. Neither men's nor women's. So if the dancers, if they're dancing . . . they should not have their navels visible. Because in the Uppsala Culture Night a group of them who danced . . . well, these things get a little mixed up with Arab dance and other things."[66]

The members around the table quickly erupted with reactions to this intervention that was clearly intended to differentiate Iranian dance from belly dance, what is often called "Arab dance" in Persian. Mansour clarified that the dancers never claimed they'd only perform Iranian dance: "And besides, I can't put in their contract that they can't show their navels . . . let's let the artists choose how to do their art." Despite this clarification, a middle-aged woman jumped in and, after apologizing for jumping the speaker list, argued, "But if they're going to dance under the name of 'Iranian dance,' and then do belly dancing and those movements [*laughs*], well, I don't like that, that's just my opinion. That becomes . . . [something else]." Shahin quickly agreed and suggested his silence on previous topics had been kept in commitment to the committee's spirit of democratic principles and compromise, but he could not stay silent on this matter: "Because that's not in [Iranian dance]! In all these discussions I haven't criticized anything, and have always been agreeable, but we don't have *this*!"[67]

Mansour was incredulous at a suggestion of censorship, asking sternly: "My friends, do you *really* want me to go dictate to a female artist not to show their navel?" The student, suddenly seeming to recognize the layers of the issue, especially regarding women's freedoms, was nevertheless still concerned. He responded: "No, but maybe at least ask what they'll be wearing?" This exchange prompted even more side conversations as committee members shared their opinions and raised further questions. Massood tried several times to bring the meeting to order, finally knocking loudly on the table while exclaiming, "Friends! Ladies and gentlemen! Allow me [*ejaze bedin*]!" The room quieted, and, true to the rules, Massood gave the floor to the next speaker on the list who briefly diverted the conversation to a question about balloons for children. But the next speaker, a human rights activist in his late fifties, quickly turned back to the dance exchange. He agreed with the student that since the committee hired the dancers to perform *Iranian* dance, Arab dancing should not be included on stage. Nevertheless, he felt that under no circumstances should the committee be interfering with artists' clothing choices; he hoped that the cold weather might take care of that issue organically. Next, a middle-aged woman extended Shahin's original point to express concern over the appearance of belly dancing (which had constituted several seconds of a short dance medley in the 2011 festival), while others disagreed with the appearance of "Arab dancing" in general. Meanwhile, those who were professionals in arts and cultural fields bristled at the idea of dictating any artistic choices.

Kayvan, a political activist in his early sixties, happened to be next on the speaker's list. Visibly shaken, he voiced his shock that his friends in the room were expressing anti-Arab racism, and further, that he and his comrades had left Iran precisely because of the Islamic Republic's dictating what citizens, especially targeted groups such as women and artists, could and could not wear, do, or say. He would quit on the spot if this was something the committee even considered doing now. Hearing the issue framed in these stark terms, the group quieted, and Massood quickly returned to the remaining issues on the agenda. But as soon as the meeting ended, the debate continued. Shahin, supported by the woman who first had agreed with him, rearticulated his original claim to Kayvan. Agreeing, she loudly scoffed, "If it were an Arab festival, they would *never* include Iranian dancing!"

The discussion had fully shifted from a concern about authentic dance and dress to the subject of ethnic and racial difference, covering familiar ground typical of debates about the limits of liberal multiculturalism. Shahin continued, "We're not saying Arab dance is bad, or that showing navels is bad; nor are we saying it's good. We're saying that you can't spend 1 million kronor saying you're going to show *this* thing [and then show another]!" As we walked out of the meeting, he clarified his position to me, abandoning the issue of the navel altogether and resorting to an essentialist view of cultural boundaries:

> SHAHIN: You can't spend one million kronor and then use symbols that aren't part of your culture. And because Swedes are kind of hazy [*gij*] and don't know a lot about or recognize these cultures, they mix them up! For example last year, when a Latin-American musician came [to Eldfesten], still to this day people say "Last year a singer came from Latin America! I still don't understand what that was!" Ok, fine—but then an Arab or Indian dance or whatever can be just as strange to people. Because you're supposed to be working for *Iranian* culture.
> 
> AMY: Who was saying this about Latin Americans? Iranians or [non-Iranian] Swedes?
> 
> SHAHIN: Iranians were saying it. Swedes don't even make a distinction! *That's the point!* . . . So in some way you have to explain it, [in English] "clarify," or as the Swedes say, you have to *förklara*! That *this* is different from *that*.

In this clarification in three languages, Shahin, who was himself a member of the Kurdish minority, offered an essentialist perspective that excluded Arab dance from "Iranian culture," despite knowing that Arabs form a significant minority group in Iran. He illustrated a recognition of Swedish audiences as either ill-informed or unwilling to make distinctions between cultural boundaries that he suggested were crucial. As he had explained in the meeting room: "Swedes don't understand, they mix it up! We are doing this to separate it for them!" But later, as our one-on-one conversation on the sidewalk continued, Shahin revealed that his concern actually was the nationalist Iranians, whose expressions of nationalism historically have included racially motived anti-Arab epithets.[68] He suggested they would revolt should they see an Arab dance on what they felt should be an Iranian-only stage—an affront of "inauthenticity" that would surpass that of the Spanish-language singer of the year before: "When Iranians come here their nationalism grows. So they'll say, 'What! They're dancing Arab-style?? Pack it up! What's the deal?' [*Che vaz'eshe?*] This is why—otherwise, what's it to me? I'm

Kurdish. There are twenty styles of Kurdish dance. You can show some of those! Show it or don't, to me it's not that important. But what is important is that the showcase you put on stage, with that money you're spending, people need to be happy with it so they don't complain [*azash harfi dar nayad*]."

Here, Shahin's concern shifted to one of anticipated community contestations. His assertion that Iranians who arrive to Sweden experience a rise in their Iranian nationalism was a reminder of the ways that feelings of exclusion are not only created by assimilation pressures but also interculturalism, and that they both can result in efforts to keep a grip on the power of authentication.

In the end, one of the dance groups at Eldfesten 2012 did perform a brief section of belly dance in colorful costumes that revealed the dancers' navels. Though the student's concerns about nationalist backlash over their performance never materialized, his intervention (informed by contestations already swirling from the previous year) and the debate it sparked revealed a fissure among the committee members surrounding the cultural forms and ethnic expectations of what should appear on the festival stage. In other words, these opposing positions reflected different approaches to the translation of a series of invented traditions associated with Chaharshanbeh Suri and what and who should be included and excluded from representations of multicultural Iranian identity in a multicultural Swedish society encouraging intercultural exchange.

The intertwined issues of nationalism and racism emerged in these meeting spaces sometimes as undercurrents and at other times, as in the concerns expressed by Shahin or Kayvan, in more overt ways. Anti-racism, in particular, was invoked a handful of times in committee meetings as an integral part of Swedish identity and democracy.[69] But more often, concerns over Iranian racism emerged at suggestions of exclusion, whether when someone questioned the presence of Arab dance or at the suggestion of ramping up the "Iranianness" of the event to the exclusion of other minority groups.

Such was the case when, two days before the festival, a committee member offered me and other volunteers a ride back to Södra Teatern after a long dress-rehearsal at the venue. In the car, Nasser, a theater director in his fifties who cohosted a local Persian-language radio program known for its leftist and feminist perspectives, told us that several people had called into his show that week to talk about Eldfesten, unprompted by him. He had considered it unethical to engage personally with these callers since he was a committee member, but told us that his commitment to democracy required that he give them the same airtime as any other caller, even as they began to spread accusations and what he knew to be false rumors about the festival. He expressed pride, however, that several of his loyal listeners had called in to defend the festival's mission. The debate between these callers, he told us, was about the relationship between integration and the maintenance of tradition, but had become framed through accusations of prejudice against Swedes, which he and others in the group described using the English word "racist": "The [anonymous] callers were instigators who said nonsense like, 'We should not pay attention to Swedes,' and 'Swedes only deceive us!' . . . But because our regular listeners are at a different level, they called in and responded: 'Why are you saying all this racist stuff?! Our hope is to become *connected* to Swedes and do good things!' And then [the instigators] responded with garbage about 'Our traditions . . .'—Come on, we're going after modernity! Not tradition!"[70]

Nasser presented this debate as one between racist instigators and his anti-racist and intellectual listeners ("on a different level") who advocated for integration and modernity—pitted squarely against isolationism and tradition. Here, accusations about Swedes' mistreatment of Iranians—whether as prejudice, discrimination, or overt racism—were provided by callers as rationale for attacking what they had viewed to be a Swedish-produced Eldfesten.

## Whose Cultural Belonging(s)?

In an effort to dispel rumors, a week prior to the Eldfesten festival, both Rani and Mansour had agreed to be interviewed by an Iranian radio journalist on the state-sponsored Swedish national radio's Persian-language program. The journalist directly addressed the various complaints that had been leveled, including about the budget of the event, the name Eldfesten, subtle differences in the event's website's explanation of Chaharshanbeh Suri in Swedish versus Persian (whose speakers would presumably already know about the holiday), and the priorities of Riksteatern. In one heated exchange, after remarking that Rani had stated in her interview that Eldfesten doesn't *only* belong to Iranians, the journalist pressed Mansour to defend the name "Eldfesten," insinuating that Riksteatern had demanded its use. He responded:

> We didn't want to translate this proper noun [Chaharshanbeh Suri], and we didn't. Instead, we took a name that different groups in different cities [in Sweden] have been using for a long time and said that is the same as what Iranians do, a fire party [*eldfest*]. Right here in Stockholm, until last year, all the groups called it Eldfesten–Chaharshanbeh Suri! We welcomed the connection between Swedish and Iranian society that had come about, and so we used it. Ms. Kasapi is totally right, we used this name to *include* others. We welcomed it and we'll keep it, but we'll never change the name of Chaharshanbeh Suri.[71]

Mansour's reference to inclusion and connection to Swedish cultural traditions emphasized bidirectional interculturalism in answer to an interviewer taking the argument of critics who insisted on protectionism. Mansour saw the name *Eldfesten* as a matter of inclusion (enacting the motto "for everyone, everywhere"), while those critical of the name viewed the same choice as enacting exclusion, sidelining them through cultural theft and misrepresentation in the name of intercultural inclusion.

Despite these efforts at transparency, one social media critic, an ardent nationalist infamous for his accusatory exposés, maintained a fervently oppositional stance against Eldfesten. Indeed, over the course of a decade, long after the Eldfesten Committee ceased to operate, nearly every March, Omid Dana took to his social media channels to reassert his claim that the Iranian holiday Chaharshanbeh Suri should *not* be for everyone, and that in fact Eldfesten was not for everyone—namely him—due to what he called its "anti-Iranian" representational choices. In a particularly inflammatory YouTube rant in 2019, he resorted to familiar anti-Arab, anti-Muslim, and chauvinistic tropes of extreme Iranian nationalism in hyperbolically suggesting that the cultural betrayal of Eldfesten had been even more damaging to Iranian culture than the Arab conquest of Iran (633 to 654 CE): "They've taken out all the Iranian parts! They don't say in Swedish that Chaharshanbeh Suri is Iranian. . . .

They've removed all mention of Iran! They keep saying this tradition belongs to all! No sir, this tradition of Chaharshanbeh Suri belongs to us Iranians! It doesn't belong to all! Even the Arab invasion of our country wasn't as bad as the blow that they are delivering to Iranian culture! [*Yani zarbeh-i ke inha darand mizanand 'arab pas az hamleh be keshvar-e maa be in shekl nazadand be farhang-i Iran!*]"[72] Versions of this complaint, along with Ehsan's accusations outlined earlier and told through the story of the newcomer elephant, were officially registered to Riksteatern in 2012 through numerous letters, including ones signed by a handful of small associations in Stockholm. Shared by Mansour with the committee in the name of transparency, they prompted debate in committee meetings regarding how best to respond. Since the letters were addressed to the national theater, it was determined that they warranted an official response from the theater itself. Ehsan, who had authored at least one of these complaints, described to me the official response he had received from Riksteatern several months later: Riksteatern "wrote that this celebration belongs to no minority group [*goruh-i aqaliat*]. By 'minority' they meant countries like Iran or Syria or Türkiye. And that this belongs to everyone. That it belongs to anyone who celebrates it. In other words, they see it as one of their own!"[73] Ehsan's incredulity at the notion of shared ownership was directly opposite to the goals of the Eldfesten Committee, which included a long-term aim of seeing Eldfesten become a national holiday on Sweden's calendar, much like International Nowruz Day had become an official holiday when the United Nations proclaimed it so in 2010, and in inscribing Nowruz on the Representative List of the Intangible Cultural Heritage of Humanity in 2016.[74]

As frustrating as these official responses were for the critics, their complaints were equally frustrating for members of the Eldfesten Committee, who felt they had done everything possible to maintain the "Iranianness" of Eldfesten. On the event's website, its Facebook event page, and in print media advertising, they carefully included Swedish descriptions explaining the event, connecting it explicitly to the "Iranian New Year" (as opposed to Nowruz more generally, which is celebrated by many other nationalities), and including the transliterated Persian name "Chaharshanbeh Suri." Nevertheless, in the final meeting prior to the 2012 festival, Mansour and Massood were yet again pressed by a newcomer to the meetings about the "Iranianness" of the festival. Mansour responded by listing the elements of the festival that would be seen by critics as demonstrating sufficient "Iranianness":

> On a big screen [at Eldfesten] . . . the Chaharshanbeh Suri logo will come up several times, very big, for example before the next artist comes, it just says Chaharshanbeh Suri in Swedish, in Farsi, the same logo that we have [everywhere]. . . . On all the [volunteer] vests it's also written, "Chaharshanbeh Suri." Then, we found a very good version of "Ey Iran" [O Iran, a popular Iranian anthem] performed by Banan that we'll play at the end. The serpentines that will go up in the air are the [three colors of the] Iranian flag. Apart from this, [to be more Iranian] we would have to choose a Shah and put him on stage!⁷⁵

As the group laughed at his joke, Mansour continued in his effort to assuage doubts by describing a video being produced especially for the festival to play on a large digital screen next to the stage: "Strauss's 'Also sprach Zarathustra' plays as those serpentines [are set off], then the image we had last year: a sun rising from the ground. When the sun appears–" Mansour paused to sing the dramatic crescendo, finishing with a flourish: "The serpentines are released, and an image comes up: FREE IRAN!" No one batted an eye at the overtly political message of the video, and Mansour concluded, "The festival couldn't get any more Iranian than this! We couldn't do [more]—we don't want to make it nationalist, you know what I'm saying?"

In the case of Ghorashi's ethnographic example in Southern California, community members who had sent letters of complaint to local officials eventually won, satisfying community concerns over maintaining the authenticity of a tradition of picnicking that involved homecooked meals and family gatherings. However, in the case of Eldfesten, letter writing, misinformation, and intimidation campaigns failed to curtail audience attendance or Riksteatern's support for Eldfesten. This is not to say that criticism was quieted, nor that the organizers ignored it; but Eldfesten has continued unabated, save for the interruption made necessary by the global COVID-19 pandemic in 2020. In 2012, the power of the Swedish intermediary organizations and the professional execution of Eldfesten had enabled the organizers to frame negotiations of memory and debates over authenticity as part of democratic practice, and thus ultimately to retain the interculturalist principles that they sought to promote.

As Lalaie Ameeriar observed in her study of South Asian immigrants in Toronto, state multiculturalism enacts a "dual mode of interpellation" that "puts immigrants in an impossible situation in which they must sometimes suitably display their Otherness, but otherwise cannot be culturally different."[76] Similarly, Aihwa Ong's articulation of cultural citizenship demonstrated how processes of subjectification involve a dialectical process of "self-making and being made."[77] In this formulation, subject formation is never only state-controlled nor only agentive but involves articulations and contestations navigating both—and often through the important role of state intermediaries. In the Eldfesten Committee, these dual modes of interpellation and subjectification were made evident through state intermediaries (like Mansour) by encouraging debate, drawing on democratic principles such as freedom of speech, modelling collaboration, or insisting upon cool Swedish composure. Through these, the leaders of the Eldfesten Committee were not only ensuring the festival would be conducted "in a good and smooth way" as Massood had stated, they were also providing avenues for inclusion through the rehearsal of these norms by an immigrant community under the gaze of their Swedish hosts.

# 4

## Navigating Multiculturalism in Toronto

On January 12, 2020, over 1,500 Canadians gathered in the darkened Convocation Hall of the University of Toronto to memorialize a national tragedy. Several hundreds more, unable to enter the packed main hall, filled an overflow space to watch the proceedings. Just four days prior, two short-range surface-to-air missiles had struck down a Boeing 737 passenger jet minutes after taking off from Tehran's Imam Khomeini International Airport. Upon crashing into a large field, all 167 passengers and 9 crew members who had been on board Ukraine International Airlines Flight 752 tragically perished. Apart from the Ukrainian crew, most on board had been Iranians living in diaspora. They had used their Iranian, Canadian, Swedish, British, and German passports to board the plane, offering a glimpse of the transnational lives of these passengers. The vast majority, some 138, were Iranian Canadians of all ages and a range of statuses—dual citizens, permanent residents, students at Canadian universities—who had been enroute back to Canada after spending winter break in Iran. Members of the shocked and angry Iranian Canadian community also composed the majority of the mourners filling the Convocation Hall just one day after the Islamic Revolutionary Guard Corps (IRGC, a branch of the Iranian Armed Forces) finally admitted (after four days of lies and equivocations) that they had shot down Flight 752.

Even before this disaster, it had already been an intensely stressful week for Iranians around the world: On January 3, a US drone attack had assassinated Iranian major general Qasem Soleimani in Iraq, a sharp escalation in an ongoing tit-for-tat of attacks. Observers warned of possible war and, while some urged restraint, then–US President Donald Trump took to Twitter threatening to intentionally target Iranian cultural sites. For several tense days, the hashtag #wwIII trended on TikTok and Twitter, especially under memes shared by young Americans who half-joked about the best ways to dodge a military draft.[1] Iran's retaliation arrived on January 8 in the form of ballistic missile attacks on US military positions in Iraq. It would be mere hours after these attacks and amid this heightened tension that the IRGC shot down Flight 752.

Global news coverage of the shocking incident and its victims was extensive. A dual sense of alarm and fear consumed the widespread but well-networked global Iranian diaspora, who felt the loss of Flight 752 personally: It seemed everyone knew someone who had been on board, connected by just one or two degrees of separation.[2] Decades of threats of war between the United States and the Islamic Republic of Iran (IRI) appeared to be coming to fruition, and collective memories of the downing of Iran Air Flight 655 in 1988 by the US Navy were triggered in this moment of renewed collective grief.

Makeshift memorials and organized vigils were held around the world; in Canada, local politicians joined community-organized memorial events in the large cities of Toronto, Vancouver, and Montréal but also in several midsized cities home to large populations of Iranians. In Edmonton, home to at least thirty of the victims and their families,[3] then-Prime Minister Justin Trudeau joined mourners and promised that their Canadian government would pursue justice: "Your entire country stands with you, tonight, tomorrow, and in all the years to come."[4]

It was in this context that I joined thousands of viewers watching the digital livestream of the memorial at the University of Toronto. The broadcast reached tens of thousands of mourning Iranians located not only across Canada but around the world. Presided over by two Iranian Torontonian women impossibly tasked with sensitively shepherding a community through such a devastating loss, speeches from community leaders offered tearful remembrances and calls for collective support. These emotional words were interspersed with moving musical performances, poetry recitations, and readings of the names of the deceased by the tearful hosts. Between these brief eulogies, Canadian politicians expressed not only sympathy for an immigrant community experiencing a shocking loss, but also recognition of the Canadian identities of the victims and their surviving relatives. They emphasized that this moment was one of *Canadian* mourning and promised that the Canadian government would seek justice, feeding a collective urge for revenge against a government that, in the eyes of many in this global audience, had added yet another life-taking tragedy to a long list of oppressions and crimes.

Following speeches by Iranian Canadian community leaders, professors, and local elected officials, as well as the Canadian deputy prime minister and the premiere of Ontario, the final speaker to address the international audience was Payam Akhavan, a law professor at McGill University. After reciting a poem in Persian, he switched to English to deliver a passionate speech describing the tragedies of geopolitical conflict in the Middle East as intimately tied to Canada through its immigrants. He marked collective bereavement—mourning as Canadians—as a lesson in Canadian citizenship:

> In Tehranto and Montréal, Windsor and Guelph, Edmonton and Vancouver, Halifax and London, across this vast space which we call Canada, people have lost family and friends, neighbors and colleagues, teachers and students. This isn't just another horrible thing happening out there, in that other world of suffering that momentarily intrudes on our lives of privilege, trivialized by a Tweet or a fleeting Facebook post, soon to be forgotten. *Now it is happening to us: We, who call ourselves Canadians, who imagine belonging as something beyond the ties of blood and soil. A transcendent connection built on a shared humanity.* Now, we mourn the loss that has become ours for the simple reason that we have come to live in the same place, in a common home. . . . Just as joyous celebrations define who we are, communal bereavement, healing together—whether it is with our Indigenous brothers and sisters who were here before us, or with the recent immigrant returning home from a previous home—teach[es] us what it means to be human, what it means to be Canadian.[5]

Akhavan invoked an understanding of belonging as "shared humanity" through affective solidarities—here, of grief as expressed in collective bereavement—that provided symbolic recognition and public affirmations of Iranian Canadians *as Canadians*. His remarks echoed the messages of the politicians who had spoken before him, including Deputy Prime Minister Chrystia Freeland who had affirmed, "This is Toronto's loss, this is Ontario's loss, and this is Canada's loss."[6] The public mourning of these lost Canadians formed an important step not only in a communal grieving process but also in the trajectory of national representation of an immigrant community that had worked for more than a decade to ensure they not only would be visible but also *seen* by their

Canadian representatives and neighbors in exactly this way—as Canadians. The title of the memorial event promoted on social media and local television in English had honed this message: not "Iranians Mourn," nor "A Diaspora Mourns," but "Canada Mourns."

Organized in just three days, the Canada Mourns memorial in Toronto was among the most watched of the numerous events held in Canada that January and the response from viewers and attendees was overwhelmingly positive. Online viewers also recognized the event as a Canadian one: "Canada got tons of credit and respect worldwide and esp [sic] among Iranian people who saw negligence and denying from Iranian authorities. Canada leading this tragedy in a very responsible and humanitarian way, God bless Canada."[7] Toronto leaders noticed as well; the assistant vice president of the University of Toronto wrote to the organizers the next day: "What a remarkable event—so professional—all the more impressive given the timeline you had to pull this together and that it was volunteer-driven."[8] How were the Iranian Canadian organizers of Canada Mourns able to pull together prominent Canadian politicians, Iranian community leaders, international media organizations, and dozens of volunteers into a seamless production in front of a global audience in such short time?

Canada Mourns was organized by Tirgan, an Iranian Canadian nonpartisan, nonprofit arts and cultural organization based in Toronto. Established in 2007 by a group of young immigrants in partnership with a Canadian cultural organization, by 2020, Tirgan had become the most powerful and most widely recognized Iranian community organization in Canada.[9] Best known for its biennial festival of contemporary Iranian arts and culture, the largest of its kind in the world, Tirgan's reputation has extended well beyond Canada. Each festival since 2008 has featured over 150 international artists, authors, and performers, and draws between 120,000 and 160,000 in-person spectators (fig. 4.1), as well as hundreds of thousands of viewers through digital livestreams and extensive coverage on Persian-language digital and satellite media. Over three hundred volunteers are necessary to organize and run each festival and Tirgan's dual emphasis on promoting Iranian arts and culture and on community-building (e.g., through volunteer development, fundraising, and social networking) has led thousands of Iranian Canadians over the course of the 2010s and into the 2020s to feel deep affinities with Tirgan, as well as a deepened sense of belonging in Canada as Iranian Canadians. It was the loss of five of these volunteers on board Flight 752,[10] in addition to scores of friends and acquaintances, that had led Tirgan's organizers to jump into action, putting their years of experience and extensive networks to work on Canada Mourns. As a Tirgan board member put it, "I can't describe the sadness that everyone felt. The entire Tirgan Family, we were so upset. But sadness doesn't do anything. We had to *do* something."[11]

In addition to revealing the ways Iranians had become included as Canadians (and among many other more immediate outcomes), the Canada Mourns event also demonstrated just how strong Tirgan had become and how uniquely positioned it was among Iranian immigrant community organizations in diaspora. The organization's consistent and intentional strategies to leverage the human capital of the community to build social, cultural, and symbolic capital had created a hard-won but remarkably strong set of networks and reciprocal social relations; the event confirmed to many Iranians in Tehranto that the organization both belongs to them and represents them and can do so beyond its festivals and arts and culture mandate.

The leaders of the Tirgan Family have been earnest followers of the tenets of Canadian multiculturalism and "the Canadian Way," as exemplified by its founding mission rooted in discourses of "unity in diversity," its institutionalization as a registered charity, its operating structure that has promoted democratic practice and teamwork, and its marketing and fundraising materials that put forward multiculturalism and diversity as shared cultural values in Iran and Canada. Doing so resulted in an impressive mutual investment of time and resources, including over $4 million CAD in in-kind support (including through state intermediaries) and over $2.6 million CAD in federal, provincial, and municipal grants between 2011 and 2022.[12] The community invested both financial and human resources, including raising over $3.1 million CAD in cash donations and sponsorships in the same eleven-year period.[13]

But like all diasporic organizations, Tirgan has also had its share of detractors, whether artists who disagreed with its artistic direction, community members who questioned its financial decisions (e.g., charging high prices for the few ticketed events on its calendar, or taking sponsorships from corporate donors seeking to repair their tarnished reputation in the community),[14] or political activists who have questioned the organization's nonpartisan commitment. From its inception, a carefully limited focus to arts and culture as separate from "contentious issues" has been Tirgan's attempt at a neutral political veneer (e.g., prohibiting political demonstrations, signs, flags, or rallying at its festivals) to build a sense of unity in a community as politically fragmented as it is politically charged. The Canadian multicultural models that had enabled Tirgan to emerge and to succeed had strongly influenced—and in some cases even required—each of these contested choices. But the deep community investment in, and sense of ownership over, the organization has also meant that political and social events that emerged in the early 2020s have presented Tirgan with repeated challenges—what I collectively term *stress tests*—that required the organization's leaders to repeatedly question the kind of organization it will be.

Through interviews, media analysis, and ethnographic fieldwork—including participant observation at Tirgan festivals and in planning meetings, as well as interviews with leadership and volunteers—this chapter demonstrates the powerful impacts on belonging and behavior that have emerged through Tirgan's strategies of inclusion. It outlines how Tirgan has built a strong organization through adherence to the principles and expectations of Canadian multiculturalism, especially by presenting Iranian multiculturalism—in the past but, importantly, also the present—as evidence of shared Iranian and Canadian values. These strategies of inclusion have built mainstream visibility for the community while also developing feelings of belonging and practices of participation among volunteers and festivalgoers. As a result, and through their participation in Tirgan, Iranian Canadians have benefitted from and (to various degrees) reproduced the liberal notions of immigrant participation and cultural recognition represented by the Canadian multicultural model. While creating value in the form of social, symbolic, and cultural capital for Iranian Canadians, the case of Tirgan in the early 2020s also demonstrates how these policies of Canadian multiculturalism, liberal approaches to immigrant integration, and adherence to Canadian institutional norms—glossed as "the Canadian Way"—have served not just an enabling function but also, once established, a proscribing limitation for a diverse, transnational, and growing diasporic community.

## Participating in the Canadian Multicultural Mosaic

Encouraged by the government's support for diversity and multiculturalism, we embarked on a mission to celebrate and promote Iranian arts and culture, while contributing to the Canadian Cultural Mosaic model with a simple motto: Our Culture, Our Identity.
—"Our Mission," Tirgan, 2022

In a speech delivered to the Canadian House of Commons on October 8, 1971, then–Prime Minister Pierre Elliott Trudeau outlined what is frequently cited as the first instantiation of a federal multiculturalism policy in the world: "Although there are two official languages [in Canada], there is no official culture, nor does any ethnic group take precedence over any other. No citizen or group of citizens is other than Canadian, and all should be treated fairly."[15] Trudeau emphasized the dual importance of cultural retention and individual freedom, the latter of which would be "hampered if [individuals] were locked for life within a particular cultural compartment by the accident of birth or language."[16] Multiculturalism thereby became an official policy of Canada in 1971, codified in the 1982 Canadian Charter of Rights and Freedoms and elaborated more specifically in the Canadian Multiculturalism Act of 1988. The act provided for ten policy directives committing Canada to recognition and respect for cultural diversity and affirming that "multiculturalism is a fundamental characteristic of the Canadian heritage and identity" and "provides an invaluable resource in the sharing of Canada's future."[17] Unlike other countries, multiculturalism in Canada emerged not only as a strategy to manage immigration-based difference, but also as a response to rival and heritage communities including French Québécois, Métis, Inuit, and more than 630 First Nations communities.[18] By establishing multiculturalism rather than biculturalism, Pierre Trudeau attempted to dismantle the strength of the French Québécois challenge to British English Canadian dominance by recognizing First Nations and non-British and non-French Canadians (e.g., citizens coded by the government as "visible minorities").[19] He also offered the country a distinct national identity through the notion of a "multicultural mosaic," asserting the

Canadian nation as a unified entity of multiple distinct but equal cultural groups, distinguishing it from the "melting pot" of the United States.[20] Citing its history of national contests for power between British, French, and Indigenous groups, sociologist Rainer Bauböck has pointed to Canada's exceptional status in this regard: "No other Western country has gone as far as Canada in adopting multiculturalism not only as a policy towards minorities but also as a basic feature of shared identity."[21]

On a national scale, Canadians take pride in their commitment to the diversity and inclusivity that their brand of multiculturalism espouses. In a 2007 poll, 84 percent of Canadians agreed with the statement, "Canada's multicultural makeup is one of the best things about this country."[22] More recently, the 2020 General Social Survey found that "92% of the population aged 15 and older agreed that ethnic or cultural diversity is a Canadian value."[23] Environics surveys over several decades consistently have found that significant numbers of Canadians are more likely to answer "multiculturalism" when "describing, in their own words, what makes Canada unique" than any other answer; more than 31 percent did so in its 2021 survey.[24] According to sociologist Irene Bloemraad, integral to this sense of national pride in multiculturalism are symbolic and instrumental support provided by the state for organizations that enable ethnic communities to legitimately cultivate "multiple identities while promoting Canadian citizenship" and to publicly present their cultural and artistic talents and heritage across Canada.[25] Toronto's Tirgan Iranian Festival began as one such endeavor.

Much like other Iranian community organizers in the global diaspora, at its outset in the mid-2000s, Tirgan's organizers were young immigrants who had been keen to bring together Iranians in Toronto and, as importantly, to illustrate "who we really are" in the midst of "tainted" representations in Western media. In a 2008 article in the first issue of *Tirgan Magazine* (published on the occasion of each festival through 2019, with five thousand copies distributed for free on-site) the coauthors described these representations as ones that painted Iran with broad stereotypes, namely as "a country overrun with irrational zealots, hungering for nuclear power and political domination," and that thereby mischaracterized the "Iranian populace as a voiceless, silent mass, incapable of rising above the tides of repression and censorship."[26] The best way to harness these representations and counter this image in Canada, organizers told me, was to join the busy Toronto summer calendar of ethnic festivals, which they did with a goal of "contribut[ing] to the diverse, cultural mosaic of the Canadian society by celebrating Iranian art and culture."[27]

Such an approach was made possible through a partnership with Toronto's nonprofit Harbourfront Centre (HC), whose multiculturalism- and diversity-driven mandate reflected the 2000s understandings of the Canadian model. Originally established in 1972 as a Crown corporation by the Canadian government with a goal of revitalizing the city's industrial harbor and attracting tourism, in 1991, HC became a nonprofit charitable cultural organization operating a ten-acre waterfront campus. By 2010 HC was considered the largest arts and cultural facility in Canada, attracting over seventeen million visitors to its over four thousand arts and cultural events per year.[28] Governed by a twenty-six-person community-based multicultural volunteer board of directors, as of 2013, HC received up to a third of its operating budget from government grants, leaving approximately two-thirds to be raised by its self-described "strong entrepreneurial spirit": a mix of corporate sponsorships; summer camps; merchandising; fundraising; on-site restaurants; and management of two marinas, several parking decks, and a number of tour boats.[29] With a slogan of "The World in 10 Acres," HC maintained a multidisciplinary artistic and cultural focus, and at the core of its mission was a mandate to offer free or low-cost public events that introduce Toronto audiences to contemporary cultures, artists, and art forms that may not otherwise be available in commercial venues catering to mainstream Canadian audiences.

By the late 2000s, among the over four thousand events that took place there each year, HC's summer calendar had become best known for its large multicultural festivals.[30] Festivals are an ever-present feature of Toronto summer life, whether in the form of multiday megafests or smaller neighborhood street parties. Several of Toronto's largest festivals, such as Ashkenaz (a global Jewish music and culture festival begun in 1995) and Masala! Mehndi! Masti! (the largest South Asian

Figure 4.1. Tirgan 2013 (above) drew over 120,000 attendees to Harbourfront Centre; Tirgan 2017 (below) drew over 160,000. (Credit: Amy Malek)

cultural festival outside of South Asia, begun in 2001), originated at HC, eventually spreading to multiple venues across the city. These successful festivals have been supported by federal Canadian multiculturalism policies and by provincial and city financial support to attract tourism to the region. Their successes have provided sources of inspiration and templates for other Toronto immigrant groups to follow, and they were named specifically to me by Tirgan's leaders as inspirations for moves the organization made (e.g., in expanding to multiple venues across the city in 2017, like Ashkenaz) and future goals it aspired to achieve (e.g., to attract one million people for a full week of events, like the annual Caribana Caribbean carnival).[31]

Many of the summer festivals that took place at HC in the 2000s and first half of the 2010s, like Tirgan, were organized through HC's Community and Educational Programs (CEP) department. CEP sought to engage local nonprofit community groups in producing programming at the center through significant in-kind donations of staff support, volunteer training, and venue space. Community partners applied for the program through a competitive application process and were evaluated based on a published list of parameters. Once selected, community organizations were then responsible for providing artistic vision, production finances, and volunteer staff, while HC provided in-kind administrative, media, and production support.[32]

Although collaboration and teamwork were repeatedly identified by Iranians during my fieldwork as key areas of community deficiency and sources of contention, in 2013, the director of CEP, having worked with hundreds of such community organizations, shared with me that Tirgan already was among its most successful partnerships. Tirgan's directors agreed: The festival owed much of its early success to Harbourfront Centre's community partnership model. In 2011, after volunteering for the highly successful second Tirgan Festival, I sat down with each of the festival's directors, several of whom had been integral to its move from an informal group of graduate students to a formal Canadian registered charitable organization. The founders and directors of Tirgan repeated similar claims as my other interlocutors: A relative lack of experience in collaboration, group dynamics, and team-oriented management had impeded large-scale, coordinated Iranian diaspora projects, whether political, cultural, or otherwise. These limitations, they had argued, also presented a challenge to diasporic Iranians' participation in mainstream Canadian cultural and political realms.

For example, when Nima, a cofounder and Tirgan's marking director in 2011, had arrived in Canada as a student in 2003 eager to meet fellow Iranians, he had experienced these challenges directly, which he described in 2011 as an ongoing problem: "We [Iranians] haven't learned to play well with each other.... For example, if I want to [organize] an association for all the [Iranian] lawyers [in Toronto], we would never come to an agreement. Even though they are lawyers and know law and law would give them a framework, they can't come to an agreement that, 'Okay, we want to do *this* thing.' We are not good in teamwork. That's why we are very, very [weak] in the mainstream."[33] Having just spent months participating in Tirgan's meetings and observing their organizational strategies, I was surprised by Nima's assessment; my experience with Tirgan seemed to directly counter his observation. He answered excitedly:

> In the case of Tirgan, it's not us, it's Harbourfront Centre. See, you can't beat Harbourfront! We have joined and become one.... If we wanted to do this by ourselves, I can guarantee you it would be a disaster ... because we can't really perform very well in a team. Tirgan does well, but because ... Harbourfront Centre gave us a template and we adopt this template as best as possible. But if we wanted to create our own template ... we are not in a stage yet to have our own.[34]

For Nima, the inability to successfully come together toward a common goal was the ultimate reason Iranians had not yet put forward a unified voice in mainstream Canadian society, which he had expressed as important for immigrant communities wishing to gain resources and legitimacy in Canada. Looking back over a decade later, in 2023, another director of Tirgan, Babak Payami, observed that not only had Tirgan successfully performed in a team, they also had joined other major Canadian festivals in providing a template for other communities to emulate.[35] They had done so through strategically adapting Iranian culture and community goals to priorities of Canadian multiculturalism.

## Tirgan as a "Celebration of Multiculturalism Itself"

Working with Tirgan festival has helped me to understand that the best way to celebrate the diversity of my Canadian culture is to recognize and appreciate the diversity that exists within my native country of Iran.
—Maryam Nayeb-Yazdi, *Tirgan Magazine*, 2008

The Tirgan Festival serves as a powerful reaffirmation and celebration of our community and its unique place within the larger Canadian mosaic. It is through arts and culture, after all, that our core values of equality, openness, and inclusivity often find their most meaningful articulations. The celebration and promotion of arts and culture is, in fact, a celebration of multiculturalism itself.
—Ali Ehsassi, *Tirgan Magazine*, 2017

The partnership between Tirgan and Harbourfront Centre, with its focus on diversity and multiculturalism, would ultimately influence not only the name and symbolism of the festival, but also the goals of the organization, the performances that would appear on its stages, the sensorial spaces they would (and would not) create on festival grounds, the visual branding that would promote it, and the artistic themes that would be selected to guide each festival.

### *Reimagining Iranian Culture: Naming Tirgan*

Tirgan began as the only project of the Iranian Canadian Centre for Arts and Culture, a nonprofit organization established in 2007 and rebranded as the Tirgan Centre for Art and Culture in 2021. This registered charity was created as an umbrella organization to house what would become the Tirgan Festival and any future projects, a forward-thinking move that was helpful when the organization leveraged its summer successes to organize large annual Nowruz events, elaborate Yalda (winter solstice) nights, and occasional concerts. Though the name of Tirgan is drawn from an ancient Zoroastrian rain festival celebrated in the summer month of Tir, the founders of the Tirgan Festival reimagined this ancient summer festival in a "Canadian Way."³⁶ The festival neither aimed to replicate the ancient religious traditions of Tirgan, nor had Tirgan been celebrated widely as a contemporary secular holiday in Iran or the diaspora prior to 2008. Since then, however, and directly inspired by the Toronto festival, secular Tirgan celebrations have entered summer calendars around the world from Stockholm to Lausanne, and Los Angeles to Brisbane—and even in Iran itself.

A thoroughly diasporic phenomenon at its start, the organizers of Toronto's Tirgan Festival worked to refashion ancient Iranian themes and symbols to serve contemporary diasporic circumstances, opportunities, needs, and desires. This refashioning would adopt, for example, the story and iconic mythistorical figure of Arash the Archer, *Arash-i Kamangir*, in marketing materials, awards, and artistic productions at the festival, but would take little else from the ancient tradition.³⁷ That refashioned story has been retold in dozens of Tirgan marketing and public relations materials over the years, including the following version, written to promote the festival on a foreign policy blog in 2011:

> There are many legends on the origins of Tirgan. One legend describes that Iran and Turan, two longstanding rival powers, decided to declare peace by demarcating the boundaries between the two empires. Arash, the best archer in the Iranian army—whose last name, Kamangir, means expert in bowing—was chosen to ascend a mountain to shoot an arrow whose landing location would determine the boundary between the two warring lands. After soaring from dawn until noon, the arrow finally descended in today's Central Asia, expanding Iran's boundaries beyond expectation. And the Tirgan Festival today, indeed, is the extension of those cultural boundaries.³⁸

The Canadian multicultural festival version of Tirgan thereby claims the ancient story of Arash as its antecedent through the shared notion of cultural diversity, extending the "cultural boundaries" of Iran to include its diaspora in Canada and beyond. This story would animate future years of the festival, as well as its marketing, as in a 2011 campaign in which Arash the Archer was depicted by a young present-day Iranian Torontonian aiming his bow across Lake Ontario towards the Harbourfront Centre, thereby symbolically incorporating not just Tehranto but Toronto, and specifically the Tirgan Festival, within the "cultural boundaries" of Iran (fig. 4.2).³⁹

Figure 4.2. A 2011 Tirgan marketing campaign described a "postmodern" Arash the Archer being introduced to Toronto by his "Torontonian entourage." (Credit: Sam Javanrouh/Tirgan)

## *Who Is Canada Today?: Artistic Representation at Tirgan*

The impact of HC's mission and especially its in-kind production support on the establishment of the Tirgan Festival should not be understated. Beyond making possible events that otherwise would not likely have found funding, the required HC orientation meetings and selection processes meant that CEP staff heavily influenced the artistic direction and ideas that community partners would propose and thus how they would eventually represent their communities to Canadian publics. As HC's director of CEP in 2013 told me in an interview, "Our mandate is both as a contemporary art center and with a community engagement principle. So . . . our mandate is contemporary. It's not looking back at heritage kinds of things. It's looking at who is and what is Canada today, in a global context."[40] HC's mandate to "explor[e] new and bold frontiers in the arts and creative expression" led groups such as Tirgan to mold their application and first festivals to this mission, focusing on new and innovative arts and culture, especially those amenable to 2000s Canadian multiculturalist priorities of cultural hybridity and diversity. The Tirgan festival would offer audiences references to an "ancient celebration of arts and culture" (e.g., the mythology of Tirgan) while featuring performances and exhibitions that highlighted the contemporary art, literature, and culture of Iran and its diaspora, as mandated by HC.[41]

This resulted in line-ups featuring fusion acts with cutting-edge forms (like jazz and blues artist Rana Farhan or London-based Ajam Band) rather than only traditional or "heritage" ones, and inviting up-and-coming or lesser-known artists (such as young Persian trap producer ASADI or LA-based Rana Mansour prior to her breakout success), rather than those who could already sell out arenas. The exposure that Tirgan gave these groups to large North American audiences played a significant role in their careers. Such an emphasis has meant that, over the years, Tirgan has featured an impressively wide array of artistic genres: classical Persian, rock, rap, trap, jazz, opera, and choir music; poetry recitations, author talks, and book fairs; photography, sculpture, and poster exhibitions; culinary demonstrations; classical, folk, ballet, flamenco, and modern dance; theater adaptations and puppetry performances; contemporary *Shahnameh* orations; and especially hybrid or fusion performances that combined several of these with other cultural forms.

## Creating Presences and Absences: Spaces at Tirgan

HCs priorities and rules also impacted what the physical spaces of Tirgan have and have not looked like. Unlike in the United States, where large replicas of pre-Islamic Persian architecture and artifacts have dominated many festival spaces, HC site policy precluded any large installations on its grounds.[42] This did not prevent the presence of tents or large banners for financial sponsors or vendors, which are prominent on HC's campus year-round, nor the production of three-dimensional spaces mimicking eras of modern Iranian history, such as a life-sized Qajar-era photo-op in 2015 or the nostalgic home décor of the Tehran Tea House in 2017 (fig. 4.3). But the focus of these spaces and their intended effects of spatial mimesis has been to (re)produce nostalgia for lived experiences (e.g., of grandma's house) and multiple eras of recent Iranian history, rather than the imagined and imperial nostalgia of ancient times and ruins. This diversity of historical and cultural representations at Tirgan did not merely stem from HC policies and notions of Canadian multiculturalism but also reflected the more recent migratory flows and cultural preferences of the Iranian diaspora in Toronto.

The absence of Iranian flags on the grounds of Tirgan's summer festivals, especially in comparison with other Iranian diaspora events in Toronto, are a case in point. HC's rule book for summer partners specifically prohibited their display, stating: "As a result of past conflicts related to display of national flags at Harbourfront Centre, it is our policy that only the Canadian flag is allowed to be displayed on our site."[43] Even when the organization expanded its events to additional venues, they maintained this policy. This rule led to complaints from Iranian community members in ways anticipated in the HC policy statement, but the prohibition dovetailed with a general Tirgan principle of assuming a nonpartisan, nonpolitical stance and carefully avoiding divisive issues. This strategy emerged from organizers who were seeking to use arts and culture as a unifying force amid a politically fragmented Toronto Iranian community. By disallowing political displays by attendees—whether through flags, signs, or the shouted slogans of demonstrators—while inviting Canadian politicians from each of the major political parties to speak on Tirgan's stages, the organization drew additional criticism but held firm. They carefully tailored a curatorial vision that avoided

Figure 4.3. Tirgan Festival photo ops. Left: Emplacing festival-goers in Qajar-era royal portraiture at Tirgan 2015. Right: A corner of the Tehran Tea House featuring nostalgic mid-twentieth-century furnishings, reminiscent of a grandmother's house, at Tirgan 2017. (Credit: Amy Malek)

controversial political positions that could expose community fragmentations and undermine Tirgan's goal of building and presenting (to Canadian and Iranian audiences alike) a unified and united community.

## Sharing Values: Artistic Themes of Tirgan

As required by the CEP, each iteration of the Tirgan Festival has been organized around an artistic theme. The festival's organizers were hyperaware that conforming to expectations of Canadian multiculturalism while drawing connections between Iranian and Canadian values would bring about greater support, funding, and thus longevity for their organization. For example, in explaining the theme of the first Tirgan Festival—"Exploring Diversity"—in 2008, the organizers cast the legend of Arash the Archer as the origin story of both Tirgan and ethno-religious diversity in Iran, connecting it directly to Canadian values of diversity and multiculturalism.⁴⁴ Presenting this reimagined Tirgan as an invented tradition of celebrating Iranian diversity was an ideal fit for Canadian multiculturalism, and for Toronto, which adopted a motto of "Diversity, Our Strength."⁴⁵ This theme and choice of name would provide the symbolism for all the organization's future events.

The use of "diversity" in these statements was careful; the term "multicultural" or "multiculturalism" was absent in HC's CEP materials, largely because by the early 2010s, during what would become known in Europe as a "multiculturalism backlash,"⁴⁶ the director of the partnership program viewed the term as problematic, preferring "diversity" instead. With the next artistic theme in 2013 of "Hope," newly appointed artistic director and filmmaker Babak Payami more boldly reached back to ancient history where, amid "natural and self-inflicted devastations," he found hope in Iran's "Artistic and Cultural heritage." He emphatically asserted a view that the tenets of multiculturalism were, and have always been, Iranian: "Pluralism, diversity and the ability to change and embrace change is engrained in the Iranian psyche from the beginning of civilization."⁴⁷ As we have seen, this sentiment echoed an argument circulating in the same year in the United States with the traveling exhibition of the Cyrus Cylinder. For the 2017 ("Benevolence") and 2019 ("Unity in Diversity") themes, Payami drafted longer musings on these selections, naming his inspiration in the Cyrus Cylinder to present a set of shared multicultural values and Iranian contributions to Canada and what would become enshrined as its "prime national value" of multiculturalism.⁴⁸ Writing in the same period that his Los Angeles counterparts were preparing to unveil the Freedom Sculpture to present a similar—if more robust—argument to Americans in 2017,⁴⁹ Payami argued that it was the shared values of multiculturalism that connected Iranians and Canadians and Iranian arts and culture that should be viewed as their contribution to Canada:

> Benevolence is perhaps the unifying and principal thesis underlying the ancient cylinder of Cyrus the Great. A thesis that heralded a major turning point for humanity. . . . Canada is a modern iteration of a society shaped by multiculturalism and ethnic diversity. The Canadian model . . . passionately aspires to protect its aboriginal citizens while shaping an efficient multi-cultural society in which diversity and respect for minority are virtues that guarantee Canada's success as a country on the leading

edge of civilization. The ancient quilt of Iranian culture in which ethnic, religious and cultural diversity are deeply engrained, fits flush within the Canadian cultural mosaic model. The Tirgan biennial showcases the contribution of Iranians to Canadian culture.[50]

### Visual Strategies of Inclusion: Branding Tirgan

These 2010s themes were also formative for the visual branding of the festival, led by professional designer Pendar Yousefi, the creative director for the "festival's branding, overall art direction, and . . . the design and implementation of the festival's website."[51] Yousefi's clever designs consistently put forward visual arguments that worked to convince viewers of what Payami's artistic theme statements aimed to evoke through text: that Iranian and Canadian cultural values were united.

For example, in 2013, that vision emerged through designs that drew similarities by literally drawing Iranian landmarks of architecture (e.g., Milad tower, the Siosepol bridge) and geography (e.g., the Alborz mountains) onto photos of the Toronto cityscape (fig. 4.4). In 2017, Payami's thematic argument that ancient Iran and contemporary Canada shared the values of diversity and multiculturalism was clearly articulated through Yousefi's poster designs that meshed time and place: An illustrated poster combines the bottom half of an ancient frieze, showing gift bearers from the waist down bringing tribute from across the Persian Empire to Persepolis, with the upper bodies of a diverse present-day crowd of ostensibly Canadian festivalgoers ascending a subway escalator to visit Tirgan (fig. 4.4). In each of these campaigns, Iranian symbols were made to mesh seamlessly with Canadian ones.

The impact of multicultural policy and funding, through HC, extended beyond these symbolic and aesthetic choices. They would also guide the organization of a growing group of volunteers, including especially the ways they would practice "Canadian Ways" of working together.

### "Learning Teamwork and Enjoying Its Benefits": Developing Diasporic Cultural and Social Capital

From its earliest days, the Tirgan Festival has been envisioned as a community-building exercise as much as a presentation of contemporary

Figure 4.4. Posters advertising Tirgan 2013 and 2017. On the left, Siosepol Bridge is drawn to cross Lake Ontario to reach the Harbourfront Centre. On the right, ancient figures in Persepolis friezes and Tirgan's diverse Canadian audience become one. (Credit: Tirgan)

Iranian art and culture. This aim is neither incidental nor limited to a Canadian audience; it has been carefully crafted as global in focus. With a guiding motto of "From Toronto to the World,"[52] the organization's website in 2015 elaborated on this orientation: "Tirgan is more than just a festival. Tirgan is about building communities. By entertaining and educating its audience, Tirgan aims to promote a cross-cultural dialogue between the Iranian community and the global community at large."[53] Canadian cultural policies that set diversity and multiculturalism as priorities had created opportunities such as HC's community partnership program that in turn insisted on the development of practices of volunteerism, accountability, and collaboration. State intermediaries, such as provincial and municipal arts councils and local agencies in Canada, thereby became key players in the formation of diasporic belonging by supporting cultural productions that worked to create active and networked multicultural citizens.

In her study of political incorporation among Portuguese and Vietnamese immigrants and refugees in Toronto and Boston, Irene Bloemraad found that when Canadian multiculturalist policies were paired with government support for immigrant groups (for example, by funding community organizations and programs), immigrant organizing and participation occurred at higher rates than in countries without this crucial pairing, such as in the United States.[54] More specifically, she found that "organized activities that foster community pride—or which are just plain fun—can serve as 'schools,' teaching newcomers the requisite skills for civic and political involvement."[55] The communication and organization skills learned at such "schools," might then be transferrable into other areas, like politics, where "those who are 'institutionally connected' enjoy an advantage."[56] Scholars elsewhere have connected the role of immigrant volunteerism, specifically, to integration outcomes.[57] The creation of these forms of social capital formed important if underrecognized outcomes of multicultural policy, with not only potential local political outcomes, as Bloemraad found, but also—and as Tirgan would eventually be pushed to attempt—diasporic ones as well.

As early as 2010, Tirgan included integration outcomes such as the ones Bloemraad anticipated in its vision statement alongside its cultural goals: "To help Iranian Canadians especially youth, have a better understanding of their cultural identity and their place in Canadian society, which will facilitate their integration into the fabric of Canadian civic life."[58] The practices of teamwork, collaboration, and cooperation for a "greater good" in the Canadian sense were being imagined by organizers even in early days as tools for cultural citizenship. Mehrdad Ariannejad, a cofounder of Tirgan and to date its only CEO, often describes the process of festival planning as "learning teamwork and enjoying its benefits": "There's a process we start a year and a half before [the festival], and all of [the three hundred volunteers] go through this process. And I think this process is as important as the outcome, which is the festival. We learn how to work together, how to learn from each other."[59]

Numerous Tirgan directors, themselves active in diasporic political activities in a personal capacity and in other organizations, shared with me that although they may hold political aspirations for their community, arts-and-culture [*farhang-o-honar*] was one thing all Iranians could agree on, and thus the ideal medium through which to create unity, build their community, and practice teamwork. Political fragmentations within the community required steering clear of contentious topics and remaining nonpolitical in hopes of creating community growth—and in some cases, repairing some of the divisions plaguing it. Behrouz, Tirgan's director of public relations in 2011 and later a member of its board of trustees, emphasized this in describing to me his initial motivation for volunteering with Tirgan:

> One thing I realized was that when it comes to art and culture, it's much simpler to find that commonality because it's something that all of us are proud of. I haven't seen Persians who make fun of our art and culture.... On the other hand, I guess the polar opposite is politics, right? When it comes to politics, we all have our different opinions, and it's really difficult to convince each other that, you know, what I say is right or what you say is right or maybe we should pick something in the middle.... I realized that [arts and culture] was the best framework to ... implement that community-building exercise. What better environment than a place where you're talking about beautiful art and culture. It gets a lot easier to satisfy our differences.[60]

As evidenced by Tirgan, Harbourfront's template and corresponding emphasis on collaboration with local immigrant and cultural communities worked to raise the public's awareness and support of multicultural values while simultaneously implementing Canadian norms, behaviors, and practices among the volunteers with whom they worked. The organizers of Tirgan and the hundreds of Iranian volunteers HC's community partnerships team helped train emerged from the first events having gained hands-on experience with long-term planning, goal-oriented processes, team leadership, strategy development, and project management—all practices that were permeated with discourses of democratic values like transparency and cooperation. Since many of the festivals that HC coproduced through this model were immigrant community partnerships, this disciplining of newcomers formed part of the subject formation of new Canadians.

Each iteration of the Tirgan Festival has relied upon the time, skills, and labor of around three hundred part-time volunteers, most of whom begin meeting weekly six months to one year before the event to plan fundraisers, artistic programs, marketing strategies, ad campaigns, publicity opportunities, logistics, and outreach efforts that lead up to that year's four-day festival. Run entirely by these volunteers until 2016, the organization won municipal, provincial, and federal government grants that allowed for the opening of a Tirgan office in 2014–15 and the hiring of a handful of full and part-time staff members. Beyond these paid positions, Tirgan's volunteers, including its directors, arrive with a range of previous experiences and expectations. Alongside their Tirgan duties, most Tirgan volunteers hold bachelor's and master's degrees and juggle full-time careers, whether as graduate students or in professional fields such as architecture, software engineering, dentistry, law, real estate, and marketing.[61] Notably, art and performance professionals have not occupied the key executive positions in Tirgan; those with extensive artistic expertise have generally been limited to the role of the artistic director.

The cultural capital that these young volunteers bring to the organization is vital to its success; educated, linguistically dexterous, and professionally motivated, Tirgan's volunteers are typically ambitious and often overachievers—after all, they have in many cases earned their student admission or landed status through their skills, experience, and potential as measured by the Canadian immigration system. Throughout the 2010s, the vast majority of Tirgan's first-time volunteers were first-generation Iranian immigrants in their twenties and thirties who migrated to Canada within the previous two to ten years; meetings were thus conducted primarily if not entirely in Persian. In more recent years, young Iranian Canadians have joined Tirgan's volunteer ranks, whether second-generation teenagers in high school or 1.5-generation young adults in university.

Managing this large cadre of volunteers has required clear and precise organization, a particular challenge in early years when the festival also implemented a self-described transparent "open-door policy," bringing on volunteers throughout the year with little or no restrictions or prescreening, enabling individuals to enter multiple levels of decision-making within the organization's structure. I joined two Tirgan volunteer teams in preparation for the 2011 festival and attended their weekly planning meetings. There, I observed and experienced the significant level of input and responsibility shouldered by each volunteer and committee. The amount of time, labor, and collaboration required to fundraise, build networks, conduct outreach, promote, organize, and safely put on a festival of this scale is significant and requires intense commitments made by the volunteers.

Due in part to previous experiences of conflicts and interpersonal disagreements in student organizing among Iranians at Toronto universities in the 1990s, the early leaders of Tirgan set out to tackle the issue of teamwork directly. Early attempts had involved a flat organizational structure: in 2008 a CEO and nine directors oversaw subcommittees responsible for music, dance, theatre, cinema, literature, children's activities, décor, marketing, graphic design, publishing, and volunteers.[62] These volunteer teams prioritized equality through decision-making processes that required consensus, but the result had been conflicting opinions and personality clashes that made for a difficult planning process. In contrast, by 2011 a hierarchical structure had been implemented and documented in an eighty-nine-page "Tirgan Organizational Structure Manual" that included job titles and duties for an individual CEO overseeing a board of directors heading up five departments: Administration, Marketing and Sales, Public Relations, Artistic, and Operations, each of which counted numerous subcommittees under its leadership. In this new structure, which largely has remained in place, most volunteers are no longer focused on the cultural planning of the festival but on its operation, promotion, and fundraising.[63]

Despite this hierarchical structure, in the numerous weekly meetings I attended across several departments of the 2011 Tirgan planning committees, I noted how decision-making nevertheless remained an open process, incorporating all voices and emphasizing transparency through information sharing. For example, each department implemented the use of hyperstructured meeting strategies including detailed printed agendas that offered key organizational information and progress updates to volunteers at all levels, and often across teams. All teams were visited by fellow directors with updates from their teams, and in my observations, meetings featured an open approach to brainstorming, idea gathering, and assignments by and to volunteers through clear deadlines, agendas, and a consistent and transparent method of following up on goals. I also observed the substantial progress and positive results of these approaches: With very few exceptions, volunteers tasked with assignments at a weekly meeting returned the following week having completed the task or having made reasonable progress. Collective troubleshooting and brainstorming supported those few who did not, while positive and consistent messaging by directors and fellow volunteers ensured high morale.

The result was a festival in which most volunteers had not just shown up on the first day of the event to learn their duties on-site nor just been invited to share ideas that others (e.g., professionals) would implement. Instead, most Tirgan volunteers were given consequential decision-making roles and tasks, creating a deep feeling of responsibility for and thus personal investment in the positive outcome of the festival. Multiple volunteers expressed to me their feeling of personal accomplishment and collective success—and the camaraderie that emerged from it—after the 2011 festival, and these positive experiences became one of Tirgan's most effective recruitment tools. For example, Arian, director of operations in 2011, described to me previous negative experiences of working with fellow Iranians both in Iran and the diaspora that had made him skeptical of joining Tirgan. It was only after observing a few meetings that he realized Tirgan's organizers took a different approach: "I went to a few meetings and I really liked it—they weren't self-important [*tu qiafeh*] and really wanted to do something. They worked in a really organized and systematic way [*organized o sistematik*]. Because Iranian society, on this front, is really behind. . . . A scientific system in which we spend six months to create a manual, six months researching, eight months or something working on development—these ideas weren't really prevalent among Iranians, in Iran or outside. That's why I really liked this group. And so I started working with them."[64]

By 2023, even after organizing six biennial four-day festivals, democratic practice and collaborative teamwork remained primary goals for Tirgan's leaders. Mercedeh, a longtime volunteer and director of operations in 2023, described her vision for Tirgan's future as continuing this mission unabated, for the benefit of Iranians in Canada—but also in Iran: "Within the Iranian community, collaborative work is very rare. [W]e are doing this teamwork for over twenty years and I would like it to continue in the future. Every day we are practicing democratic work in a small community. We work together, [but] we all have different ideas. We come together, we discuss, and we take collective decisions. And this is something that needs to continue in our community. I hope it starts from here and spreads to the larger Iranian society because *we all need this practice*."⁶⁵

## The Emotional Bonds of the Tirgan Family

While sharing a common investment in representing Iranian art and culture, numerous volunteers also described to me a primary motivation to volunteer with Tirgan was social: to meet new people in their new home. Thanks to the reach of Tirgan on social media—reportedly 2.8 million on Instagram and 346,000 on Facebook in 2022⁶⁶—by the 2020s, young Iranian newcomers to Canada already knew about and had followed Tirgan on Instagram prior to their migration. Several sought it out for volunteer opportunities upon arrival in Toronto. As one volunteer told me, the mission of working toward a common cause that they loved—Iran and Iranians—and meeting weekly for several months toward that goal meant Tirgan's volunteers built a strong social network and camaraderie that has lasted through several iterations of the festival. Though not everyone experiences the same outcomes, for many volunteers, their Tirgan colleagues have become among their closest friends, an extension of family in their new home. Mahsa, a longtime volunteer I met at her first Tirgan in 2011, posted memories from that first year to her Facebook in anticipation of her fourth festival in 2017, writing: "I have developed some of the best and closest relationships/friendships of my adult life through my volunteer involvement with Tirgan."⁶⁷ Those feelings of closeness and emotional attachment—of belonging—meant that, as early as 2008 (the year of the first Tirgan festival) volunteers were already referring to fellow "Tirganis" as their "Tirgan family" (*khanevadeh-ye Tirgan*).

Soon the term *Tirgan family* was taken up in marketing, fundraising, and press materials. Though commonly used in organizations as an aspirational term to try to create a sense of cohesion among employees, Tirgan volunteers used "family" not as a goal, but as a descriptor, marking the closeness they had developed through working together. When asked their favorite thing about Tirgan, several volunteers responded not about a performance or particular year's festival, but with reference to how Tirgan made them *feel*. Common responses centered on the central necessities of belonging, friendship, and connection, all acute needs for recent immigrants, especially those who arrived solo in Toronto. In a 2021 promotional video for Tirgan, volunteer Shiva described this bonding as a feeling of familial connection, and as Tirgan's "biggest advantage": "For me, [family are] people with whom I'm comfortable, who I can talk to, who I can open up to and commiserate with (*dard o del*), people I can work with (*hamrahi*) and move forward with. And the biggest advantage that Tirgan has—and anyone who has worked with Tirgan knows this—is that everyone is so very close to one another."[68]

Another volunteer, when asked in summer 2023 to describe what it means to volunteer with Tirgan, described his impression of its volunteers as "everyone who misses their mothers while abroad."[69] The phrase "Tirgan family" then was more than just metaphor; it put into words the feelings of belonging formed in the group as one of fictive kinship, supplementing the kinship ties strained due to migration with those found in community organizing toward a common cultural goal in diaspora.

In a particularly intimate 2011 blog entry entitled, "Dear Tirgan," longtime volunteer Maryam Eskandari wrote about the deep range of emotional impacts her time with the organization had upon her life:

> I am going to write about the tears that you have brought into my eyes and the joy that you have filled my heart with. I may even someday talk about those sad, weak moments of my life that you helped me to get through.
>
> You have changed me in many ways my friend. Because of you, I am much stronger now. You have given me this unique experience that has made me feel I am living my history.... that I am taking charge... that I am not a silent observer... not anymore. It is because of you that I so feel proud yet selfless of all the achievements that I have gained through you.[70]

This deeply meaningful combination of achievement, pride, friendship, and belonging is so pervasive among Tirgan volunteers, and experienced through such emotional attachments, that the end of each Tirgan festival has come to be called "post-Tirgan depression" (*afsordegi pas az Tirgan*). Nastaran, a volunteer who attended her first Tirgan just one month after immigrating to Canada described in an organization-produced video the commonly-felt loneliness she experienced, revealing not only how busy she had been in her volunteer role but also how reliant she had become on her Tirgan family for social support: "After [the festival ended], I was depressed for a week! Because everything became deserted [*khalvat shode*], I kept calling and asking, 'Where should we go? What should we do? I'm bored!'"[71]

Like many families, many of Tirgan's volunteers "fly the nest" once they "learn how to fly" in Toronto. Others have maintained a role in Tirgan since its inception and still consider the Iranian friends they've made within it their closest friends. Some have even met their spouses through volunteering and the children of Tirgan couples have joined as young volunteers as well (fig. 4.5).

Volunteers and attendees at Tirgan festivals also have expressed how simply being present on the festival grounds evoked a sense of belonging and affinity, whether because they were reuniting with visiting family or old friends and acquaintances they hadn't seen in years; or because they were introducing their young Canada-born children or non-Iranian friends to their Iranian "cultural family;" or simply because they experienced a sense of comfort being among so many Iranians, "familiar strangers" with whom they shared languages, beliefs, networks, and migration experiences. At multiple iterations of the festival, I heard attendees marvel at how being at Tirgan almost felt like they were in Iran again. Mercedeh explained:

> The best days at Tirgan are at the summer Tirgan festivals: Saturday afternoon, around 5 or 6 p.m. . . . between the Bazaar and the Stage in the Round [at HC] there's a hill. From the first year I joined, every year, each festival, at that time on that day, I stand there for ten or fifteen minutes and just look around me. . . . People are eating *faloodeh*, eating ice cream; people who haven't seen each other for a long time find each other there and ask boisterously, "How are you! Where have you been?!" That scene is the best scene of Tirgan.[72]

Public spaces like these at Tirgan that create a collective sense of familiarity and belonging among volunteers, attendees, and artists may offer momentary relief from homesickness, but they are also contributing to Iranian cultural citizenship in Canada. Social media volunteer Mona described this effect as a "bridge": "Tirgan is like a bridge. I'm in

Figure 4.5. Tirgan volunteers celebrate with their youngest member after the final event of the 2013 festival. (Credit: Amy Malek)

Canada, but there are elements from home and Iran here. And it gives me a feeling that 'Ah, this is my place,' you know? I don't feel exiled. It gives me a good feeling."[73] The sense of being emplaced in an Iranian environment in Canada—surrounded by fellow Iranians of all ages, speaking Persian, eating Iranian foods, watching Iranian cultural performances—where they were once again masters of a familiar language, culture, and etiquette was also a key draw for Tirgan's Iranian diaspora attendees. These feelings are neither incidental nor coincidental; Tirgan's organizers recognized the importance of creating these collective spaces and, through them, a sense of unity through the building and maintenance of collective diasporic memories.

Crucially, the sense of belonging developed through Tirgan was not only about belonging to an Iranian community, but specifically to a Canadian one. Several volunteers I spoke with recognized the support provided by the Canadian government for programs such as Tirgan as the kind of support their homeland had not provided for them. Like Maryam's blog entry, in our 2011 interview Arian especially emphasized the importance of this effect in the face of an otherwise difficult migration experience that had initially left him feeling angry and resentful:

> Now when I look at it—aside from thinking I can do something small for Iran—[volunteering for Tirgan] did a lot for *me*: I'm much calmer, much more comfortable. I have a much better feeling about Canada. All that anger [*khashm*] that I had, it's as if it's gone now. Because first of all, we did this large event, and not that it was some major thing, but to be honest, until now I hadn't done anything at that level for any country—not Iran, not any country. And second, Canada had offered a ton of possibilities—the truth is they made a budget available, they offered the Harbourfront space, a lot of possibilities.[74]

Arian also expressed his feeling, shared by other directors and volunteers, that Tirgan "belongs in Iran," but that Canada had offered Iranians in diaspora opportunities he felt they did not have in Iran and did not want from the Iranian government. Beyond Iran and Canada, several Tirgan directors also noted the absence of this kind of support in the United States, noting how the opportunities that Canada provided were therefore exceptional, even if they felt all countries should offer them. As Arian put it, "It is my opinion that what a government must do for its country, Canada did this, in part, for us."[75]

## Testing Tirgan

Foundational principles of diversity and multiculturalism coupled with high-quality and unique cultural programming, a focus on volunteer development, and a principled commitment to avoiding contentious matters had worked for over a decade to build and protect Tirgan's reputation. This approach led to deep investment and the widespread support of a diverse diasporic community. But in community organizations, as with families, crises present stress tests that can reveal fractures and the limits of ideological commitments.

Overlapping crises in the early 2020s presented Tirgan with multiple stress tests. First, in January 2020, Tirgan rose to the challenge of organizing the collective mourning of Toronto's Iranian community through the Canada Mourns event described earlier. Then, in March, the COVID-19 pandemic and Canadian public health regulations forced Tirgan (like all organizations) to cancel their annual Nowruz event (and eventually its 2021 summer festival). Challenged to pivot under these unprecedented circumstances, Tirgan innovated its first virtual Nowruz celebrations and digital-only programming in March 2020. These were made possible due to continued financial support from government granting agencies charged with keeping the Canadian arts and culture sectors afloat during the pandemic.

Having managed to weather these winter and spring storms, the summer of 2020 led to an unprecedented challenge for the Iranian diaspora community and for Tirgan. In August, Iran's #MeToo movement gained momentum on social media, garnering international attention after dozens of Iranian women anonymously or openly alleged experiences of sexual harassment or assault by Iranian men; one press article counted over one hundred men publicly accused in the second half of August alone.[76] One such accusation on Twitter was delivered by a prominent journalist against internationally recognized Iranian artist Aydin Aghdashloo, an Iranian Canadian dual citizen residing in Tehran. Over the following weeks, more women anonymously shared their stories alleging sexual misconduct and by the end of October, numerous English-language news outlets had reported on "Iran's #MeToo moment," including *The New York Times*, which published a widely circulated and much-discussed story largely focusing on Aghdashloo, who denied wrongdoing and repeated his support of women's rights.[77]

The connection between #MeToo and Tirgan was multifold: As a prominent Iranian Canadian artist, Aghdashloo's work had been featured at previous iterations of Tirgan's summer festival, where he had been a participating artist and a VIP guest. In addition, Aghdashloo's art was sold through his ex-wife's Toronto art gallery, which is co-owned by the gallery's executive director, Tirgan CEO Mehrdad Ariannejad. Other artists and public figures who had been accused in these weeks also had been previous guests or artists at Tirgan events, and in August, a Change.org petition initiated anonymously by "a group of artists, activists, academics, and members of the Iranian Canadian community" under the name Aletheia Justice listed these connections and others. It specifically called upon Tirgan and its board of directors to issue a public statement and to "believe the survivors and stop giving predators a platform."[78] The petition continued:

> We believe that the Tirgan Festival belongs to every one of us. It belongs to all who have volunteered at Tirgan during past years, to all artists who have participated and all those who supported the festival by attending it every year so that Tirgan can be more prosperous and successful.
>
> Tirgan festival must stop collaborating, inviting, and supporting predators, and until Tirgan representative [sic] clearly express that they will do so, we will continue our awareness campaign through civil means supported and preserved under the Canadian law, such as boycotting the festival, informing the Canadian public in this regard, and asking Tirgan sponsors to reconsider their financial support for this festival.[79]

In short, the authors argued that because the organization "belongs to every one of us," it owed them solidarity, not silence, and they would make use of their Canadian rights to apply pressure until it offered them this solidarity.

Although the petition quickly drew over 850 signatures as it spread across social media, Tirgan did not immediately respond. As a result, the petition eventually found the mainstream media attention its authors had promised: It was featured in a second *New York Times* article on November 1, and in articles by CBC (Canadian Broadcasting Corporation) and *ArtForum* on November 2. In these pieces, activists and former Tirgan volunteers were quoted expressing their expectations for Tirgan to live up to its reputation as a principled leader in the community promoting Canadian values such as inclusivity and equality. *The New York Times* quoted Safaneh Mohaghegh Neyshabouri, a university professor and one of the authors of the petition, who named the issue as a moral one: "I don't think the Tirgan festival can morally afford to not take a stand. Not taking a stand in this case means the festival is not a safe space for women."[80] Mahshid Yassaei, a signatory of the petition described by CBC as a thirty-four-year-old Toronto-based entrepreneur, summarized the situation: "This is a turning point for Tirgan to really tell the story of what kind of organization it is. Is it an organization that's built for the community and by the community, or is it an organization that's turning into a corporation that's just thinking about profit?"[81]

Asked directly by *The New York Times* about the petition's call, Tirgan CEO Ariannejad replied, "Our board decided this has nothing to do with Tirgan," and he questioned why Tirgan was being singled out to take a stand in this moment: "We invite as many artists as we can to our gatherings and performances. Are they going to ask all the organizations, all the museums around the world, all the people that have been in contact with Mr. Aghdashloo to come out and take a position?"[82] But Toronto activists and the authors of the petition had raised additional concerns beyond ties to Aghdashloo, and specifically about Ariannejad.

In April 2020, as the global pandemic left many in lockdown conditions seeking connections via digital media, Ariannejad had launched an English-language digital radio program and media company, both named Roqe ("candid" in Persian), with Jian Ghomeshi. A well-known public figure, Ghomeshi had been one of the few Iranians in Canada to have gained wide mainstream popularity, at first through his rock band, then as the host of syndicated CBC radio show "Q" and through thousands of related media and personal appearances. His presence at Iranian events in Toronto during the 2000s and early 2010s, including as a VIP at Tirgan festivals, was frequent and widely celebrated. That all changed in 2014. That October, Ghomeshi was fired by CBC after allegations emerged of inappropriate workplace behavior, after which more than twenty women came forward alleging assault or harassment. Ghomeshi never denied these encounters but insisted that they had been consensual.

Three women filed complaints with Toronto police and an investigation brought forward criminal charges amounting to "seven counts of sexual assault and one count of overcoming resistance by choking."[83] Two sexual assault charges were dropped in May, and Ghomeshi pled not guilty to the remaining charges. After a closely watched trial, in March 2016, a judge acquitted Ghomeshi of five charges. In May, he signed a peace bond and apologized to his accuser in a separate case, leading the Crown to withdraw the final charge.[84] Ghomeshi's star defense attorney had managed to discredit the witness testimony of all three women, whom the judge in the case provocatively described as "deceptive," while also noting, "My conclusion that the evidence in this case raises a reasonable doubt is not the same as deciding in any positive way that these events never happened."[85]

While Ghomeshi's trial captivated Canadians and Canadian media over the course of two years, the news didn't reach far beyond Canada until Ghomeshi's attempt to return to the spotlight in an October 2018 essay in *The New York Review of Books* titled "Reflections from a Hashtag." Perhaps underestimating the social and cultural shifts taking place in North America amid #MeToo, including Harvey Weinstein's trials and the Time's Up movement, Ghomeshi's long-form essay fashioned himself as the first victim of cancel culture and entirely omitted or mischaracterized details of the allegations against him, ultimately stopping short of a full-throated apology.[86] The backlash that followed was quick and widespread, resulting in the resignation of *The New York Review of Books* editor-in-chief—who appeared not to have fact-checked the piece—and a new note placed on the digital version of the essay.[87]

It was this context that led to questions by observers, including the petitioners, about the 2020 establishment of Roqe and Ariannejad's professional partnership with Ghomeshi, which marked a personal, financial, and reputational investment by Ariannejad to usher his close friend back to a public role. Sharing the sentiments of many other Iranians in Toronto, Ariannejad went on the record in a published interview repeating an insistence that the Canadian judicial system had acquitted Ghomeshi of the charges that were brought against him and thus it was "not for me to judge."[88] Yet, in his next sentence, he did judge: He "never believed" the women because he could not believe that Ghomeshi could be "a person who does these things."[89] These statements, in part, led to the petition, which referred directly to the tangled relationship between Ariannejad and Ghomeshi because Tirgan had built a trusted reputation rooted in principles of liberal multiculturalism, one that had been represented most publicly by Ariannejad.

By 2020, the Tirgan organization had become publicly identified with these controversies to such an extent that Ariannejad wrote a statement to CBC indicating that Roqe had no ties to Tirgan, while defending his decision to start Roqe with Ghomeshi: "Jian might have made mistakes but I believe that people should be given a second chance. I don't believe in cancel culture."[90]

Nine days after the CBC article and nearly eleven weeks after the Aletheia Justice petition was posted, on November 11, 2020, Tirgan finally published a statement in English and Persian. Posted on the organization's website and social media alongside a graphic reading "Our Core Values," the statement declared: "Tirgan wishes to clarify that we do not have any ties to any of the artists that have performed or presented their works at any of our festivals. Specifically, to clear the ambiguity of CBC's article, Tirgan does not have any ties with Aydin Aghdashloo."[91] The statement continued by placing Tirgan's operations within the tenets of Canadian values: "Tirgan upholds the basic values of Canadian society including gender equality; zero-tolerance towards discrimination, harassment, and violence in all its forms." It concluded by strongly condemning "all acts of sexual misconduct" and responding directly to the petition's invitation: "In an effort to foster a safe and welcoming environment for all our volunteers and stakeholders, we will continue to uphold our policies against harassment and discrimination and commit that we will never act as a forum for those who are guilty of sexual misconduct."[92] The focus on disclaiming "ties" to artists with whom it had indeed endeavored to build connections (for example through VIP invitations) was notable. Suddenly some of the social networks—a key piece of accumulated social capital—the organization had worked so hard to develop appeared as a liability. While the statement stopped short of acknowledging that its CEO held potentially compromising intertwined professional relationships that were difficult to separate, it had finally been forced to break its policy "to stay away from contentious matters."[93]

Despite the statement it put out, internally the organization was shaken; its board did not all agree on the steps it should take nor the statements it should make. The stress test of summer and autumn 2020 proved to be a turning point for the organization, one in which it was forced to debate what kind of organization it would be. The experience also exposed the organization to several liabilities, and its leadership undertook two efforts to address them. First, in a social context in which women were sharing their stories of experiencing sexual misconduct in workplaces at an unprecedented rate, neither the eighty-nine-page organizational manual, nor the code of conduct, nor the official bylaws had included policies or procedures about sexual harassment. The organization also did not employ a director of human resources to handle personnel matters. A third-party consultant was hired to address this gap and others, including questions regarding succession of leadership, in order to protect the organization, its brand, and its volunteers. The immediate result was a policy document titled "Tirgan: Respect in the Workplace Policy and Procedures," covering harassment and discrimination that detailed procedures for reporting, investigating, and resolving complaints, that all incoming volunteers were required to sign.[94]

Second, the social movements that had ignited North America in the summer of 2020, like protests following the murder of George Floyd, #BlackLivesMatter, and #MeToo, led to a sense that Tirgan, like so many nonprofit organizations and corporations at the time, should review its internal documents and policies. In the same period, Tirgan's board had received a complaint from a hearing-impaired artist and, separately, questions had emerged about a previous donor who had since been flagged for money laundering. In response to these challenges, Tirgan hired consultants and crafted policy documents and Diversity, Equity, and Inclusion (DEI) and Values statements consistent with recommended business practices in Canada at the time. As Nima, founding Tirgan board member, told me in April 2023, "Our response to [these challenges] was that we should hire the people who can deal with PR crises, we should hire the right lawyers to look at our bylaws and code of conduct, and make sure that we are protecting our brand, we are protecting our people."[95] Following the lead of other organizations and recommendations from a consultant, the organization crafted a "Diversity, Equity, and Inclusion Statement," which it published in its 2020 Annual Report along with a newly articulated list of values, including "equality" and "stewardship."[96]

Several existential questions remained unanswered. Was the structure of the organization capable of living up to promises of gender equality? Would the community continue to support the organization without its popular, if controversial, cofounder and CEO—if it ever came to that? Among the difficult realities the organization's leadership has had to consider is that, over the course of a decade, women volunteers have been integral to Tirgan's success (a fact that its leadership proudly acknowledges), but Tirgan's board of directors and executive office (e.g., CEO and directors of the organization's departments) have been predominantly men. Even though the organization's cofounders and early directors included several women, and even though around half of Tirgan's large volunteer base have been women, the Tirgan board of directors elected by the trustee membership (which consists of twenty-five to thirty longtime volunteers, whose names and photos are posted on the Tirgan website) has never included more than one woman at a time. This trend remained consistent even after the expansion of the board from five members to eight members in October 2018. Furthermore, among its executive officers, there have never been more than two women serving at the same time. When, in October 2020 and in the midst of Iran's #MeToo movement, Tirgan was due for a board of directors election, the board of trustees once again elected seven men and just one woman.

The controversy forced Tirgan to confront its commitments to gender equality, transparency, and its role as a community institution—raising broader questions about accountability within diasporic organizations navigating both internal expectations and public scrutiny. Rather than undertaking deep changes in how the organization operated, with the stress test of #MeToo, Tirgan's immediate efforts focused instead on protecting the organization's brand and reputation in order to maintain the status quo. While disappointing for some observers, this approach was consistent with Canadian expectations for corporate and nonprofit organizations in 2020, suggesting Tirgan had professionalized and performed in exactly the ways a nonprofit, nonpartisan Canadian organization was expected to do.

The stakes of doing otherwise were high: What Tirgan's organizers were able to accomplish for the community in the wake of the Flight 752 tragedy demonstrated why many community members were so invested in it, and therefore reluctant to destabilize or discredit it. When Ariannejad posted to Twitter and Facebook defending his track record and his position vis-à-vis Ghomeshi in particular, commenters largely supported him through statements referring to the invaluable service Tirgan provided the community. It—and Ariannejad as its respected leader—would not be put at risk because of what they called "ambiguous" ties to accused Iranian men in a socially, culturally, and politically fractious moment. The status quo was maintained, Ariannejad remained the CEO, and by summer 2023, Jian Ghomeshi was welcomed again as a VIP at the Tirgan Festival.

## For Iran: (Non)Partisan, (Non)Political and Challenging the Canadian Way

Nonpartisanship is not only required by most governments to be registered as a nonprofit organization (e.g., "registered charity" in Canada) with related tax benefits, it also has been a tool used by nonprofit organizations. Claiming a "nonpolitical, nonreligious, nonprofit" status allows organizations to garner broader support, present an inclusive and democratic image, and provide neutral cover during community disputes that allow them to remain silent when doing otherwise could be considered divisive.[97] This is particularly true of Iranian diaspora cultural organizations, from community schools to university student groups to arts and culture foundations.

But like so many in these organizations, despite commitments to organizational nonpartisanship, the leaders of Tirgan have never been apolitical, especially in their personal opinions about their homeland. They also have been very willing to engage with politicians in Canada: Tirgan's teams have carefully built networks with municipal, provincial, and federal Canadian politicians from multiple political parties, drawing them to its festival stages each year and working diligently to build social capital for the Iranian Canadian community. Though these politicians' speeches led to some grumbles in the community (especially in audiences when speeches went on too long), the organization held firm on its nonpartisan stance.

The Canada Mourns event revealed the first public crack in this nonpartisanship for Tirgan: Having lost members of its own Tirgan family in the tragedy, organizing a memorial was deemed appropriate, and by incorporating musicians and poets alongside politicians, the organization felt justified in doing so. But even there, political statements were left to participants to make—whether by local politicians swearing revenge or by the loud applause for the slogans shouted by angry mourners in attendance. The #MeToo movement had prompted a second, more directed challenge to Tirgan's practice of steering clear of "contentions issues." But by adhering closely to Canadian norms ("the Canadian Way"), the organization ultimately arrived at a 'safe' conclusion that largely maintained the status quo, rather than engaging in the deeper, if difficult, institutional changes that concerned community members and the moment invited.

Just two years later, unprecedented protests for political and social change by Iranians in Iran and the diaspora would force Tirgan to reconsider once again its nonpolitical/nonpartisan stance, and ultimately what kind of organization it would be. The killing of Jina Mahsa Amini, a Kurdish Iranian woman, in September 2022 while in custody in Tehran after being arrested by the morality police (*gasht-e ershad*) for alleged nonconformity to the Islamic dress code ignited the Woman, Life, Freedom (WLF) protests. These renewed protests in Iran, especially among women and youth, called for social and political change and quickly spread to the diaspora. Enraged by the circumstances of Amini's death, and, not long after, by the imprisonment and killing of protesters demanding rights and freedoms long repressed, the diaspora was ignited to amplify the protesters' calls for justice. All Iranian diaspora organizations were forced to reckon with a political moment that, through slogans like "Say Her Name" and "Be Our Voice," demanded public expressions of solidarity. How would these organizations reconcile commitments to nonpartisanship and avoidance of "contentious issues" when the demand of the community, and especially voices in the homeland, was to disrupt or even abandon it altogether? Indeed, after a brief period of proclaimed unity, this moment and the actions taken or not taken during it, would ultimately come to expose and deepen political fragmentations in the diaspora.[98]

For its part, Tirgan posted Persian and English statements to its social media on September 19, three days after Amini's death was announced. The English statement ended with, "On behalf of the Tirgan family, we would like to commemorate Mahsa Amini and offer our condolences to all Iranians, especially Mahsa's family. We hope for justice and a day where women in Iran are free and treated equally."[99] Read as tone-deaf and shockingly timid in the face of international outrage, community commenters were not impressed; they expected more from an organization they felt belonged to them and should represent them. Writing angrily in English, one asked: "Why [is] our non-profit organization staying silent!???"[100] Another commenter asked in Persian why Tirgan wasn't being more proactive: "What about a call for a rally in Toronto? Won't you organize it?"[101] When Tirgan's social media team responded that community members should look to Iranian Canadian news media sources for that kind of information (as opposed to an arts and culture organization), the commenter responded expressing his and others' expectations of Tirgan that had grown beyond arts and culture: "Thanks for your response, but I think it would be a positive move for Tirgan's executives to also participate in the call and not wait for the invitation of other groups."[102] Reflecting mixed feelings that persisted in the community about Tirgan's stubborn nonpartisanship when it came to Iranian politics but eagerness to engage with Canadian politicians, another commenter added acerbically, "If these people do hold a rally, they will tell you not to bring flags or chant slogans. From start to end, they will promote the Liberal Party and tons of realtors, jewelry sellers, and other businesses in order to make money."[103] A fourth commenter, a longtime Tirgan volunteer with knowledge of its operations responded from his personal account to this harsh critique: "What an ugly thing to say."[104]

Four days later, as protests in Iran escalated and anger deepened in Iran and the diaspora, Tirgan finally abandoned nonpartisanship and posted a second, bolder, and explicitly political statement in English:

> In solidarity with the people of Iran: We write to inform you that Mahsa Amini's murder by police forces due to the misogynistic Islamic Republic laws has angered Iranians once again and led to widespread protests across many cities in Iran. Our nation is facing another historical challenge and is united across the country in standing up against oppression and social injustice, especially pertaining to women's rights and economic inequality. *Since our culture does not prescribe seeking a safe haven during landmark historical events*, the Tirgan family condemns Mahsa Amini's killing and warns the regime from using violence against protestors. We stand by the Iranian people during these critical times and support them in reaching their demands. Long live Iran.[105]

In this statement expressing direct political solidarity, Tirgan carefully offered a cultural justification for doing so ("Since our culture does not prescribe seeking a safe haven . . ."). Despite this departure from their long-held nonpolitical stance, the comments reflected the growing intensity of emotion that was erupting in the global diasporic community and especially on social media. Sarcastic and disappointed responses in Persian pointed to the delay in Tirgan's statement ("Don't wear yourselves out all of a sudden"; "You really pressured yourselves to post twice"; "Where have you been?!!!").¹⁰⁶ One commenter articulated the unfulfilled expectations that Tirgan would take a leadership role in the community that it had already demonstrated it had the means to do: "Does your warning to the government in using violence against protesting citizens have a special effect? Did you fulfill your duty as the largest Iranian community abroad by issuing a statement? We are all waiting for a bigger and more effective move from Tirgan. You have both the required budget and enough manpower to organize a big gathering!"¹⁰⁷ Another summed up the existential question facing the organization: "Tirgan we expected you to be a constant companion [*hamrah-e hamishegi*, e.g., to always stand with] of Iranians, not just the host of expensive concerts!"¹⁰⁸

Having finally abandoned nonpartisanship, by October, like most other diasporic media accounts at the time, Tirgan's Instagram had become a source of reshared information for rallies, updates, and events, especially those from @PS752justice, the account of the Association of Families of Flight PS752 Victims established in Toronto. For Iranian Canadians, including Tirgan's volunteers, the WLF protests and fight for justice for Flight 752 victims were deeply intertwined. It was this organization that played a major role in organizing the unprecedented protests that took place in Toronto (more than fifty thousand participants) and Berlin (eighty to one hundred thousand participants) in October 2022 and that gained massive global attention.

Indeed, in autumn 2022, the rules of engagement fundamentally changed for Iranian diaspora organizations everywhere: Where nonpartisan stances had protected organizations like Tirgan from fragmentation in the 2010s, it now felt impossible and indeed irresponsible to avoid "contentious issues" as the Canadian Way suggested they do. Amid the heightened emotions, deep-seated anger, and disinformation permeating the diaspora in this period, silence resulted in harsh, quick, and direct attacks—from within these organizations' memberships as much as from outside.¹⁰⁹ As these conditions continued into early 2023, most cultural organizations in the diaspora had expressed solidarity, but weighed what to do about their Nowruz celebrations. In its effort to maintain another of its organizational commitments—here, to communal decision-making—the leaders of Tirgan created an ad hoc committee to keep track of events and its board of trustees and board of directors, over thirty people in total, held long discussions during which they disagreed about what the organization should do.

I discussed this tumultuous period with Nima in April 2023. "In September of last year, when the uprising happened back home, Tirgan didn't do anything," he said. "Because we gathered, and we said there is no real domain for us to start doing any *cultural* thing because people are angry; they don't even want to see their artists." As Nowruz approached, the board met again to decide what kind of organization Tirgan would be: "We knew that people didn't want to celebrate this Nowruz as before, because they're angry. And so what we did, we said, 'Okay, this is the time where we deliberately give our platform to some political figures or cultural activists.'"[110] Ultimately, where other arts and culture organizations reinterpreted their role in this moment by holding Nowruz concerts *about* WLF (as Riksteatern's Eldfesten in Stockholm and Farhang Foundation in Los Angeles did), Tirgan announced in January 2022 that it would go one step further and *replace* its Nowruz festival with an event that would join its expertise in concert production with its accumulated social and political clout—inviting Canadian, US, and European politicians and key Iranian diaspora opposition figures to share the stage with diasporic musicians for what they internally called a *festival-e eterazi*: a protest festival.

Advertised as "For Iran," the ticketed and livestreamed four-hour event was held at the 19,800-seat Scotiabank Arena in downtown Toronto (home to Toronto's NBA and NHL teams). "For Iran" was a sharp departure from Tirgan's usual programming. Still professionally organized and largely run by volunteers, this event not only allowed political speeches on stage from non-Canadian politicians, it exclusively featured politicians' and activists' speeches for the first full hour of the event. These included fiery screeds from controversial figures such as the leader of the Canadian Conservative Party and member of Parliament Pierre Poilievre, as well as diasporic political activist Masih Alinejad. Later, a "surprise" appearance (that had been rumored for weeks) from the former Crown Prince of Iran, Reza Pahlavi, led to huge applause. As hundreds of *shir-o-khorshid* flags—no longer deemed divisive or banned, and even distributed for a donation to the organization—waved in the crowd, Iranian diaspora musicians performed protest songs written for this political moment. The *shir-o-khorshid* (Lion and Sun) is an Iranian flag with a long history that has become associated with the Pahlavi monarchy; it is not the internationally recognized official flag of Iran but has become predominant and promoted in the diaspora, especially during and after the WLF protests of 2022–23. Between performances and speeches, videos on the large screens surrounding the stage explicitly connected the deaths of Flight 752 victims with the deaths of WLF protestors. The charged audience chanted passionate political slogans calling for regime change, and all of it was livestreamed to a broad global audience.

The day before, in a quieter if just as unprecedented move, Tirgan had hosted a related livestreamed event: a press conference called "Unity: A Bridge to Freedom" that, for the first time, brought together a recently announced coalition of opposition figures (calling themselves the Alliance for Democracy and Freedom in Iran[111]) to confer with several diasporic Iranians holding elected positions across Europe and North America. The event sought to build networks between diasporic politicians and activists and to stake out common ground and policy strategies amid this unprecedented opening inspired by the courage of protesters in Iran.[112] Tirgan's approach of avoiding politics or contentious issues had not only been fully abandoned, it appeared the organization had put its weight entirely into the political moment.

These two events, the "protest festival" concert and the opposition press conference, appeared to show that Tirgan had left the arts and culture domain and fully embarked on a political future. I asked Nima if Tirgan's leadership saw it that way, too. He replied: "If you are looking at our activity becoming more political, we [Tirgan] are still trying to move within the arts and culture environment, but at this moment in time you cannot separate these two [culture and politics] from each other. . . . We still are very much standing on our position and constitution and our objectives. We are not shifting from that. No, we're still laser focused on enriching Iranian art and culture within the Canadian context. But, you know, the time requires us to do *festival eterazi* at this moment in time."[113]

While Tirgan had consistently succeeded within arts and culture, with politics, it struggled to find its footing on rapidly shifting ground.

The "For Iran" event sold more tickets (more than 9,500) than any other ticketed Tirgan event (90 percent of Tirgan events are free), but because it had ambitiously rented such a prominent and large venue, they did not sell enough tickets to break even; instead, the organization suddenly found itself in debt. Although thousands of Iranians had attended, many thousands more in Toronto had not. The idea of paying for tickets for what many saw as a political rally had rubbed some the wrong way, especially those who disagreed with the presence of activists and politicians with whom they disagreed. Others expressed concerns amid the tense climate about being seen publicly at an event that featured these political figures, fearing the reputational costs as much as the possible problems they may face if or when they returned to Iran to visit relatives. Still others expressed that the community had become so fraught, so suspicious of one another, and so distrustful in the course of the previous six months, that not only did they not want to hear political speeches but they did not even want to be surrounded by other Iranians—even at Nowruz.

The circumstances risked undermining a key thesis upon which Tirgan was founded and that multiple leaders of the organization had stressed to me, namely that arts and culture was an arena through which political differences could be bridged and through which community norms of teamwork and collaboration could be built for the benefit of Iranian Canadian cultural citizenship. As it happened, many of the differences that Behrouz had pointed out to me in 2011 as areas he hoped arts and culture could help to soften had instead deepened due to ongoing disputes in the Canadian Iranian community and geopolitical events that had occurred in the intervening decade.

Moreover, where Tirgan had managed to weather the stress tests of 2020 by performing as Canadian norms would ask of them, the test of 2022–23 demanded a pivot. As Nima shared with me in 2023, this led to existential questions that the organization was still grappling with: "I've had this discussion with every level of supporter in Tirgan—with ticket buyers, sponsors, donors, board members, trustee members. We are all dealing with this mixed feeling that Tirgan is becoming a political avenue." Echoing some of the demands expressed on social media, however, Nima remained firm in his personal belief as a cofounder and board member that in organizing For Iran, Tirgan was answering the call of the moment for which it uniquely had developed the necessary skills and networks: "You know, we know artists; we know political people; we know [officials] in City of Toronto, [in the Ontario] province, in the federal level; we have a very good trusted brand; we have a good connection with ticket buyers."[114] By drawing on its social capital for the benefit of the broader diasporic community—bringing these particular people into the same room, creating global networks that otherwise were not being built, and offering their platform to the needs of the moment—Tirgan's leadership saw their mandate not as having changed but rather as being more completely fulfilled. In this way, Tirgan was building not only cultural citizenship, but also *diasporic* citizenship. Defined by Lok Siu as "the processes by which diasporic subjects experience and practice cultural and social belonging amid shifting geopolitical circumstances and webs of transnational relations," diasporic citizenship involves emotional attachments, behaviors, and practices relating to fellow Iranians, not only those where one is (in this case, Canada) and where one is from (Iran), but also to those in diaspora, anywhere they may reside.[115]

Ultimately, even if nonpartisanship was a demand of community-building, Canadian regulations, and granting institutions, Tirgan could not afford to ignore the political and social changes around it. Nima made clear that doing so would not only have put Tirgan's position in the community in question (inverting the logic behind nonpartisanship), it also would require silencing its own members' beliefs and desires as individuals to build solidarity for Iranians in Iran, which could itself lead to irreparable internal disputes in addition to personal turmoil. When I asked him directly whether he felt the risk they had taken with Tirgan's brand and community trust (eroded in some sectors after For Iran) had been worth it, he thought for a few moments before responding through the language of citizenship:

> I think it was worth it. Definitely. Because when I see the amount of courage that is happening back home, Amy *jun*, I am shameful. I, personally, I am a shameful citizen. And I think I cannot, I have not done enough. Honestly. And if I can get Tirgan to do those kind of things, I would do it eyes closed. Regardless of what people think. What is happening back

there is just unbelievable. I was one of those kids. I did all my studies in Iran. I just did my university studies in Toronto. So I could have been one of them.[116]

\* \* \*

The Tirgan family had worked to facilitate immigrant integration and cultural citizenship—making Iranian Canadians feel, behave, and become recognized as Canadians—not by diminishing cultural connections to Iran, but by fostering belonging in a Canadian Way: introducing newcomers to their new communities through a Canadian process of organizing, volunteering, and communicating a multicultural identity that produced pride and dignity through collective representation. For most of Tirgan's volunteers—whether first, 1.5, or second generation— their participation in Canadian multiculturalism led to experiences of successful teamwork with fellow Iranian Canadians and a deepened sense of belonging to Canada without silencing or interrupting connections with their homeland. The emotional effects of Tirgan thus included a deeper affinity to both Canadian and Iranian identities—an outcome Canadian approaches to multiculturalism would applaud. As Bloemraad anticipated, through the "school" of Tirgan, an increased sense of belonging in Canada among Tirgan's volunteers and the broader Toronto Iranian community led to more active participation in and beyond the Iranian community, whether as entrepreneurs, donors, or candidates and volunteers for local political campaigns. The Canadian Way had also required the organization's institutionalization as a registered charity and the production of formalized mission statements, organizational manuals, and constitutional bylaws that, alongside institutional transparency and consistent follow-through, ensured Tirgan's continued support from granting agencies.

Indeed, Tirgan's successful institutionalization enabled it to develop symbolic and social capital for the community, all of which would be called upon to get it through the first stress tests of 2020 (e.g., Flight 752 and COVID-19). When the next test came in summer and autumn 2020 from within the community and called on the organization to take difficult but decisive action towards affirming gender justice, the organization again performed in the Canadian Way: It held steady in its commitment to avoid "contentious issues" and instead hired consultants, drafted diversity statements, protected the brand, and ultimately maintained the status quo. While reproducing these hegemonic practices enabled Tirgan to continue to operate in the midst of widespread calls for social and cultural changes in North America that summer, it also reinforced the organization's existing structures, limiting its ability to take a leadership role in addressing the core problem of gender equality in the community and beyond.

As occasions for Iranians in diaspora to practice different ways of relating both to each other and to dominant power structures, these contestations have the potential to transform the very meaning of belonging itself. By 2022–23, calls for change came not only from Toronto's Iranian community but from the global diaspora and, critically, from within Iran. The nonpartisanship that had long protected Tirgan now threatened to erode its standing in the community. Yet abandoning it entirely posed an equally existential risk. Tirgan's deep integration into Canadian institutional and behavioral norms had enabled its success. But when confronted with the #MeToo movement, these same norms limited immigrants with commitments to justice and freedom—hallmarks of multiculturalism—to actually be able to disrupt a patriarchal status quo in an effort to achieve them. Only when demands for disruption came from beyond Canada and in a moment that threatened to upend their work altogether, did Tirgan's commitment to the Canadian Way finally give way to resistance to, rather than reproduction of, Canadian norms.

Tirgan's strategies of inclusion ultimately produced dual but interrelated forms of citizenship—a cultural citizenship tied to Canada's multicultural framework and a diasporic citizenship committed to a transnational Iranian identity. As pressures mounted, the organization could no longer deny the personal and collective demands to mobilize its accumulated capital—symbolic, social, cultural, and financial—toward diasporic politics. In doing so, it redefined its role, no longer only as an institution navigating Canadian multiculturalism, but as one actively building solidarity beyond its cultural contours with Iranians across borders. This decision was neither taken lightly nor came without significant costs. For individuals like Nima, failing to act—remaining on the sidelines—would have amounted to an unbearable personal shame. Yet leaping into divisive diasporic politics clearly carried its own risks. Tirgan's shift away from strict nonpartisanship resulted in deep financial strain and, having taken that leap, reputational risks—both of which jeopardized its long-term stability. While Tirgan had long relied on professionalization and nonpartisanship to establish its legitimacy, institutions are not neutral actors. They are shaped by individuals, who ultimately decide when adherence to established norms must give way to something greater.

# 5

# Comparing Iranian Diasporic Strategies in Multicultural Societies

On a bright summer afternoon in 2017, I arrived at a tall glass skyscraper to meet David, an Iranian American attorney and community leader in Los Angeles. In addition to running his legal practice, David was active in city politics, serving as a board commissioner for the city followed by fulfilling a two-year appointment by the mayor heading a major city department. He was a recognizable figure in LA's Iranian and Jewish communities; over the years I had heard him give speeches about civic responsibility and the importance of voting for LA's Persian-language radio stations and at community events in Westwood and the Valley.

In our interview in his firm's conference room just around the corner from the Freedom Sculpture, David shared with me his thoughts on Los Angeles, multiculturalism, and how the Iranian American community there had developed politically. For David, LA's pluralism was both the source of his love for the city and "a great human experiment . . . which we cannot allow to fail": "You can have all of these people from all of these cultures and creeds and religions and with 140 languages spoken in the schools, that you can have them all in one place and have them be able to do business with each other, to live with each other, and to live in harmony. And that you can have these people who would be at each other's throats in their countries of origin and yet be able to cooperate with one another here."[1] David recognized and appreciated that the city's multicultural population required cooperation on an exceptional scale. He suggested that the stakes of that "experiment" on social cohesion (e.g., testing whether a diverse citizenry could "live in harmony" and "cooperate with one another") were great.

David had been among a number of key community donors who had ensured the success of the Freedom Sculpture, unveiled just two weeks prior. The sculpture had been a costly project (about $2.6 million USD) funded through a series of private fundraisers and a public crowdfunding campaign. After explaining my research interests and the notably different approaches that I had observed among Iranians in Sweden and Canada, I asked whether David felt there should be greater financial support from the city, state, or the US federal government for immigrant community initiatives that worked to foster belonging. He thought carefully, and his answer reflected a common sense in the United States that immigrant belonging and inclusion are the responsibility of immigrants alone.

> DAVID: There's no expectation of the city. Perhaps because we haven't been brought up with the Scandinavian model.... But I mean, here in the United States—you know, the basic thing that you think government would provide, which is health care for the people, here we've got people who think that *that's* anathema. 'Let everybody go out there and buy their own!' So I think given that, it's hardly surprising that at a city level we don't have [multiculturalism or integration] programs.... And it's hardly surprising that we go and do the Nowruz thing, we go and do the Freedom Sculpture, and I write, you know, a big check for the Freedom Sculpture without even thinking—
> 
> AMY: —that this should be our tax dollars doing this, not my dollars?
> 
> DAVID: Exactly.... It's a very interesting point this thing between expecting the government itself to initiate this outreach to immigrant communities or putting the burden on the shoulder of immigrant communities to make themselves part and parcel. I think there's got to be a coming together of the two. And I think so far, in the Iranian[-American] community anyway, we have kind of thought that it is up to us. It is up to us to push ourselves forward, to make ourselves a part, and I think we've enjoyed a measure of success.... I think we're by and large a very successful community. And I think we have the means, we have the power, we have the opportunity, and the potential—right?—to make ourselves a significant part of the city. I don't think we need a helping hand from the government to do that. I think there are others who need it a lot more than we do.[2]

This answer was not surprising to me as an Iranian American, but in comparison with what I had heard from Iranians in Sweden and

Canada, it was notable that David felt inclusion and belonging of immigrants was "up to us" alone, rather than a shared responsibility of immigrant communities, their fellow residents, and the federal or city government. Even if he could imagine the "coming together of the two" would be optimal, David's phrase, "a helping hand," reflected a common sense in the United States of equating government support with an act of charity as opposed to an obligation of a state toward its citizens that would be of benefit to the state as much as to the newcomer. Social welfare, specifically, is imagined in the United States as a last resort for the neediest citizens as opposed to an expected or necessary part of the social contract between the state and its citizen subjects. This is a pervasive sentiment, even if those with "the means," "the power," "the opportunity," and "the potential" often benefit the most from welfare policies like tax breaks, subsidies, government contracts, or loan relief programs (e.g., the Paycheck Protection Program [PPP] loan forgiveness).

Despite the presence of Iranian Americans across different class positions in Los Angeles, narratives of self-sufficiency obscure internal economic heterogeneity. Although Iranian American families and individuals—like other Americans—rely on social security, unemployment benefits, disability benefits, SNAP (Supplemental Nutrition Assistance Program), low-interest government loans, and other government welfare programs for economic support, concerns surrounding *aberu* (saving face, honor) often prevent public disclosure of utilizing these forms of support.[3] Such concerns may be understandable but nevertheless reinforce invisibility, creating a public image of affluence that does not account for the full spectrum of Iranian American experiences. As a result, many Iranian Americans perceive and present themselves and their communities both as separate from and having a higher status than other immigrants. This outlook underlies the numerous generalized descriptions from prominent community members who mark Iranian American success primarily by wealth and status. Such a successful immigrant group surely doesn't need charity.

In the United States, a country without an official multiculturalism policy, seeking government support was not just an invisible or a disfavored strategy for immigrant cultural organizing, it was not a readily available one. Because US politicians and media have framed these programs in neoliberal terms as "wasteful social spending" that should be cut in favor of individual responsibility, the idea of cultural belonging as fostered through education or the arts has been consistently shifted to the responsibility of individuals, philanthropy, or open market competition, rather than maintained as a public good the state should guarantee through funding and other forms of support. This framing is consistent with Wendy Brown's description of the neoliberal project as one that aims "to change the soul" through neoliberalizing society itself, diminishing and denigrating dependency on the state and the very idea of society as a source of welfare and security. Instead, citizens are encouraged to become independent "self-investors" who "socially and monetarily invest in themselves to become more valuable";[4] or, in Aihwa Ong's words, to become "entrepreneurs of themselves."[5] So mainstream has this approach become that even self-described progressives, like David, who otherwise support public welfare do not imagine it could or should pertain to immigrant inclusion or culture.

In contrast, several of my interlocutors in Stockholm and Toronto shared with me their belief that the responsibility of the state to foster belonging among all of its subjects was a commonsense approach to demographic multiculturalism and social cohesion. If a socially cohesive society requires that all its members are able to participate equally, cooperate toward the common good, and feel a sense of belonging, they reasoned that the state would need to ensure immigrants were fully included through enacting policies and putting forward budgets to support programs toward these goals. The Canadian and Swedish Iranian organizers in this book thus made significant use of state-funded programs in their efforts to build cultural citizenship and inclusion in their societies. When Iranians began arriving in large numbers to these global locations, official multiculturalism policies seeking to do exactly that were being established—unlike in the United States, where Iranian Americans arrived to a society undergoing another round of culture wars in which assimilation was expected and multiculturalism was and continues to be hotly contested.

These differences are not simply differences of political opinion. Rather, they reflect the ways different structures and hegemonic ideologies directly impact immigrant identities. In contrast to David's answer, Arian, one of the directors of Toronto's Tirgan Festival in 2011, felt all countries should provide the opportunities that Canada had offered its newcomers. A common sentiment among festival volunteers was that while Tirgan should have already existed in Iran, it was only through the financial and symbolic support available in diaspora that it became possible. In their view, the Canadian government and its intermediaries had offered Iranians in Canada opportunities that all governments should offer their citizens. The result was that Arian and many of his colleagues felt a greater sense of belonging and duty to Canada, *but also* to fellow Iranians, both in Canada and the broader Iranian diaspora: "Canada had offered a ton of possibilities—the truth is they made a budget available, they offered the Harbourfront space, a lot of possibilities. . . . It is my opinion that what a government must do for its country, Canada did this, in part, for us. And so, by working with Tirgan I have a better feeling towards . . . Iranians outside of Iran."[6]

As we have seen, across the diaspora, Iranians have sought to redress misrecognition by taking the reins of their own representation and have been doing so especially through public-facing arts and cultural events. This strategy not only puts forward self-representation through culture as an argument for inclusion in majority societies, but in each case also sought to fulfil other community needs, both at home and across the diaspora. For example, in locations where members sought to build coalitions and strengthen their fragmented communities, arts-and-culture was considered "the only thing the Iranian people . . . will not argue over" and thus an avenue to build unity and practices of teamwork and democracy. The stakes of these festivals, exhibitions, and public representations were thus much higher than they may have appeared to be from the outside: unity, teamwork, and democratic practices were framed by organizers as necessary in order to be visible (literally be seen) by politicians, neighbors, and the larger society as a community deserving of rights, especially in societies where everyday forms of exclusion were increasingly being joined with heightened xenophobia and, in some cases, state-sanctioned exclusions.

State policy and civic institutions create and shape competition and contestation over representation within diasporic communities. Building on the cases presented in this book, this chapter presents a comparative view of three Iranian diaspora contexts in countries with different immigration histories and approaches to multiculturalism and immigrant inclusion. The absence or presence of official multiculturalism policies—and the variation in emphases among countries' approaches to immigrant inclusion—has influenced understandings of Iranian identity, diasporic identity, and the hegemonic common sense about Iranian immigrants' roles in society. They have also led to strategies, practices, beliefs, and investments among Iranians in the global diaspora with impacts on Iranian identity and culture that cross continents.

To draw out these comparative analyses, this chapter more directly draws upon Ong's formulation of cultural citizenship (as "the dual process of self-making and being-made" by hegemonic institutions) to offer reflections on how differing histories of migration and multiculturalism policy have created social and political contexts wherein Iranian immigrants have found themselves navigating shifting state policies, geopolitics, and modes of belonging.[7] Ong identified everyday situations wherein interactions between US intermediary institutions and immigrants and refugees from different parts of Asia had resulted in differential classing and racializing within the Black-white continuum of US racial hierarchy.[8] As we have seen in the preceding chapters, ambitious community leaders in the United States, Sweden, and Canada have deployed cultural strategies of inclusion based on the possibilities, politics, and histories of their local communities within state structures, norms, and networks. Different strategies emerged in each of these diasporic locations, but across all three, Iranian culture became an arena of contestation wherein those most aligned with the state's hegemonic forms, whether official multiculturalisms or the lack thereof, have been best positioned to prevail. Moreover, these different processes of representing Iranian culture in the diaspora have generated competing views on what it means to be Iranian but also competing modes of belonging that variously subvert and reinforce existing power relations across local, national, and transnational scales.

After a comparative discussion of these migratory flows, hegemonic forms, and cultural contestations, the chapter turns attention to how diasporic Iranians have navigated the intersecting vectors of class, religion, and race that Iranians in diaspora seek to reproduce or, in some cases, to resist—by tripping up without tripping over—these lines of inclusion and exclusion.

## Being and Belonging as Iranian in Diaspora

Using the ethnographic examples presented in the previous chapters, I offer two key lines of relational comparison: (1) migration flows from Iran to the United States, Sweden, and Canada that have created distinctive community contexts and have led to different attitudes among—and also toward—Iranians and different experiences of inclusion and exclusion, and (2) hegemonic ideologies and webs of power in each location that Iranian communities have navigated in seeking alignment as a strategy of inclusion.

### Iranian Migration Trajectories and Reception Experiences

The significant migratory flows of Iranians in the late twentieth century to nearly every continent were precipitated by social, economic, and political changes in Iran as well as changes in migration pathways, opportunities, and interventions of states, especially in Europe and North America.[9] The mix of varying motivations for emigration, pathways to immigration, and historical periods of migration have led to the growth of diverse communities in and across the diaspora that, while not generalizable, nevertheless have created some distinguishing characteristics that lead to varying modes of being and belonging as Iranian.

As we have seen, the Southern California Iranian population is widely considered to be the oldest and largest concentration in the diaspora. Large flows of Iranian refugees and immigrants in the late 1970s and 1980s joined an earlier cohort of students who stayed in the United States during political upheaval in Iran. This growing community included Pahlavi elites and relatively large concentrations of multiple religious minorities (e.g., Jewish, Baha'i, Zoroastrian, Christian Assyrian and Armenian) and, contrary to stereotypes, a mix of economic classes, including extremely wealthy Iranians alongside those of the working class. Known as Tehrangeles or Irangeles, the diaspora in Los Angeles has been historically anchored by pockets of ethnic entrepreneurs in Westwood, the San Fernando Valley, and downtown LA, though Iranians have settled across the region. Though not a homogenous group, many have built careers both within and beyond these neighborhoods, especially in fields like real estate, law, media and entertainment, dentistry, and medicine. Given the size and diversity of this population, including a wide variety of subcommunities, divergent political dispositions (including an especially active network of monarchists), multiple generations and immigrant cohorts, and ethnic and religious identities, intracommunity fragmentations have challenged leaders seeking to build unity or represent a united political voice in city, state, and federal elections. Ongoing migrations, even in the face of the Muslim Ban announced in 2017, and political shifts both in Iran and in the United States in the 2020s have deepened and opened new fragmentations (fig. 1.3).

Given the antagonistic US-Iran relationship since the 1979 Hostage Crisis, Iranian Americans developed various covering strategies, including self-identification with the ethnic marker "Persian" rather than the stigmatized national marker "Iranian." In contrast to news-media- and Hollywood-driven stereotypes of Iranians as terrorists and religious extremists, competing stereotypes of "LA Persians" highlighted materialism, conspicuous consumption, and extreme wealth.[10] While this latter set of stereotypes homogenizes the ethnic and class diversity of Iranian diaspora communities, these competing sets of media narratives nevertheless have formed a "common sense" about Iranians in Los Angeles for a variety of audiences, including themselves.

In contrast, the Stockholm Iranian community was established largely by urban middle-class political refugees and their families who arrived in the late 1980s and 1990s with little to no financial capital, but with high levels of education and other cultural capital (fig. 1.5). While many in this large early cohort of Iranian refugees and immigrants have succeeded in learning Swedish, earning degrees of higher education, and establishing businesses and careers, others—in line with larger employment trends among immigrants in Sweden—have faced difficulties and discriminatory barriers to employment leading to high levels of under- or unemployment. Nevertheless, the concentration of intellectuals, activists, artists, and political refugees, many of whom found fundamental similarities between their leftist principles and Swedish social welfare, has contributed to the active social, cultural, and political participation of Iranians in Stockholm and other large Swedish cities. Iranian immigrants have been more successful in electoral politics in Sweden than in the United States, including as MPs representing parties across the political spectrum in Swedish Parliament.

Thanks to this participation, and especially the public roles of 1.5- and second-generation Iranians in Swedish media, the Iranian community has come to be seen by many Swedes—and some Iranians—as an exceptional example of successful immigrant integration. This image is sometimes placed in contrast against other nonwhite, and especially Muslim, immigrants who are depicted by far-right Swedish politicians as unable to integrate. This perception is supported and even argued by some Iranians in Swedish media, especially those on the political right, but denounced by other Iranians, especially those on the political left. Though smaller in total population than in Los Angeles, Iranians in Stockholm have also faced challenges in uniting divergent political, religious, and ethnic positions, including new cohorts of first-generation immigrants and refugees, especially in the mid-2010s, with very different experiences of and attitudes toward Iran, Iranian identity, and, ultimately, one another.

In Toronto, large waves of late 1990s and post-2000 arrivals have joined earlier, if fewer, Iranian immigrants in building a new diasporic capital, leading to competition with Los Angeles for the reputation of being the largest and most active in the diaspora. Through Canada's refugee and asylum policies, various family reunification pathways, and a points system that favored skilled workers, a significant number of primarily well-educated, middle- and upper-class Iranians have arrived to Canada since the 2000s (fig. 1.6). While many have attained postgraduate degrees in Canada, started businesses, or gained employment in Canadian organizations and corporations, others have struggled to find employment commensurate to their qualifications or faced other difficulties that have led to their working "survival jobs." Like Los Angeles, then, the large Toronto community also includes extremely wealthy Iranians alongside working-class newcomers. But relative to Los Angeles and Stockholm, Toronto is home to a larger percentage of recent cohorts, with the majority of the community having arrived after 2000 and especially in the 2010s (fig. 1.6). While perhaps fragmented along similar lines as in these other diasporic cities, the active Tehranto community has been especially divided in their orientation to Iran and the Islamic Republic of Iran (IRI), including multiple competing opposition groups but also those who continue to maintain networks among elites and government officials "back home."

These overlapping migration flows of Iranians of differing generations, immigrant cohorts, political orientations, ethnic identities, religious affiliations, class positions, and experiences of being Iranian in Iran prior to arriving to the United States, Sweden, and Canada have had important impacts on how their diasporic communities have experienced and responded to inclusion and exclusion. Migration flows are impacted (though not wholly determined) by migration policies, but once immigrants and refugees arrive to new societies, hegemonic ideas pertaining to the role of immigrants and the presence or absence of policies that work to instill these ideas are critical to the identity negotiations that follow.

## Navigating Power and Multicultural Frameworks in Diaspora

If Iranians across the diaspora have experienced misrecognitions and have sought redress through strategies that assert Iranian culture to mainstream publics, variations in the societies in which they reside have led to significant differences in how they have done so. Ong's formulation of cultural citizenship emphasized the importance of attending to subject formation as taking place within "webs of power linked to the nation-state and civil society."[11] These institutions and state policies—or, in some cases, their absence—both create and shape competition and contestation within immigrant communities. These all contribute to how hegemonic webs of power, including multicultural policies and the various intermediary institutions that implement them, impact Iranian diasporic subjectification and belonging in these locations. Through these institutions, Ong argued, "the state and its hegemonic forms . . . establish the criteria of belonging."[12] Thus, within arenas of cultural contestation, it is unsurprising that those most aligned with the state's hegemonic forms are the ones best positioned to succeed within a given system.

This observation is borne out in each of the cases examined in this book. Sharing similar goals of representation and inclusion, each community and their public cultural events have nevertheless taken unique routes, pragmatically aligning with the hegemonic structures that shape immigrant belonging in their societies. For the Iranian diaspora, as organizers mobilize through cultural events to navigate these webs of power, contestations have included disagreements over the nature of Iranian culture. Rather than producing a singular vision of "Iranianness," each community's strategies for achieving these goals reveal how local systems impact not only the cultural lives of Iranians in their immediate communities, but across the diaspora, and thus influence understandings of Iranian identity itself.

## ELITE PHILANTHROPY AND THE LIMITS OF PRIVATIZED MULTICULTURALISM

Faced with a society particularly unwelcome to Iranians in the 1980s, many Iranian Americans in Los Angeles at the time turned inward to their families, their religious communities, and their businesses and entrepreneurial networks. Without directed resources, policies, and symbolic inclusion provided by official multiculturalism or other programs by the city, state, or federal government, Iranian Americans seeking to build their communities were, like other immigrant groups in the United States, required to creatively develop other pathways for doing so through their social networks. This led to local efforts—whether small Persian-language schools or Nowruz celebrations—that relied entirely on the community for small donations and sponsorship, especially through advertising from ethnic businesses. Facing renewed discrimination after 9/11, individuals who had "the means" and "the power" began putting their personal resources and skills toward building a larger collective voice and asserting public dignity through developing national organizations focused on civic participation, political representation, and public relations.[13] One such national organization, the Public Affairs Alliance of Iranian Americans (PAAIA), included in its vision statement the goal and logic of so many efforts described in this book: "We see a future where Iranian American contributions to society are widely recognized and the community is seen as an important constituency in the eyes of U.S. policymakers."[14]

But while Iranian cultural organizations with smaller budgets, entirely volunteer staff, and an emphasis on community participation managed through great effort to organize public cultural events focused on representing Iranian culture in Southern California (like the organizers of the Mehregan Festival in Orange County throughout the 2000s), their precarious reliance on corporate sponsorships, advertising, and ticket sales led to difficulties and, in most cases, eventual decline.

It was against this backdrop in the late 2000s that Farhang Foundation's trustees decided to use their personal wealth toward building the representations of Iranian culture in the mainstream that they wished to see. Because Farhang's founding trustees were not reliant on public or external granting agencies and their priorities, the strategies the organization used catered to ensuring the continuing support of trustees and donors, rather than to state cultural policies or granting agency imperatives. The example of the multiple and ongoing high profile projects of the Farhang Foundation demonstrate that, in the context of US neoliberal multiculturalism, it is communities who have access to extensive private financial resources and who have cultivated influential networks who are best positioned to influence their own representation before wide public audiences—audiences who, in turn, see the version of culture and identity (e.g., "Iranianness") these elites wish them to see.

Moreover, while all of the large public cultural events described in this book were notable for their high production quality, where Eldfesten and Tirgan could rely on the expertise of state intermediaries (like Riksteatern in Sweden or Harbourfront Centre in Canada) for everything from stage production to volunteer training, in order to produce an equally professional event Farhang needed (and was able) to hire event planners, production companies, and public relations and social media managers. But the absence of state intermediaries influenced by state-mandated and funded cultural policy had other effects as well. While all three of these events emphasized the importance of democracy, as we have seen, without the influence of external granting agencies or state intermediaries, any emphasis on democracy in Farhang's Freedom Festival largely remained at the level of discourse. Where building community volunteerism, participation, and democratic *practices* were integral to the large-scale public-facing projects of my interlocutors in Stockholm and Toronto, these have never been articulated as primary goals for Farhang Foundation projects. Instead, the organization has sought to build attention for Iranian arts and culture and, in this case, for the Freedom

Sculpture and its *messages* of democracy through crowdfunding, social media engagement, and public relations management. In these efforts, the messaging, representation, and image of the community has been prioritized over targeting the practices and participation of the community. When seen through the frame of US neoliberal multiculturalism, this was a very American strategy to constituting participation, and by that standard, a successful one.

In a country where the "nation of immigrants" mythology papers over the different ways some immigrants are included while others remain "forever foreigners,"[15] upward economic mobility and class status become pathways to belonging that legal citizenship does not guarantee.[16] For Iranian Americans who have the "means, . . . the power, . . . [and] the opportunity," the ideal of the American Dream is found in the attainment of elite status through a combination of American individualism and Iranian culture.[17] Appropriately, then, the messages put forward in the Cyrus Cylinder exhibition tour, in promotions of the Freedom Sculpture, and on the 2017 Freedom Festival stage, such as the values of "Freedom, Dignity, and Wealth" (as attributed to Cyrus the Great), all doubled down on discourses of American individualism and freedom, arguing that they are not only shared values but originally Iranian ones. Rather than resisting exclusion through developing participation and civic engagement through culture, or through recourse to the purported values of the Cyrus Cylinder itself such as human rights and diversity (contested as these interpretations may be), this ancient contribution and the economic and social contributions of contemporary Iranian Americans were strategically deployed as appeals for inclusion.

Representations of wealth and individual responsibility in these displays of cultural entrepreneurialism demonstrated worthiness of belonging in the United States and implicitly positioned Iranian Americans as "good" immigrants in a period of heightened anti-immigrant rhetoric. In a system of unofficial neoliberal multiculturalism that favors entrepreneurialism and individualism and parcels out belonging unevenly among immigrant communities, those with private wealth and elite networks will be encouraged to harness both in their immigrant communities—including the power to represent that community in ways that mobilize culture as a strategy of inclusion.

## STATE-SUPPORTED MULTICULTURALISM: CULTURAL INTERMEDIARIES AND THE TERMS OF INCLUSION

In contrast, both Sweden and Canada have adopted official multiculturalisms, albeit with different policies and emphases that have led to important differences in their Iranian communities. In Sweden, state multicultural policy and rhetoric in the early 2010s centered interculturalism, described as a bidirectional process in which both immigrants and the mainstream Swedish society adjust to one another, as opposed to the traditional one-way assimilation of immigrants. This ideology was supported and expressed through cultural policies implemented by intermediary institutions like Riksteatern (Sweden's national touring theater) and their representatives, including Iranian cultural workers hired into influential positions. These individuals not only brought professional arts experience and a mandate from the state, they also had the support of the state's budget and the intermediary institutions' networks and reputations within Swedish society and politics.

Through navigating these "webs of power" (so different from those of the United States) they and their Iranian community partners created Eldfesten, a festival that aimed to represent Iranian arts and culture while also adhering to Swedish cultural policy imperatives of interculturalism. In my 2012 observations, this approach included deliberately diversifying performances and inviting English and Swedish speakers as hosts and audience, as well as responding to contestations over cultural ownership brought forward by members of the community through direct reference to Swedish hegemonic discourses of democracy, antiracism, and diversity. The result has been an annual celebration of Chaharshanbeh Suri as Eldfesten, an event that looks much different from the holiday celebrated in Iran. It has thus spurred community contestations around authenticity and cultural ownership, but also has become recognized by Swedish officials as a "Swedish tradition" broadcast live on national radio and TV and across the diaspora through digital media.

Close attention to the production of Eldfesten 2012 offered a clear example of how the presence of Iranian representatives in Swedish institutions also led to the deliberate and directed rehearsal of Swedish hegemonic norms and behaviors in the organizing committee's meetings. Leaders emphasized the importance of practicing democracy, transparency, professionalism, and cool comportment "like Swedes" among Iranian organizers and volunteers—and especially in front of "Swedish eyes." These practices and the debates the event sparked reflect the ways official Swedish multiculturalism in this period rewarded groups who aligned with hegemonic Swedish norms, whether by reproducing Swedish ideologies and behaviors or by innovating cultural events and practices that promoted the state's view of interculturalism through promotion of an expansive version of "Iranianness" as a strategy of inclusion.

The Canadian mosaic model, on the other hand, centers a top-down insistence that no cultural group—Indigenous, settler colonial, or immigrant—is more or less Canadian than the other. This principle informed the state's 2000s–2010s commitment to putting both symbolic and instrumental support behind groups through programs that embedded principles of diversity in Canadian national identity. These policies succeeded in developing a common sense among Torontonians that demographic multiculturalism and the policies that support it are matters of pride for Canada and for Toronto, an assertion made repeatedly by politicians and community members alike. It is also evident, for example, in the development of the city's popular summer ethnic festival tradition and the array of community partnership programs, partially funded by federal and provincial resources, that have enabled them.

One such partnership, between young Iranian immigrants and Toronto's Harbourfront Centre (HC), enabled the creation of the biennial Tirgan Festival in 2007. By selectively drawing upon and reframing Iranian mythistorical traditions in its name and initial funding application, these organizers quite consciously sought to conform to Canadian multicultural priorities of diversity as a shared value for both Iranians and Canadians. Beyond Tirgan's name, this value also was realized through an energetic and motivated volunteer base of several hundred first-generation Iranian Canadians who worked to bring a diverse and contemporary view of Iranian arts and culture to Toronto. Tirgan's artistic programming, organizational structure, marketing strategies, and fundraising initiatives were deeply influenced by HC and thus put forward Canadian norms of transparency, teamwork, and professional development as priorities equal to their mission of promoting Iranian art and culture, all while carefully maintaining nonpartisanship and refraining from divisive stances in order to bring together a fragmented community.

The result has been the development not only of the largest festival of Iranian arts and culture in the world, but also of the Tirgan Family, a network of fictive kinship that has helped facilitate the integration of thousands of young Iranians into the Canadian Way. As they volunteered alongside and for their new community, they also built emotional attachments and deep feelings of belonging in Canada. Tirgan's alignment with Canadian multiculturalism has meant that in moments of contestation—such as during social movements like #MeToo wherein community members challenged Tirgan's commitment to gender equality—rather than take up community calls to resist hegemonic structures, the organization has remained aligned with the organizational norms of the Canadian Way. These have guaranteed not only a continuation of the status quo but also additional support from government granting institutions and community donors who support these positions—that is, until the Woman, Life, Freedom protests put the organization in a catch-22 that highlighted the potent element of transnational belonging and commitments to compatriots in Iran, suggesting for the first time the possibility of new strategies of resistance.

Clearly, community leaders in all three of these locations were committed to showcasing Iranian art and culture to a wide public through high-quality public cultural events. The ways they have done so provides a view of the distinctions between these different locations and hegemonic forms in the same global diaspora. Arts and culture programs like Eldfesten in Stockholm and Tirgan in Toronto could not have taken shape in the ways they did, have had such strong impacts on inclusion, nor persisted for over a decade, without official multiculturalism and the related and multiple strands of support from each state's intermediaries. The Swedish and Canadian governments have provided key funding, both through grants (such as the over $2.6 million CAD that was awarded between 2011 and 2022 to Tirgan by federal, provincial, and municipal agencies) and state cultural institutions (such as Riksteatern, which consistently provides over 90 percent of the funding necessary for Eldfesten in Stockholm). State-supported institutions in Sweden and Canada also have provided in-kind support, such as the professional producers, event coordinators, techs, and marketers at Riksteatern and Harbourfront Centre. Finally, they have provided support through symbolic recognition of the communities these policies and funds support, whether through politicians' recognition of Tirgan or in national media coverage of Eldfesten on Swedish national TV and radio.

Where Farhang Foundation relied entirely on private funding and the volunteer hours of its dues-paying trustees and council members to organize its events, Toronto's Tirgan has only been possible through a mix of government funding, prominent corporate sponsorships, private donors, and the presence of a large and active cadre of energetic volunteers trained by the intermediary institution HC, which also provided the venue and on-site professionals to ensure a smooth, high-quality production. In Sweden, cultural policy provided the budget and the avenue for an Iranian theater and event producer employed in a state intermediary cultural institution to ensure that Eldfesten would be a professionally produced event, paid for by the national theater and its cultural association partner(s), who also received state grants.

## INTERPRETING IRANIANNESS

Despite these many differences, in all three cases, Iranians aligned with dominant power structures in their respective locations in order to achieve their goals of representation, which also resulted in different interpretations of "Iranianness." For example, the cultural symbols of ancient Iran, as imperial nostalgia, are present across the global diaspora, and these displays put forward a particular vision of what constitutes Iranian culture and identity that has forefronted pre-Islamic—or, non-Islamic—elements of Iranian history and culture. Though present in the United States, Sweden, and Canada, examples of Cyromania were far more prevalent in the public festivals, art installations, street parades, and exhibitions in the United States than in those I observed in Canada or Sweden. In Canada, while elements of Cyromania are evident in Tehranto restaurant decor or in shops that sell jewelry and models of the Cyrus Cylinder, apart from its name and founding story, Tirgan as a public-facing cultural event does not primarily or exclusively center ancient history, symbols, and myths, whether in its programming or on its festival grounds. The policy imperatives of partner HC and provincial and federal Canadian granting agencies—agents of Canadian multiculturalism which have accounted for 20–30 percent of Tirgan's funding—would not have rewarded a limited focus on ancient history or traditional culture.

Its audience also may be less likely to seek out such a narrow focus; as a large and growing community of mostly first-generation Iranian Canadian immigrants, many of whom have continued to travel back and forth to see family in Iran, their tastes and interests also include the art and culture of contemporary Iran, not just its diasporic artists, nor just its ancient history.

Likewise, in Sweden, Eldfesten has focused on presenting musical acts and cultural representations that include diverse ethnic and cultural practices, but with a careful curatorial vision that prefers multicultural inclusion and fusion over nostalgic representations or heavy promotions of Iranian nationalism. This vision reflected an alignment with Swedish interculturalist goals that favored incorporating new cultural forms and innovating new traditions for a popular Iranian holiday in a new location. Even as some community members disagreed with these organizers' vision of "Iranianness," and challenged Eldfesten as inauthentic, or worse, "cultural fraud," adhering to this principle has helped it to receive continued support and a mainstream recognition of Iranians in Sweden.

\* \* \*

Just as the deep financial commitment of ambitious Iranian Americans were required to produce the Freedom Sculpture and Festival, policies promoting multiculturalism or interculturalism alone could not have produced festivals and programs like Eldfesten or Tirgan; they too required determined Iranians, in this case those willing to cooperate with state intermediaries to work, often as volunteers over several months, with and on behalf of their communities. Unlike their LA counterparts, but in line with the systems they have worked within, organizers in Toronto and Stockholm deliberately created opportunities for community members to collaborate as volunteers on a long-term project in which they would experience, practice, and perform teamwork through the values and norms of Canada and Sweden, emphasizing open democratic debate, transparency, and professionalism. According to Ong, "becoming a citizen depends on how one is constituted as a subject who exercises or submits to power relations."[18] While aligning with hegemonic norms certainly suggests submission to power, the examples discussed in this book nevertheless show significant agency and pragmatism in how Iranian diaspora organizers and community members have mobilized cultural strategies of inclusion.

## Economies of Inclusion: The Gift of Culture

In mission statements and donor appeals, Iranian American organizations, whether political, social, or cultural, frequently include phrases like the PAAIA tagline, "Give back to America as it has given to us."[19] Similarly, when the House of Iran in San Diego was donated in October 2003, it was presented "as a gift from the Iranian American community in appreciation of the opportunities that the Iranian American community has found and enjoyed in this beautiful city."[20] Farhang Foundation used similar language to gift the Freedom Sculpture to Los Angeles in 2017.

As an anthropologist interested in the global Iranian diaspora, the repeated invocation of this notion of gift-giving across global locations was especially intriguing. The metaphor of gifts is a well-established practice among immigrant groups in the United States. Dianne Selig has shown how Ellis Island immigrants' "cultural gifts" had been used in early twentieth-century appeals for inclusion, for example through incorporating in US schools lessons about the artistic contributions of Italian Americans or scientific contributions of German Americans to encourage the second-generation children of immigrants.[21] The recognition of these gifts of immigrants, whether cultural and scientific (as in these examples), political (e.g., in civil society, the military, or elected positions), or economic (e.g., as taxpayers, entrepreneurs, consumers, and donors), has been frequently termed in the literature as "national contributions"[22] that, it is presumed, earn immigrants "worthy citizenship."[23]

When these immigrant contributions (of any kind) are framed as gifts, they point to an exchange of obligations. Gifts, according to the classic text from Marcel Mauss, enable ongoing social relations through a series of obligations: to give, to receive, and to reciprocate.[24] These exchanges of "obligatory gifts" ensure the ongoing social relations between parties and, in theory, enhance solidarity.[25] In Maussian terms, then, immigrant declarations of "giving back" through their gifts to cities, states, and nations amount to a reciprocation, momentarily balancing the scales of obligation and building feelings of solidarity, which further obligates the societies that receive them to also reciprocate with greater inclusion and ongoing social relations.

Immigrants embarking on cultural examples of contributionism enter this economy of exchange as one among numerous strategies of inclusion in their societies. For example, having witnessed the contributionist strategies of immigrants who arrived to the United States before them, Iranian Americans have followed suit in putting forward public arguments for inclusion through evidence of their achievements and "economic Americanness."[26] This focus on wealth and status is especially common among Iranian American organizations, especially in seeking the support of politicians. For example, when called upon to testify before a Los Angeles City Council hearing regarding the harmful and discriminatory impact of the Muslim Ban on the Iranian community, David had delivered a passionate speech: "If anybody is looking for proof that immigration is good for America, they need look no further than [the Iranian American] community. Leaders at Apple, Google, Uber, Twitter, Expedia, eBay; acclaimed professors at our most acclaimed universities. Job creators, leaders of business. . . . This is the true face of immigration."[27]

The belief in and commitment to this approach is evident in the Iranian Americans' Contributions Project (IACP) and its sister organization, the Iranian Canadians' Contributions Project (ICCP). Established in 2016 amid heightened anti-immigrant political rhetoric, IACP's mission seeks "to document and highlight the professional achievements and the contributions of Iranian Americans to the United States and, by extension, to the world," especially through a "focus on the professions, the arts, and the world of business and entrepreneurship."[28] Presenting data-mined national counts of doctors, lawyers, patents, and professors along with over two thousand profiles of Iranian Americans, the IACP website explains their goal as "to better inform our fellow citizens and put a human face to the Iranian American diaspora community."[29] Much like other organizers quoted in this book, the founder of this organization—himself a Silicon Valley executive—was driven by a desire to counter negative stereotypes and discrimination and, in his words, "to build a shield . . . a protective mechanism to say, 'Here is what we've done.'"[30] This shield of elite status and upper-class achievements, he seemed to reason, would be stronger than formal citizenship alone: "If we don't know the contributions of Iranian Americans, how can we expect the American public to know? If the public is not with us, why would policymakers want to stick up for us?" In these examples, politicians and policymakers have been envisioned as brokers of rights who could be swayed by Iranians' contributions of wealth and status, which were seen as the more accurate markers of "the true face," (or, tellingly, "a human face") of Iranian Americans and Iranian Canadians.

The presentation of immigrant gifts by Iranians in cultural terms has become a recurring strategy of inclusion across the diaspora, revealing a belief that Iranian culture could serve as that shield against discrimination, as well as a bridge between immigrants and mainstream society and a glue that could tie together a fragmented diaspora. In the United States, the Cyrus Cylinder tour in 2013 had put forward the argument that ancient Iranians already had contributed foundational American concepts like multiculturalism, diversity, and human rights. Meanwhile, in Canada, the 2017 artistic statement of the Tirgan Festival insisted that "the Tirgan biennial showcases the contribution of Iranians to Canadian culture."[31]

Though over a decade apart and completely unrelated to one another, in both Sweden and the United States, Iranian community members took this approach to culture when they established nonprofit arts and culture organizations named Farhang ("culture" in Persian). Despite having quite different ethos and modes of working, representatives of both organizations have described their projects through the metaphor of cultural gifts presented to the host societies in which they live. The marketing of the Freedom Sculpture and Freedom Festival by LA's Farhang Foundation repeated this frequently, as the organization's vice chair at the time explained to a reporter: The Freedom Sculpture "is a precious gift from our community to the most diverse city in the U.S. as a permanent reminder of the ideas of liberty, tolerance and multiculturalism which was espoused by Cyrus the Great over 2500 years ago. The same ideas that were later adopted by the Founding Fathers of the United States and enshrined in our Constitution."[32] In Stockholm, Rostam, the founder of Farhang Förening (a partner organization of the Eldfesten Committee), also had articulated to me in an interview his vision of Eldfesten as a cultural gift to Sweden:

Eldfesten takes an inspiration from Iranian culture but we put it on in Sweden, and we want it to be for everyone, not just for [Iranians]—*it's a gift from us*.... And that's why we've said it is for the public. And when we say it is public . . . it's not only that our public should be mixed, but that on the stage, too, we should create the possibilities for mixing! For example to bring a big Swedish artist to this program, . . . [then they'd] say, "I participated in an old traditional Iranian event!" and take good memories from that and *develop some credit for us*.³³

On its face, Rostam's framing of Eldfesten as a gift to the host society that can "develop some credit" for the immigrant community is in line with the general philosophy behind contributionism and Farhang Foundation's use of it. In both Eldfesten and the Freedom Festival, organizers recognized the exchange value of Iranian culture and the "credit" each sought: inclusion for Iranians, especially during politically challenging times for immigrants. These literal "immigrant gifts"—of a sculpture, festivals, and adherence to shared values—were framed as being given as a symbol of contributions offered as gratitude to the societies that have nurtured them but also as a symbol of the reciprocations made by Iranians to these societies.³⁴

But despite these outwardly similar approaches, there are important distinctions between these two organizations and their gifts that are also emblematic of the differences between US and Swedish societies and their expectations of immigrant assimilation and inclusion. Farhang Förening in Stockholm was founded by artists, receives most of its funding from the Swedish state, and thus must work within the structures and regulations required to receive grants and satisfy expectations of a professional Swedish cultural organization. Farhang Foundation in Southern California, on the other hand, was founded by wealthy elites with a deep affinity for Iranian culture who, as trustees, have been responsible for ensuring its sustainability. Key differences, then, lie in a) to whom these organizations are accountable and b) the receiving steps of Mauss's series of exchanges (e.g., to accept a gift).

In public statements extolling the virtues of "giving back," the details of the initial gift are almost always unstated and either presumed or glossed over with platitudes or generalities (e.g., "a gesture of gratitude"; "as it has given to us"). Just as the culturally and socially constructed specifics of gift exchange (e.g., the expectations of when and how to reciprocate a gift) vary cross-culturally, so too do approaches undertaken by Iranians in diaspora seeking to offer cultural gifts as reciprocation for sometimes quite different "initial gifts."[35] In return for America's acceptance of the arrival of Iranians, Iranian Americans reciprocated not only through contributions to American ideals and gifts such as public art, but also through the economic gifts of campaign donations, corporate contracts, and entrepreneurial job creation. Following Mauss, such an exchange entails ongoing obligations indefinitely, solidifying a social relationship in the form of inclusion in American society.

As with other types of giving, if a reciprocation is not in line with expectations, it may not be accepted. It was noted to me twice in separate interviews that the City of Los Angeles is offered gifts of public art frequently, but rarely accepts them. Because those gifts come with costly obligations—for example, to store and maintain them—the City often declines. Even more rare are agreements to install public art gifts on City property. The Farhang Foundation managed to secure the acceptance of the Freedom Sculpture and its placement in a major thoroughfare thanks to the accumulated social capital of Iranian leaders, including employees in city government and businessmen who had donated regularly to city campaigns, held fundraisers for non-Iranian political candidates, organized voting drives in the community, and participated at City Hall events and hearings. All these efforts built *and built on* social capital—a powerful form of credit—that created not only the possibilities for the gift of the Freedom Sculpture to be gifted, but also an obligation for the City to receive it, and thus also to reciprocate once again. While Farhang Förening sought to build credit for the community through Eldfesten, the Farhang Foundation's Freedom Sculpture was a strategy of inclusion that relied as much, if not more, on already accumulated credit in order to also develop future credit.

To be sure, the powerful tools of social and cultural capital also enabled Farhang Förening to partner with Riksteatern to produce Eldfesten. But rather than put forward Iranians' contributions to the Swedish economy (which others have done) or Iranians' ancient contributions to strongly held principles like human rights and tolerance (as was done in the United States), Rostam and his partners in Eldfesten suggested that their community's gift was their cultural work and everyday forms of cultural citizenship. As Rostam put it: "We immigrants, both from our activities [in society] with the everyday things that everyone does, and from our positive cultural things, we can help this society. And we have!"[36] While acknowledging the importance of adhering to state multiculturalism and its goals, this list stands in telling contrast to the ways Los Angeles Iranians framed their ancient history and contemporary economic contributions to the United States as exceptional grounds for belonging.

Framed as "giving back" in both Los Angeles and Stockholm, Iranian cultural gifts can ensure ongoing social relations that, over time, may create inclusion. But not all community members felt that inclusion was worth the exchange. In the case of the $2.6 million USD Freedom Sculpture and Festival, many were left wondering if the coffers of the community's elite could have been put toward other, more pressing, needs. Nevertheless, few Iranian Angelenos publicly objected to the *strategy* of presenting Cyrus the Great as the originator of human rights nor the representation of his values as an inspirational ancient gift from Iranians to the US Founding Fathers. Even among those who did question it, they nevertheless seemed to implicitly understand the exchange value of this narrative of ancient history in the market of contemporary American society.

But in Sweden, Eldfesten's organizers and critics each saw the exchange value of Iranian culture in Sweden differently. Critics balked at the cost of the professionally produced 2012 Eldfesten, comparing its budget—published online by the organizing committee in line with Swedish ideals of transparency—to that of the community-organized Chaharshanbeh Suri event held annually at a soccer field in the suburbs, and they argued (without evidence) that the former's budget was artificially inflated. Competing cultural producers leveled accusations that implied (and in some cases directly claimed) that Eldfesten's organizers had pocketed taxpayer funds in exchange for "selling out" an authentic vision of Iranian culture. Eldfesten's organizers had strategically presented an intercultural event that has been both popular and recognized by Iranian and non-Iranian Swedes, but it was described by community critics as a betrayal and distortion of Iranian culture in exchange for Swedish inclusion—an exchange they were unwilling to make.

Despite these differences in approach and reception, in both cases, the metaphor of gifts deployed by each stemmed from the hegemonic ideas and narratives about immigrant integration, inclusion, and "good" citizenship in each country. In other words, though quite different from one another, each cultural gift was in line with the expectations and hegemonic forms in their society. Similarly, the exchange and reciprocation of inclusion was understood in both contexts to be processual—a greater acceptance over time—but also conditional, for example dependent on the "professional" behavior of the gift-givers who obligated them and, of course, on the shifting winds of politics for the receiving societies obligated to receive and reciprocate.[37] The "gifts" of Iranian culture through these public events were thus viewed by both organizations as a way to obligate their Swedish and American societies, respectively, to recognize Iranians as a community who can organize, collaborate, and work well together, and thus a community worthy of inclusion.

### Tripping Up and Tripping Over the Lines of Belonging

Strategies of inclusion seek to navigate hegemonic forms through a complex set of negotiations between agency and submission in often messy ways. Concluding her article on cultural citizenship with a reflection on her personal ambivalence about becoming a US citizen and thus an "Asian American," Ong described navigating multiple and overlapping tripwires of inclusion and exclusion within the American scheme of belonging: "One learns to be fast-footed," she wrote, "occasionally glancing over one's shoulder to avoid tripping over—while tripping up—those lines."[38]

Not all immigrants seek to challenge, or trip up, lines of inclusion and exclusion, and indeed, some seek instead to reproduce them and to constrain resistance. But, as Ong suggested, those who do work to "trip up" must simultaneously be careful not to "trip *over*" these lines: Different vectors of power and lines of belonging in these global locations necessitate different strategies. This is especially the case when troubling those boundaries of inclusion and exclusion may (intentionally or otherwise) reproduce some lines of exclusion in order to trip up others. Among many such lines, I focus on the ways cultural approaches in the three cases examined in this book have navigated overlapping "tripwires" of class, race, and religion as they intersect with each other and with hegemonic ideologies in diasporic webs of power.

*Navigating the Intersections of Class, Race, and Religion*

In numerous conversations over several years of follow-up research, I was convinced that in all three locations, Iranians working within the organizations discussed in this book deeply believed in the missions of their projects as well as in the ideologies through which they sought to represent Iranian culture and show alignment. But the political and cultural landscapes in each country also have undergone significant changes since the early 2010s. In Sweden, the rise of the Sweden Democrats (SD), especially in the 2020s, has shepherded a rise in xenophobic rhetoric that reasserts a narrow view of Swedish identity, language, and norms that has challenged the inclusion of immigrants like Iranians altogether. Among the key points of the SD platform has been the insistence that not only has multiculturalism led to the deterioration of social cohesion, but that immigrant inclusion and integration should be the sole responsibility of immigrants themselves—an increasingly popular position in Sweden, if already a norm in the United States. There, emphasizing a community's wealth and status and putting that wealth towards political power and conspicuous accumulation is a time-honored strategy.[39] But, as Ong has demonstrated in the case of Hong Kong elite and wealthy Chinese Americans in the United States, wealth, conspicuous consumption, and high status do not necessarily translate into meaningful social and political inclusion, especially for racialized and marginalized citizen subjects. Even though Riksteatern could proclaim in 2017 that Eldfesten "is nowadays a Swedish tradition,"[40] many of the Iranians who produced it and attended it did not enjoy the same privilege of being called Swedish in their everyday lives.

Though not as loudly declared, the contributionist strategies of Iranian Americans have also involved claims related to race and religion. Scholars have long pointed to the relationship between race and class, and research on immigration has shown that socioeconomic status both impacts and is impacted by racial ascriptions. For example, in her study of cultural citizenship, Ong demonstrated the "racializing logic of class attributes" that have been used to "order Asian immigrants along a white-black continuum" in the United States through "discriminatory modes of perception, reception, and treatment."[41] Others have shown how racializing logics in European and Canadian contexts similarly have led to deepening inequalities. As this field of scholarship has illustrated, the association of wealth with whiteness in Western democracies is evident in the ways financial capital, consumption, and class status have been used as arbiters of both inclusion and exclusion for nonwhite immigrants and other minoritized groups.[42]

More specifically, for many immigrants from southwest Asia, north Africa, and south Asia, racialization ("the extension of racial meaning to a previously racially unclassified relationship, social practice, or group"[43]) is coconstructed with not only class but religion, where people perceived to be Muslim may face forms of anti-Muslim racism.[44] In his provocative essay "The European Question," Nicholas de Genova noted that "as a category, 'Muslim' condenses both racial and class derision, encompassing nonwhite 'foreigners' who may not even be Muslims."[45] The impact of these intertwined processes is evident both in the racial ascriptions of Iranians in multicultural societies and in the ways Iranians respond to these ascriptions, in many cases through seeking to align themselves with white mainstreams, whether through class markers or through anti-Arab and anti-Muslim discourses.

Like all categories of identity and belonging, Iranianness is contested, in flux, and subject to inclusions and exclusions asserted through competing claims to authenticity, including competing notions of its relationship with race and religion. What has become a deeply embedded Iranian racial identity rooted in imaginings of the ancient pre-Islamic past as a Golden Age of Persian empire was popularized by Pahlavi elites through the institutionalization of Iranian nationalism in the twentieth century. Historians and philosophers have long analyzed Iranian identity as having been shaped by pre-Islamic, Islamic, and European influences that, over time, have been manipulated by the ruling classes. In Pahlavi nationalist narratives, Iranian lineage—as Aryan—was connected to white European racial identities[46] while pointing to the seventh-century invasion of Arab Muslims as the cause of Iran's subsequent decline. They thus actively sought to diminish the role of Islam in Iranian national identity while emphasizing the connections between pre-Islamic and European influences through imperial nostalgia. The Islamic Republic, in response, has worked to erase European influences in favor of Islamic ones.[47]

In diasporic cultural representations, emphasis on pre-Islamic Iranian history and the exclusion (if not outright denigration) of Islamic influence has become a common strategy for representing Iranian culture and identity to audiences outside Iran, a strategy that is openly framed as a reaction to the IRI. But it is also reflective of a belief in and insistence upon Aryan roots, referred to in the literature as "the Aryan myth," in diaspora societies where whiteness is privileged and where Iranian racialization is ambiguous at best.[48] Therefore, this approach is also tied to lines of racial (non)belonging and the hierarchies and hegemonic ideologies in host societies surrounding race, class, and religion—and especially anti-Muslim racism. In other words, it also has become a strategy of inclusion.

For many of those who choose this strategy, personal negative experiences with extremist forms of Islam have led them (like many Iranians) to shift their personal beliefs and behaviors[49] toward secularism or, more precisely, what Reza Gholami has called "non-Islamiosity."[50] For others, these Iranian-as-Aryan narratives become incorporated into what Ehsan Estiri has called "vernacular conceptualizations of Islam" in the context of negative representations and misrecognition of Shia Islam in diasporic societies.[51] In more extreme versions, understandings of Iranian history and Aryan origins coalesce in an anti-Arab sentiment that is also anti-Muslim. As a result, in diaspora, some of the most extreme Islamophobic rhetoric has been employed not only by far-right politicians in the mainstream, but also by Iranians who may not otherwise consider themselves aligned with far-right political positions.[52] These anti-Islam narratives serve a dual purpose of also separating Iranians from Arabs, and while not always stated explicitly, it is an outlook that is especially prevalent in societies where average citizens do not easily distinguish between Arabs and Persians. Despite (or perhaps due to) the long presence of Arabs in Iran, there may be no faster way to anger an Iranian of this persuasion than to misrecognize him as an Arab.

## IMPERIAL NOSTALGIA, RACIAL HIERARCHIES, AND THE POLITICS OF INCLUSION IN THE UNITED STATES

Informed by these narratives and mythologies to varying degrees, affirming one's own understanding of Iranian identity became a diasporic strategy of reclaiming the dignity of that identity, writ large. But it also has served to bolster Iranians' positions vis-à-vis other immigrant groups. For example, nonwhite racial others in the American racial hierarchy, and especially close neighbors like Arabs, have especially been the target of distancing language and discourses of Persian exceptionalism.[53] Neda Maghbouleh's study highlighted the ways many first-generation Iranian American parents held opinions that Iranians (as Aryans) should be regarded as sitting atop the racial hierarchy as "the original white people."[54] These ideas have also aligned with a shared ideology of anti-Black racism in US society.[55] Aligning with, rather than challenging, white supremacy is not a unique strategy for Iranians; rather, it is another example of the ways Iranian Americans have adhered to rather than undermined hegemonic ideologies and racial tripwires in the United States.[56]

For some, then, presenting Iranian culture in its pre-Islamic, pre-Arab, and most imperial form is an attempt at a tripartite identity claim that sets Iranians apart from the IRI, Islam, and Arabs, while centering a glorified Aryan identity that simultaneously connects to European racial identity and plays into imperialist ideals and Western racial hierarchies. Imperial nostalgia as ancient Persian revivalism in the United States has offered one visible way for Iranian Americans to differentiate themselves at once from the Islamic Republic *and* the Islamophobic and anti-Arab media representations of the post-9/11 era. These narratives intentionally silenced the role of Islam in Iranian culture and identity; in some cases, the same Iranians seeking to protect themselves from Islamophobic violence through these representations have also been those prone to anti-Muslim sentiments.

Self-identifications and external ascriptions of Iranian racial belonging and nonbelonging in diaspora are often in conflict, but they are always deeply contextual and cannot be applied with a broad brush across the diaspora. Perhaps the most studied diasporic claims to white identities is that of first-generation Iranian Americans, many of whom relied on this notion of Aryan identity as they found themselves placed along the Black-white racial hierarchy of the United States in the decades directly following the height of the civil rights movement. In her book *The Limits of Whiteness*, Maghbouleh demonstrated how geopolitical circumstances between Iran and the United States during these decades directly impacted the racialization of Iranian Americans. Despite legal confirmation of whiteness in 1978 through earlier court decisions collectively referred to as racial prerequisite cases, Iranians soon became so demonized in US public media and discourse following the 1979 Revolution that they were "socially browned," a condition Maghbouleh conceptualized as a *racial loophole*: "legally white but socially brown, and on the receiving end of racialized enmity and discrimination."[57]

When the Iranian-as-Aryan racial ideology of many first-generation Iranian Americans were confronted by discrimination, nonwhite racial ascriptions, and "social browning," they were left in a racial paradox. Some resorted to covering strategies, working to satisfy what John Tehranian called an "appetite for whiteness" and its benefits through name changes (e.g., Mohammad to Mike), dying black or brown hair to blonde, or limiting language use in public that would reveal a "disfavored"—minoritized—identity.[58] It is important to note, however, that these strategies were neither desired nor used by all Iranian Americans—nor were they available to all Iranians, for example, Black or Afro-Iranians. But for many Iranians in the United States, a racial construction of Iranian-as-white or "white adjacent" draws on nationalist and racial ideas brought from Iran and mixed with American understandings of whiteness and class, along with anti-Muslim racisms that could be tied to both, creating a cocktail of identity that served as a tool for some first-generation Iranians as they have navigated the US social hierarchy and its white supremacist foundations.

In the case of the Freedom Sculpture and Festival in Los Angeles, and Cyromania more generally, among the characteristics of the Cyrus Cylinder that has been most consistently promoted is its presentation of multiculturalism through innovating practices of religious diversity and tolerance. Indeed, scholars and especially members of the Iranian Jewish community pointed to the cylinder as confirmation of the role of Cyrus the Great as described in the Hebrew Bible. But while the notion of religious diversity and discourses of tolerance attributed to Cyrus were repeated throughout marketing, promotions, and on the stage of the Freedom Festival, there was no direct mention made in these materials or at the festival of the Muslim Ban that had been implemented just months prior and which directly challenged these principles and especially targeted Iranians—regardless of their religious beliefs. Nor was there any effort made to incorporate the diverse array of Iranian religious traditions into the cultural representations and symbols on display on the festival grounds that could have highlighted religious diversity as a feature of a heterogeneous diaspora. Neither have Tirgan nor Eldfesten made such an effort, for that matter. To the contrary, the elements selected for cultural representation in the Iranian diaspora most frequently very intentionally and carefully omit religious displays altogether. Along with "nonpolitical," most Iranian diaspora cultural organizations conscientiously describe themselves as also "non-religious," avoiding an internal tripwire of exclusion for the community.

Purveyors of Cyromania stress the demographic multiculturalism of Cyrus's empire, the tolerance displayed by his cylinder, and the art and architectural importance of related artifacts. This allows Iranians to present culture—ancient or otherwise—as a matter of elite and imperial power duly respected in an age of American empire. American mainstream racial norms and the social expectations of immigrants have together encouraged Iranian diaspora members to selectively highlight and reframe Pahlavi nationalism with the goal of immigrant representation, belonging, and inclusion. In an anti-Islamic present, claiming a "nonreligious" identifier while promoting the pre-Islamic past (and the tolerance of Cyrus the Great) has become a way to shore up a 'safe' Iranian diasporic identity.

## IRANIAN IDENTITY AND (ANTI-)RACISM IN SWEDEN

In contrast to the "social browning" occurring in the United States, the experience of Iranians in Sweden and other parts of northern Europe more closely resemble the "forever foreigner" experiences of Asian Americans, or what Sahar Sadeghi has described as "conditional belonging."[59] Strategies of claiming whiteness may not have been undertaken by all Iranians in the United States, but in Sweden, such a claim was not only never a realistic option, it was also, in the context of hegemonic racial understandings, not seen as the pathway to inclusion many Iranian Americans hoped or perceived it to be. Arriving to a country with a national identity predicated on assumptions of racial and ethnic homogeneity (despite the presence of Indigenous communities and earlier immigrant groups) and amid a rise of neo-Nazi and race-based violence (like the serial murders of dark-haired immigrants by a far-right extremist[60]), Iranians in Sweden in the 1980s and 1990s were never confused whether they would be taken (or "mis-taken") for white as the Swedish mainstream understood it. The racial ambiguities experienced by some Iranian Americans was not shared by Iranians in Sweden.

Furthermore, many (though not all) Iranian refugees arriving to Sweden in this period were leftists whose politics motivated them to fight for equity in solidarity with other ethnic and racial groups who had already arrived or were arriving to Sweden at the same time rather than distancing themselves or claiming a superior position, racially, economically, or otherwise. The Eldfesten Committee included several such individuals, and the debates that ensued in meetings involved first-generation Iranians of this cohort in disputes with newer cohorts, like students who arrived in the late 2000s and early 2010s, and who thus had quite different political orientations and experiences of living in Iran *and* of arriving in Sweden. This earlier cohort specifically identified race as a line of inclusion and exclusion that they sought to trip up through their cultural work. As Tobias Hübinette has argued, inclusion and full belonging of nonwhite Swedes *as Swedish* would require white Swedes to acknowledge white hegemony and their attendant privileges in everyday life—in the cultural industries as much as the subway—something they have been slow and, in the case of SD leaders, loathe to do. These privileges are a key source of the decidedly unequal experiences of Swedish citizenship that contribute to nonbelonging that these earlier cohorts personally experienced.

In these micro-level debates around the festival planning table, Iranians of differing viewpoints deliberated about the inclusion of Arab music and belly dance on stage. For some, their presence served as a reinforcement of multicultural inclusion and as a direct refusal of anti-Arab racism. For others, it amounted to cultural betrayal and the deterioration of the event's "Iranianness." Furthermore, the inclusion of ethnic minorities and multiple languages and cultural traditions on Eldfesten's stages was framed in Committee meetings through ideals of anti-racism as a deliberate response to anti-Arab racism within the community, but also to increasing anti-immigrant discourses in the Swedish mainstream. Though these debates had emerged through perceptions of anti-Arab racism as an internal Iranian community issue, earlier cohort immigrant leaders cited Swedish anti-racism and Swedish icons like

Olaf Palme for recourse in their effort to convince newer immigrants of their position. For these Iranians, tripping up racial lines of exclusion within Iranian communities was as essential as tripping them up in Swedish society.

## MULTICULTURAL CITIZENSHIP AND IRANIAN IDENTITY IN CANADA

In Canada, the country's history of settler colonialism and immigration may appear similar to the United States', but there are key differences in both scale and approach that are related to racialization processes. As Irene Bloemraad has shown, where a history of racial slavery in the United States has led to race becoming a master status that continues to proscribe inclusion and exclusion in US identity, Canada's history led to a somewhat different racial landscape.[61] Racial slavery is also part of Canadian history, if on a smaller scale compared to the United States, but in the context of competition between British and French colonial descendants to assert power in Canada, the First Nations and growing immigrant populations presented an opportunity for British descendants to resist a French Québécois insistence on equal footing through biculturalism.[62] The result was a Canadian version of official multiculturalism that has formed the core of national identity for the entire population, rather than the primary reliance on racial hierarchy. Racism and white supremacy continue to lead to inequalities in Canada, as it does in the United States and elsewhere,[63] but in comparison to the US—where citizenship as belonging is, as Bloemraad described, "race-based"—for Canadians, race forms one of many lines of belonging and nonbelonging. Multicultural citizenship, in theory, offers an alternative narrative for the nation and for rendering inclusion.[64]

For Iranians in Canada, seeking proximity to whiteness may be one of many strategies of inclusion, but the ethos and sets of norms promoted through symbolic inclusion by the Canadian state creates an opening for other elements of Iranian culture and identity (a large range of which is seen at Tirgan events) to be promoted, rather than to resort only or primarily to ancient history (and through it, Aryanism) for access to inclusion. There are a number of possible explanations for this that involve both Canadian society and the migration history of Iranians to Canada. The largest waves of Iranian migration to Canada arrived in the first decades of the twenty-first century, rather than in the 1980s or 1990s, as young, well-educated, middle- and upper-class professionals or students who attended grade school in the 1990s and 2000s Islamic Republic, not in prerevolutionary Pahlavi Iran. They therefore have brought with them (and in many cases reproduced in Toronto) the ideas and norms of that more recent period. Because many continue to travel to Iran, or remain in close contact with parents, siblings, and friends through digital and social media, they also have a relatively more flexible and continuing relationship with Iran. This is not to suggest that Aryanism and other Pahlavi nationalist ideas are absent in present-day Iran or Canada; these ideas remain a cornerstone of nationalist discourses among Iranians, wherever they may reside. Further, Iranian Canadians do not ignore race, religion, or ancient history, nor is it hard to find symbolisms of these in the visual landscape of Toronto. However, in a milieu of demographic superdiversity and symbolic inclusion of immigrants, imperial nostalgia and its racial claims have not become the primary nor the most common representations of Iranian Canadians in seeking inclusion.

Moreover, while Iranians in Toronto were compelled to organize public cultural events in the face of racialization experiences and negative representations of Iranians in the news just like Iranians in the United States and elsewhere, they could do so by making use of Canadian multiculturalism policies and, through them, the discourses that encouraged communities to be proud of their culture in whatever forms they chose. In 2000s and 2010s Toronto, this meant Iranians put forward numerous displays of Iranian culture and traditions, but without forefronting Aryanism or going to great lengths to convince Canadians that Cyrus the Great and his ancient Iranian values were the source of Canadian democracy—even if they were shared. Furthermore, as in Sweden, contemporary, experimental, and hybrid forms of Iranian culture were encouraged by state institutions through Canadian multiculturalism policy. But because Tirgan was not a holiday celebrated by most Iranians prior to this Canadian reinvention, it did not face the same kind of accusations surrounding authenticity or cultural manipulation that its Swedish counterparts did with Eldfesten. Instead, the success of Tirgan has led to a proliferation in diaspora of other Tirgan festivals (e.g., in the United States, Sweden, and France), and even in Iran itself. The early organizers of Tirgan could therefore more freely and effectively build their community's symbolic and instrumental inclusion in Canada by putting forward more contemporary views of Iranian culture and its roots, rather than primarily emphasizing nostalgic visions of ancient empire with its linked ideas of race and religion.

\* \* \*

Through comparison, it becomes evident that while Iranians in multiple parts of the diaspora may feel the effects of discrimination and the need to rehabilitate Iranian dignity through representations of culture, there is not one generalized experience of these forms of exclusion nor one generalized response to them. Across the Iranian diaspora, strategies of inclusion are shaped not only by state policies but also by the expectations, resources, and ideologies within each society. Whether through elite philanthropy in Los Angeles, state-supported cultural programming in Stockholm, or multicultural institutional partnerships in Toronto, Iranian communities have navigated their belonging within dominant power structures, often seeking alignment. While discourses of contributionism and cultural gifts may be present across diasporic locations, the ways that these have manifested complicates assumptions that contributionism is a neutral strategy for inclusion. Their different strategies demonstrate how diasporic identity is never fixed but continuously negotiated through social, political, economic, and cultural forces. Different racial ascriptions and hierarchies, class structures, and religious identities frame these experiences and thus also frame the cultural strategies of inclusion each community has undertaken.

Nevertheless, across all three locations, and indeed across the diaspora, Iranians have understood that positioning themselves closely to the norms and ideologies prevailing within hegemonic webs of power in their diasporic homes will enable them to publicly represent their understandings of "Iranianness," contested as it may be. At the same time, these strategies reveal not just how Iranian identity is shaped by dominant structures, but also how Iranians actively navigate, contest, and repurpose those structures to stake their claims to belonging on their own terms. As we have seen, these strategies for building inclusion rely on multiple scales, whether in local experiences of belonging within the community (e.g., the Tirgan family), experiences of belonging within different national multicultural societies (e.g., American, Swedish, Canadian), or experiences of belonging that connect Iranians to one another, both across the diaspora and in Iran.

# Conclusion

*Belonging, Like Homes, Must Be Built*

On an overcast November morning, my father and I drove to the Atlantic Station mixed-use development in downtown Atlanta, less than a mile from the campus of Georgia Tech, his alma mater. The area that was once the contaminated site of the Atlantic Steel mill—an off-limits area for most of his life—is now the site of an open-air mall and a spate of apartment and condo complexes. Somewhat improbably, on the way to the large Ikea or Target stores, visitors are greeted by an enormous mimic of the Arc de Triomphe, known as the Millennium Gate. Various flags have been raised in its archway since the monument appeared in 2008, but that morning in 2023, as my father and I drove past, for the first time a giant *shir-o-khorshid* (Lion and Sun) waved in the breeze.

The Lion and Sun is not the official flag of the Islamic Republic of Iran (IRI), a fact that has contributed to its becoming predominant in the US diaspora and especially among opposition groups during and after the Woman, Life, Freedom protests of 2022–23. This was the context of its enormous display that morning in downtown Atlanta, where the flag had formed a colorful backdrop for the unveiling of a statue: a nine-meter tall bronze monumental sculpture of Cyrus the Great, located in the park just behind the Millennium Gate. Presiding over a small lake, the larger-than-life Cyrus was depicted in a triumphant pose, holding a tall staff in his left hand and gazing upwards towards a replica of his Cylinder, which he held aloft in his right (fig. c.1). As we walked the grounds, I took note of Cyrus's smaller neighbors in the privately owned oval: To his left stood a 2022 monument to Hungary's "heroes of 1956 who fought valiantly against Soviet tyranny and communism," sponsored by a Hungarian-American coalition; to his right, a 2021 sculpture of José Martí sponsored by Georgia's Cuban-American community. While contributing to an evident theme of immigrants celebrating

Figure c.1. A nine-meter-tall bronze sculpture depicting Cyrus the Great in downtown Atlanta, Georgia. Left: in November 2023, when a large *shir-o-khorshid* flag hung from the monumental arch. Right: in October 2024, reinstalled after a storm collapsed the original in April 2024. (Credit: Amy Malek, 2023, 2024)

liberal notions of freedom and human rights in this park owned by the nonprofit National Monuments Foundation, unlike its neighbors, the sculpture of Cyrus did not yet have a plaque to inform passers-by of his history, nor of its benefactors.

The sculpture's ceremonious unveiling on October 29, 2023, had been rushed to coincide with Cyrus the Great Day. There, the former crown prince of the Pahlavi monarchy, Reza Pahlavi, gave a speech citing his father's famous statements about Cyrus the Great and thanking the Atlanta-based venture philanthropist who had sponsored this monumental sculpture. He also thanked the National Monuments Foundation, whom he celebrated for enabling the statue's placement in "their home": "The Poet says, 'This home is beautiful, but it is not my home.' For us Iranians forced to live our lives in exile, that quote has rung all too true for more than four decades as we have sought temporary refuge with those kind enough to grant it. But today, . . . we Iranians have a small piece of home here in Atlanta. Thanks to you all, this beautiful home may not be ours, but we are proud to have a bit of our home in it."[1] Here, Pahlavi described Cyrus the Great not just as a forebear but, in sculptural form, as "a small piece of home" in Atlanta, which was "not ours" but someone else's home. It was a poetic speech delivered by a would-be ruler in exile in a particularly symbolic moment in his aspirational political career. But for many of the over thirteen thousand Iranian Americans in Georgia, like my family, Atlanta *is* home. My father has nostalgic memories of the Iran he left as a teenager and that he still calls "back home," but it has been in Atlanta where he was educated, had a career, and built a family. In Atlanta, he has felt at turns othered and tolerated but also, undeniably, at home.

The sculpture's unveiling and Pahlavi's words reflected a familiar tension in the Iranian diaspora—between an identity tied lovingly and nostalgically to Iran and the desire to inscribe permanence and belonging in new homes. In her study of the children of Asian American immigrant entrepreneurs, sociologist Lisa Sun-Hee Park described the act of migrating, adjusting, building a career, and raising children as "investments or down payments towards the purchase of a new 'home'; that is, belonging/acceptance in a new country."[2] Although exiled politicians might resist the insistence that Iranians can maintain a love for "back home" while also being settled in their new homes, for many others, they, their children, and their children's children are now firmly settled in North America, Europe, and beyond. Iranians have worked hard to build a sense of belonging in these diasporic homes, and although they are deeply invested (emotionally and otherwise) in Iran's future, it is unlikely any changes that may take place there would lead to return migration for many of these families.

In my conversation with David that began the previous chapter, he described the contributions of Iranian Americans and the obligations of immigrants to become "part and parcel" in their societies. Despite imagining itself as a "nation of immigrants,"[3] the United States lacks a federal policy supporting their incorporation, leaving this responsibility to immigrants alone, who quickly learn that the social expectations of their new society actually require a separation of their cultural lives: "American in public, ethnic at home."[4] Inherent to this notion is that certain cultural and linguistic practices, glossed as "ethnic" and thus "foreign," should only appear in public once sufficiently melted (read: accepted) into the "stew" of American identity. To belong then, is to have your cultural identity and practices accepted *publicly*, as American. Thus, as this book has shown, marking a physical impression on the city, whether through monumental statues, public art, street parades and festivals, or named enclaves, has been a common strategy for inclusion for immigrant communities in the United States. As one of my LA interlocutors had put it, "This is home; so if it's home, you put a mark on it!"

This strategy has been taken up in earnest by Iranians across the diaspora in the first two decades of the twenty-first century. These efforts have asserted not only a presence but a permanence, and their publicness is as important as their everydayness: The four-day festival attracting 150,000 attendees or the installation of a larger than life Iranian landmark that each required substantial resources and planning eventually blends into the landscape of multicultural cities, becoming one of many cultural festivals on the summer calendar or one of many sculptures in a garden of immigrant cultural representations. But inclusion in these cities and gardens is the point. The continued investment in and value placed on public representations by community members stands as evidence of both the ongoing need for them and a common belief in their power. Though they may not play obvious roles in building avenues for equitable housing or ensuring fairness in employment, the work that these efforts do in building symbolic and social capital and thereby shaping inclusion and belonging is significant and can, in theory, then contribute to other community goals.

In our conversation, David elaborated on the importance of a home-making that takes many forms—economic, cultural, social, political—but that is ultimately focused on building inclusion and belonging and especially political empowerment:

> My children were born here, and my parents are buried here. I have no other home. This is my home. And, if it's going to be my home, that entails a number of things, right? First of all, I expect my home to accept me. I expect my home to open her arms to me just as she would to any other resident of this city. But I also owe something to my home. And,

it isn't just to become wealthy in my home. It is also to employ people in my home. It's also to be a positive influence in my home. But in order to truly do that, I've got to become politically involved. . . . And that kind of political involvement in turn also leads to a feeling of empowerment for the community, and a feeling of belonging and a feeling of pride. And it also means that generations such as yours [e.g., the second generation] will be able to say . . . "I am an Iranian American," and not consider that to be a title that is going to be stigmatized or discriminated against.

\* \* \*

In Iranian diaspora communities, experiences of exclusion, misrecognition, and nonbelonging have motivated a flurry of cultural organizing in the twenty-first century. These exclusions are not just about emotional turmoil. They have had negative tangible outcomes as well, including employment discrimination, targeted bans on migration, and both threats and acts of anti-Iranian violence. These experiences have led Iranians to collaborate to present what they see as the "real" Iran, or the "true face" of Iranians, to their neighbors, colleagues, and friends in their diasporic homes. Iranians in multiple countries have articulated to me their work toward accurate representations of Iranian culture as attempts to restore dignity, maintain cultural heritage for the second generation, and assert their belonging in multicultural societies.

Everyday practices like struggles over representation are part of the "ideological work of citizen-making" in the United States and in Western democracies more generally.[5] Building cultural citizenship, in particular, is the aim of much of the arts and culture organizing that has proliferated in the Iranian diaspora. The multiscalar analysis in this book has shown the relationship between multiculturalism and increasing neoliberal disinvestment and the resulting strategies employed by immigrants in doing this ideological work: Iranians are navigating webs of power within social structures through developing and mobilizing assets that facilitate access to social mobility and inclusion, including financial but also social, cultural, and symbolic forms of capital.

Immigrant communities use festivals, exhibitions, and public art to build cultural citizenship, creating and shaping inclusion within society. These efforts require navigating hegemonic norms and aligning with institutional frameworks that structure belonging. While Iranians across different contexts may draw on similar cultural repertoires (though they do not always do so), their strategies reflect the influence of the governments (national, state/provincial, and municipal), civil society institutions, and social and cultural relations through which they operate. The impact of local policies and attitudes is significant: In Canada and Sweden, state-sponsored multiculturalism has encouraged cultural productions that emphasize diversity and democratic engagement while presenting new and emerging art forms. In contrast, the US model of unofficial neoliberal multiculturalism has pushed Iranian diasporic organizing to rely on private funding, contributionist narratives, and imperial nostalgia as primary strategies for representation. Differences in migration flows, state policies, lived experiences, and social contexts shape strategies of inclusion within nation-states, but also across them—transforming Iranian diaspora identity itself. Local histories of race and class, as well as their intersections with religion and geopolitical relations with the Islamic Republic, continue to influence Iranian diasporic identity formation.

These broader forces of identity formation also reflect and contribute to the cultural and political commitments of Iranian diaspora organizers, who engage in cultural work not only as an assertion of belonging but as a vehicle for political participation. For so many Iranian cultural workers in the diaspora, artistic and community organizing is deeply tied to their connection to Iran, including a deep interest in shaping Iran's future. Politics—local, diasporic, and global—looms over the entire diaspora, fueling both misrecognition and the organizing efforts that seek to counter it. Many of the cultural organizers I came to know therefore viewed their cultural work as inherently political, creating spaces where Iranians could practice democratic engagement in everyday life—what Irene Bloemraad[6] described as "schools" for democratic participation. For example, in Stockholm, Eldfesten organizers saw cultural organizing as opportunities for Iranians to rehearse the skills of democratic life that were absent "back home" and yet critical not only to a successful life in their Swedish homes but to a future they envisioned for Iran. Similarly, the organizers of Tirgan sought to balance these kinds of opportunities while maintaining an inclusive, nonpartisan stance. Yet its 2022-23 pivot to greater political engagement illustrates how Iranian cultural institutions in diaspora can mobilize accumulated social and symbolic capital for both local and transnational purposes.

Representing Iranian culture in the diaspora not only generates competing interpretations of Iranianness but also shapes different modes of belonging, at times reinforcing dominant power structures and at other times subverting them. Across immigrant communities—including among Iranians—questions of cultural ownership, authenticity, and representation remain central: Who defines Iranian culture? Who gets to represent it, and on what terms? Do these representations challenge or reinforce existing hierarchies?[7] At their core, these debates are about power—who holds it, who can access it, and how it operates across a global diaspora. By examining these contestations in relation to migration patterns, cultural policies, and social structures, this book has shown that Iranian identity is negotiated well beyond nation-state borders, revealing fractures in what it means to be "of" or "from" a homeland.

* * *

The efforts of Iranian diaspora organizers have significantly reshaped public representations of Iran, Iranians, and Iranianness since the 2000s. Yet while the diversity of representations has widened, gaps persist, and the perceptions of misrecognition reliably resurface during moments of crisis—whether in response to policies curtailing the rights of Iranians in Western societies, such as during the 2017 US Muslim Ban; during tragedies like Flight 752 in 2020, or through repeated threats of war in Iran, as in 2020 and 2024. In these moments, diasporic Iranians return to culture, again and again, reasserting and reinforcing their enduring faith in its power.

The 2022–23 Woman, Life, Freedom protests underscored the continued role of arts and culture and the significance of these accumulated social and institutional networks. Organizations like Farhang Foundation, Tirgan, and Riksteatern (through Eldfesten) had long provided platforms for Iranian artists, but the political and social turmoil of this period raised critical questions: Should these platforms and forms of social and symbolic capital be used to respond to new demands? In a period marked by both hope and fear, Iranian transnational solidarities revealed not only the potential of cultural organizing and representation but also its limitations in navigating political crises.

If in this book we have seen that the modes of belonging that upheld hegemonic forms were most likely to prevail, it does not follow that cultural work merely reinforces hegemonic structures, leaving no way out of dominant power structures. Nor that cultural work is not also a way to transform those structures. Representation, rather than passively replicating dominant norms, has the potential to generate new, non-normative modes of belonging that subvert—or trip up—intersecting "tripwires" like racial, religious, and class-based lines of exclusion. Contestations—whether over a Chaharshanbeh Suri celebration or a cultural organization's political neutrality—are occasions for Iranians in diaspora to practice different ways of relating to each other and to reimagine their relationship to larger power structures. They thus have the potential to transform the very meaning of belonging itself. These contestations, in many ways inherent to diasporic life, have inspired 1.5- and second-generation Iranian diaspora members to carve out alternative pathways, confront new challenges, and engage with culture in novel ways. As new cohorts continue to emigrate and second and third generations come of age, evolving strategies and modes of belonging present opportunities to resist the reproduction of lines of exclusion in multicultural societies.

These interventions have taken place both in public settings and in private conversations with first-generation parents, aunts, uncles, and grandparents that challenge inherited biases, especially learned racism and classism promoted as nationalism. In the United States, Iranian activists, artists, and scholars have turned attention to anti-Black racism within their Iranian American communities, whether in theaters,[8] faith communities,[9] community centers,[10] language schools,[11] or their own families.[12] In Sweden, where some have framed community-level socioeconomic success as evidence of superiority that sets Iranians apart, others have resisted pitting immigrant groups against each other, seeking instead to build belonging through solidarities with other immigrants in the public sphere. Much of this work has unfolded through art. Whether in Farnaz Arbabi's or Nasim Aghili's critical theater interventions,[13] Bahar Pars's biting short films exposing everyday Swedish microaggressions,[14] Parastou Backman's innovative and inclusive design practice,[15] or Athena Farrokhzad's searing poetry,[16] 1.5-generation Iranian Swedes have been addressing the experiences not only of Iranians but of minoritized immigrants and refugees in Sweden more broadly. Rather than reinforcing discourses of Swedish anti-racism that have failed to acknowledge systemic forms of racism or anti-Blackness, they seek to confront the colonial and racial underpinnings of that discourse while building spaces and possibilities for a more inclusive understanding of Swedish identity. Actor and playwright Shima Niavarani articulated this as a personal goal in 2014:

> Since I set foot in the public space 10 years ago, or rather forcibly created space for myself, I have devoted myself to making my social role more complex than what has otherwise been attributed to me. . . . It is something that I have made my mission: to both visibly and invisibly prepare space for people who are marginalized based on a contemporary approach in the media and cultural sphere to be able to ascribe their own characteristics to themselves. To . . . be able to become more than just a mannequin for one's gender, origin and sexual orientation.[17]

## Future Directions in Iranian Diaspora Studies

As a student in search of another kind of home—an academic one—in the 2000s, I gravitated toward the relatively few publications about the Iranian diaspora and toward their authors who were charting out a still new but promising path. Twenty years later, the now-established subfield of Iranian diaspora studies seeks to study the diaspora as a global one, with transnational dimensions and local particularities that benefit from innovative and comparative methodologies. Whether driven by Iran's political, social, and economic instability or the growth of second and third generations, the Iranian diaspora continues to expand in new and sometimes unexpected ways. These shifting dynamics demand continued adaptation and expansion of research agendas and methodological approaches in Iranian diaspora studies.

This book contributes to that effort by offering a comparative study of three major Global North locations with large Iranian diaspora populations. By examining immigrant belonging through the lenses of cultural citizenship and cultural production, I have highlighted the role of multiculturalism—its presence, absence, or contested nature—as a key variable in shaping strategies of inclusion. Given the ongoing migration of Iranians to Global North locations, despite ongoing challenges to their mobility, this geographical focus is warranted. But emerging scholarship in global South locations of the diaspora demonstrates that South-South flows are not only understudied but may complicate this comparative view in important ways. Similarly, comparison between Iranian and non-Iranian diaspora communities remain surprisingly underexplored, despite their potential to illuminate broader patterns of migration, identity formation, and cultural adaptation.

While multiculturalism in these Global North locations presented an important comparative framework that lent itself to a focus in the final chapter on the tripwires of race, class, and religion, a framework of diversity itself could present a compelling line of investigation: How does the ethno-linguistic and religious diversity within Iran and the diaspora impact the questions of belonging addressed in this book, both within diasporic communities and across them? How do gender and sexuality complicate and "trip" these lines of belonging and exclusion, especially when intersected with racialization and religion? Legal status clearly impacts the ability to access cultural citizenship; how do "failed" asylum seekers, undocumented Iranians, and dual or multiple citizenship holders experience and navigate exclusion, forming yet another set of exclusionary lines in diasporic belonging? Many of these areas have surfaced in this book, but demand a focus in their own extended, related, and comparative analyses.

My methodological approach sought to capture a broad range of perspectives from those engaged in Iranian diaspora cultural production rather than focusing on a strictly representative sample. The most striking imbalance in the resulting participants had to do with gender: While Iranian women have played pivotal roles in community organizing, activism, art, and leadership, first-generation Iranian men disproportionately occupied formal positions of power in the institutions studied. I met many passionate people of a variety of gender identities who sought to represent Iranian art and culture, and I met many women who served in leadership roles in their professional careers, in their private lives, and in women's organizations. But despite observing and collaborating with dozens of women volunteers heavily engaged in the hard work of pulling off these community events, it nevertheless was evident that first-generation Iranian men more often filled boards, held leadership positions, and were ultimately in charge of the cultural organizations and large events under study. This was the case despite all the ink that has been spilled analyzing the ways women have been positioned as the bearers of culture, and especially in contemporary forms of nationalism.[18]

Gendered hierarchies clearly persist in diasporic cultural organizations. Given that these organizations are formed in communities with near parity in terms of gender composition (measured by most national censuses as men and women), this observation deserves further research. Scholarship on gender and sexuality has formed an important dimension of Iranian diaspora studies, addressing shifts in family dynamics, impacts of migration on interpersonal relationships, gendered experiences of exile and trauma, the relationship between sexualities and social exclusions, and the growth of transnational feminism and activism by—and for—Iranian women, both online and offline.[19] Given the fundamental role that gender plays in Iranian diasporic practices, and especially given that women and women's rights have been at the forefront of diasporic activism, an urgent area of further research lies in the continued reproduction of gender hierarchies in diaspora, even among those who denounce them in Iran.

While immigrant generations and cohorts have been prominent in each of the case studies in this book, it remains to be examined how the third generation will experience what sociologists have observed as the clearest moment to measure cultural and language "loss." These concerns motivated many of my first-generation interlocutors who sought to not only contest misrecognition and misrepresentation, but also to keep a recognizable Iranian cultural identity alive for their children and grandchildren. It is this third generation, some of whom are already coming of age in the United States, who will test the strength of that cultural inheritance. Yet as this book has shown, ongoing migrations complicate generational categories—despite colloquial diasporic uses of "first generation" to refer to older immigrants who arrived "first," first-generation Iranians in diaspora are not only those who migrated in the 1970–80s but anyone in the immigrant generation, including recent arrivals. Similarly, "second generation" as a catch-all includes youth, young adults, and adults. Across the diaspora, these terms could describe an individual of any age. Categorically speaking, as the diaspora continues to grow, *generations* thus may not be as useful as *cohorts* and future research framed around cohort effects will offer important nuances about belonging and nonbelonging within and beyond generations.

Finally, the politics of recognition that have been debated by political philosophers since the 1990s are being relitigated in the 2020s through the forces of neoliberalism and digital economies. The Cyromania phenomenon described in this book—especially as an effort to reframe Iranian identity through references to Cyrus the Great and pre-Islamic history—reflects broader concerns with reputation management in an era of rapid digital circulation. Social media has amplified both misrepresentations of Iranians and the strategic counter-representations that seek to correct them. Yet, as we have seen, some critics argue that these counter-narratives produce their own distortions, reinforcing an elite, exclusionary vision of Iranian identity. As Iranians continue to find themselves the subject of negative representations in the media, the attempt to accumulatively build on reputation—whether of Cyrus the Great, or of the economic successes of contemporary Iranians, or otherwise—for collective reputation management is further necessitated by a growing reputation economy that has been altered by digital and social media.[20] The role of digital media in shaping Iranian diasporic activism, political engagement, and cultural identity is an urgent area for further research, particularly as social media increasingly structures diasporic discourse, mobilization, and even transnational political alliances.

\* \* \*

In contrast to the landscapes I entered when I began fieldwork in the late 2000s, it is fair to say that mainstream representations of Iranian culture have now become common in these three capitals of the Iranian diaspora. Iranians may still face xenophobia or be vilified by politicians, but, thanks in part to these community efforts, Iranians now also may be recognized for more than the politics of the day. But that hasn't led to guarantees of rights or protections from discrimination based on national identity, racial ascription, or any number of other tripwires of exclusion. Once desperate for even a small drop of positive representation in what felt like a desert, diasporic Iranians now find themselves in an expanding stream of them. Or perhaps, more cynically, we have come to realize that these small sips of positive representations don't seem to fully quench the thirst for belonging after all.

Indeed, representation may come with benefits to belonging, but it will never alone guarantee it. Nor is it ever neutral—representation is constantly redefined and reshaped by the very struggles it seeks to address. Representation inevitably invites contestations and produces outcomes beyond our intentions, desires, or control. Still, that doesn't render these efforts meaningless. Representation may not be a cure-all, but the continued emotional, financial, and sociocultural investments in projects like the US Cyrus Cylinder tour, the LA Freedom Sculpture, Eldfesten in Sweden, and Tirgan in Canada (and yes, the Cyrus the Great statue in Atlanta) attest to the ongoing struggle to build belonging in our homes. Everyday experiences of exclusion feel more surmountable when set against moments of recognition—whether through the display of ancient Iranian artifacts in major museums or as large public sculptures, in the broadcast of Nowruz traditions on Swedish television, or in the inclusion of Iranians as Canadians in ever greater arenas of civic life. Cultural representation stands as just one of the many strategies immigrants use to forge inclusion and stake their place in diaspora.

At its core, the Iranian diaspora's struggle for recognition is a struggle over identity, power, and belonging. Across multiple and overlapping generations, political perspectives, class positions, religious affiliations, gender identifications, and ethnic backgrounds, Iranians hold diverse and sometimes competing visions of what Iranianness is, how it should be represented, and by whom. The challenge, as in other immigrant communities, is to develop new strategies of claim-making across these fragmentations while advancing more inclusive and expansive understandings of Iranian belonging. As this book has shown, these negotiations do not merely reflect diasporic realities—they actively shape them, reinforcing and, at times, transforming the very terms of inclusion and exclusion in multicultural societies.

ACKNOWLEDGMENTS

I have been a very lucky person. For well over a decade, I have been privileged to work on a project that introduced me to hundreds of Iranians in multiple locations of the global diaspora, all of whom share a love for arts and culture. I am grateful especially to those who shared their time and their experiences with me in interviews; invited me to join their organizations; and allowed me to attend and participate in their planning meetings, rehearsals, conferences, and performances. Their friendship and encouragement over so many years has been invaluable. It is impossible to name here all who made the fieldwork for this study possible; I extend my deep gratitude to all who shaped this book, whether their words are directly quoted or not. *Sharmandam.*

I have also been the fortunate beneficiary of generous mentorship and collegiality in numerous academic settings. Undergraduate advising can be a challenging job, but my first mentor, the inimitable Frank Lewis, set the bar for that endeavor. He was, among many other things, a deeply committed and empathetic scholar and teacher who was also an exceptionally good person, one whom we lost far too soon. I am grateful especially to Shiva Balaghi, Persis Karim, and Hamid Naficy for encouraging me from very early on to pursue my genuine interest in the diaspora, even if the path for doing so was not yet clear. I am so grateful for their mentorship as much as for their scholarship.

The opportunity to share ideas and write the bulk of this book with a cohort of fellows with expertise across Iranian studies was invaluable and, for me, sustaining—and all the more so during a global pandemic. I am so appreciative to have benefitted from the time, space, resources, and mentorship provided by Behrooz Ghamari-Tabrizi and the Bijan and Sharmin Mossavar-Rahmani Center for Iranian and Persian Gulf Studies at Princeton University. My sincere gratitude to cofellows Amin Moghadam and Khodadad Rezakhani for welcoming me into the fold, and to my beloved *BBD* writing group (Maryam Alemzadeh, Arash

Davari, Peyman Jafari, Amir Moosavi, and Milad Odabaei) for hours of virtual cowriting, discussion, feedback, and collegiality during what was otherwise an impossible time.

At Oklahoma State University, I'm grateful to colleagues who provided support and space for writing. My thanks to Randy Kluver, Jami Fullerton, Marten Brienen, John Schoeneman, Cara Eubanks, Bailey Bryan, and Patricia Acurio Padilla. Thanks also to fellow Iranian faculty, especially Pouya Jahanshahi, Ali Mirchi, and Sara Alian, and graduate students at OSU for building community together in Stillwater. A special thanks to Lili and Mae Badiyan and their family for keeping us all nourished and beautifully so. At the College of Charleston, I had the very good fortune of working alongside Kathleen Foody, Max Kovalov, Beatrice Maldonado-Bird, Kristen McLean, Malte Pehl, Blake Scott, and Sarah Wuigk. I am especially grateful to Jennifer Cavalli and Mari Crabtree, with whom I co-wrote in nearly every café in Charleston.

At the University of California, Los Angeles (UCLA), I am most grateful to Susan Slyomovics and Sondra Hale (my fearless cochairs) and Jessica Cattelino, the three of whom taught me lessons not just in anthropology, but in what integrity, committed scholarship, and intellectual generosity look like. I remain enriched by their continued friendship and guidance. For invaluable feedback and support during the early stages of this work, sincere thanks go to Ali Behdad, Aparna Sharma, and Hamid Naficy. The groundbreaking 1993 book *Irangeles* led me to Jonathan Friedlander at UCLA; it was Susan and Jonathan who encouraged me to think seriously about—and especially to resist dismissals of—cultural events like festivals and parades. Their vision allowed me to see these as sites of contestation that can serve as lenses onto immigrant cultural identity, belonging, and resistance. I'm also grateful for the friendship that only cotravelers can provide during the highs and lows of graduate school; my thanks to Anoush, Bailey, Charles, Hadi, Hanna, Hannah, Jessica, Jenny, JP, Katja, Sonya, and especially Rachel and John, who are nothing less than family.

For their feedback, clarifying questions, or invitations to share portions of this work at its various stages, I earnestly thank Camron Amin, Beeta Baghoolizadeh, Narges Bajoghli, Kaveh Bassiri, Danielle Battisti, Aomar Boum, Louise Cainkar, Houchang Chehabi, James Clark, Jennifer Dueck, Talinn Grigor, Sally Howell, Persis Karim, Maryam Kashani,

Akram Khater, Mikiya Koyagi, Hani Khafipour, Shahram Khosravi, Sarah Koellner, Ulf Hannerz, Neda Maghbouleh, Ida Meftahi, Manijeh Moradian, Hamid Naficy, Nima Naghibi, Nasrin Rahimieh, Arash Saedinia, Gwyneth Talley, Mohamad Tavakoli-Targhi, Helena Wulff, and Ida Yalzadeh. For their kindnesses large and small while bringing this book to fruition, I am deeply appreciative of Nakkisa Akhavan, Katja Antoine, Ramin Bajoghli, Jean Beaman, Lara Deeb, Babak Elahi, Stacy Fahrenthold, Sarah Gualtieri, Farzaneh Hemmasi, Sarah Khanghahi, Amy Motlagh, Negar Mottahedeh, Sahar Sadeghi, Nahid Siamdoust, and Fernanda Soto Joya. I benefitted greatly from insightful colleagues at workshops at the University of California, Irvine, the University of Manitoba, Johns Hopkins University (SAIS), the University of Toronto, and the University of Texas at Austin. I'm grateful to audiences at the University of Southern California, University of Michigan–Dearborn, San Jose State University, University of Nebraska–Lincoln and Omaha, and the Iranian Diaspora in Global Perspective Conference at UCLA; and to copanelists and audiences at the 2012 and 2014 American Anthropological Association annual meetings, 2018 American Studies Association annual meeting, 2014 and 2024 Association for Iranian Studies conferences, 2014 and 2024 Middle East Studies Association conferences, 2018 Council for European Studies conference, and 2023 International Studies Association conference.

At NYU Press, I am grateful to Jennifer Hammer, Brianna Jean, Ainee Jeong, and their colleagues for careful stewardship of the manuscript. I also wish to thank the two anonymous reviewers for their helpful feedback, and editors Susan Frekko and Allison Brown who offered invaluable editorial guidance that substantially improved the manuscript. For enabling transnational fieldwork through institutional and financial support, I thank the Swedish Institute, Stockholm University, and the American-Scandinavian Foundation; at UCLA, the International Institute, Center for Near Eastern Studies, Institute for American Cultures, Center for Asian American Studies, Graduate Division, and Department of Anthropology; at College of Charleston, the School of Languages, Cultures and World Affairs; at Princeton, the Sharmin and Bijan Mossavar-Rahmani Center for Iranian and Persian Gulf Studies; and at Oklahoma State University, the Endowed Chair in Iranian and Persian Gulf Studies.

I am filled with appreciation for friends dispersed here, there, and elsewhere, who ensured writing also included joy. My love especially to Ameesh, Amir, Arash, Arash, Azadeh, Carolyn, Craig, Farnaz, Ilana, Jacquie, Jessica, Joseph, Judith, Justin, Kaveh, Kiana, Kimia, Mari, Nasim, Ramin, Sarah, Sepideh, Shayda, Shima, Shirin, and Tara. I may have been born as an only child, but I have been sustained by sisterhood with Ariana, Beeta, Hannah, Jennifer, Michelle, Megan, Narges, Nakkisa, Neda, Rachel, and Sarah. I wish for everyone to have sisters as fiercely brilliant and loving as they are.

As a student, I never imagined the sheer number of personal triumphs and losses that an author experiences while completing a scholarly book. Among my greatest joys has been loving a partner who is generous, spirited, whip-smart, and makes a knockout *gheimeh*. His steady encouragement and sense of humor have been invaluable bulwarks amid the uncertainties and challenges of academic life. On the other side of the ledger, the loss of my mother, the very essence of kindness and an anchor in my life, stopped me in my tracks. As it turned out, she gave me not only her wide smile and her mother's name, but also the strength to navigate life without her—though it has taken years to realize it. I miss her each day, yet I keep discovering new reasons to be grateful for all that we share. She would have been so happy this book is (finally) complete. My father certainly is; and through it all, he has been my inspiration and champion in equal measure. My love for him is endless, and there is no greater gift than that of his unconditional love and support. My parents taught me what it means to be Iranian and American, even as they—like all of us—were still figuring it out. It is to them that I lovingly dedicate this book.

My extended family and friends who are like family have been especially cherished during tragedies and periods of grief, both personal and communal, during fieldwork and the writing of this book. And they have been numerous: The unbearable loss of life on Flight PS752, the intense periods of loss and uncertainty that came with the COVID-19 pandemic, the emotional highs and (unfortunately more often) lows of the effects of geopolitics on those we love in Iran and its growing diaspora. To this incomplete list I add the losses of community members I met in the field. The passing of Nasser Yousefi in Stockholm and Ali

Mohammadi in Toronto during this project were both sharp reminders of the irreplaceable energy Iranians in diaspora have devoted to their communities out of love for Iran and its arts and culture. I am so grateful to have crossed paths with them and so many others, if only too briefly. To all we've lost: *Ruheshun shaad va yaadeshun gerami.*

# NOTES

### INTRODUCTION

1. Asterisks indicate pseudonyms.
2. Interview with Maria Sabaye Moghadam by author, Toronto, August 18, 2011.
3. While acknowledging the ongoing discussion around hyphens and hyphenated identities, throughout the book I follow Chicago Manual of Style guidelines in using "Iranian American" consistently.
4. Slyomovics 1996; Malek 2011.
5. Interview with Zohreh by author, New York, March 28, 2009.
6. Mobasher 2012; Maghbouleh 2017; Bajoghli 2019a.
7. Khosravi 2009; Bauer 2000; Emami 2016.
8. Throughout the book, I use the terms "community" and "communities" because these were the preferred terms of my interlocutors, who used it in English but also as a loan word when speaking Persian. They employed it as a descriptor as much as an aspirational term.
9. Bozorgmehr 1997; Malek 2015.
10. Mobasher 2012.
11. Gholami 2015; Spellman 2004.
12. Khosravi 2018.
13. Moghadam 2021.
14. Fozi 2021.
15. Interview with Mehrdad Ariannejad by author, Toronto, August 18, 2011.
16. Taylor et al. 1994; Hall 1997; Fraser 2000; Benhabib 2002.
17. See caption to fig. I.1.
18. PARSA Community Foundation 2007.
19. Seattle City Hall, 2019, "Nowruz in Seattle—Persian New Year," Facebook, March 19, 2019, www.facebook.com.
20. Yuval-Davis 2006.
21. Yuval-Davis 2006, 197–99.
22. Castañeda 2018, 1.
23. While *assimilation* historically referred to the processes by which immigrants adjust their behaviors, norms, and practices to conform to a national majority, contemporary scholarship has demonstrated that both immigrants and the communities they join adjust to one another, such that "the characteristics of members of immigrant groups and the members of a given receiving society come to resemble one another." *Integration* has been used more commonly than *assimilation* in

European and Canadian multicultural settings, though not without its detractors. It is used positively by those who insist immigrants' sociocultural differences are neither to be feared nor diminished in favor of a majority culture as they adapt to their new homes but instead can be encouraged for greater positive outcomes for both immigrants and for the larger society. Bean et al. 2015, 17.

24 Bloemraad 2006.
25 Bloemraad 2006; Castañeda 2018.
26 In describing his hopes for Eldfesten, Mansour said, "In the future, in the Swedish calendar, this day will be known as Iran Day." Mansour Hosseini, interview for "Manoto+," Manoto1, March 29, 2014. Translated from Persian by author.
27 Eldfesten, "Eldfesten 2017—Chaharshanbeh Soori," Facebook video, March 17, 2017, https://www.facebook.com/watch/?v=1408958339168704.
28 Rosaldo 1997.
29 Ong 1996.
30 Tehranian 2009.
31 Tehranian 2009; Yoshino 2007.
32 Khosravi 2012.
33 See Malek 2019.
34 See Karim 2020.
35 Hübinette 2023.
36 In the sociological literature, the *first generation* includes individuals who immigrated as adults, while the *1.5 generation* consists of those who immigrated as youth. The *second generation* describes those born in diaspora to immigrant parents; their children are the *third generation*, including those born to at least one second-generation parent. Rumbaut and Massey (2013, 150–51) suggest possibilities for even further disaggregating the first and second generations, though necessary data to do so is not always available.
37 Beaman 2017, 4.
38 Ong 1996, 738.
39 Ibid.
40 Ibid.
41 W. Brown 2015.
42 Ong 1996, 739.
43 W. Brown 2015, 10.
44 Ong 1996, 739.
45 Ibid.
46 Park 2005, 5; Schall 2016; Hackl 2022.
47 Ong 1996, 739; Ong 2006, 145.
48 Ong 1996, 740. Ong points to the "racialization of class" in the "whitening" of Irish Americans, Jewish Americans, and some Asian Americans to conclude that "official racial categories are reproduced by everyday American activities of inclusion and exclusion." Ibid.
49 Pakulski 1997, 80; Beaman 2016.

50  Here I draw on sociologist Pierre Bourdieu's forms of capital that describe nonfinancial assets, such as social capital (e.g., social networks and interpersonal relationships) and cultural capital (e.g., knowledge, education, skills, style of speech and dress), that can enable social mobility. The concept of human capital can also refer to education, skills, and networks, though is more often used in economic studies of labor. See Bourdieu 1986.
51  Bloemraad and Wright 2014. Scholars have suggested additional forms of multiculturalism; Bloemraad and Wright (2014) put forward multiculturalism as public discourse, while Korteweg and Triadafilopoulos (2014) suggest multiculturalism as a form of governance.
52  Hall 2001, 3.
53  Bloemraad, Korteweg, and Yurdakul 2008, 160.
54  Ekman 2022.
55  For example, Swedish Prime Minister Magdalena Andersson responded to three days of protests (what the police called "riots") in April 2022 against an extremist anti-Islam group's planned Quran-burnings: "Segregation has been allowed to go so far that we have parallel societies in Sweden." Henley 2022.
56  Bloemraad, Korteweg, and Yurdakul 2008.
57  Phillips 2009; Benhabib 2002.
58  My thanks to Jessica Cattelino for this formulation.
59  Rahimieh 2001, 20.
60  Geertz 1973, 448.
61  See Marashi 2008; Dabashi 2015; Zia-Ebrahimi 2016.
62  Books that have dealt with this subject in whole or in part include Naficy 1993; Grigor 2014; Rahimieh 2016; Maghbouleh 2017; Hemmasi 2020.
63  See Amanat and Vejdani 2012; Rahimieh 2016.
64  Laguna 2017.
65  Siu 2005; Dufoix 2008.
66  Brubaker 2005; Dufoix 2008; Hage 2021, 2.
67  Mobasher 2018.
68  For more on this growing field, see Karim and Elahi 2011; Karim 2013.
69  The 2009–10 Green Movement in Iran emerged through a series of large nonviolent protests contesting the reelection of Mahmoud Ahmadinejad in June 2009. Alleging fraud and a stolen election, protesters demanded "Where is my vote?" as they took to the streets in what observers described as the largest protests in Iran since the 1979 Revolution. The movement was violently suppressed and hundreds of protesters, journalists, and reformists were arrested, imprisoned, or even killed.
70  The Joint Comprehensive Plan of Action (JCPOA), colloquially referred to as the "Iran Nuclear Deal," was an agreement reached between Iran and the P5+1 (United States, United Kingdom, France, Russia, China, and Germany) and the European Union that limited Iran's development of its nuclear capabilities in exchange for reducing economic sanctions on Iran. US President Donald Trump

withdrew from the deal in 2018, leading Iran to also ignore the deal's obligations. The United States then not only restored economic sanctions but also imposed new ones under a policy of "maximum pressure." See Bajoghli et al. 2024.
71  Bourdieu 1986.
72  Castañeda 2018.
73  Marcus 1995.
74  Hage 2021.
75  Lee 2020.
76  For examples of how scholars have navigated comparison in studies of migration and diaspora, see Foner 2005; Abdelhady 2011; Castañeda 2018; Moss 2021; Sadeghi 2023.
77  Werbner 2013.
78  Werbner 2012.

CHAPTER 1. DEPARTURES AND ARRIVALS

1  National census methodologies vary across countries but often have serious flaws in measuring and counting race and ethnicity, often resulting in elisions of these identifications in favor of place of birth or language use, making it not only difficult to count those who would self-identify as Iranian but also impossible to identify second and third generations and undocumented persons.
2  Ardalan 2023. Translated from Persian by author.
3  Abrahamian 2018.
4  Mottahedeh 1985, 316–17.
5  Shannon 2017.
6  Matin-Asgari (1991) 2002, citing a 1967 Confederation of Iranian Students National Union publication.
7  Matin-Asgari (1991) 2002.
8  Matin-Asgari (1991) 2002, 65.
9  Moradian 2022, 118; Lai and Batalova 2021.
10  Sadeghi 2023.
11  Moradian 2022.
12  Moradian 2022.
13  Abrahamian 2018, 160.
14  Amanat 2017.
15  Mossayeb and Shirazi 2006; Azadi, Mirramezani, and Mesgaran 2020.
16  *Entekhab.ir News* 2013.
17  *DW Farsi* 2012.
18  For how this legal system specifically impacted the racialization of Iranian Americans, see Maghbouleh 2017.
19  Chishti, Hipsman, and Ball 2015.
20  Pew Research Center 2015.
21  Chagnon 2013, 2.
22  Citizenship and Immigration Canada 2012.

23 Triadafilopoulos 2012; Kelley and Trebilcock 2000, 442. See also Calliste 1994.
24 Triadafilopoulos 2012, 4–8.
25 FitzGerald and Cook-Martin 2014.
26 Despite removing restrictions based on race, the act nevertheless still placed visa caps per country, and initially by hemisphere.
27 Triadafilopoulos 2012, 3.
28 Chishti, Hipsman, and Ball 2015.
29 US Census Bureau 2021.
30 Triadafilopoulos 2012, 2–3.
31 Citizenship and Immigration Canada 2012, 12. According to this government report: "The percentage from Asia and Pacific, and from Africa and the Middle East have grown dramatically (from 9% to 46% for Asia, and from 3% to 25% for Africa). The percentage of permanent residents from South and Central America also doubled over this fifty-year period, and represented 10% of the total immigrant population in 2010." Ibid.
32 Statistics Canada 2021.
33 Citizenship and Immigration Canada 2012, 13; Chagnon 2013, 14. Iranians were included as visible minorities under the West Asian subgroup. The term *visible minorities* faced multiple criticisms: It suggested the existence of a "Canadian race"; it lumped together groups that are and are not at an economic disadvantage in society; it was used to describe groups that demographically comprise a majority, rather than a minority; and so on. As Banting and Thompson (2021, 875) point out, even the United Nations Committee on the Elimination of Racial Discrimination criticized the term in 2017 for "rendering invisible the plight of distinct racialized groups." In response to such criticisms, the 2021 Canadian Census replaced this term with "racialized groups."
34 Statistics Canada 2023.
35 Statistics Canada 2022a.
36 Schnakenbourg 2022.
37 *France 24* 2023.
38 Skodo 2018.
39 Westin 2006. See Ohlsson 2006.
40 Skodo 2018.
41 Westin 2006. Saukkonen 2013.
42 Government Offices of Sweden 2013, 23.
43 Hübinette and Lundström 2014; Borevi 2014, 709–10.
44 Statistics Sweden, n.d.a.
45 This number includes those who had arrived as students or tourists and adjusted their status, as well as those who arrived later as asylum seekers. The Refugee Act of 1980 created the federal refugee resettlement program in the United States that Iranians would benefit from in the following decade.
46 Babcock 1980. For a dramatized take on these events, see the film *Checkpoint*, dir. Parviz Sayyad, 1987.

47  Mobasher 2006; Solomon 1979.
48  Mobasher 2013, 1001.
49  Ibid.
50  Mobasher 2006; Sadeghi 2023.
51  Kelley 1991, 162.
52  Naficy 1997, 73–90; Bajoghli 2019a; Semati, Cassidy, and Khanjani 2021.
53  Yoshino 2007, ix. Yoshino describes covering in the United States as a form of assimilation.
54  Tehranian 2009.
55  Rytina 2022.
56  Mobasher 2013.
57  Modarres 1998, 38.
58  Ibid.
59  Tsubakihara 2013.
60  Kelley 1991, 163–64.
61  Bozorgmehr 1997.
62  Mobasher 2013, 1003.
63  Hirabayashi 1991.
64  Naficy 1993.
65  Hemmasi 2020.
66  Mobasher 2013, 1008.
67  Mobasher 2012, 6.
68  Mobasher 2012, 6.
69  Amirani 2012.
70  Notably, the first and second Iranian Americans to be elected to the United States Congress have not come from California's large Iranian communities. The first, Republican Stephanie Bice, was elected to represent Oklahoma's fifth district in the House of Representatives in 2020. Bice's father is half Iranian, though she did not speak openly about her heritage leading up to her election. In 2024, Democrat Yassamin Ansari was elected as the second Iranian American in Congress, representing Arizona's third congressional district. Both are second-generation women.
71  See, for example, Bravo's reality series *Shahs of Sunset*, which featured a cast of Beverly Hills Iranian American "affluencers" over a nine-season run (2012–22), and the debates it sparked. Malek 2015; Alinejad 2017; Yalzadeh 2021.
72  Mahmoudi 2021.
73  Shannon 2017.
74  Bozorgmehr and Ketchum 2018, 39.
75  Moallem 2000.
76  Bozorgmehr and Ketchum 2018, 40.
77  Maghbouleh and Malek 2023.
78  Ibid. Note: The margin of error for this estimate (±13.2) is affected by sample size and variability.

79  US Census Bureau 2023.
80  Unlike in Canada, the US Census is not compulsory, and unlike in Sweden, the US government does not track heritage populations (e.g., nonimmigrants) outside of American Community Survey estimates.
81  Marks, Jacobs, and Coritz 2023.
82  The 2020 American Community Survey (five-year, person-weighted) estimated that 194,925 Iranians lived in California. Of these, 80,935 lived in Los Angeles County (41.5 percent), with the strongest concentrations in Westwood, West LA, Woodland Hills, Encino, Tarzana, Pacific Palisades, and Beverly Hills. An additional 30,776 (16 percent) lived in adjacent Orange County, with strong concentrations in Irvine, Laguna Hills, Laguna Niguel, and Mission Viejo.
83  Ruggles et al. 2019. American Community Survey, 2013–17, five-year estimate, person-weighted IPUMS dataset. Note that all ancestry data is self-reported. My thanks to Beatrice Maldonado-Bird.
84  Nikou 2017.
85  US Department of Homeland Security Office of Immigration Statistics 2022.
86  Interview with Susan Taslimi by author, Stockholm, June 13, 2012. All quotes from this interview were translated from Persian by the author.
87  Ibid.
88  Andersson 2007.
89  Interview with Susan Taslimi by author, Stockholm, June 13, 2012.
90  Ibid.
91  Personal communication with author, Stockholm, June 12, 2017.
92  Behtoui 2022.
93  Kelly 2011, 443–454.
94  For example, see Sanandaji 2012.
95  Khosravi 2012, 65–80.
96  Kelly 2011, 444.
97  Khosravi 2012.
98  Government Offices of Sweden 2013, 89.
99  Government Offices of Sweden 2013.
100 Statistics Sweden 2022.
101 Interview with Maryam by author, Stockholm, May 23, 2012.
102 Ibid. Regarding stigmatized identities based on names and rising rates of name changes, especially among Muslims as coping and covering strategies in 1990s Sweden, see Khosravi 2012.
103 Hajighasemi 2012.
104 Kelly 2011; Ahadi 2018.
105 Government Offices of Sweden 2013, 24.
106 Nilsson and Westin 2022.
107 Statistics Sweden n.d.b; Statistics Sweden n.d.c. Here "foreign background" has been calculated to include foreign-born, those born in Sweden to two foreign-born parents, and those born to at least one foreign-born parent. "Iranian origin"

is used here to indicate Iran as location of birth or birthplace of at least one parent.
108 Statistics Sweden n.d.d.
109 *Dagens Nyheter* 2012. Note that this program predated the shift in Swedish migration from primarily European labor migrants to largely nonwhite, non-European, and non-Christian refugee populations.
110 For example, according to Ahadi (2018), Husby "experienced a sharp increase in its immigrant population between 1990 and 2000, from 4,000 to 10,000, while the native Swedish population decreased by 60%, from 6,000 in 1990 to 2,000."
111 Andersson and Kährik 2015.
112 Stockholms stad 2025, 132. On July 1, 2023, the Rinkeby-Kista and Spånga-Tensta districts merged to form the Järva city district area (*stadsdelsområde*), which includes the nine districts (*stadsdel*) of Akalla, Bromsten, Flysta, Husby, Kista, Lunda, Rinkeby, Solhem, Sundby, and Tensta.
113 Stockholms stad 2025, 29. Note that "foreign background" in this table ("Utrikes födda och födda i Sverige med två föräldrar födda utomlands 2023-12-31") did not include individuals with only one foreign-born parent.
114 Mirfakhraie 1999.
115 Chagnon 2013, 3–6.
116 Minister of Public Works and Government Services Canada 1999.
117 Lu and Hou 2015, 1.
118 According to the *Globe and Mail*, the dollar amount varied based on year of application and which province invited their investment; the range in 2014 was $300,000–800,000 CAD.
119 Ong 1999, 6, 112.
120 For more on the phenomenon of "astronaut families" and "parachute kids," see Ong 1999, 19.
121 As translated and quoted in Nejad 2013.
122 For example, Iranian Canadian dual citizen Mahmoud-Reza Khavari was a managing director at Bank Melli (the National Bank of Iran) who lived in Iran while his family lived in a $3 million home in Toronto. In 2011, Khavari was suspected of being party to a major Iranian banking scandal involving over thirty individuals arrested for fraud that culminated in the embezzlement of $2.6 billion. Gladstone and Hauser 2012.
123 Using an example of an Iranian Canadian man's YouTube videos in Toronto as her case study, Nasrin Rahimieh has referred to the extreme versions of this effort as "*gasht-i intiqam*" ("roving avengers"), in which some diaspora members turned their anger at the Islamic Republic (especially its *gasht-e ershad*, morality police) toward fellow diasporic Iranians whom they suspected of supporting the IRI. Rahimieh 2023.
124 Statistics Canada 2022b.
125 Statistics Canada 2023.
126 For a comprehensive list of early Toronto community media, see Yazdanfar 2004.

127  Canadian Minority Media Database, "Shahrvand," accessed March 9, 2025, www.artsrn.ualberta.ca.
128  Zerehi 2010.
129  In 2023, local politicians circulated surveys calling for community input in the potential official naming of an area of North York as "Little Persia."
130  Toronto Iranians 2014.
131  For example, several Iranian Americans were prevented from purchasing iPhones and iPads at Apple Stores across the United States in 2012 in a case of "overcompliance" of sanction laws. See Abdi 2012. Mobile payment services like Venmo have similarly prevented transactions with "Iran" or "Persian" in the description. See Moritz-Rabson 2019.
132  *Maclean's* 2012; *CBC News* 2012.
133  Malek 2019; see chapter 4 of this book.
134  *CBC News* 2022.
135  Public Safety Canada 2024.
136  Statistics Canada 2022c.
137  In addition to "Iranian," the 2021 Canadian Census added "Persian" as an option for "ethnic or cultural identity." While "Iranian" is a national category and "Persian" an ethnic category (both of which were encouraged by the Census prompt), usage slips between the two for political and other reasons, so it is necessary to consider both answers for a more accurate count of this community. However, because each respondent could select up to four answers, it is possible the same individual chose both Iranian and Persian. The Census was unable to provide me with those dual counts. Email communication, January 20, 2023.
138  Statistics Canada 2022b.
139  Chagnon 2013, 5.
140  Statistics Canada 2024.
141  Banting and Kymlicka 2010, 881. See also Reitz and Banerjee 2007.
142  Creese and Wiebe 2009; Ameeriar 2017.
143  Government of Canada 2024.
144  The Ukraine International Airlines Flight 752 passenger airliner was shot down on January 8, 2020, by Iranian air to surface missiles just minutes after leaving Tehran, killing all on board. Among them were over 138 Iranians who had been en route back to their Canadian homes. See chapter 4 of this book.
145  Winter 2011, 13.
146  Portes and Rumbaut 2001.
147  Abu-Laban, Gagnon, and Tremblay 2023.
148  Cameron 2004, 401.
149  Ibid., 402.
150  Ibid., 411.
151  Citizenship and Immigration Canada 2012, 11.
152  Abu-Laban, Gagnon, and Tremblay 2023, 7.
153  Winter 2011, 16.

154 Saukkonen 2013, 188.
155 Schierup and Scarpa 2017, 46.
156 Kulturrådet, n.d.
157 Hale 2006; Melamed 2011.
158 Bloemraad 2006.
159 Ibid., 122.
160 Ameeriar 2017.
161 Acts of anti-Muslim racism, especially but not exclusively in Quebec, have especially been on the rise.
162 Straw 2013.
163 Vertovec and Wissendorf 2010; Kymlicka 2012a.
164 Harding 2021.
165 Skodo 2018.

CHAPTER 2. ASSERTING "FREEDOM, DIGNITY, AND WEALTH" IN LOS ANGELES

1 "The Cyrus Cylinder and Ancient Persia," 2013.
2 Sackler Galleries at the Smithsonian in Washington, DC (Foundation for Iranian Studies and Levy Foundation), the Museum of Fine Arts in Houston (Ansary Foundation), the Metropolitan Museum of Art in New York, The Asian Art Museum in San Francisco (PAAIA), the Getty Villa in Los Angeles (Farhang Foundation). The name of the exhibition at the New York Metropolitan Museum of Art was slightly altered: "The Cyrus Cylinder and Ancient Persia: Charting a New Empire."
3 Farhang Foundation, n.d.a.
4 "The Cyrus Cylinder and Ancient Persia," 2013.
5 In her extensive literary study, Deborah Levine Gera (1993, 1–3) argues that the *Cyropaedia* "was not written as a history" but rather a "didactic work" in which "Xenophon improvises freely with the facts of Cyrus' life, altering historical circumstances to suit his literary and didactic purposes" resulting in more "idealized fiction than fact." See also Ansari 2012, 167.
6 Terhune 2013.
7 Ibid.
8 Steele 2021.
9 Boehm 2013.
10 For example, it has been established by historians that not only did Thomas Jefferson personally profit from the labor of enslaved workers, he "embraced the worst forms of racism to justify slavery" (Ambrose 2002) and maintained a "lifelong failure to confront slavery, either as a politician or as a private citizen" (Finkelman 2014, 245). Furthermore, the "self-evident" truth he wrote into the US Declaration of Independence that "all men are created equal" appears to have included caveats and exceptions for nonwhite men and all women, starting in his own estate. Whereas his contemporaries, like Benjamin Franklin, had become ardent abolitionists, historian Paul Finkelman (2014, 268) has shown that Jefferson's public

statements against slavery did not match his personal beliefs and actions: "In sum, Jefferson's views on race are embarrassing, not just by the standards of our age but by the standards of his own age."

11  Estimates provided by Iran Heritage Foundation-America on the tour website, http://cyruscylinder2013.com, now archived on the Wayback Machine (see for example May 31, 2016, capture). In introducing the cylinder to new audiences, media outlets likened it to a rugby ball (*The Economist*), a loaf of rye bread "from which someone has broken off a chunk" (*Al-Monitor*, NPR), and a corn cob "that's been gnawed bare" (*LA Times*). *LA Weekly* was especially colorful in their description: "The Cylinder is the Keith Richards of history and antiquity: broken and cracked, yet timeless, and monumental to the evolution of culture." Minazad 2013.
12  That record would be broken again by the 2022 exhibition of "Persia: Ancient Iran and the Classical World."
13  Halkett 2013.
14  Narang 2013.
15  On (in)visibility of Middle Eastern Americans, see Naber 2000 and Tehranian 2009.
16  Ibid.
17  Narang 2013.
18  Fayyaz and Shirazi 2013.
19  Dabashi 2015, 49.
20  "Recognizing the cultural and historical significance of Nowruz and acknowledging the Cyrus Cylinder as a symbol of respect for human rights and religious tolerance," H.Res.130, 113th Congress (2013–2014), https://www.congress.gov/.
21  Bourdieu 1993.
22  Lorcin 2013, 97–111.
23  Grigor 2021.
24  Both New York City and Los Angeles mayors provided letters of support, and LA Mayor Eric Garcetti became more involved in fundraising in the Iranian American community once the Freedom Sculpture was proposed.
25  The cost of the event has been estimated at over $21 million. Amanat 2017, 665–66. See, for example, the 2016 BBC documentary, *Decadence and Downfall: The Shah of Iran's Ultimate Party*.
26  Grigor 2005.
27  Steele 2021, 44; quoting from "Misaq-e Shahanshah ba Bonyangozar-e Shahanshahi-ye Iran" [The Shah's covenant with the founder of Imperial Iran], *Keyhan*, 20 Mehr 1350, October 12, 1971, 1.
28  For analysis of the ways these have influenced contemporary Iranian and diasporic identity, see Rahimieh 2016.
29  Grigor 2021.
30  Gera 1993, 19–20.
31  There is a theory popular among a handful of Iranian and Indian scholars that a figure in the Quran (Dhul-Qarnayn) should be recognized as Cyrus the Great. See Merhavy 2015.

32  Grigor 2005, 25.
33  Baghoolizadeh (2024, 113–14) notes that translations of the cylinder have been "somehow misconstrued to suggest that Cyrus II freed all enslaved people from forced labor—a dramatically incorrect idea, as Babylonia was expected to send a tribute of five hundred enslaved boys to the Achaemenid king every year." See also Baghoolizadeh 2013. Ansari (2012, 176) suggests these claims have amounted to "fetishism" around the cylinder: "As impressive a political text as it represents, to describe it as a 'charter of human rights' must by definition be wholly anachronistic."
34  Curtis 2013a, 85.
35  Ibid., 86. Mohammad Reza Pahlavi emphasized the connection between Cyrus and Western democracy, writing, "While Iran at the time knew nothing of democratic political institutions, Cyrus nevertheless demonstrated some of the qualities which provide the strength of the great modern democracies." Pahlavi 1961, 21.
36  Steele 2021, 25.
37  Merhavy 2019, 80. Steele (2021) and Merhavy (2019) both offer multiple examples of books and films that promoted this narrative, such as Shapur Shahbazi, *Korush-i Bozorg* (Shiraz, Iran: Danishgah-i Pahlavi, 1970) and Hadi Hedayati, *Korush-i Kabir* (Tehran: Tehran University Press, 1956).
38  Curtis 2013a, 87.
39  Steele 2021, 125.
40  Steele 2021, 45. Not all scholars accepted the invitation. Steele quotes British historian Peter Avery, who had declined: "I couldn't believe that it would be correct for anybody who thought of himself as a historian of Iran to support a so unhistorically, unauthentic event, in terms of history." See Steele 2021, 81.
41  Press Release, "Iran Presents Replica of Ancient Edict to United Nations," October 14, 1971, UN HQ/264, S-0882-0002.
42  Curtis 2013b.
43  Steele 2021.
44  Abrahamian 1999; Nikpour 2018.
45  Merhavy 2019, 76–77.
46  For a filmic meditation on the commodification of Cyrus the Great, see the documentary short film produced in conjunction with the Getty Villa stop of the exhibition, titled "O CYRUS," dir. Arash Saedinia, 2013, https://vimeo.com/125550050. For a scholarly analysis of the commodification of these symbols and diasporic consumerism, see Mostafavi 2024.
47  But it was not only Iranians touting Cyrus in the 2010s; American Evangelical Christians, Israeli political leaders, British art historians, and Jewish leaders of numerous nationalities all brought the story of Cyrus into the public sphere in this decade. On developing a hegemonic common sense about Iran and Iranians through media, see Naficy 1997.
48  Chelkowski and Dabashi 1999.
49  Naficy (2012, 233) suggests this regarding cinema: "As the Islamic Republic attempted to forge a homogenous Shiite political nation, cultural producers, some

of whom opposed the regime, attempted to revive an imagined multicultural multiethnic, multilingual, and multinational nation patterned after the ancient transnational Persian Empire." On the "return of pre-Islamic symbols" during the Khatami and Ahmadinejad periods, see Merhavy 2019, 156–65.
50  Zia-Ebrahimi 2016.
51  Ibid. On Iranian nationalism, see Vaziri 1993; Tavakoli-Targhi 2001; Marashi 2008; Dabashi 2015.
52  The theory of Aryan racial identity has been debunked and is known as "the Aryan myth." See Motadel 2014.
53  Zia-Ebrahimi 2016.
54  Naficy 1993.
55  Maghbouleh 2017.
56  Moallem 2005. As Islamophobic discourses are often enacted against Iranians racialized as Muslim in Western societies, they are also picked up by some Iranians themselves in an effort to set themselves apart. These practices are not limited to the Iranian American context, though the racialization of Iranians is not identical across all contexts. On intersections of religion and race in the Iranian diaspora in the United Kingdom, see Gholami 2015; in the United States, see Maghbouleh 2017; and in the Netherlands, see Roodsaz 2020. On covering, see Tehranian 2009 and Yoshino 2007.
57  Ansari 2021; Merhavy 2019; Bajoghli 2019b.
58  Bajoghli 2019b.
59  Abdolmohammadi 2015. See also Mostafavi 2024.
60  The significance was highlighted in a Facebook announcement by History Advocates: "Through the efforts of History Advocates and their supporting scholars, language has been added to the California curriculum which speaks to the multicultural tolerance of the Persian Empire, as well as its influence on world history, including modern history." Facebook, January 4, 2017, www.facebook.com.
61  Farhang Foundation, n.d.b.
62  Remarks by Eric Garcetti on July 4, 2017, video message, transcribed by author.
63  The Freedom Sculpture—A Shared Dream, 2017, "The Freedom Sculpture's puzzle-like pattern design is [. . .]," Facebook. July 26, 2017, www.facebook.com.
64  Farhang Foundation, n.d.c.
65  Ardalan 2017.
66  *NIAC News* 2017.
67  Battisti 2019.
68  For more on immigrant gifts discourse, see Selig 2008.
69  Battisti 2020.
70  Battisti 2019, 12.
71  Battisti 2020.
72  Ibid.
73  Battisti 2019.
74  Yalzadeh 2021.

75 Maghbouleh 2017.
76 Sahar Sadeghi's research confirms the extension of these experiences into the 2020s. See Sadeghi 2023.
77 Shakhsari 2020.
78 W. Brown 2015.
79 Ong 1996, 739.
80 Ong 1996, 737.
81 Melamed 2011, 43.
82 Melamed 2011, 43.
83 Selig 2008.
84 Read and Parvini 2020.
85 Khanghahi 2017, 794.
86 Hembree 2018.
87 Gardiner 2019.
88 In 2020, during the COVID-19 pandemic, NIPOC's Mehregan Festival was temporarily revived in virtual form in front of a large replica of the Cyrus Cylinder. NIPOC 2023.
89 Personal communication with author, July 14, 2017.
90 Farhang Foundation, n.d.d.
91 Farhang Foundation 2023. See also Malek 2021.
92 During the challenges of the COVID-19 pandemic, the organization also added a dues-based membership category for the general public.
93 See the "Farhang Sources of Funds" section of the Farhang Foundation Annual Reports for 2016 through 2024. Farhang Foundation 2017; 2019; 2021; 2023; 2024.
94 Compare, for example, the London-based Iran Heritage Foundation (IHF). While IHF offers similar programming, their annual reports available online do not offer the same level of detail as those of Farhang Foundation. They nevertheless consistently have reported total annual source funds amounting to less than one third that of Farhang Foundation.
95 Farhang Foundation 2020.
96 Interview with Alireza Ardekani by author, Los Angeles, July 13, 2017.
97 An important exception is the foundation's annual Nowruz festival, which relies on the energy of dozens of day-of volunteers, many of whom are university students and young professionals.
98 Parsi 1997.
99 *House of Iran*, n.d.
100 Ezatollah Delijani was an Iranian Jewish real estate investor and philanthropist instrumental in the development of downtown LA's Jewelry District and Garment District and the preservation of theaters the Broadway District. He was also actively involved in city politics, leading to investigations of his relationship with now-convicted former Sheriff Lee Baca in late 2010. This investigation may have impacted the progress of his statue project. See Broverman 2010.
101 Farhang Foundation 2014.

102 Farhang Foundation, "Freedom: A Shared Dream—International Jury Announcement," press release emailed by Farhang Foundation, July 2, 2014.
103 Malek 2011. Prior to 2017, Farhang Foundation had done this most noticeably through the placement of street banners along major Los Angeles avenues and boulevards to announce Nowruz each year or to promote their major programs like the exhibition of the Cyrus Cylinder in 2013.
104 Kajart 2016.
105 Ibid.
106 Farhang Foundation, n.d.b., see "Timeline."
107 Arora Project, n.d.
108 During the campaign, a "Latest Donors" section of the sculpture website (now removed) featured a list of the most recent donations, including those of just $1.
109 Interview with Alireza Ardekani by author, Los Angles, July 13, 2017.
110 During the campaign, a running tally was posted on the sculpture website, which on July 13, 2017, read "$2,697,894 raised from 1,157,299 donors & supporters (77% of $3,500,00 goal)."
111 Interview with Alireza Ardekani by author, Los Angles, July 13, 2017.
112 Farhang Foundation, n.d.e.
113 Public comment from user "surfnspy" on Elijah Chiland, "Century City Freedom Sculpture unveiled on Santa Monica Boulevard median," Curbed LA, July 5, 2017. https://la.curbed.com/.
114 Public comment from user "MMVic" on Elijah Chiland, "Century City Freedom Sculpture unveiled on Santa Monica Boulevard median," Curbed LA, July 5, 2017. https://la.curbed.com/.
115 Public comment from user "beechwooddude" on Elijah Chiland, "Century City Freedom Sculpture unveiled on Santa Monica Boulevard median," Curbed LA, July 5, 2017. https://la.curbed.com/.
116 Nili 2017.
117 Farhang Foundation, n.d.b., see "Sculpture Facts."
118 Facebook comment by Armita Mehrabi-Hashemi, on "The Freedom Sculpture—A Shared Dream," July 10, 2017, www.facebookcom/FreedomSculpture.
119 Facebook comment by Fahi Vazirian, on "The Freedom Sculpture—A Shared Dream," February 4, 2018, www.facebook.com/FreedomSculpture.
120 Facebook comment by Guity Rouhani, on "The Freedom Sculpture—A Shared Dream," July 26, 2017, www.facebook.com/FreedomSculpture.
121 Facebook comment by Nina Attara, on "The Freedom Sculpture—A Shared Dream," August 23, 2017. www.facebook.com/FreedomSculpture.
122 Facebook comment by Aza Moti, on "The Freedom Sculpture—A Shared Dream," July 5, 2017. www.facebook.com/FreedomSculpture.
123 Ghorashi 2004, 329–40, 335–6.
124 Farhang Foundation 2017.
125 Mike Pompeo (@SecPompeo), Twitter, October 29, 2019, https://twitter.com/SecPompeo/status/1189199170537689088.

126 Merhavy 2019, 165–166, 170–171.
127 US State Department (@USABehFarsi), Twitter, October 27, 2020 https://twitter.com/USABehFarsi/status/1321263216639565824.
128 Ibid.
129 Byrne 2014.
130 Jacoby 1986.
131 Rosaldo 1989, 108.
132 Valanejad 2020. Surviving family members of executed political prisoners also have sought to add their loved ones' names to the sculpture-as-memorial, such as Parviz Rostamalipour, whose name was added in January 2024.
133 Kurosh Valanejad, 2020, "The Freedom Sculpture is an Iranian-American led [. . .]," Facebook, October 7, 2020, https://www.facebook.com.
134 Westall 2022.

## CHAPTER 3. CONTESTING CULTURAL BELONGING(S) IN STOCKHOLM

1 Eldfesten Committee meeting, Stockholm, February 27, 2012. Translated from Persian by author.
2 Interpretive license has been applied in these translations to best reflect the speaker's intention.
3 Various versions of this celebration take place in Iran, Afghanistan, Tajikistan, Azerbaijan, Kurdistan (Iraq, Türkiye), and their diasporas.
4 While jumping, celebrants recite "*Sorkhi-ye to az man, zardi-ye man az to*" ([let] your ruddiness [be] mine, my paleness yours." See Kasheff and Saʿīdī Sīrjānī 1990.
5 Rezaian 2010.
6 Merhavy 2019, 156.
7 Eldfesten returned to Kungsträdgården in 2024.
8 Eldfesten has regularly taken place in Stockholm, Gothenburg, and Malmö; in 2014 it also took place in Sundsvall and Västerås.
9 Birgitta Ohlsson, then-Minister for European Affairs, emphasized these political implications to Swedish Radio in 2012: "It is even more important that when you live in a free country, as Sweden is—a democracy—that we celebrate [Eldfesten] here and that also the pictures from here reach Iran and reach those who thirst for democracy and freedom." Quoted in Z. Hashemi 2012.
10 Chaharshanbeh Suri and other Nowruz traditions have been banned in public areas of Istanbul in regulations specifically targeting Kurds; the Taliban "abolished" Nowruz in Afghanistan in 1996 and again in 2022. These kinds of repressions in Iran and beyond have been reported on in international media. See Sethi 2022.
11 Kulturrådet, n.d.
12 Zapata-Barrero 2013.
13 For a comprehensive overview of this debate, see Meer, Modood, and Zapata-Barrero 2016; Zapata-Barrero 2015; and the collected essays in *Comparative Migration Studies*, especially Modood 2017.

14 Hosseini 2021. In a magazine article on his festival work, Mansour suggests the possibility of an even higher number, over forty million. ITI Germany 2014, 86.
15 Eldfesten, 2017, "Eldfesten 2017—Chaharshanbeh Soori," Facebook video, March 17, 2017. https://www.facebook.com/watch/?v=1408958339168704.
16 This chapter focuses mostly on the Iranian community in Stockholm, but of course supporters and critics of Eldfesten also included non-Iranian Swedes. Online, some praised the event and how much they enjoyed watching it, while others complained about having to hear Arabic on Swedish TV (which, during Eldfesten, was not Arabic but Persian) and used it as evidence in stating their anti-immigrant, anti-Muslim, and anti-multiculturalism views.
17 Eldfesten Committee meeting, Stockholm, March 11, 2012. Translated from Persian by author.
18 I attended committee meetings as both an observing anthropologist and as a volunteer, serving as a photographer for the event on the day of the festival. I also interviewed a dozen of the regularly attending committee members outside of these meeting settings.
19 Riksteatern, n.d.
20 Carlson 1963.
21 Rani Kasapi would establish and run the International Department from 2005–13; her success there was recognized in being awarded Diversity Manager of the Year in 2014 (from Sweden's *Chef* [Chief] Magazine), and in 2017, she was appointed the deputy director-general of the Division of the Arts in Sweden's Ministry of Culture.
22 Kulturrådet, n.d.
23 Interview with Rani Kasapi by author, Stockholm, May 30, 2014. Emphasis in original.
24 Interview with *Ehsan by author, Stockholm, June 27, 2012. Translated from Persian by author.
25 Ghorashi 2003.
26 Eldfesten Committee meeting, Stockholm, February 27, 2012. Translated from Persian by author.
27 Asterisks indicate pseudonyms.
28 In the 2010s, *Shahr-e Ghesseh* gained renewed attention among Iranians in diaspora, for example, in new productions in Toronto, San Jose, and San Diego; screenings of the rare film of the production in New York City; as well as a reimagining of the play as an animation by a diasporic satellite station that aired around Nowruz 2012 and may have prompted Ehsan's invocation. Multiple diasporic artists have drawn inspiration from its human-animal hybrid characters as a method of artistic political commentary. See, for example, Dubai-based Rokni Haerizadeh's animation "The Reign of Winter" (2012–13) and "Fictionville" series (2009–) or US-based Pouya Afshar's illustration, "Shahr-e-Ghesseh, 2017."
29 The details of the play related here are not entirely accurate to Mofid's script but reflect Ehsan's recollection and interpretation of the scene in question. Interview with Ehsan by author, Stockholm, June 27, 2012. Translated from Persian by author.
30 Ibid. *Khareji* (foreigner) is a term used commonly in diaspora to refer to non-Iranians; here it refers to Swedes.

31  For example, in Stockholm, at Shahrzad and Zartosht, or in Uppsala, at Sofreh. Images of these are annually shared on social media such as Instagram with the hashtag #persisktjulbord.
32  Translated from Persian by author. In this quote, transliterated terms are followed by translations in brackets; the speaker's translation of terms is followed by [sic] to indicate the way he used language here was not precise.
33  Theodossopoulos 2013, 347.
34  Ghorashi 2003, 172.
35  Ghorashi 2003, 171.
36  Haji Firuz has become a controversial figure in the Iranian diaspora. His presence at 2012 Eldfesten was not debated, but critics decried his appearance there without "traditional" blackface. For more on the history of Haji Firuz, and especially the use of blackface, see Baghoolizadeh 2021 and 2024.
37  Eldfesten Committee meeting, Stockholm, February 27, 2012. Translated from Persian by author.
38  Ibid. Emphasis original.
39  Ibid. On *aberu*, see M. Hashemi 2020, 37–38.
40  Ibid.
41  Eldfesten Committee meeting, Stockholm, March 11, 2012. Translated from Persian by author.
42  Here and in other statements regarding potential Iranian exclusion of Swedes, the English term "racist" was used, though what it was describing sometimes was more in line with the English word "discrimination." This distinction was never overtly discussed.
43  Eldfesten Committee meeting, Stockholm, March 11, 2012. Translated from Persian by author. Emphasis mine.
44  "Eldfesten Committee," Eldfesten, www.eldfesten.info, now archived on the Wayback Machine (see for example the March 19, 2015, capture).
45  Eldfesten Committee meeting, Stockholm, March 2, 2012. Translated from Persian by author.
46  Interview with Mansour Hosseini by author, Stockholm, May 8, 2012. Emphasis mine.
47  Hoge 1998.
48  Interview with Massood by author, Stockholm, May 18, 2012. Translated from Persian by author. Emphasis original.
49  Eldfesten Committee meeting, Stockholm, February 27, 2012. Translated from Persian by author.
50  Eldfesten Committee meeting, Stockholm, March 2, 2012. Translated from Persian by author.
51  Eldfesten Committee meeting, Stockholm, February 20, 2012. Translated from Persian by author.
52  Ibid.
53  Eldfesten Committee meeting, Stockholm, March 11, 2012. Translated from Persian by author.

54  *Dagens Nyheter* 2009.
55  Strandberg 2009; *Dagens Nyheter* 2009.
56  Ubuntu Forums, 2009, "The Stage of *Kungsträdgården* Burned on the Day of Eldfesten," Integration and Immigration (March 2009), conversation in Swedish, https://www.flashback.org.
57  Interview with Tomaj by author, Stockholm, June 19, 2012.
58  Interview with Tomaj by author, Stockholm, February 13, 2012. Emphasis original. "Burning flags" refers to activism at political protests.
59  In interviews, Tomaj was clear that—like most diasporic cultural organizations—they also had to be careful to steer clear of party politics, as a divisive issue. Hanberg 2010, 11.
60  Interview with Tomaj by author, Stockholm, June 19, 2012. Emphasis original.
61  Eldfesten Committee meeting, Stockholm, February 27, 2012. Translated from Persian by author.
62  Interview with Tomaj by author, Stockholm, February 13, 2012.
63  Interview with Tomaj by author, Stockholm, June 19, 2012.
64  Farhang Förening 2014.
65  Interview with Rostam Mirlashari by author, Stockholm, February 13, 2012. Translated from Persian by author. Emphasis original.
66  Eldfesten Committee meeting, Stockholm, March 2, 2012. Translated from Persian by author. Emphasis original.
67  Ibid. Emphasis original. Like in other parts of the Middle East, belly dance would have been common in cabarets in prerevolutionary Iran. There, it would likely have been known as Arab dance, or as *raqs-e shekam*. On belly dancing as a representation of the Middle East in the West, see Shay and Sellers-Young 2003. On contemporary Iranian dance, see Meftahi 2016.
68  See Zia-Ebrahimi 2016.
69  Hübinette 2013.
70  Comments by Nasser, Stockholm, March 11, 2012. Translated from Persian by author.
71  Radio Sweden Farsi 2012. Emphasis in original.
72  Dana 2019.
73  Interview with Ehsan by author, Stockholm, June 27, 2012. Translated from Persian by author.
74  United Nations, n.d.
75  Eldfesten Committee meeting, Stockholm, March 11, 2012. Translated from Persian by author.
76  Ameeriar 2017, 4.
77  Ong 1996, 737.

CHAPTER 4. NAVIGATING MULTICULTURALISM IN TORONTO

1  Bogost 2020.
2  *BBC News*, 2020, "Canada Mourns Victims of Plane Crash," Facebook video, January 9, 2020, https://www.facebook.com/watch/?v=2206236933016050.

304 | NOTES

3 Galloway 2020.
4 *The Guardian* 2020.
5 Global News 2020. Emphasis mine.
6 *The Guardian* 2020.
7 Comment by user @diyako30 on Canada Mourns livestream. GlobalNews 2020. This positive impression would not last long, as Iranian community members became increasingly frustrated at what they viewed as the too-slow pace of the justice promised by politicians. Surviving family members organized a nonprofit association to memorialize their loved ones, conduct fact-finding missions, and apply pressure to the Canadian government. Association of Families of Flight PS752 Victims 2021.
8 Email communication to Tirgan volunteers, January 13, 2020.
9 There are other contenders, such as the Iranian Canadian Congress (ICC), established in 2007 as an advocacy organization. Seeking to represent the interests of Iranians in Canadian government and society, the effectiveness of the ICC has been limited by a long series of internal and community disputes.
10 Sommerville 2022.
11 Tirgan 2023a. Translated from Persian by author.
12 Tirgan, "Annual Reports," http://tirgan.ca. Accessed November 1, 2023.
13 Ibid.
14 For example, some community members expressed dismay when TD Bank became a presenting sponsor of Tirgan's summer festival in 2017, the highest level of corporate sponsorship. See *CBC News* 2012.
15 Reprinted in Cameron 2004, 401.
16 Ibid., 402.
17 Ibid., 411.
18 Government of Canada, n.d.
19 See 289n33 for definition and revision of this term.
20 Of course, both metaphors are imprecise and strongly criticized: Where the melting pot implies immigrants should lose their distinguishing cultural practices and beliefs in favor of a mainstream American culture, the "plaster" that bonds each "tile" of the mosaic in place can present a false image of bounded, timeless, and essentialized immigrant cultures that resist the influences of other "tiles" but also never even touch them, thereby disabling social cohesion and leading to separate "parallel lives." Nevertheless, these metaphors persist in everyday usage and frequently are contrasted against one another.
21 Bauböck 2005, 93
22 Soroka and Roberton 2010, 3.
23 Statistics Canada 2022a.
24 Environics Institute 2021.
25 Bloemraad 2006, 122.
26 Ziaee and Zerehi 2008.
27 "Goals of Tirgan," *Tirgan 2013 PR Content Index*, Tirgan, 2013, internal document in author's possesion.

28 "Harbourfront Centre," *See Toronto Now*. Accessed September 9, 2010. www.seetorontonow.com.
29 Harbourfront Centre 2013.
30 Destination Ontario 2024.
31 Notably, several of these large festivals added major Canadian corporate sponsors to their titles, e.g. "The Rogers Masala! Mehndi! Masti! Festival" (Rogers is a major Canadian telecommunications and media corporation headquartered in Toronto) or the "Scotiabank Caribbean Carnival" (Scotiabank is a Canadian multinational banking and financial services company also headquartered in Toronto). As of 2024, Tirgan has not followed suit, although corporate presenting sponsors' branding has appeared across the festival and its publications.
32 Harbourfront Centre, "Community Partnership Programme Application Package," November 19, 2012. This document was provided to prospective community partners to inform them of the process of working with HC.
33 Interview with Nima by author, Toronto, August 25, 2011.
34 Ibid.
35 Tirgan 2023a.
36 Ariannejad, public speech, Tirgan 2011.
37 According to Foltz 2009, Iranian Zoroastrians in Toronto were "highly offended" that they were not consulted about Tirgan traditions and that their offer of assistance was declined by organizers of the first Tirgan in 2008.
38 Akhlaghi 2011.
39 Intended to attract attention on social media, these ads were somewhat controversial for the depiction of Arash as a slim, clean-shaven young man with a short haircut, wearing a Roman costume and leather loafers.
40 Interview with Melanie Hernandez by author, Toronto, July 19, 2013.
41 Tirgan 2013.
42 Harbourfront Centre 2013.
43 Ibid.
44 Tirgan, n.d.a. [2008].
45 City of Toronto, n.d.
46 Vertovec and Wessendorf 2010.
47 Payami 2015.
48 Mehrdad Ariannejad, "Message from Tirgan CEO," Tirgan Festival 2019 booklet, 2–3, printed booklet handed out at the festival in the possession of the author.
49 This was of course not coincidental as these organizations not only were aware of one another, they also supported one another. Tirgan donated to the Freedom Sculpture crowdfunding campaign and a Farhang Foundation trustee gave a presentation at the 2017 Tirgan Festival about the Freedom Sculpture.
50 Payami 2017.
51 Yousefi 2019.
52 Ariannejad 2017, 1.
53 Tirgan 2015.

54 Bloemraad 2006.
55 Bloemraad 2006, 94.
56 Bloemraad 2006, 92.
57 Handy and Greenspan 2009.
58 ICCAC 2010.
59 Mehrdad Ariannejad, presentation at the Fifth IAAB International Conference on the Iranian Diaspora, University of California, Los Angeles, October 14, 2012.
60 Interview with Behrouz by author, Toronto, August 24, 2011.
61 Tirgan 2023a. Translated from Persian by author.
62 *Tirgan Magazine* 2008, 8.
63 *Tirgan Magazine* 2011, 14.
64 Interview with Arian by author, Toronto, August 9, 2011. Translated from Persian by author.
65 Tirgan 2023a. Translated from Persian by author. Emphasis mine.
66 Tirgan 2023b.
67 Facebook post by Mahsa, July 26, 2017, www.facebook.com.
68 Tirgan Media 2021b. Translated from Persian by author.
69 Tirgan 2023a. Translated from Persian by author.
70 Eskandari 2011.
71 Tirgan 2023a. Translated from Persian by author.
72 Tirgan Media 2021c. Translated from Persian by author.
73 Tirgan Media 2021a, 2021d. Translated from Persian by author.
74 Interview with Arian by author, Toronto, August 9, 2011. Translated from Persian by author.
75 Arian was clear in the same 2011 interview that he did not want the IRI's support: "Because it's a government that for thirty-two years has harassed our artists both inside and outside of Iran. There's no reason to then go to this government and say, 'Support our artists!'" Ibid.
76 Sepehri Far 2020; Fassihi 2020.
77 Fassihi 2020.
78 "Calling on Tirgan Festival to Believe the Survivors & Stop Giving Predators a Platform," August 27, 2020, www.change.org.
79 Ibid.
80 Fassihi and Porter 2020.
81 Nasser 2020.
82 Fassihi and Porter 2020.
83 J. Brown 2018; Donovan and Hasham 2015.
84 Mehta and Marshall 2019.
85 Kingston 2016.
86 J. Brown 2018.
87 Ghomeshi 2018.
88 Goldsbie 2020.
89 Ibid.

90  Nasser 2020.
91  Tirgan Media 2020.
92  Tirgan Media 2020.
93  Nasser 2020.
94  Tirgan, n.d.b.
95  Interview with Nima by author, Zoom, April 18, 2023.
96  Tirgan 2022.
97  What constitutes "nonpartisan" for these organizations can range from internal decisions to avoid any political bias or contentious issues (as Tirgan did), to legal requirements not to engage in "any activities that support or oppose a political party or candidate for public office" (as the Canadian government requires of registered charities). Canada Revenue Agency 2023.
98  Malek 2023; Razavi 2023.
99  @tirganfestival, Instagram, September 19, 2022, https://www.instagram.com/p/CisklFbrt64.
100  Comment by user @pegaah_d on post by @tirganfestival, Instagram, September 19, 2022, https://www.instagram.com/p/CisklFbrt64.
101  Comment by user @mo.mellati on post by @tirganfestival, Instagram, September 19, 2022, https://www.instagram.com/p/CisklFbrt64. Translated from Persian by author.
102  Ibid.
103  Comment by user @sawnio on post by @tirganfestival, Instagram, September 19, 2022, https://www.instagram.com/p/CisklFbrt64. Translated from Persian by author.
104  Comment by user @behzzad__ on post by @tirganfestival, Instagram, September 19, 2022, https://www.instagram.com/p/CisklFbrt64/. Translated from Persian by author.
105  @tirganfestival, Instagram, September 23, 2022, https://www.instagram.com/p/Ci3TzBzrP-J. Emphasis mine.
106  Comments by users @aa_shabkhosh, @mobin.mirzahashemi, and @negariii_ta on post by @tirganfestival, Instagram, September 23, 2022, https://www.instagram.com/p/Ci3TzBzrP-J. Translated from Persian by author.
107  Comment by user @mahsasal on post by @tirganfestival, Instagram, September 23, 2022, https://www.instagram.com/p/Ci3TzBzrP-J. Translated from Persian by author.
108  Comment by user @nikkii.es on post by @tirganfestival, Instagram, September 23, 2022, https://www.instagram.com/p/Ci3TzBzrP-J. Translated from Persian by author.
109  Rahimieh 2023; Razavi 2023.
110  Interview with Nima by author, Zoom, April 18, 2023.
111  See Razavi 2023.
112  Tirgan 2023c.
113  Interview with Nima by author, Zoom, April 18, 2023.

114  Ibid.
115  Siu 2005, 5.
116  Interview with Nima by author, Zoom, April 18, 2023.

CHAPTER 5. STRATEGIES OF INCLUSION

1  Interview with David by author, Los Angeles, July 19, 2017.
2  Ibid.
3  The notion of "saving face" has been the subject of much anthropological analysis. Manata Hashemi has described *aberu* as that which "protects one from the judgments and valuations of others." Losing "one's figurative face means to lose one's dignity," which in turn "leads to loss of one's respect, esteem, and standing among one's peers." M. Hashemi 2020, 37–38.
4  W. Brown 2015.
5  Ong 1996, 739.
6  Interview with Arian, Toronto, August 18, 2011. Translated from Persian by author.
7  Ong 1996.
8  Ong 1996. Though initially theorized with regard to immigrant belonging in the United States, the concept of cultural citizenship also has been applied elsewhere to account for subject formation as a negotiation between the agency of refugees and immigrants and the racialization processes and class relations that operate through hegemonic ideologies and structures of the state and its intermediaries.
9  Moradian 2022.
10  As magnified by the Bravo television series *Shahs of Sunset*. Malek 2015; Yalzadeh 2021.
11  Ong 1996, 788.
12  Ibid.
13  For example, the National Iranian American Council (NIAC, founded in 2002) or the Public Affairs Alliance of Iranian Americans (PAAIA, founded in 2006).
14  PAAIA, n.d.
15  Behdad 2005; Tuan 1998.
16  Park 2005.
17  This particular vision of the American Dream as the combination of American individualism and Iranian culture was Darioush Khaledi's, described in the marketing of the Darioush Winery in Napa Valley, California. "Our Journey," Darioush Winery, http://www.darioush.com.
18  Ong 1996, 788.
19  PAAIA, n.d.
20  A replica monument of the Cyrus Cylinder also was unveiled outside the House in 2004 by the Mayor of San Diego.
21  Selig 2008.
22  Kymlicka 2015, 7, 13.
23  Ong 2004, 54. Here Ong refers to the "politics of recognition" advanced by gay rights activism since the 1960s, which "demanded public recognition of cultural

diversity in connection with middle-class achievements." See also Taylor et al. 1994.
24  Mauss (1950) 2002.
25  Douglas (1950) 2002.
26  Warikoo and Bloemraad 2018; Park 2005.
27  Public comment on Item 17-0118, "Motion relative to the impact of President Trump's executive order on immigration (Protecting the Nation from Foreign Terrorist Entry to the United States) on Los Angeles International Airport," Innovation, Grants, Technology, Commerce, and Trade Committee, Los Angeles City Hall, February 7, 2017.
28  Iranian Americans' Contributions Project, n.d.
29  Ibid.
30  Quinn 2017.
31  Payami 2017.
32  Ardalan 2017.
33  Interview with Rostam Mirlashari by author, Stockholm, June 1, 2012. Translated from Persian by author; emphasis mine.
34  Selig 2008.
35  Notably, cultural norms surrounding gift giving and reciprocating in Iran and its diaspora, especially through ta'arof, varies widely from those of the three countries studied in this book. See Beeman 2019.
36  Interview with Rostam Mirlashari by author, Stockholm, June 1, 2012. Translated from Persian by author.
37  See Hackl 2022.
38  Ong 1996, 751.
39  Park 2005.
40  "Eldfesten 2017—Chaharshanbeh Soori," Facebook video, posted March 17, 2017, https://www.facebook.com/watch/?v=1408958339168704.
41  Ong 1996, 739.
42  For example, see Ong 1999; Beaman 2016; Thobani 2007; Banting and Thompson 2021.
43  Omi and Winant 2015, 111.
44  Love 2020; Rana 2011; Fekete 2004; Jamal and Naber 2008.
45  De Genova 2016, 81.
46  Zia-Ebrahimi 2016.
47  Chelkowsi and Dabashi 1999; Merhavy 2019.
48  Ansari 2012; Motadel 2014; Zia-Ebrahimi 2016.
49  For Iranians for whom the 1979 Revolution and the establishment of the Islamic Republic have represented immense losses (e.g., of rights, livelihoods, property, and family members executed by the state), the abandonment of Islam has been a common step. For Iranians of other faiths, similar experiences along with targeted persecution for their religious practices have led to perhaps even stronger feelings against the religion. See Gholami 2015; R. Shirazi 2014; Mobasher 2006.

50 Gholami 2015, 96. Gholami puts forward the concept of "non-Islamiosity" to describe that a significant proportion of the Iranian diaspora "is incessantly ridding itself of the Islamic—including from 'culture.'" Ibid.
51 Estiri 2024, 178–81.
52 Gholami 2015.
53 Yalzadeh 2021.
54 Maghbouleh 2017, 60–61.
55 Baghoolizadeh 2024, 2021; Vossoughi and Vakil 2015.
56 Gualtieri 2009; Battisti 2019.
57 Maghbouleh 2017, 45.
58 Tehranian 2009.
59 Sadeghi 2023; Tuan 1998.
60 See Khosravi 2010.
61 Bloemraad 2006. See Omi and Winant 2015.
62 On the history of slavery in Canada, see Cooper 2006.
63 Thobani 2007; Banting and Thompson 2021; Tajrobehkar 2021.
64 Bloemraad 2006.

CONCLUSION

1 Reza Pahlavi (@PahlaviReza), Twitter, video, 12:12 p.m., October 29, 2023, https://twitter.com/PahlaviReza/status/1718662197830619305/video/1.
2 Park 2005, 3.
3 See Behdad 2005.
4 Bloemraad 2006; Berlant 1997.
5 Ong 1996, 740.
6 Bloemraad 2006.
7 Laguna 2017.
8 M. Shirazi 2016.
9 Farrell 2022.
10 Afsarzadeh 2022.
11 Vossoughi 2022.
12 Vossoughi and Vakil 2015.
13 Sharifi 2017; Elswit 2018.
14 See the short film trilogy written and directed by Bahar Pars: *Rinkebysvenska* (2015), *Turkkiosken* (2017), and *Donkeyland* (2023).
15 Gosling 2018.
16 Farrokhzad 2013, 2018.
17 Shima Niavarani, Facebook, February 27, 2014, www.facebook.com.
18 See McClintock 1993.
19 Naghibi 2016; Farahani 2018; Sameh 2019; Shakhsari 2020; Roodsaz 2022.
20 Davies 2021.

# REFERENCES

Abdelhady, Dalia. 2011. *The Lebanese Diaspora: The Arab Immigrant Experience in Montreal, New York, and Paris*. NYU Press.
Abdi, Jamal. 2012. "Sanctions at the Genius Bar." *New York Times*, July 11, 2012.
Abdolmohammadi, Pejman. 2015. "The Revival of Nationalism and Secularism in Modern Iran." *LSE Middle East Centre Paper Series* 11 (November): 1–20.
Abrahamian, Ervand. 1999. *Tortured Confessions: Prisons and Public Recantations in Modern Iran*. University of California Press.
———. 2018. *A History of Modern Iran: Revised and Updated*. Cambridge University Press.
Abu-Laban, Yasmeen, Alain-G Gagnon, and Arjun Tremblay. 2023. "Reflecting on Multiculturalism at Its Semicentennial: Over the Hill or Just Getting Started?" In *Assessing Multiculturalism in Global Comparative Perspective*, edited by Yasmeen Abu-Laban, Alain-G Gagnon, and Arjun Tremblay. Routledge.
Afsarzadeh, Hooshyar. 2022. "Virtual Lecture—Hoosh Afsar Lecture on Critical Race Theory in Persian." Persian Cultural Center of Atlanta, YouTube video, May 23, 2022. https://www.youtube.com/watch?v=ZLPccPFwrR4.
Ahadi, Daniel. 2018. "Disrupting the Digital: Persian-Language Community Radio in Stockholm and the Continued Relevance of Analog Media in the Digital Age." In *Ethnic Media in the Digital Age*, edited by Sherry S. Yu, Matthew D. Matsaganis. Routledge.
Akhlaghi, Reza. 2011. "Far from Home, Reviving an Age-Old Tradition of Diversity." *Foreign Policy Blogs*, July 15, 2011.
Alinejad, Donya. 2017. *The Internet and Formations of Iranian American-ness: Next Generation Diaspora*. Palgrave Macmillan.
Amanat, Abbas. 2017. *Iran: A Modern History*. Yale University Press.
Amanat, Abbas, and Farzin Vejdani, eds. 2012. *Iran Facing Others: Identity Boundaries in a Historical Perspective*. Palgrave Macmillan.
Ambrose, Stephen. 2002. "Founding Fathers and Slaveholders." *Smithsonian Magazine*, November 2002. www.smithsonianmag.com.
Ameeriar, Lalaie. 2017. *Downwardly Global: Women, Work, and Citizenship in the Pakistani Diaspora*. Duke University Press.
Amirani, Shoku. 2012. "Tehrangeles: How Iranians Made Part of L.A. Their Own." *BBC News*, September 29, 2012. https://www.bbc.com/news/magazine-19751370.
Andersson, Roger. 2007. "Ethnic Residential Segregation and Integration Processes in Sweden." In *Residential Segregation and the Integration of Immigrants: Britain, the*

*Netherlands and Sweden*, edited by Karen Schönwälder, 61–90. Wissenschaftszentrum Berlin für Sozialforschung.

Andersson, Roger, and Anneli Kährik. 2015. "Widening Gaps: Segregation Dynamics During Two Decades of Economic and Institutional Change in Stockholm." In *Socio-Economic Segregation in European Capital Cities*, edited by Tiit Tammaru, Szymon Marcińczak, Maarten van Ham, and Sako Musterd, 110–31. Routledge.

Ansari, Ali. 2012. *The Politics of Nationalism in Modern Iran*. Cambridge University Press.

———. 2021. "A Royal Romance: The Cult of Cyrus the Great in Modern Iran." *Journal of the Royal Asiatic Society* 31 (3): 405–19.

Ardalan, Davar. 2017. "Freedom Sculpture to Be Gifted to Los Angeles." *Huffington Post*, June 27, 2017.

Ardalan, Jahanshah, dir. 2023. *The Chronicler*. Homa Sarshar, YouTube, March 29, 2023, https://www.youtube.com/watch?v=P7f939IqxI.

Ariannejad, Mehrdad. 2017. "Message from Tirgan CEO." *Tirgan Magazine*, 2017.

Arora Project. n.d. "Freedom Sculpture: A Crowdfunded Monument to Humanity." Accessed December 13, 2022. www.aroraproject.co.

The Association of Families of Flight PS752 Victims. 2021. *The Lonely Fight for Justice*. Association of Families of Flight PS752 Victims. https://www.ps752justice.com/.

Azadi, Pooya, Matin Mirramezani, and Mohsen B. Mesgaran. 2020. "Migration and Brain Drain from Iran." Working Paper No. 9. Stanford Iran 2040 Project, April.

Babcock, Charles R. 1980. "Carter's Visa Crackdown Won't Hurt Immediately." *Washington Post*, April 9, 1980.

Baghoolizadeh, Beeta. 2013. "Reconstructing a Persian Past: Contemporary Uses and Misuses of the Cyrus Cylinder in Iranian Nationalist Discourses." *Ajam Media Collective*, June 6, 2013. https://ajammc.com.

———. 2021. "The Myths of Haji Firuz: The Racist Contours of the Iranian Minstrel." *Lateral* 10 (1).

———. 2024. *The Color Black: Enslavement and Erasure in Iran*. Duke University Press.

Bajoghli, Narges. 2019a. "American Media on Iran: Hostage to a Worldview." *Anthropology Now* 11 (3): 31–38.

———. 2019b. *Iran Reframed: Anxieties of Power in the Islamic Republic*. Stanford University Press.

Bajoghli, Narges, Vali Nasr, Djavad Salehi-Isfahani, and Ali Vaez. 2024. *How Sanctions Work: Iran and the Impact of Economic Warfare*. Stanford University Press.

Banting, Keith, and Will Kymlicka. 2010. "Canadian Multiculturalism: Global Anxieties and Local Debates." *British Journal of Canadian Studies* 23 (1): 43–72.

Banting, Keith, and Debra Thompson. 2021. "The Puzzling Persistence of Racial Inequality in Canada." *Canadian Journal of Political Science* 54 (4): 870–91.

Battisti, Danielle. 2019. *Whom We Shall Welcome: Italian Americans and Immigration Reform*. Fordham University Press.

———. 2020. "Columbus Day Had Value for Italian Americans—But It's Time to Rethink It." *Washington Post*, October 20, 2020.
Bauböck, Rainer. 2005. "If You Say Multiculturalism Is the Wrong Answer, Then What Was the Question You Asked?" *Canadian Diversity* 4 (1): 90–94.
Bauer, Janet L. 2000. "Desiring Place: Iranian 'Refugee' Women and the Cultural Politics of Self and Community in the Diaspora." *Comparative Studies of South Asia, Africa and the Middle East* 20 (1): 180–99.
Beaman, Jean. 2016. "Citizenship as Cultural: Towards a Theory of Cultural Citizenship." *Sociology Compass* 10 (10): 849–57.
———. 2017. *Citizen Outsider: Children of North African Immigrants in France*. University of California Press.
Beeman, William. 2019. "Ta'ārof: Pragmatic key to Iranian social behavior," In *Handbook of Pragmatics, 22nd Installment*, edited by Jan-Ola Östman and Jef Verschueren, 203–23. John Benjamins Publishing Company.
Bean, Frank D., James D. Bachmeier, Susan K. Brown. 2015. *Parents Without Papers: The Progress and Pitfalls of Mexican-American Integration*. Russell Sage Foundation.
Behdad, Ali. 2005. *A Forgetful Nation: On Immigration and Cultural Identity in the United States*. Duke University Press.
Behtoui, A. 2022. "Upward Mobility, Despite a Stigmatised Identity: Immigrants of Iranian Origin in Sweden." *Nordic Journal of Migration Research* 12 (1): 54–71.
Benhabib, Seyla. 2002. *The Claims of Culture: Equality and Diversity in the Global Era*. Princeton University Press.
Berlant, Lauren. 1997. *The Queen of America Goes to Washington City*. Duke University Press.
Bloemraad, Irene. 2006. *Becoming a Citizen: Incorporating Immigrants and Refugees in the United States and Canada*. University of California Press.
Bloemraad, Irene, Anna Korteweg, and Gökçe Yurdakul. 2008. "Citizenship and Immigration: Multiculturalism, Assimilation, and Challenges to the Nation-State." *Annual Review of Sociology* 34:153–79.
Bloemraad, Irene, and Matthew Wright. 2014. "'Utter Failure' or Unity out of Diversity? Debating and Evaluating Policies of Multiculturalism." Supplement, *International Migration Review* 48 (S1): S292–334.
Boehm, Mike. 2013. "Huge Significance Rolled into Tiny Cyrus Cylinder at the Getty Villa." *LA Times*, November 13, 2013.
Bogost, Ian. 2020. "A New, Meme-Fueled Nostalgia for War." *The Atlantic*, January 4.
Borevi, Karin. 2014. "Multiculturalism and Welfare State Integration: Swedish Model Path Dependency." *Identities* 21 (6): 708–23.
Bourdieu, Pierre. 1986. "The Forms of Capital." In *Handbook of Theory and Research for the Sociology of Education*, edited by J. Richardson, 241–58. Greenwood Press.
———. 1993. *The Field of Cultural Production*. Columbia University Press.
Bozorgmehr, Mehdi. 1997. "Internal Ethnicity: Iranians in Los Angeles." *Sociological Perspectives* 40 (3): 387–408.

Bozorgmehr, Mehdi, and Eric Ketchum. 2018. "Adult Children of Professional and Entrepreneurial Immigrants: Second-Generation Iranians in the United States." In *The Iranian Diaspora: Challenges, Negotiations, and Transformations*, edited by Mohsen Mobasher. University of Texas Press.

Brown, Jesse. 2018. "Fact-Checking Jian Ghomeshi's Comeback Attempt." *Canadaland*, September 17, 2018.

Brown, Wendy. 2015. *Undoing the Demos: Neoliberalism's Stealth Revolution*. MIT Press.

Broverman, Neal. 2010. "Emperor May Invade Downtown's Pershing Square." *Curbed LA*, September 30, 2010. https://la.curbed.com.

Brubaker, Rogers. 2005. "The 'Diaspora' Diaspora." *Ethnic and Racial Studies* 28 (1): 1–19.

Byrne, Malcolm. 2014. *Iran-Contra: Reagan's Scandal and the Unchecked Abuse of Presidential Power*. University Press of Kansas.

Calliste, Agnes. 1994. "Race, Gender and Canadian Immigration Policy: Blacks from the Caribbean 1900–1932." *Journal of Canadian Studies* 28 (4): 131–47.

Cameron, Elspeth. 2004. *Multiculturalism & Immigration in Canada: An Introductory Reader*. Canadian Scholars' Press.

Canada Revenue Agency. 2023. "Engaging in Allowable Activities." Government of Canada, December 29, 2023. https://www.canada.ca.

Carlson, Harry Gilbert. 1963. "Riksteatern: The Swedish National Provincial Theatre." *Educational Theatre Journal* 15:39–46.

Castañeda, Ernesto. 2018. *A Place to Call Home: Immigrant Exclusion and Urban Belonging in New York, Paris, and Barcelona*. Stanford University Press.

CBC News. 2012. "Iranian Canadians Fume as TD Closes Accounts." July 11, 2012.

———. 2022. "Tensions Rise in Toronto's Persian Community as Activists Try to Expose Regime Links in Canada." November 13, 2022.

Chagnon, Jonathan. 2013. *Migration: International, 2010 and 2011*. Statistics Canada Catalogue no. 91-209-X. Report on the Demographic Situation in Canada.

Chelkowski, Peter J., and Hamid Dabashi. 1999. *Staging a Revolution: The Art of Persuasion in the Islamic Republic of Iran*. New York University Press.

Chishti, Muzaffar, Faye Hipsman, and Isabel Ball. 2015. "Fifty Years On, the 1965 Immigration and Nationality Act Continues to Reshape the United States." Migration Policy Institute, October 15, 2015. www.migrationpolicy.org.

Citizenship and Immigration Canada. 2012. *Evaluation of the Multiculturalism Program*. Evaluation Division, Research and Evaluation. www.cic.gc.ca.

City of Toronto. n.d. "City of Toronto Symbols." Accessed December 14, 2023. https://www.toronto.ca/.

Cooper, Afua. 2006. "Slavery in Canada." Ontario Historical Society. Accessed December 14, 2023. http://ontariohistoricalsociety.ca.

Creese, Gillan, and Brandy Wiebe. 2009. "'Survival Employment': Gender and Deskilling Among African Immigrants in Canada." *International Migration* 50 (5): 56–76.

Curtis, John. 2013a. "The Cyrus Cylinder: The Creation of an Icon and Its Loan to Tehran." In *The Cyrus Cylinder: The King of Persia's Proclamation from Ancient Babylon*, edited by Irving Finkel. I. B. Tauris.

———. 2013b. "The Cyrus Cylinder from Ancient Babylon and the Beginning of the Persian Empire." The Met, YouTube video, June 20, 2013. https://www.youtube.com/watch?v=5qIoEevJ6qE.

"The Cyrus Cylinder and Ancient Persia: A New Beginning." Smithsonian Institute, National Museum of Asian Art. Last accessed March 9, 2025, www.si.edu.

Dabashi, Hamid. 2015. *Persophilia: Persian Culture on the Global Scene.* Harvard University Press.

*Dagens Nyheter.* 2009. "Eldfest." March 17, 2009.

———. 2012. "Fler kineser—och allt färre finländare." May 15, 2012.

Dana, Omid. 2019. "حقیقت جشن چهارشنبه سوری استکهلم، مافیای مالی، نابودی فرهنگ ایران_رودست". YouTube video, March 24, 2019. https://www.youtube.com/watch?v=VTuDfcbxKeE.

Davies, William. 2021. "The Politics of Recognition in the Age of Social Media." *New Left Review* 128:83–99.

De Genova, Nicholas. 2016. "The European Question: Migration, Race, and Postcoloniality in Europe." *Social Text* 34, no. 3.

Destination Ontario. 2024. "Interesting facts about Harbourfront Centre." Last updated December 17, 2024. http://www.destinationontario.com.

Donovan, Kevin, and Alyshah Hasham. 2015. "Jian Ghomeshi Now Charged with Sexually Assaulting Six Women." *Toronto Star*, January 8, 2015.

Douglas, Mary. (1950) 2002. "Foreword: No Free Gifts." In *The Gift: The Form and Reason for Exchange in Archaic Societies* by Marcel Mauss, ix–xxiii. Routledge.

Dufoix, Stéphane. 2008. *Diasporas.* University of California Press.

*DW Farsi.* 2012. "سیر صعودی مهاجرت نخبگان علمی ایرانی" [The rising trend in the migration of Iranian scientific elites], May 29, 2012. https://www.dw.com.

Ekman, Mattias. 2022. "The Great Replacement: Strategic Mainstreaming of Far-Right Conspiracy Claims." *Convergence* 28 (4): 1127–43.

Elswit, Kate. 2018 "Performing Anti-Nationalism: Solidarity, Glitter and No-Borders Politics with the Europa Europa Cabaret." *Theatre Research International* 43 (1): 25–44.

Emami, Gazelle. 2016. "The *Not Without My Daughter* Problem: How a Sally Field Movie Became an Iranian-American Headache." *Vulture*, January 11, 2016. www.vulture.com.

*Entekhab.ir News.* 2013. "سرنوشت رتبه های برتر کنکور چیست؟" [What is the fate of the top ranked of the entrance exam?], November 5, 2013. www.entekhab.ir.

Environics Institute. 2021. "50 Years of Multiculturalism." *Insights*, October 7, 2021.

Eskandari, Maryam. 2011. "Dear Tirgan." Maryam Eskandari (blog), July 20, 2011. https://tirgan.ca.

Estiri, Ehsan. 2024. "Islam L.A. Style: Talking Back to America Through Islamic Discourses." *HAU: Journal of Ethnographic Theory* 14 (1): 176–90.

Farahani, Fataneh. 2018. *Gender, Sexuality, and Diaspora.* Routledge.

Farhang Förening. 2014. "Om Farhang—In English." Accessed April 23, 2014. http://www.farhang.nu.

Farhang Foundation. n.d.a. "Freedom Sculpture." Accessed December 13, 2022. http://www.freedomsculpture.org.

———. n.d.b. "About." The Freedom Sculpture. Accessed March 31, 2025 https://freedomscuplture.org.

———. n.d.c. "About." Accessed March 1, 2025. http://farhang.org/about

———. n.d.d. "Letter from the Chairman." In *Annual Report 2016–2017*, 8–9. Farhang Foundation. http://www.farhang.org.

———. n.d.e. "Milestones and History." Accessed December 13, 2022. http://www.freedomsculpture.org.

———. 2014. "'Freedom: A Shared Dream'—International Public Urban Art Competition Sponsored by Farhang Foundation." May 2, 2014. www.payvand.com.

———. 2017. *Annual Report 2016–2017*. Farhang Foundation. http://www.farhang.org.

———. 2019. *Annual Report 2018–2019*. Farhang Foundation. http://www.farhang.org.

———. 2020. "Farhang Foundation's 2020 State of the Foundation Address." YouTube video, November 17, 2020. https://www.youtube.com/watch?v=bujc3WFhB6o&t=3s.

———. 2021. *Annual Report 2019–2021*. Farhang Foundation. http://www.farhang.org.

———. 2023. *Annual Report 2021–2023*. Farhang Foundation. http://www.farhang.org.

———. 2024. *Annual Report 2023–2024*. Farhang Foundation. http://www.farhang.org.

Farrell, Leslie. 2022. "Course Helps Persian Immigrants Respond to Anti-black Racism in America." *Baha'is of the United States*, October 11, 2022. http://bahai.us.

Farrokhzad, Athena. 2013. *Vitsvit*. Argos Books.

———. 2018 "Europe, Where Have You Misplaced Love?: An Open Letter from a Poet." *Literary Hub*, August 23, 2018. http://lithub.com.

Fassihi, Farnaz. 2020. "A #MeToo Awakening Stirs in Iran." *New York Times*, October 22, 2020.

Fassihi, Farnaz, and Catherine Porter. 2020. "Famed Iranian Artist Under #MeToo Cloud Faces Art World Repercussions." *New York Times*, November 1, 2020.

Fayyaz, Sam, and Roozbeh Shirazi. 2013. "Good Iranian, Bad Iranian: Representations of Iran and Iranians in Time and Newsweek (1998–2009)." *Iranian Studies* 46 (1): 53–72.

Fekete, Liz. 2004. "Anti-Muslim Racism and the European Security State." *Race & Class*, 46 (1): 3–29.

Finkelman, Paul. 2014. *Slavery and the Founders: Race and Liberty in the Age of Jefferson*. Routledge.

FitzGerald, David Scott, and David Cook-Martin. 2014. *Culling the Masses: The Democratic Origins of Racist Immigration Policy in the Americas*. Harvard University Press.

Foltz, Richard. 2009. "Iranian Zoroastrians in Canada: Balancing Religious and Cultural Identities." *Iranian Studies* 42 (4): 561–77.

Foner, Nancy. 2005. *In a New Land: A Comparative View of Immigration*. New York University Press.

Fozi, Navid. 2021. "A Fragmented and Polarized Diaspora: The Making of an Iranian Pluralist Consciousness in Malaysia." *Diaspora: A Journal of Transnational Studies* 21 (2): 231–58.

*France 24*. 2023. "Sweden's 'Truth Commission' Delves into Painful Sami Past." October 5, 2023. www.france24.com.

Fraser, Nancy. 2000. "Rethinking Recognition." *New Left Review* 3:107–20.

Galloway, Matt. 2020. "The Current." CBC Radio. Aired January 9, 2020.

Gardiner, Aidan. 2019. "Iranian Families Divided by the Trump Travel Ban Tell of Holidays Apart and Lives on Hold." *New York Times*, December 20, 2019.

Geertz, Clifford. 1973. *The Interpretation of Cultures*. Basic Books.

Gera, Deborah Levine. 1993. *Xenophon's Cyropaedia: Style, Genre, and Literary Technique*. Oxford University Press.

Gholami, Reza. 2015. *Secularism and Identity: Non-Islamiosity in the Iranian Diaspora*. Routledge.

Ghomeshi, Jian. 2018. "Reflections from a Hashtag." *New York Review of Books*, October 11, 2018.

Ghorashi, Halleh. 2003. *Ways to Survive, Battles to Win: Iranian Women Exiles in the Netherlands and the United States*. Nova Science.

———. 2004. "How Dual is Transnational Identity? A Debate on Dual Positioning of Diaspora Organizations." *Culture and Organization* 10 (4): 329–40; 335–36.

Gladstone, Rick, and Christine Hauser. 2012. "Courts Rebuke Iran's President with Sentences and Ally's Firing." *New York Times*, July 30, 2012.

Global News. 2020. "Canada Mourns: Iran Plane Crash Memorial Ceremony." YouTube video, January 12, 2020. www.youtube.com/watch?v=8GUXG0qonqM.

Goldsbie, Jonathan. 2020. "Ghomeshi's Back." *Canadaland*, May 8, 2020.

Gosling, Emily. 2018. "Parasto Backman on How to Embed Feminist, Post-colonial + Intersectional Perspectives into Graphic Design." *Eye on Design*, January 15, 2018. www.eyeondesign.aiga.org.

Government of Canada. n.d. "Indigenous Peoples and Communities." Accessed March 9, 2025. www.rcaanc-cirnac.gc.ca.

———. 2024. "How Express Entry Works." www.canada.ca/.

Government Offices of Sweden Ministry of Labour. 2013. "2013 Nordic Pocket Facts—Statistics on Integration." November 28, 2013. http://ast.dk.

Grigor, Talinn. 2005. "Preserving the Antique Modern: Persepolis '71." *Future Anterior* 2 (1): 22–29.

———. 2014. *Contemporary Iranian Art: From the Street to the Studio*. Reaktion Books.

———. 2021. *The Persian Revival: The Imperialism of the Copy in Iranian and Parsi Architecture*. Penn State University Press.

Gualtieri, Sarah. 2009. *Between Arab and White: Race and Ethnicity in the Early Syrian American Diaspora*. University of California Press.

*The Guardian*. 2020. "Trudeau Tells Iran Crash Vigil He Will Pursue 'Justice and Accountability.'" January 12, 2020.

Hackl, Andreas, ed. 2022. *Permitted Outsiders: Good Citizenship and the Conditional Inclusion of Migrant and Immigrant Minorities*. Routledge.

Hage, Ghassan. 2021. *The Diasporic Condition: Ethnographic Explorations of the Lebanese in the World*. University of Chicago Press.
Hajighasemi, Ali. 2012. "The Political Life of Iranian Immigrants in Sweden." In *The Iranian community in Sweden: Multidisciplinary perspectives*, edited by Hassan Hosseini-Kaladjahi, 65–93. Stockholm: Mångkulturellt centrum.
Hale, Charles. 2006. "Neoliberal Multiculturalism: The Remaking of Rights and Racial Dominance in Central America." *PoLAR* 28 (1): 10–28.
Halkett, Kimberly. 2013. "Cyrus Cylinder Goes on Display in US." *Al Jazeera English*, YouTube video, March 30, 2013. www.youtube.com/watch?v=aGBacaBrbA4.
Hall, Stuart. 1997. *Representation: Cultural Representations and Signifying Practices*. Sage.
———. 2001. "The Multicultural Question." Milton Keynes, UK: Open University Pavis Papers in Social and Cultural Research.
Hanberg, Martin. 2010. "Eldfesten flyttar till City." *Svenska Dagbladet*, March 16, 2010.
Handy, Femida, and Itay Greenspan. 2009. "Immigrant Volunteering: A Stepping Stone to Integration?" *Nonprofit and Voluntary Sector Quarterly* 38 (6): 956–82.
Harbourfront Centre. 2013. *Summer Festival Partnership Handbook 2013*. Harbourfront Centre.
Harding, Tobias. 2021. "Culture Wars? The (Re)politicization of Swedish Cultural Policy." *Cultural Trends* 31 (2): 115–32.
Hashemi, Manata. 2020. *Coming of Age in Iran: Poverty and the Struggle for Dignity*. New York University Press.
Hashemi, Zinat. 2012. "شرکت هزاران نفر در مراسم چهارشنبه سوری در سوئد". *SverigeRadio— Radio Sweden Farsi/Dari*, March 14, 2012.
Hembree, Diana. 2018. "Bank of America Accused of Discrimination Against Iranian Americans." *Forbes*, May 22, 2018.
Hemmasi, Farzaneh. 2020. *Tehrangeles Dreaming: Intimacy and Imagination in Southern California Iranian Pop Music*. Duke University Press.
Henley, John. 2022. "Sweden's Failed Integration Creates 'Parallel Societies', Says PM After Riots." *The Guardian*, April 28, 2022.
Hirabayashi, Bernice. 1991. "Minority Students Excel at Abundant Beverly Hills High." *Los Angeles Times*, October 17, 1991.
Hoge, Warren. 1998. "A Swedish Dilemma: The Immigrant Ghetto." *New York Times*, Oct 6, 1998.
Hosseini, Mansour. 2021. "Så blir Eldfesten i år: 'Viktigare än någonsin.'" *SVT Nyheter*, March 16, 2021.
House of Iran. n.d. "About House of Iran in San Diego." Accessed November 23, 2022. http://thehouseofiran.com.
Hübinette, Tobias. 2013. "Swedish Antiracism and White Melancholia: Racial Words in a Post-racial Society." *Ethnicity and Race in a Changing World: A Review Journal* 4 (1): 24–33.
———. 2023. "Swedish Whiteness as White Terror and Non-white Rage in Antiracist Sweden." In *Race in Sweden: Racism and Antiracism in the World's First 'Colourblind'*

*Nation*, edited by Tobias Hübinette, Catrin Lundström, and Peter Wikström, 114–138. Routledge.

Hübinette, Tobias, and Catrin Lundström. 2014. "Swedish Whiteness and White Melancholia." In *Unveiling Whiteness in the Twenty-First Century: Global Manifestations, Transdisciplinary Interventions*, edited by Veronica Watson, Deirdre Howard-Wagner, and Lisa Spanierman, 49–74. Lexington Books.

Iranian Americans' Contributions Project. n.d. "About." Accessed July 19, 2024. https://ia-cp.org.

Iranian Canadian Centre for Art and Culture (ICCAC). 2010. *Tirgan Organizational Structure Manual: (Version 1)*. Iranian Canadian Centre for Art and Culture (ICCAC).

ITI Germany. 2014. "Creating a Different Festival." In *ITI Jahrbuch/Yearbook 2014*, ITI Germany.

Jacoby, Tamar. 1986. "The Reagan Turnaround on Human Rights." *Foreign Affairs* 64 (5): 1066–86.

Jamal, Amaney, and Nadine Naber, eds. 2008. *Race and Arab Americans Before and After 9/11*. Syracuse University Press.

Kajart. 2016. "Freedom: A Shared Dream." Video, 2016. www.kajart.com

Karim, Persis. 2013. "Guest Editor's Introduction: Iranian Diaspora Studies." *Iranian Studies* 46 (1): 49–52.

———. 2020. "In Praise of Big Noses." In *My Shadow Is My Skin: Voices from the Iranian Diaspora*, edited by Katherine Whitney and Leila Emery, 112–19. University of Texas Press.

Karim, Persis, and Babak Elahi. 2011. "Introduction: Iranian Diaspora." *Comparative Studies of South Asia, Africa and the Middle East* 31 (2): 381–87.

Kasheff, Manouchehr, and ʿAlī-Akbar Saʿīdī Sīrjānī. 1990. "ČAHĀRŠANBA-SŪRĪ," *Encyclopaedia Iranica*, 6:630–34.

Kelley, Ninette, and M. Trebilcock. 2000. *The Making of the Mosaic: A History of Canadian Immigration Policy*. University of Toronto Press.

Kelley, Ron. 1991. "Iranian Protest Demonstrations in Los Angeles." In *Iranian Refugees and Exiles Since Khomeini*, edited by Asghar Fathi. Mazda Publishers.

Kelly, Melissa. 2011. "Transnational Diasporic Identities: Unity and Diversity in Iranian-Focused Organizations in Sweden." *Comparative Studies of South Asia, Africa and the Middle East* 31 (2): 443–54.

Khanghahi, Sarah. 2017. "Thirty Years After Al-Khazraji: Revisiting Employment Discrimination Under Section 1981." *UCLA Law Review* 64:794.

Khosravi, Shahram. 2009. "Displaced Masculinity: Gender and Ethnicity among Iranian Men in Sweden." *Iranian Studies* 42 (4): 591–609.

———. 2010. *'Illegal' Traveller: An Authoethnography of Borders*. London: Palgrave Macmillan.

———. 2012. "White Masks/Muslim Names: Immigrants and Name-Changing in Sweden." *Race & Class* 53 (3): 65–80.

———. 2018. "A Fragmented Diaspora." *Nordic Journal of Migration Research* 8 (2): 73–81.

Kingston, Anne. 2016. "What Jian Ghomeshi Did: How a Trial That Was Supposed to Flip the Script Only Made Things Worse." *Maclean's*, March 30, 2016.

Korteweg, Anna C., and Triadafilos Triadafilopoulos. 2014. "Is Multiculturalism Dead? Groups, Governments and the 'Real Work of Integration.'" *Ethnic and Racial Studies* 38 (5): 663–80.

Kulturrådet. n.d. "Cultural Policy Objectives." Accessed May 6, 2014. http://kulturradet.se.

Kymlicka, Will. 2012a. "Comment on Meer and Modood." *Journal of Intercultural Studies* 33 (2): 211–16.

———. 2012b. "Multiculturalism: Success, Failure, and the Future." In *Rethinking National Identity in the Age of Migration: The Transatlantic Council on Migrationå*, edited by Bertelsmann Stiftung and Migration Policy Institute, 33–78. Gütersloh Verlag Bertelsmann Stiftung.

———. 2015. "Solidarity in Diverse Societies: Beyond Neoliberal Multiculturalism and Welfare Chauvinism." *Comparative Migration Studies* 3:17.

Laguna, Albert. 2017. *Diversión: Play and Popular Culture in Cuban America*. New York University Press.

Lai, Tianjian, and Jeanne Batalova. 2021. "Immigrants from Iran in the United States." *Migration Information Source*, July 15, 2021. www.migrationpolicy.org.

Lee, Ching Kwan. 2020. "An Ethnography of Comparative Ethnography: Pathways to Three Logics of Comparison." In *Beyond the Case: The Logics and Practices of Comparative Ethnography*, edited by Corey M. Abramson and Neil Gong, 139–61. Oxford University Press.

Lorcin, P. E. 2013. "Imperial Nostalgia; Colonial Nostalgia." *Historical Reflections/Réflexions Historiques* 39 (3): 97–111.

Love, Erik. 2020. "Islamophobia: The Racial Paradox and the Racial Dilemma." *Political Theology* 21 (5): 461–66.

Lu, Yuqian, and Feng Hou. 2015. *Insights on Canadian Society: International Students Who Become Permanent Residents in Canada*. Statistics Canada, Minister of Industry.

*Maclean's*. 2012. "Don't Be Too Quick to Condemn TD Bank for Shutting Iranian Accounts." July 23, 2012.

Maghbouleh, Neda. 2017. *The Limits of Whiteness: Iranian Americans and the Everyday Politics of Race*. Stanford University Press.

Maghbouleh, Neda, and Amy Malek. 2023. "What the Latest Census Results Reveal about Iranian Americans." *With a Trace: Documenting and Sharing the Experiences of the Iranian Diaspora* (blog), October 3, 2023. https://centerforiraniandiasporastudies.wordpress.com.

Mahmoudi, Hassan. 2021. "Iran Loses Highly Educated and Skilled Citizens during Long-Running 'Brain Drain.'" Migration Policy Institute, April 21, 2021. www.migrationpolicy.org.

Malek, Amy. 2011. "Public Performances of Identity Negotiation in the Iranian Diaspora: The New York Persian Day Parade." *Comparative Studies of South Asia, Africa and the Middle East* 31 (2): 388–410.

———. 2015. "Claiming Space: Documenting Second-Generation Iranian Americans in Los Angles." *Anthropology of the Middle East* 10 (2): 16–45.

———. 2019. "Paradoxes of Dual Nationality: Geopolitical Constraints on Multiple Citizenship in the Iranian Diaspora." *Middle East Journal* 73 (4): 531–54.

———. 2021. "Persian Language Use and Vitality in Tehrangeles." In *Multilingual LaLa Land*, edited by Claire Chik, 229–46. Routledge.

———. 2023. "On Unity and Fragmentation in the Iranian Diaspora." *Society for Cultural Anthropology*, June 29, 2023.

Marashi, Afshin. 2008. *Nationalizing Iran: Culture, Power, and the State, 1870–1940*. University of Washington Press.

Marcus, George. 1995. "Ethnography in/of the World System: The Emergence of Multi-Sited Ethnography." *Annual Review of Anthropology* 24:95–117.

Marks, Rachel, Paul Jacobs, and Alli Coritz. 2023. "Lebanese, Iranian and Egyptian Populations Represented Nearly Half of the MENA Population in 2020 Census." September 21, 2023. www.census.gov.

Matin-Asgari, Afshin. (1991) 2002. *Iranian Student Opposition to the Shah*. University of Michigan Press.

Mauss, Marcel. (1950) 2000. *The Gift: Forms and Functions of Exchange in Archaic Societies*. W. W. Norton.

McClintock, Anne. 1993. "Family Feuds: Gender, Nationalism, and the Family." *Feminist Review* 44:61–80.

Meer, Nassar, Tariq Modood, and Ricard Zapata-Barrero. 2016. *Multiculturalism and Interculturalism: Debating the Dividing Lines*. Edinburgh University Press.

Meftahi, Ida. 2016. *Gender and Dance in Modern Iran: Biopolitics on Stage*. Routledge.

Mehta, Diane, and Tabitha Marshall. 2019. "Jian Ghomeshi Case." *Canadian Encyclopedia*, February 26, 2019.

Melamed, Jodi. 2011. *Represent and Destroy: Rationalizing Violence in the New Racial Capitalism*. University of Minnesota Press.

Merhavy, Menahem. 2015. "Religious Appropriation of National Symbols in Iran: Searching for Cyrus the Great." *Iranian Studies* 48 (6): 933–48.

———. 2019. *National Symbols in Modern Iran: Identity, Ethnicity, and Collective Memory*. Syracuse University Press.

Minazad, Orly. 2013. "What the Cyrus Cylinder at the Getty Villa Means to LA's Iranian Community." *LA Weekly*, October 18, 2013. www.laweekly.com.

Minister of Public Works and Government Services Canada. 1999. *Citizenship and Immigration Statistics—1996*. Citizenship and Immigration Canada, Cat. No. MP22-1/1996.

Mirfakhraie, Amir Hossein. 1999. "Transmigration and Identity Construction: The Case of Iranians in Canada, 1946–1998." MA thesis, Simon Frasier University.

Moallem, Minoo. 2000. "'Foreignness' and Be/longing: Transnationalism and Immigrant Entrepreneurial Spaces." *Comparative Studies of South Asia, Africa and the Middle East* 20 (1–2): 200–210.

———. 2005. *Between Warrior Brother and Veiled Sister*. University of California Press.

Mobasher, Mohsen. 2006. "Cultural Trauma and Ethnic Identity Formation Among Iranian Immigrants in the United States." *American Behavioral Scientist* 50 (1): 100–117.

———. 2012. *Iranians in Texas: Migration, Politics, and Ethnic Identity*. University of Texas Press.

———. 2013. "Iranian and Iranian Americans, 1940–Present." In *Immigrants in American History: Arrival, Adaptation, and Integration*, edited by Elliott Robert Barkan. ABC-CLIO.

———, ed. 2018. *The Iranian Diaspora: Challenges, Negotiations, and Transformations*. University of Texas Press.

Modarres, Ali. 1998. "Settlement Patterns of Iranians in the United States." *Iranian Studies* 31, (1): 31–49.

Modood, Tariq. 2017. "Must Interculturalists Misrepresent Multiculturalism?" *Comparative Migration Studies* 5 (15): 6.

Moghadam, Amin. 2021. "Iranian Migrations to Dubai: Constraints and Autonomy of a Segmented Diaspora." Working Paper No. 2021/3, Ryerson Centre for Immigration and Settlement (RCIS).

Moradian, Manijeh. 2022. *This Flame Within: Iranian Revolutionaries in the United States*. Duke University Press.

Moritz-Rabson, Daniel. 2019. "Venmo Flags Payments for 'Persian' Restaurants, Other Terms Related to Iran Due to Sanctions." *Newsweek*, February 28, 2019.

Moss, Dana. 2021. *The Arab Spring Abroad: Diaspora Activism against Authoritarian Regimes*. Cambridge University Press.

Mossayeb, Sina, and Roozbeh Shirazi. 2006. "Education and Emigration: The Case of the Iranian-American Community." *Current Issues in Comparative Education* 9 (1): 30–45.

Mostafavi, Parmida. 2024. "'Wearing the Homeland': Multicultural Capitalism and the Racial Politics of Diasporic Iranian Consumerism." PhD diss., New York University.

Motadel, David. 2014. "Iran and the Aryan Myth." In *Perceptions of Iran: History, myths and nationalism from Medieval Persia to the Islamic Republic*, edited by Ali M. Ansari, 119–46. I. B. Tauris.

Mottahedeh, Roy. 1985. *The Mantle of the Prophet: Religion and Politics in Iran*. Oneworld.

Naber, Nadine. 2000. "Ambiguous Insiders: An Investigation of Arab American Invisibility." *Ethnic and Racial Studies* 23 (1): 37–61.

Naficy, Hamid. 1993. *The Making of Exile Cultures: Iranian Television in Los Angeles*. University of Minnesota.

———. 1997. "Mediating the Other: American Pop Culture Representation of Postrevolutionary Iran." In *The U.S. Media and the Middle East: Image and Perception*, edited by Yahya Kamalipour, 73–90. Greenwood Press.

———. 2012. *A Social History of Iranian Cinema*. Vol. 3, *The Islamicate Period, 1978–1984*. Duke University Press.

Naghibi, Nima. 2016. *Women Write Iran: Nostalgia and Human Rights from the Diaspora*. University of Minnesota Press.

Narang, Sonia. 2013. "This 2,600-Year-Old Clay Cylinder is Bringing Tears, and Pride, to Iranians in the US." *The World*, Public Radio International, December 7, 2013.

Nasser, Shanifa. 2020. "Iran's #MeToo Movement Makes Waves in Toronto as Calls Mount for Festival to Cut Ties with Celebrated Artist." *CBC News*, November 2, 2020.

Nejad, Reza Haghighat. 2013. "Khomeini's Granddaughter Photoshops Her Daughter's Skinny Trousers." *IranWire*, September 4, 2013. https://iranwire.com.

*NIAC News*. 2017. "Celebrating Heritage and Home: An Iranian-American Community's Gift to Los Angeles." June 1, 2017.

Nikou, Semira. 2017. "The Travel Ban and Iranian Americans." *MERIP*, May 9, 2017. https://merip.org.

Nikpour, Golnar. 2018. "Claiming Human Rights: Iranian Political Prisoners and the Making of a Transnational Movement, 1963–1979." *Humanity: An International Journal of Human Rights, Humanitarianism, and Development* 9 (3): 363–88.

Nili, Hadi. 2017. "منشور کورش، الهام‌بخش 'مجسمه آزادی' در لس‌آنجلس." *BBC Farsi*, July 5, 2017. www.bbc.com/persian/.

Nilsson, Per, and Lars Westin. 2022. "Ten Years After. Reflections on the Introduction of Tuition Fees for Some International Students in Swedish Post-Secondary Education." *Education Inquiry* 15 (4): 1–21.

NIPOC. 2023. "Mehregan 2020." YouTube video, February 2, 2023. https://www.youtube.com/watch?v=IuGMd6v3wTA.

Ohlsson, Per. 2006. "Still the Middle Way?" Lecture at Columbia University, September 28, 2006. http://www.columbia.edu.

Omi, Michael, and Howard Winant. 2015. *Racial Formation in the United States*. 3rd ed. Routledge.

Ong, Aihwa. 1996. "Cultural Citizenship as Subject-Making: Immigrants Negotiate Racial and Cultural Boundaries in the United States [and Comments and Reply]." *Current Anthropology* 37 (5): 737–62.

———. 1999. *Flexible Citizenship: The Cultural Logics of Transnationality*. Duke University Press.

———. 2004. "Latitudes of Citizenship: Membership, Meaning, and Multiculturalism." In *People out of Place: Globalization, Human Rights, and the Citizenship Gap*, edited by Alison Brysk and Gershon Shafir. Routledge.

———. 2006. *Neoliberalism as Exception: Mutations in Citizenship and Sovereignty*. Duke University Press.

PAAIA. n.d. "About." Accessed December 14, 2020. https://paaia.org.

Pahlavi, Mohammad Reza. 1961. *Mission for My Country*. London: Hutchinson.

Pakulski, Jan. 1997. "Cultural Citizenship." *Citizenship Studies* 1 (1): 73–86.

Park, Lisa S. 2005. *Consuming Citizenship: Children of Asian Immigrant Entrepreneurs*. Stanford University Press.

PARSA Community Foundation. 2007. "Darioush Khaledi's Persepolis-Inspired Winery." *Payvand*, June 22, 2007. www.payvand.com.
Parsi, Kourosh. 1997. "Cyrus in the Park." *The Iranian*, March 1997. https://iranian.com.
Payami, Babak. 2015. "A Message from the Artistic Director." *Tirgan Magazine 2013*, April 1, 2015.
———. 2017. "Tirgan 2017 Artistic Statement." *Tirgan Magazine 2017*.
Pew Research Center. 2015. "Selected U.S. Immigration Legislation and Executive Actions, 1790–2014." September 28, 2015. www.pewresearch.org.
Phillips, Anne. 2009. *Multiculturalism Without Culture*. Princeton University Press.
Portes, Alejandro, and Ruben Rumbaut. 2001. *Legacies: The Story of the Immigrant Second Generation*. University of California Press.
Public Safety Canada. 2024. "Government of Canada Lists the IRGC as a Terrorist Entity." Government of Canada, June 19, 2024. http://canada.ca.
Quinn, Michelle. 2017. "Iranian Americans Use Tech to Count Their Impact in US." *Voice of America*, April 6, 2017. https://voanews.com.
Radio Sweden Farsi. 2012. "گفتگو با منصور حسینی تهیه کننده در تئاتر ملی سوئد." *Sverige Radio P6*, March 8, 2012. http://sverigesradio.se.
Rahimieh, Nasrin. 2001. *Missing Persians: Discovering Voices in Iranian Cultural History*. Syracuse University Press.
———. 2016. *Iranian Culture: Representation and Identity*. Routledge.
———. 2023. "Politics of Vengeance in Iranian Diaspora Communities." *International Journal of Middle East Studies* 55 (4): 749–53.
Rana, Junaid. 2011. *Terrifying Muslims: Race and Labor in the South Asian Diaspora*. Duke University Press.
Razavi, Sahar. 2023. "Discord in the Diaspora: Agonism in the Women, Life, Freedom Movement for Democracy." *International Journal of Middle East Studies* 55 (4): 754–58.
Read, Richard, and Sarah Parvini. 2020. "Customs Agents Held More Iranian Americans and Others at U.S.-Canada Border Than It Admitted, Records Show." *Los Angeles Times*, November 17, 2020.
Reitz, Jeffrey G., and Rupa Banerjee. 2007. *Racial Inequality, Social Cohesion and Policy Issues in Canada*. Institute for Research on Public Policy.
*Reuters*. 2016. "Iranians arrested after celebrating ancient Persian king Cyrus the Great." October 31, 2016. www.reuters.com.
Rezaian, Jason. 2010. "In Iran, a Street Demonstration That Both Sides Stay Away From." *Time*, March 16, 2010.
Riksteatern. n.d. "Historia." Accessed April 22, 2014. https://www.riksteatern.se.
Roodsaz, Rahil. 2020. "Vacillating in and out of Whiteness: Non-religiosity and Racial (Dis)identification among the Iranian-Dutch." In *Transforming Bodies and Religions*, edited by Mariecke van den Berg, Lieke Schrijvers, Jelle Wiering, and Anne-Marie Korte, 178–98. Routledge.
———. 2022. *Sexual Self-Fashioning: Iranian Dutch Narratives of Sexuality and Belonging*. Berghahn.

Rosaldo, Renato. 1989. "Imperialist Nostalgia." *Representations* 26 (Spring): 107–22.
———. 1997. "Cultural Citizenship, Inequality, and Multiculturalism." In *Latino Cultural Citizenship*, edited by William V. Flores and Rina Benmayor, 27–38. Beacon Press.
Rumbaut, Rubén, and Douglas Massey. 2013. "Immigration & Language Diversity in the United States." *Daedalus* 142 (3): 141–54.
Ruggles, Steven, Sarah Flood, Ronald Goeken, Josiah Grover, Erin Meyer, Jose Pacas, and Matthew Sobek. 2019. *IPUMS USA: Version 9.0.* IPUMS. https://doi.org/10.18128/D010.V9.0.
Rytina, Nancy. 2022. *IRCA Legalization Effects: Lawful Permanent Residence and Naturalization Through 2001–2002.* Office of Policy and Planning, US INS, October 25, 2022.
Sadeghi, Sahar. 2023. *Conditional Belonging: The Racialization of Iranians in the Wake of Anti-Muslim Politics.* New York University Press.
Sameh, Catherine. 2019. *Axis of Hope: Iranian Women's Rights Activism Across Borders.* University of Washington Press.
Sanandaji, Nima. 2012. *Från fattigdom till framgång—om iranska invandrare som lyckas och om svensk integrationspolitik som inte gör det.* Stockholm: Timbro.
Saukkonen, Pasi. 2013. "Multiculturalism and Cultural Policy in Northern Europe." *Nordisk Kulturpolitisk Tidskrift* 16 (2): 178–200.
Schall, Carly Elizabeth. 2016. *The Rise and Fall of the Miraculous Welfare Machine: Immigration and Social Democracy in Twentieth-Century Sweden.* Cornell University Press.
Schierup, Carl-Ulrik, and Simone Scarpa. 2017. "How the Swedish Model Was (Almost) Lost: Migration, Welfare and the Politics of Solidarity." In *Reimagineering the Nation: Essays on Twenty-First-Century Sweden*, edited by Aleksandra Ålund, Carl-Ulrik Schierup, and Anders Neergaard, 41–83. Peter Lang Publishing Group.
Schnakenbourg, Éric. 2022. "Scandinavians and the Atlantic Slave Trade." *Digital Encyclopedia of European History*, June 6, 2022. https://ehne.fr.
Selig, Diana. 2008. *Americans All: The Cultural Gifts Movement.* Harvard University Press.
Semati, Mehdi, William P. Cassidy, and Mehrnaz Khanjani. 2021. *Iran and the American Media: Press Coverage of the 'Iran Deal' in Context.* Palgrave Macmillan.
Sepehri Far, Tara. 2020. "Iran Is Having Its #Metoo Moment." *Al Jazeera*, September 9, 2020.
Sethi, Simran. 2022. "Nowruz Is Banned in Afghanistan, but Families Continue to Celebrate." NPR, March 21, 2022.
Shakhsari, Sima. 2020. *The Politics of Rightful Killing.* Duke University Press.
Shannon, Matthew. 2017. *Losing Hearts and Minds: American-Iranian Relations and International Education During the Cold War.* Cornell University Press.
Sharifi, Azadeh. 2017. "Theatre and Migration." *Independent Theater in Contemporary Europe*, edited by Manfred Brauneck and ITI Germany, 321–416. Transcript Verlag.
Shay, Anthony, and Barbara Sellers-Young. 2003. "Belly Dance: Orientalism—Exoticism—Self-Exoticism." *Dance Research Journal* 35 (1): 13–37.

Shirazi, Maziar. 2016. "A Review of Tarabnameh, or, Why Are Iranian-Americans Laughing at Blackface in 2016?" Ajam Media Collective, December 7, 2016. http://ajammc.com.

Shirazi, Roozbeh. 2014. "The Pedagogy of Visibility: Constructs and Contests of Iranianness in a Community-Organized School in a Large Southern U.S. City." *Diaspora, Indigenous, and Minority Education* 8 (2): 108–24.

Siu, Lok C. D. 2005. *Memories of a Future Home: Diasporic Citizenship of Chinese in Panama*. Stanford University Press.

Skodo, Admir. 2018. "Sweden: By Turns Welcoming and Restrictive in its Immigration Policy." Migration Policy Institute. www.migrationpolicy.org.

Slyomovics, Susan. 1996. "The Muslim World Day Parade and 'Storefront' Mosques of New York City." *Comparative Studies on Muslim Societies* 22:204–16.

Solomon, Larry. 1979. "Iranian Students Will Not Face Deportation Hearings." *Daily O'Collegian*, vol. 85, no. 75, December 15, 1979.

Sommerville, Hannah. 2022. "New Documentary Honors PS752 Families' Lonely Quest for Justice." *IranWire*, September 9, 2022. www.iranwire.com.

Soroka, Stuart, and Sarah Roberton. 2010. *A Literature Review of Public Opinion Research on Canadian Attitudes Towards Multiculturalism and Immigration, 2006–2009*. Citizenship and Immigration Canada.

Spellman, Kathryn. 2004. *Religion and Nation: Iranian Local and Transnational Networks in Britain*. Berghahn.

Statistics Canada. 2021. "Visible Minority of Person." https://www23.statcan.gc.ca

———. 2022a. "The Canadian Census: A Rich Portrait of the Country's Religious and Ethnocultural Diversity." October 26, 2022. www.statcan.gc.ca.

———. 2022b. "Ethnic or Cultural Origin by Gender and Age: Canada, Provinces and Territories, Census Metropolitan Areas and Census Agglomerations with Parts: Table 98-10-0356-01." www.statcan.gc.ca.

———. 2022c. "Census Profile, 2021 Census of Population." Statistics Canada Catalogue no. 98-316-X2021001. Released December 15, 2022. https://www.statcan.gc.ca.

———. 2023. "Changing Demographics of Racialized People in Canada." August 23, 2023. www.statcan.gc.ca.

———. 2024. "Labour Force Characteristics by Immigrant Status, Annual: Table 14-10-0083-01." Released January 5, 2024. https://doi.org/10.25318/1410008301-eng.

Statistics Sweden. n.d.a. "Number of Persons with Foreign or Swedish Background (Detailed Division) by Region, Age and Sex. Year 2002–2021." Accessed October 17, 2024. www.statistikdatabasen.scb.se.

———. n.d.b. "Population by Country of Birth and Country of Origin, 31 December 2023, Total." Accessed March 9, 2025. www.scb.se.

———. n.d.c. "Population in Sweden by Country/Region of Birth, Citizenship and Swedish/Foreign Background, 31 December 2023." Accessed March 9, 2025. www.scb.se.

———. n.d.d. "Foreign Born Population by County, Municipality, Sex and Country of Birth December 31 2024." Accessed March 9, 2025. www.scb.se.

———. 2022. "Labour Force Surveys (LFS), 4th Quarter 2021: Unemployment Decreases Among both People Born in Sweden and Foreign Born People." Febrary 8, 2022. www.scb.se.

Steele, Robert. 2021. *The Shah's Imperial Celebrations of 1971: Nationalism, Culture, and Politics in Late Pahlavi Iran*. I. B. Tauris.

Stockholms stad. 2025. "Statistisk årsbok för Stockholm 2025." Accessed March 9, 2025. https://start.stockholm.

Strandberg, Sofia. 2009. "Misstänkt mordbrand i Kungsträdgården," *Svenska Dagbladet*, March 17, 2009.

Straw, Will. 2013. "Canadian Cities Take Over Cultural Policy." *Huffington Post*. Last updated August 3, 2013. http://www.huffingtonpost.ca.

Tajrobehkar, Bahar. 2021. "Orientalism and Linguicism: How Language Marks Iranian-Canadians as a Racial 'Other.'" *International Journal of Qualitative Studies in Education* 36 (4): 655–71.

Tavakoli-Targhi, Mohamad. 2001. *Refashioning Iran: Orientalism, Occidentalism and Historiography*. Palgrave Macmillan.

Taylor, Charles, K. Anthony Appiah, Jürgen Habermas, Steven C. Rockefeller, Michael Walzer, and Susan Wolf. 1994. *Multiculturalism: Expanded Paperback Edition*. Edited by Amy Gutmann. Princeton University Press.

Tehranian, John. 2009. *Whitewashed: America's Invisible Middle Eastern Minority*. New York: New York University Press.

Terhune, Lea. 2013. "Ancient Persian Ruler Influenced Thomas Jefferson, U.S. Democracy." IIP Digital, the US Department of State, March 17, 2013. http://www.payvand.com/.

Theodossopoulos, Dimitrios. 2013. "Laying Claim to Authenticity: Five Anthropological Dilemmas." *Anthropological Quarterly* 86 (2): 337–60.

Thobani, Sunera. 2007. *Exalted Subjects: Studies in the Making of Race and Nation in Canada*. University of Toronto Press.

Tirgan. n.d.a [2008]. "About the Festival." Accessed December 4, 2023. https://tirgan.ca.

———. n.d.b. "Tirgan: Respect in the Workplace Policy and Procedures." Accessed December 3, 2023. https://tirgan.ca.

———. 2013. "About Tirgan: An Ancient Celebration of Iranian Arts and Culture." Accessed December 4, 2023. https://2013.tirgan.ca.

———. 2015. "About Us." Accessed December 4, 2023. https://tirgan.ca.

———. 2022. *Tirgan Annual Report 2020*. Tirgan.

———. 2023a. "مستند داوطلبان سازمان فرهنگی-هنری تیرگان." YouTube video, July 28, 2023. https://www.youtube.com/watch?v=vgmwt3Y9R28.

———. 2023b. "Sponsorship Package." https://tirgan2023.tirgan.ca.

———. 2023c. "Unity: A Bridge to Freedom." YouTube video, March 24, 2023. https://www.youtube.com/watch?v=ORVNiLmlEV8.

Tirgan Media. 2020. "Tirgan Statement." November 11, 2020. https://tirgan.ca.

———. 2021a. "Episode 3: Why Tirgan?" *Nothing Feels Like Tirgan*, November 24, 2021.

———. 2021b. "Episode 6: How Tirgan Fits the Dscription of a Family?" *Nothing Feels Like Tirgan*, December 14, 2021.

———. 2021c. "Episode 8: What Are Your Best Moments at Tirgan?" *Nothing Feels Like Tirgan*, December 14, 2021.
———. 2021d. "Episode 10: Has Working with Tirgan Filled the Void of Yearning for Home and Nostalgia from Iran?" *Nothing Feels Like Tirgan*, December 30, 2021.
*Tirgan Magazine*. 2008. "Tirgan Festival Staff." July 17, 2008, 8.
———. 2011. "Tirgan Staff." February 7, 2011, 14.
Toronto Iranians. 2014. "Timeline of Iranian Canadian in Ontario." Graphic created by the Iranian Canadian Oral History Project. http://icoh.ca.
Triadafilopoulos, Triadafilos. 2012. *Becoming Multicultural: Immigration and the Politics of Membership in Canada and Germany*. Vancouver: University of British Columbia Press.
Tsubakihara, Atsuko. 2013. "Putting 'Tehrangeles' on the Map: A Consideration of Space and Place for Migrants." *Bulletin of the National Museum of Ethnology* 37 (3): 331–57.
Tuan, Mia. 1998. *Forever Foreigners or Honorary Whites? The Asian Ethnic Experience Today*. Rutgers University Press.
US Census Bureau. 2021. "Race and Ethnicity in the United States: 2010 Census and 2020 Census." August 12, 2021. www.census.gov.
———. 2023. "2022 American Community Survey 1-Year Estimates, Table S0201." In *Selected Population Profile in the United States: Iranian*. US Department of Commerce. https://data.census.gov.
US Department of Homeland Security Office of Immigration Statistics. 2022. "Table 14D, Refugee Arrivals by Region and Country of Nationality: Fiscal Years 2012 to 2021." In *Yearbook of Immigration Statistics: 2021*. US Department of Homeland Security. https://www.dhs.gov.
United Nations. n.d. "International Nowruz Day 21 March." Accessed March 24, 2024. www.un.org.
Valanejad, Kurosh. 2020. "The Freedom Sculpture, Revisited." September 27, 2020. https://kuroshv.blogspot.com.
Vaziri, Mostafa. 1993. *Iran as Imagined Nation: The Construction of National Identity*. Da Capo Press.
Vertovec, Steven, and Susanne Wessendorf, eds. 2010. *Multiculturalism Backlash: European Discourses, Policies and Practices*. Routledge.
Vossoughi, Shirin. 2022. "Race, Parenting, and Identity in the Iranian Diaspora." *Journal of Family Diversity in Education* 4 (2): 160–76.
Vossoughi, Shirin, and Sepehr Vakil. 2015. "'If One Member is Afflicted with Pain': Reflections on Ferguson, Race, and Solidarity Among Iranians in the U.S." *Ajam Media Collective*, February 2, 2015. https://ajammc.com.
Warikoo, Natasha, and Irene Bloemraad. 2018. "Economic Americanness and Defensive Inclusion: Social Location and Young Citizens' Conceptions of National Identity." *Journal of Ethnic and Migration Studies* 44 (5): 736–53.
Werbner, Pnina. 2012. "Multiculturalism from Above and Below: Analysing a Political Discourse." *Journal of Intercultural Studies* 33 (2): 197–209.

———. 2013. "Everyday Multiculturalism: Theorising the Difference Between 'Intersectionality' and 'Multiple Identities.'" *Ethnicities* 13 (4): 401–91.
Westall, Mark. 2022. "During Ongoing Protests in Iran the Freedom Sculpture in Century City Takes On New Meaning #Womanlifefreedom." *FAD Magazine*, November 1, 2022.
Westin, Charles. 2006. "Sweden: Restrictive Immigration Policy and Multiculturalism." Migration Policy Institute, June 1, 2006.
Winter, Elke. 2011. *Us, Them, and Others: Pluralism and National Identity in Diverse Societies*. University of Toronto Press.
Yalzadeh, Ida. 2021. "Persian/American Exceptionalism: Post-9/11 Strategies of Belonging in the Iranian Diaspora through Cultural Production." *Amerasia Journal* 47 (3): 405–22.
Yazdanfar, Mohammad Hossein. 2004. "History of Persian Media in Ontario." November 18, 2004. http://icoh.ca.
Yoshino, Kenji. 2007. *Covering: The Hidden Assault on Our Civil Rights*. Random House.
Yousefi, Pendar. 2019. "Designing a Festival." *Pendar Yousefi* (blog). https://mahimoto.com.
Yuval-Davis, Nira. 2006. "Belonging and the Politics of Belonging." *Patterns of Prejudice* 40 (3): 197–99.
Zapata-Barrero, Ricard. 2013. "The Three Strands of Intercultural Polities: A Comprehensive View; A Critical Review of Bouchard and Cantle Recent Books on Interculturalism." GRITIM Working Paper Series No. 17 (Summer 2013).
———. 2015. *Interculturalism in Cities: Concept, Policy, and Implementation*. Edward Elgar Publishing.
Zerehi, Sima Sahar. 2010. "Mapping Tehranto." *Shahrvand*, November 4, 2010.
Zia-Ebrahimi, Reza. 2016. *The Emergence of Iranian Nationalism: Race and the Politics of Dislocation*. Columbia University Press.
Ziaee, Donya, and Sima Sahar Zerehi. 2008. "Tirgan: Creating Community Through the Arts." *Tirgan Magazine*, July 17, 2008.

# INDEX

Page numbers in italics indicate Figures and Tables.

*aberu* (saving face), 155, 230, 308n3
ABF. *See* Arbetarnas Bildningsförbund
Abrams, Elliott, 130–31
Achaemenid Empire (550–330 BCE), 6, 89, 95, 97, 98, 296n33
activism, 8, 165, 275–76, 308n23; community, 77, 274; political, 65, 123, 303n58; student, 38–40, 47
advertisements, 95, *115*, 115–16, *140*, *193*, *199*, 221, 305n39
Afghanistan, 300n3, 300n10
Afghans, 68, 110, 139, 140
Africa, 43–44, 57, 81, 146, 160, 254, 289n31
African Americans, 81, 110, 215, 256, 272, 273
Afshin (Eldfesten committee member) (pseudonym), 162
Aghdashloo, Aydin, 210, 212, 214
Aghili, Nasim, 272
Ahadi, Daniel, 292n110
Ahmadinejad, Mahmoud, 105, 287n69
Akalla, Stockholm, 69, 292n112
Akhavan, Payam, 181
Aletheia Justice petition, 210–12, 213, 214
Alexander the Great, 89
Aliens Act (1927), Sweden, 45
Alinejad, Masih, 221
Ameeriar, Lalaie, 178
American Community Survey, 57, 291nn82–83
American Dream, 86, 112, 240, 308n17
American identity, 4, 85, 86, 91, 112, 268

Amini, Zhina Mahsa, 132, 218, 219
Andersson, Magdalena, 287n55
Ansari, Yassamin, 290n70, 296n33
anti-Arab sentiment, 171, 172, 175, 254, 255, 256, 259
anti-Black racism, 256, 272, 273
anti-Iranian sentiment, 47–49, *48*, 52
anti-Muslim racism (Islamophobia), 105, 164, 254–57, 294n161, 297n56
anti-racism, 111, 158, 173, 241, 259–60, 272–73
Apple, 247, 293n131
Arab, anti-, 171, 172, 175, 254, 255, 256, 259
Arash the Archer, Tirgan Festival, 192, *193*, 196–97, 305n39
Arbabi, Farnaz, 272
Arbetarnas Bildningsförbund (ABF), 136, 158, 159–60
architecture, 69, 98, 195, 198, 202
Ardekani, Alireza, 122
Arian (Tirgan volunteer), 204, 208–9, 231–32, 306n75
Ariannejad, Mehrdad, 7, 200, 210, 212–13, 216, 305n48
Arora Project, 121
arson, 87, 163–66, *164*
*ArtForum*, 211
artistic representation, Tirgan Festival, 194
artistic themes, Tirgan Festival, 196–98
artists, 65, 117–18, 162, 183, 249, 272; with Freedom Sculpture, 119, 123–24, 125, 131–32, *133*; #MeToo and, 210–12, 214; women, 11–12, 14, 58–60, 62, 67

arts, 7, 76, 116, 169; councils, 67, 119, 146, 167, 199; culture and, 5, 9, 32, 108, 118, 187, 191, 199, 201, 205, 222, 242, 243, 245, 271, 274; public, 3, 9, 16, 20, 31, 53, 106, 119, 250, 268, 269. *See also* Eldfesten festival; Farhang Förening; Farhang Foundation; Freedom Festival; Tirgan Festival

Arya Group, 119

Aryanism, 260, 261

Aryan myth, 255, 297n52

Aryan racial identity, 104, 111, 254, 256, 257, 297n52

Ashkan (Tirgan volunteer) (pseudonym), 1, 2, 33

Ashkenaz festival, Toronto, 187

Asian Americans, 57, 81, 252, 253, 258, 267, 286n48

assassinations, 62, 179

assimilation, 81, 84, 143, 285n23; covering strategy, 13–14, 49–50, 88, 105, 235, 257, 290n53, 291n102, 297n56; Indigenous groups and forced, 42, 45

Associated Press, 87, 128

asylum seekers, 11, 46, 59, *61*, 67–68, 274, 289n45

Atlanta, Georgia, 3, 9, 265–67, *266*, 277

Australia, 40, 118

authenticity, 32, 137, 241, 271; intracommunity debates over, 3, 153, 172–73, 177–78; "Iranianness" and, 19, 143–44, 149, 254; ownership, memory and, 148–56; Tirgan Festival, 261–62

Avery, Peter, 101, 296n40

Azerbaijan, 300n3

Baca, Lee, 298n100

Backman, Parastou, 272

Baghoolizadeh, Beeta, 296n33

Baha'is, 22

Balkans, 46, 72

Balmond, Cecil, 119, 123–24

bans: on Chaharshanbeh Suri, 137, *138*, 139, 140, 300n10; migration, 5; US with Muslim, 23–24, 57–58, 106, 110, 128–29, 235, 247, 257, 271

Banting, Keith, 289n33

Battisti, Danielle, 109–10

Bauböck, Rainer, 186

Behrang (radio producer) (pseudonym), 157

Behrouz (Tirgan volunteer), 69, 71, 201, 223

belly dancing, 170–71, 173, 259, 303n67

belonging, 3, 32, 112, 208, 225, 277; cultural, 148–56, 174–78, 231; diasporic, 10, 105, 199, 274; inclusion, cultural citizenship and, 10–16; inclusion and, 10, 11, 20, 27, 230, 259; Iranian diaspora tripping up and over lines of, 252–63; Iranian diaspora with being and, 234–46; in multicultural societies, 16–24, 28, 33, 231, 263, 269; nonbelonging, 15, 256, 259, 260, 269, 276

Beverly Hills, California, 52–53, 55, 106, 125, 290n71, 291n82

the Bible, 90, 98, 257

Bice, Stephanie, 290n70

blackface, 302n36

#BlackLivesMatter, 110, 215

Bloemraad, Irene, 86, 186, 200, 225, 260, 270, 287n51

Bourdieu, Pierre, 288n71

brain drain, 41, 72

branding, Tirgan Festival, 198

Bravo, 290n71, 308n10

British Museum, 89, 90, 97

Brown, Wendy, 15, 111, 231

Bush, George W., 54

California, 57, 116; Beverly Hills, 52–53, 55, 106, 125, 290n71, 291n82; San Francisco, 9, 22, 52, 294n2. *See also* Farhang Foundation; Los Angeles

Canada, 77, 245, 247, 304n9; arriving to, 69–80; citizenship, 86, 181, 186, 260–62, 289n31, 289n33; cultural identity, 86; cultural mosaic model, 80, 185–90, 191, 197–98, 242, 304n20; immigration, 42–43, 44, 46, 47, 70, 71, 79; Iranians today in, 78–80; Montréal, 23, 74, 75, 78, 180, 181; multiculturalism in, 23, 81–85, 183, 185, 241, 244, 260–62, 270; national identity, 23, 185–86, 242, 260; nonpartisanship and, 32, 182, 184, 195, 216, 217–27, 242, 270, 307n97; points system, 23, 44, 72, 79, 236; university students, 23, 41, 71, 73; US, Sweden and, 25–26; Vancouver, 23, 73, 74, 180, 181. *See also* Iranian Canadians; Tirgan; Toronto

Canada Mourns memorial, Toronto, 179–83, 209–10, 217, 304n7

Canadian Census, 45, 78, 289n33, 293n137

the Canadian Way, 32, 183, 243; nonpartisan, nonpolitical and challenging, 217–27; Tirgan and, 184, 192, 198

cancel culture, 213

capital: diasporic, 134, 198–209, 236; human, 15, 79, 183, 288n71; symbolic, 16, 32, 183–84, 225–26, 268–71. *See also* cultural capital; social capital

Caribbean, 44, 305n31

Carter, Jimmy, 47

CBC, 211, 212, 213, 214

censorship, 39, 40, 170, 187

censuses, 288n1; Canadian, 45, 78, 289n33, 293n137; US, 42, 44, 57, 291n80

CEP. *See* Community and Educational Programs

Chaharshanbeh Suri, 168, 272; banning of, 137, *138*, 139, 140, 300n10; as Eldfesten festival, 12, 31, 136, 139, 142, 149–52, 154, 163, 166, 241; fire-jumping and, 137, 150, 300n4; Haji Firuz and, 154, 155, 156; in Iran, 140, 156, 300n3, 300n10; with "Iranianness," 143, 148, 149–52, 175–77; multiculturalism and, 157, 173–77; Riksteatern and, 166, 176, 271

Change.org petition, 210

Chicano/a Americans, 81

children, 5, 36, 38, 40, 49, 73, 246; born in diaspora, 29; immigration and, 50, 68

Chile, 46, 59, 146

Chinese Americans, 253

Chinese Exclusion Acts (1882, 1923), 42

Chinese people, 42, 76, 253

citizenship, 16, 17, 73, 110, 113, 245, 246; Canadian, 86, 181, 186, 260–62, 289n31, 289n33; diasporic, 224, 226; "good," 15, 31, 252; multicultural, 199, 260–62. *See also* cultural citizenship

City of Tales. *See Shahr-e Ghesseh*

civil rights, 22, 42, 43, 55, 81, 256

class, 11, 23, 24, 53, 56, 84, 240; gender, race and, 15; mobility, 38; race, religion and, 32, 33, 233, 235, 253–63, 272, 274; race and, 12, 16, 110, 112, 253, 270; racialization of, 254, 286n48, 308n8

colonialism, 42, 45, 260

Columbus, Christopher, 109, 134

communities, 16, 31, 200, 285n8, 285n23; American Community Survey, 57, 291nn82–83; building, 12, 199, 201, 224, 238, 239, 262; with debates over authenticity, 3, 153, 172–73, 177–78; diasporic, 20–22, 92, 115, 184, 209, 219, 224, 232, 237, 274; First Nations, 82, 185, 260; fragmentation, 113, 196, 235; Iranians in Sweden building, 63–67; LGBTQ+, 7, 8, 77, 308n23; organizing, 28, 36, 65, 74, 206, 270, 274, 275. *See also* diaspora

Community and Educational Programs (CEP), HC, 189, 194, 196, 197

community partnership, 32, 189, 199, 201, 242, 305n32

Congress, US, 94, 290n70, 295n20

Constitution, US, 90, 109, 248

constitutions, 39, 71, 83, 222, 225

contributionism, 109–10, 113, 132, 134–35, 247, 249, 262
corporate sponsorships, 116, 187, 239, 244, 304n14, 305n31
covering strategy, assimilation, 13–14, 49–50, 88, 105, 235, 257, 290n53, 291n102, 297n56
COVID-19 pandemic, 115, 142, 177, 210, 212, 298n88, 298n92
crime, 87, 165, 180
Cuban Americans, 265
cultural capital, 24, 32, 250, 269, 288n71; diasporic, 198–209; education as, 16, 23, 63–64, 235; Tirgan and, 183–84, 198–209, 226
cultural citizens, becoming, 13–16
cultural citizenship, 9, 17, 200, 207, 223, 274, 308n8; belonging, inclusion and, 10–16; building, 231, 269; cultural production and, 24, 30, 273; diasporic, 20, 24; Eldfesten and, 251; Ong on, 14, 111, 178, 233, 237, 252–54, 308n8; race and, 252–53; "self-making" and, 13, 14, 111, 178, 233; Tirgan with, 224, 225, 226
cultural gifts, 109, 246–52, 262
cultural hybridity, 152, 153, 194, 261
cultural identity: Canadian, 86; immigrants, 147; Iranian, 19, 55, 200, 268, 275–76, 293n137; Iranian Americans, 268; Iranian Canadians, 200, 225; Persian, 293n137
cultural organizing, 3, 4, 7, 33, 230, 269–71
cultural production, 3, 55, 77, 102, 167, 199, 274; cultural citizenship and, 24, 30, 273; Cyromania and, 94–98; Eldfesten Committee meetings with, 144; exile, 104; multiculturalism and, 270
culture, 10, 84, 144, 146, 173, 213; arts and, 5, 9, 32, 108, 118, 187, 191, 199, 201, 205, 222, 242, 243, 245, 271, 274; belonging and, 148–56, 174–78, 231; inclusion and, 13, 32, 175, 233, 241–44, 246–52, 262; manipulation of, 150, 152, 261; ownership of, 16, 20, 241, 271;

representations, 3, 4, 8, 19, 21, 88, 143, 149, 152, 156, 195, 245, 255, 258, 268, 277. *See also* Eldfesten festival; Farhang Förening; Farhang Foundation; interculturalism; multiculturalism; Tirgan Festival
Curtis, John, 100, 101
Customs and Border Patrol, 54, 113
Cyromania, 244, 257, 258, 276; cultural production and, 94–98; history of, 97–106; imperial nostalgia and, 95–96, 102–5, 132
*Cyropaedia* (Xenophon), 90, 98, 107, 127, 294n5
the Cyrus Cylinder, 31, 197, 240, 244, 248, 257, 295n11; commodification of, 95, *103*, 296n46; function of, 97–98; at Getty Villa, 89, 92, *95*, 116, 118, 294n2, 296n46; at LA City Hall, *102*, 105; marketing of, 101–2; at the Metropolitan Museum of Art, 89, 101, 294n2; *A New Beginning* exhibition tour, 89, 92, 108, 110, 118, 129, 132; as "new beginning" for Iranian Americans, 91–94; replicas, 101, 102, 105, *115*, 118, 124, 126, 265, 298n88, 308n20; at Smithsonian Institute, 89, 90, *93*; translations, 100, 296n33; 2500 Year Celebrations and, 98, *99*, 101; visitor reactions, 92–94, *93*, 96, 105. *See also* Freedom Sculpture
Cyrus the Great (ca. 580–530 BCE), 105, 134, 197, 251, 261, 276, 296n33; bronze sculpture, 118, 265–67, *266*; commodification of, *103*, 296n46; democracy and, 296n35; legacy and influence, 89–92, 95, 96, 106–7, 109, 119, 123, 125, 127, 129–30, 248, 257; as national hero, 90–91, 97, 98, 100–103; in Quran, 295n31
Cyrus the Great Day, 102, 129, 130, 266

Dabashi, Hamid, 94
*Dagens Nyheter* (newspaper), *164*, 292n109
Dana, Omid, 175–76

INDEX | 335

David (LA community leader), 228–31, 247, 267–68
Declaration of Independence, US, 120, 130, 294n10
De Genova, Nicholas, 254
DEI. *See* Diversity, Equity, and Inclusion
Delijani, Ezatollah, 118, 298n100
Delshad, Jimmy, 55
democracy, 123, 144–45, 173, 201; Cyrus the Great and, 296n35; inclusion and, 31, 148, 158; multiculturalism and, 140, 157–58; practiced with cool comportment, 156–62, 241–42; Sweden and, 31, 156–62, 300n9
demographics: Iranians in diaspora today, 56–58, 67–69, 78–80; multiculturalism, 231, 242, 258
Department of State, US, 54, 90, 130
deportation, 47, 54
deserving, 15, 31, 110, 113, 141, 145, 232
diaspora, 3, 29; activism, 275, 276; Iranian identity with representation and recognition in, 17, 18–21; power and multicultural frameworks in, 237–46. *See also* Iranian diaspora
diasporic: belonging, 10, 105, 199, 274; communities, 20–22, 92, 115, 184, 209, 219, 224, 232, 237, 274; cultural citizenship, 20, 24; homes, 3, 9, 80, 262, 267, 269; identity, 10, 16, 21, 24, 233, 258, 262, 270, 295n28
diasporic capital, 134, 198–209, 236
diasporic citizenship, 224, 226
Diba, Kamran, 119
discrimination, 3, 54, 134, 247–48, 262, 276; labor and, 49, 64, 113, 214–15, 235, 269; racism and, 64, 86, 174, 238, 257, 289n33, 302n42; whiteness and, 88, 110–11
diversity, 7, 10, 18, 44, 56, 110, 215; freedom and, 101, 112, 123, 131; human rights and, 248; inclusion and, 186; multiculturalism and, 126–27, 183, 185, 187, 191, 197–99, 209

Diversity, Equity, and Inclusion (DEI), 215
Diversity Immigrant Visa program, 56
DMV area. *See* Washington DC-Maryland-Virginia area
*Donkeyland* (film), 310n14

Edinburgh Iranian Festival, Scotland, 7
education, 38, 56, 73, 79; CEP, 189, 194, 196, 197; as cultural capital, 16, 23, 63–64, 235; schools, 11, 75, 116, 238. *See also* students
Ehsan (concert producer) (pseudonym), 150–53, 176, 301nn28–30
Ehsassi, Ali, 191
Eldfesten Committee meetings, Stockholm, 144, 166, 259, 301n18; with authentication and memory, 154–56; democracy practiced with cool comportment, 156–62, 241–42; festival planning, 136–37, 149–50, 156, 158, 160–62, 171, 176–78; interculturalism funding and competition, 167–69; racial anxieties of representation and, 170–74; transparency, 161–62, 168, 175–76, 241, 245, 251
Eldfesten festival, Stockholm, 7, *140*, 159–61, 168, 176, 251, 258, 286n26, 300n8; birth of, 163–67; Chaharshanbeh Suri as, 12, 31, 136, 139, 142, 149–52, 154, 163, 166, 241; as contestation site, 143, 144, 148, 173, 178; as cultural gift, 248–49; fire-jumping, 137, *138*, 150, 170; "Iranianness" and, 137, 148–50, 173, 177; in media, 12, 141–42, *142*, 149, 156, 163, *164*, 165, 174–75, 241, 244; ownership, authenticity and memory, 148–56; Riksteatern with, 12–13, 136, 142, 148, 150–52, 162, 175, 177, 239, 250, 253; viewers, 142, 301n14, 301n16; volunteers, 28, 157, 162, 173–74, 177, 242, 245
Ellis Island immigrants, 110, 246
emotional bonds, of Tirgan Family, 205–9, 225

employment. *See* labor; unemployment
Enhanced Border Security and Visa Reform Act (2002), 54
entrepreneurs, 15, 73, 231, 267; Iranian Americans as, 52, 56, 112–13, 117, 123, 134, 234, 238, 240, 247, 250; Iranian Canadians as, 187, 211, 225; neoliberal multiculturalism and, 111–13
equality, 158–59, 214–16, 226, 243, 274–75
equal rights, 81, 82, 112, 113
Eskandari, Maryam, 206, 208
Estiri, Ehsan, 255
ethnic identity, 8, 11, 44, 237
ethnic markers, 13–14, 235
ethnic minorities, 7, 8, 22, 29, 40, 59, 101, 259
ethnography, 9, 21, 24, 27–28, 30, 144, 177
Europe, 38, 40–46, 50, 287n70
"The European Question" (De Genova), 254
Eurovision Song Contest, 67
exclusion, 4, 9, 16, 42, 94, 173, 269; inclusion and, 10, 28, 233, 234, 237, 252, 254, 259–60, 277, 286n48; in multicultural societies, 272; professionalism as antidote to, 163–67; racial, 12, 14, 45
Executive Orders, US, 47, 57, 309n27
Express Entry program, Canada, 79
extremism, 13, 113, 287n55; religious, 5, 8, 55, 235, 255; rise of, 86

Facebook, 73, 126, 176, 181, 297n60; Freedom Sculpture, 121–22, 124, 125, 129, 131; Tirgan on, 205, 216
family reunifications, immigration, 22, 35, 43, 46, 50, 56, 67, 74, 75, 236
Farhang Förening, Stockholm, 136, 165–66, 168–69, 248–50
Farhang Foundation, California, 134, 239, 298n92; the Cyrus Cylinder and, 91, 108, 116; Freedom Sculpture and, 108–9, 119–25, 132, *133*, 246, 248, 250; Nowruz festival and, 116, 298n97;

299n103; private patrons and privatized participation, 113–18; programming, 115–17, 132; social capital and, 118, 119, 250; Tirgan Festival and, 305n49; volunteers, 117, 118, 244. *See also* Freedom Festival
Farrokhzad, Athena, 272
Farsi. *See* Persian language
Federal Bureau of Investigation, 54
filmmaker, 29, 53, 197
films, 5, 6, 62–63, 67, 116, 296n37, 296n46, 310n14
Finkelman, Paul, 294n10
Finland, 45
fires: arson, 87, 163–66, *164*; fire-jumping, 137, *138*, 150, 170, 300n4
First Nations communities, 82, 185, 260
Flight 752, downing of. *See* Ukraine International Airlines
Floyd, George, 215
Foltz, Richard, 305n37
food, 4, 53, 126, 137, 152, 208
foreigners (*khareji*), 151, 301n30
"forever foreigners," 240, 258
"For Iran" protest festival, Tirgan, 221, 222–23
Foucault, Michel, 14
Founding Fathers, US, 90, 106, 109, 119, 121, 129, 248, 251
France, 7, 38, 82, 87
Franklin, Benjamin, 90, 294n10
freedom, 95, 101, 185; dignity, wealth and, 132–35; gift of, 106–32; religious, 65, 89–91, 106, 129, 130; WLF movement, 74, 78, 132, 218, 220–22, 243, 265
"Freedom," 108
Freedom Festival, LA, *127*–28, 129, 239, 249, 257; Freedom Sculpture and, 31, 106–7, 119–20, 122, 130, 132, 240, 248; imperial nostalgia at, 125–28
Freedom Sculpture, LA, *108*, 135, 197, 257, 277, 295n24; Cyromania and, 96, 105; design competition, 119, 123–24,

125; Farhang Foundation and, 108–9, 119–25, 132, *133*, 246, 248, 250; Freedom Festival and, 31, 106–7, 119–20, 122, 130, 132, 240, 248; funding, 121–22, 124, 129, 228–29, 245, 251, 299n108, 299n110, 305n49; from inception to public monument, 118–25; from monument to memorial, 128–32; as protest site, 131–32, *133*
"The Freedom Sculpture, Revisited (2020–21)," 131
Freeland, Chrystia, 181

Garcetti, Eric, 106–7, 121, 123, 295n24
*gasht-e ershad* (morality police), 218, 292n123
"*gasht-i intiqam*" ("roving avengers"), 292n123
gay rights activism, 308n23
Geertz, Clifford, 19
Gelareh (artist) (pseudonym), 11–12, 14
gender, 5, 15–17, 161, 225, 273, 275; equality, 158, 214–16, 226, 243; identities, 11, 274, 277
General Social Survey (2020), Canada, 186
Gera, Deborah Levine, 294n5
Germany, 7, 21, 41, 42, 43, 50, 87
Getty Villa, LA, 89, 92, *95*, 116, 118, 294n2, 296n46
Ghanvari, Shazad, 119
Gholami, Reza, 255, 310n50
Ghomeshi, Jian, 212–13, 216
Ghorashi, Halleh, 126, 153–54, 177
gifts, 106, 109, 112, 131, 169, 246–52, 262, 309n35
goodness, 93, 96
Google, 74, 247
Gothenburg, Sweden, 23, 62–63, 65, 68, 146, 300n8
Gothenburg International Film Festival, 62–63
Great Britain, 82, 87

Green Movement (2009–10), 23, 41, 56, 67, 78, 287n69
Grigor, Talinn, 98

Hage, Ghassan, 24, 27
Haji Firuz, 154, 155, 156, 302n36
Hall, Stuart, 17
Hamburg, Germany, 7, 21, 50
Harbourfront Centre (HC), 187, *188*, 192, *199*, 207, 242, 305n32; CEP, 189, 194, 196, 197; Tirgan and, 190–91, 195, 198, 201, 209, 232, 239, 243–44
Hashemi, Manata, 308n3
HC. *See* Harbourfront Centre
Hedayati, Hadi, 296n37
*herfeh-i* ("professional"), 167
hijab, 132
history, pre-Islamic, 103–5, 244, 255, 276
History Advocates, 297n60
*History Magazine*, 105
homemaking, inclusion and, 268–69
Hosseini, Mansour, 14, 33, 146, 150; on democracy, 157–58, 160–61; with Eldfesten festival, 12–13, 157, 159, 160–62, 168, 170, 174–77, 286n26, 301n14
House of Iran, San Diego, 9, 118, 246
Hübinette, Tobias, 259
*The Huffington Post* (news website), 109
human capital, 15, 79, 183, 288n71
human rights, 43, 65, 100–101, 107, 121, 248; mediating, 128–32; tolerance and, 250, 295n20
Husby, Stockholm, 69, 136, 157, 292n110, 292n112
hypervisibility, 4, 93

IAAB International Conference on the Iranian Diaspora (2012), 306n59
IACP. *See* Iranian Americans' Contributions Project
ICC. *See* Iranian Canadian Congress
ICCAC. *See* Iranian Canadian Centre for Art and Culture

ICCP. *See* Iranian Canadians' Contributions Project
identity, 7, 88, 173, 225, 291n102; American, 4, 85, 86, 91, 112, 268; Aryan racial, 104, 111, 254, 256, 257, 297n52; diasporic, 10, 16, 21, 24, 233, 258, 262, 270, 295n28; ethnic, 8, 11, 44, 237; gender, 11, 274, 277; Iranian diaspora, 32, 270; multicultural societies with belonging and, 16–24. *See also* cultural identity; Iranian identity; national identity
IHF. *See* Iran Heritage Foundation
immigrant gifts, 109, 112, 131, 169, 248, 249
immigrant incorporation, 10–11, 28, 84, 86, 110, 200, 267
immigrants: with assimilation, 285n23; Citizenship and Immigration Canada report, 289n31, 289n33; competition and, 16; cultural identity, 147; diversity and, 18; Diversity Immigrant Visa program, 56; Ellis Island, 110, 246; entrepreneurs, 15, 52, 56, 111–13; first-generation, 275, 286n36; Muslims, 236; with neoliberal multiculturalism, 31; nonwhite, 42, 44, 68, 254, 256, 292n109; 1.5-generation, 14, 29, 57, 63, 64, 67, 155–56, 162, 164–65, 272, 286n36; populations, 38, 42, 44, 47, 68–69, 236; second-generation, 246, 275, 286n36; SFI, 62; Sweden, 23, 45–46, 47, 62, 64, 68–69, 87, 235, 236; third-generation, 275, 286n36; unemployment, 45–46, 64, 79, 87, 235; US as "nation of," 85, 113, 135, 240, 267–68. *See also* diaspora
immigration: from Africa, 43, 44, 81, 160, 254, 289n31; children and, 50, 68; family reunifications, 22, 35, 43, 46, 50, 56, 67, 74, 75, 236; of Iranians to Canada by admission type, *70*; laws, 22, 43, 45, 134; policies, 22, 25, 35, 42–44, 46, 64, 112, 134, 135; quota system, 42, 43, 60; Sweden, 45–46, 66, 83; US, 42, 43, 46, 72, 289n26; Welcome Centre Immigration Services, 79
Immigration Acts (1917, 1976), 43, 44
Immigration and Nationality Act (1965), US, 43, 289n26
Immigration and Naturalization Service (INS), 47, 50, 54
Immigration and Refugee Board of Canada, 71
Immigration Reform and Control Act (IRCA), 50
imperial nostalgia, 31, 124, 131, 134, 195, 244, 261, 270; belonging and, 112; Cyromania and, 95–96, 102–5, 132; at Freedom Festival, 125–28; US with racial hierarchies, politics of inclusion and, 255–58
The Newspaper of the Imperial Celebrations of Iran. *See Ruznameh-ye Jashn-e Shahanshahi-e Iran*
inclusion: belonging and, 10, 11, 20, 27, 230, 259; bidirectional, 152; cultural citizenship, belonging and, 10–16; culture and, 13, 32, 175, 233, 241–44, 246–52, 262; DEI, 215; democracy, transparency and, 31; democracy and, 148, 158; in diaspora, 3; diversity and, 186; exclusion and, 10, 28, 233, 234, 237, 252, 254, 259–60, 277, 286n48; homemaking and, 268–69; "Iranianness" and, 242; in multicultural societies, 3, 8, 12, 31, 145, 153; power, justice and, 8; public art and, 268; social, 8, 16, 145, 153; social mobility and, 16; strategies of, 3, 9–10, 13, 16–17, 24, 31–33, 88, 184, 198, 226, 233, 246–47, 252, 260, 262, 270, 273; US with racial hierarchies, imperial nostalgia and, 255–58; visibility and, 184
incorporation: of difference, 112; immigrant, 10–11, 28, 84, 86, 110, 200, 267
Indigenous groups, 8, 17, 81, 181, 186, 242; diversity of, 44; First Nations

communities, 82, 185, 260; forced assimilation of, 42, 45; rights, 85–86; violent coercion against, 82
Initiativ Iran, 165–67
INS. *See* Immigration and Naturalization Service
Instagram, 205, 220, 302n31
interculturalism, 85, 152, 153, 173, 245; bidirectional, 140–41, 143, 175, 241; funding and competition, 167–69; Riksteatern producing, 145–48; Sweden and, 31, 84, 140–41, 143, 241–42
International Department, Riksteatern, 146–48, 301n21
International Nowruz Day, 176
invented tradition, 144, 173, 197
invisibility, 4–5, 93, 230, 273, 289n33
Iran: Chaharshanbeh Suri in, 140, 156, 300n3, 300n10; departing, 36–42; Initiativ Iran, 165–67; media, 41; Mickey Mouse flipping off, 49; migration from, 23–24; national identity, 14, 19, 98, 254, 258, 276; protests in, 39, 219, 287n69; sanctions, 5, 7, 23, 35, 47, 77, 129, 287n70; theater, 58, 244; unemployment, 23, 35, 39, 41, 72; US and, 54, 90, 96, 179–80, 235, 256–57
Iran Air Flight 655, downing of, 180
Irangeles, 234
Iran Heritage Foundation (IHF), 89, 295n11, 298n94
Iran Hostage Crisis (1979–81), 8, 22, 47, 48, 52, 91, 235
Iranian, 78, 149; on Canadian Census, 293n137; national category of, 14; "Persian" versus, 13, 49, 235, 293n131, 293n137
Iranian Americans: cultural identity, 268; the Cyrus Cylinder as "new beginning" for, 91–94; as entrepreneurs, 52, 56, 112–13, 117, 123, 134, 234, 238, 240, 247, 250; first-generation, 55, 88, 256–57; media with negative depictions, 4–5;

NIAC, 308n13; NIPOC, 114, 298n88; PAAIA, 238, 246, 294n2, 308n13; in politics, 55, 290n70; populations, 57, 234; racialization of, 257; racism against, 293n131; second-generation, 3, 9, 53, 55–57, 80, 110, 114, 269, 290n70
Iranian Americans' Contributions Project (IACP), 247
Iranian Aryan identity, 104
Iranian Canadian Centre for Art and Culture (ICCAC), 191
Iranian Canadian Congress (ICC), 304n9
Iranian Canadians, 77, 78, 80, 202, 242, 245; cultural identity, 200, 225; downing of Flight 752, 179–82; as entrepreneurs, 187, 211, 225
Iranian Canadians' Contributions Project (ICCP), 247
Iranian diaspora, 3, 5, 7, 35, 139, 306n59; being and belonging, 234–46; identity, 32, 270; inclusion and culture, 246–52; multiculturalism and, 228–29, 232–33; studies and future directions, 273–76; three cities in global, 21–24; with tripping up and over lines of belonging, 252–63
Iranian identity, 3, 8, 12, 104, 255; Canada with multicultural citizenship and, 260–62; national, 14, 19, 98, 254, 258, 276; pre-Islamic influences on, 19–20, 254, 256; with representation and recognition in diaspora, 17, 18–21; Sweden with anti-racism and, 258–60
Iranian nationalism, 19, 97, 104, 172–73, 175, 245, 254
"Iranianness": authenticity, 19, 143–44, 149, 254; Eldfesten festival and, 137, 148–50, 173, 177; inclusion and, 242; interpreting, 244–45; in multicultural societies, 137; race, religion and, 254; representations of, 117, 118, 238; violence and, 94; watered-down, 143, 148, 149–52, 175–77, 259

Iranian Plaza, North York, 75, *76*
Iranian radio, 36–37, 149, 174
Iranian Railroad for Queer Refugees, 77
Iranian Revolution (1979), 8, 22, 35–37, 58, 69, 91
Iranians: anti-Iranian protests, 47–49, *48*, 52; asylum applications to Sweden from, *61*; in Canada today, 78–80; cultural identity, 19, 55, 200, 268, 275–76, 293n137; first-generation, 7, 12, 13, 92, 114, 149, 202, 236, 257, 259, 272, 274–75, 286n36; fleeing Iran, 40–41; immigration to Canada by admission type, *70*; immigration to Sweden by grounds for settlement, *66*; Jews, 53, 55, 257, 298n100; with LPR status in US, *51*; with neoliberal multiculturalism in US, 31, 132, 135; as nonwhite, 104, 236, 257; 1.5-generation, 14, 29, 49, 53, 55, 57, 63–65, 67, 80, 88, 155–56, 162, 164–65, 202, 225, 236, 272, 286n36; populations, 291n82; racialization of, 104, 255, 261, 297n56; second-generation, 9, 53, 56, 65, 80, 110, 236, 272; stereotyped as terrorists, 5, 8, 55, 103, 113, 165, 235; in Sweden today, 67–69; in Sweden with community building, 63–67; in US today, 56–58
Iranian student associations, 71, 76
Iranian Swedes: 1.5-generation, 14, 236; in politics, 65, 235–36; second-generation, 65, 88, 236
Iran-Iraq War (1980–88), 22, 23, 35, 69
"Iran Nuclear Deal." *See* Joint Comprehensive Plan of Action
Iranska Riksförbundet i Sverige (IRIS), 166
*IranWire* (news website), *138*
Iraq, 40, 54, 180; Iran-Iraq War, 22, 23, 35, 69; migration, 46
IRCA. *See* Immigration Reform and Control Act
Ireland, 42

IRGC. *See* Islamic Revolutionary Guard Corps
IRI. *See* Islamic Republic of Iran
IRIS. *See* Iranska Riksförbundet i Sverige
Irish Americans, 286n48
Islam, 104, 164, 254–56, 287n55, 309n49
Islam, "non-Islamiosity," 255, 310n50
Islamic, 19, 20, 40, 103, 104. *See also* pre-Islamic
Islamic Republic of Iran (IRI) (1979–), 236, 255, 256, 306n75; Canada and, 77–78; Chaharshanbeh Suri banned by, 137, 139; Constitution, 39; opposition to, 65, 132, 139, 261, 292n123; pre-Islamic past diminished by, 20, 103; repression of, 56, 62, 132; US and, 129–30, 180
Islamic Revolutionary Guard Corps (IRGC), 78, 179–80
Islamophobia. *See* anti-Muslim racism
Italian Americans, 109–10, 134, 246

Japanese people, 42, 43
Järva, Stockholm, 69, 292n112
JCPOA. *See* Joint Comprehensive Plan of Action
Jefferson, Thomas, 89, 90, 93, 107, 130, 294n10
Jews, 22, 36–38, 84, 286n48; Iranian, 53, 55, 257, 298n100; in World War II, 43
Joint Comprehensive Plan of Action (JCPOA, "Iran Nuclear Deal"), 23, 287n70
journalists, 2, 37, 53, 67, 92–93, 157, 248

Kasapi, Rani, 146–47, 174–75, 301n21
*Kayhan* (newspaper), 36–37
Kayvan (Eldfesten committee member) (pseudonym), 154–55, 171, 173
Kazemi, Zahra, 2
Kelley, Ron, 48–49
Khaledi, Darioush, 308n17
*khareji* (foreigners), 151, 301n30

Khavari, Mahmoud-Reza, 292n122
Khomeini, Ruhollah (Ayatollah), 37, 39–40, 49, 73
killings, 62, 209–10, 215, 217, 304n7; of Amini, 132, 218, 219; downing of Flight 752, 77, 80, 179–83, 220, 222, 293n144; in Iranian prisons, 2, 218, 287n69, 300n132
kinship, 92, 131, 206, 243
Kista, Stockholm, 69, 136, 157, 292n112
know-your-rights campaigns, 55
Korean Harvest Festival, 76
Korteweg, Anna C., 287n51
Kulturrådet (Swedish Arts Council), 146, 169
Kurdistan, 154, 300n3
Kurds, 68, 139, 140, 172–73, 218, 300n10

LA. *See* Los Angeles
labor, 45–46, 56, 65, 83; discrimination and, 49, 64, 113, 214–15, 235, 269; skilled, 38, 67–68, 79; "survival jobs," 79, 236
LACMA. *See* Los Angeles County Museum of Art
language, 16, 69, 71, 81; "loss," 275; Swedish, 11, 60, 62, 63, 83, 156. *See also* Persian language
Latin America, 43, 44, 81, 172
Latin Arts Festival, 76
lawful permanent resident (LPR) status, 50, *51*
LGBTQ+ community, 7, 8, 77, 308n23
Library of Congress, 90
*The Limits of Whiteness* (Maghbouleh), 256–57
Lion and Sun (*shir-o-khorshid*) flag, 221–22, 265, *266*
"Little Persia," Toronto, 293n129
Los Angeles, California, 3, 23, 27–28, 57, *133*, 250; anti-Iranian protests, *48*, 48–49, 52; festivals, 114, *115*; Getty Villa, 89, 92, *95*, 116, 118, 294n2, 296n46; Irangeles, 234; Iranian diaspora, 7, 21, 22, 228–29, 234–35; Persian Parade, *102*, 105, 114; Tehrangeles, 52–56, 118, 124, 234. *See also* Freedom Festival; Freedom Sculpture
Los Angeles City Hall, 9, *102*, 105, 114
Los Angeles County Museum of Art (LACMA), 116
*Los Angeles Times* (newspaper), 91
LPR status. *See* lawful permanent resident status

MacGregor, Neil, 90
Machiavelli, 90
*Maclean's* (news magazine), 77
Maghbouleh, Neda, 256–57
Mahnaz (Eldfesten committee member) (pseudonym), 155–56, 162
Mahsa (Tirgan volunteer), 205
Malaysia, 7
Malmö, Sweden, 23, 68, 300n8
manipulation, cultural, 150, 152, 261
Marcus, George, 24
markers, ethnic, 13–14, 235
Martí, José, 265
Maryam (Swedish Parliamentarian), 64–65
Maryland, 22, 57
Masala! Mehndi! Masti! Festival, Toronto, 187, 305n31
Massey, Douglas, 286n36
Massood (community leader), 136–37, 140, 143, 157–62, 171, 176, 178
Mauss, Marcel, 246, 249, 250
media, 41, 147, 295n11; Eldfesten festival in, 12, 141–42, *142*, 149, 156, 163, *164*, 165, 174–75, 241, 244; Freedom Festival and, 128–29; negative portrayals, 4–5, 49, 55, 94, 103, 256; Persian-language, 11, 12, 65, 67, 74–75, 142, 148, 156–57, 173–74, 182, 228. *See also* radio; social media; TV
Mehregan festival, West LA, 114

Mehregan Festival of Autumn (1994–2011), Orange County, 7, 114, 126, 239, 298n88
Melamed, Jodi, 111–12
melting pot, US as, 186, 304n20
memory, with authenticity and ownership, 148–56
men, power and, 274–75
MENA. *See* Middle East and North Africa
Mercedeh (Tirgan volunteer), 204–5, 207
Merhavy, Menahem, 101–2, 296n37
methodology, 24–31
#MeToo, 210–17, 226, 243
the Metropolitan Museum of Art, New York, 89, 101, 294n2
Mickey Mouse, 49, 49
Middle East and North Africa (MENA), 57
"Middle Way." *See* Swedish Model
migration, 5, 23–24, 42–46, 50, 234–37
Millions Program, Sweden, 68, 160
minorities, 36–37, 84–85, 163, 234; ethnic, 7, 8, 22, 29, 40, 59, 101, 259; visible, 44, 74, 289n33. *See also* Indigenous groups
Mirlashari, Rostam, 169, 248–51
misrecognition, 5, 79, 94, 255, 269, 271; culture and, 3, 10; redressing, 8, 17, 232, 237, 270, 275. *See also* recognition
misrepresentation, 3, 8, 114, 175, 275, 276
*Missing Persians* (Rahimieh), 19
modernization initiatives, Pahlavi monarchy, 36, 37–38, 39
Mofid, Bijan, 150–51, 301nn28–29
Moghadam, Maria Sabaye, 2–3, 4, 33
Mona (Tirgan volunteer), 207–8
Montréal, Canada, 23, 74, 75, 78, 180, 181
morality police (*gasht-e ershad*), 218, 292n123
mosaic model, Canadian cultural, 80, 185–90, 191, 197–98, 242, 304n20
Mossadegh, Mohammad, 91
multicultural citizenship, 199, 260–62
multiculturalism, 4, 28, 257, 287n51; in Canada, 23, 81–85, 183, 185, 241, 244, 260–62, 270; Chaharshanbeh Suri and, 157, 173–77; democracy and, 140, 157–58; demographic, 231, 242, 258; diaspora with power and, 237–46; diversity and, 126–27, 183, 185, 187, 191, 197–99, 209; elite philanthropy and privatized, 238–40; Iranian diaspora and, 228–29, 232–33; mosaic model in Canada, 80, 185–90, 191, 197–98, 242, 304n20; official, 17–18, 21, 23, 27, 31, 85, 87, 230, 231, 233, 238, 241, 243, 260; policies and, 10, 11, 17–19, 29, 60, 67, 81, 83, 141, 185, 189, 230–31, 233, 241–42, 261, 270; state, 67, 123, 169, 178, 241–44, 251, 270; in Sweden, 11, 60, 83, 241–42, 270; Tirgan as celebration of, 191–98; unofficial neoliberal, 240, 270; *Why Multiculturalism is Oppression*, 87. *See also* interculturalism; neoliberal multiculturalism
multicultural societies, 36, 137, 159, 169, 272; arriving to, 80–88; belonging in, 16–24, 28, 33, 231, 263, 269; identity and belonging in, 16–24; inclusion in, 3, 8, 12, 31, 145, 153
Muslim Ban, US, 23–24, 57–58, 106, 110, 128–29, 235, 247, 257, 271
Muslims, 54, 236; anti-Muslim sentiment, 63, 105, 106, 164, 175, 254–57, 294n161, 301n16; racism against, 105, 164, 254–57, 294n161, 297n56

Naficy, Hamid, 104, 296n49
Nasser (theater director), 162, 173–74
Nastaran (Tirgan volunteer), 206–7
national identity, 10, 109; Canadian, 23, 185–86, 242, 260; Iranian, 14, 19, 98, 254, 258, 276; Swedish, 14
National Iranian American Council (NIAC), 308n13
National Iranian Radio and Television (NIRT), 36–37
nationalism, 105, 275; Canada and, 82, 84; Iranian, 19, 97, 104, 172–73, 175, 245,

254; Pahlavi, 91, 96, 97, 104, 258; racism and, 43, 272
national markers, 13, 235
National Monuments Foundation, 266
National Security Entry/Exit Registration System (NSEERS), 54
national touring theater of Sweden. *See* Riksteatern
"nation of immigrants," US as, 85, 113, 135, 240, 267–68
Nayeb-Yazdi, Maryam, 191
Nazis, 43, 63, 87, 163, 258
neoliberalism, 15, 84, 111, 231, 276
neoliberal multiculturalism, 31, 85, 111–13, 123, 132, 135, 239–40, 270
neo-Nazi, 63, 87, 258
Neshat, Shirin, 116
Network of Iranian American Professionals of Orange County (NIPOC), 114, 298n88
*A New Beginning* exhibition tour, 89, 92, 108, 110, 118, 129, 132
New Mexico, 48
New Sounds of Iran festival, Hamburg, 7
*The New York Review of Books*, 213
new year celebrations. *See* Nowruz celebrations
New York, 4, 6, 7, 89, 101, 114, 294n2
*New York Times* (newspaper), 160, 210, 211, 212
Neyestani, Mana, *138*
Neyshabouri, Safaneh Mohaghegh, 211
NIAC. *See* National Iranian American Council
Niavarani, Shima, 273
Nima (community leader), 69, 71, 190, 215, 221–26
NIPOC. *See* Network of Iranian American Professionals of Orange County
NIRT. *See* National Iranian Radio and Television
nonbelonging, 15, 256, 259, 260, 269, 276
"non-Islamiosity," 255, 310n50

nonpartisanship, Tirgan and, 32, 182, 184, 195, 216, 217–27, 242, 270, 307n97
nonwhites, 15–16, 109, 259, 294n10; immigrants, 42, 44, 68, 254, 256, 292n109; Iranians as, 104, 236, 257
Nooshin (Tirgan volunteer) (pseudonym), 1, 33
North America, migration to, 42–46
North Korea, 54
North York, Toronto, 75–76, *76*, 293n129
nostalgia, 131, 195. *See also* imperial nostalgia
*Not Without My Daughter* (film), 5
Nowruz (new year) celebrations, 153, 154, 229, 238, 277, 300n10, 301n28; Chaharshanbeh Suri and, 136, 137; Farhang Foundation and, 116, 298n97, 299n103; International Nowruz Day, 176; Iranian diaspora and, 139; LA City Hall event, 9, 114; at LACMA, 116; with Orange County Pacific Symphony, 116; Seattle City Hall event, 9; Tirgan with, 191, 210, 220–21, 223; at UCLA, 116; US Congress and, 295n20; Westwood Festival, 114, *115*
NSEERS. *See* National Security Entry/Exit Registration System

"O CYRUS" (documentary short film), 296n46
Ohlsson, Birgitta, 300n9
Ong, Aihwa, 15–16, 73, 231, 286n48, 308n23; on citizenship and power, 245; on cultural citizenship, 14, 111, 178, 233, 237, 252–54, 308n8
Orange County, California, 57
Orange County Pacific Symphony, 116
ownership: authenticity, memory and, 148–56; cultural, 16, 20, 241, 271

PAAIA. *See* Public Affairs Alliance of Iranian Americans
Pahlavi, Ashraf (Princess), 101

Pahlavi, Mohammed Reza (Shah of Iran), 52, 221; Cyrus the Great and, 90–91, 97, 98, 100–101, 266–67, 296n35; SAVAK and, 39, 101
Pahlavi monarchy (1925–79), 20, 221–22, 265, 266; elites, 22, 40, 100, 234, 254; modernization initiatives, 36, 37–38, 39
Pahlavi nationalism, 91, 96, 97, 104, 258
Pakistan, 23, 41, 60
Palme, Olof (1969–76,1982–86), 158, 260
Park, Lisa Sun-Hee, 267
Pars, Bahar, 272, 310n14
partisanship. *See* nonpartisanship
Payami, Babak, 190, 197–98
Persepolis, 95, 97, 98, 126, 198, *199*
Persian, 13–14, 19, 49, 235, 293n131, 293n137
Persian Arts Festival, New York, 7
Persian language, 53, 98, 107; afterschool program, 11, 116, 238; media, 11, 12, 65, 67, 74–75, 142, 148, 156–57, 173–74, 182, 228
Persian parades, 4, 6, *102*, 105, 114
"Persian Phobia," 6, 8
Persians, 5, 8, 55–56, 235, 255
Persian StoryTime, 74
philanthropy, 231, 238–40, 262, 266, 298n100
photo ops, *127*, 195, *196*
poetry, 1, 53, 90, 180, 194, 272
poets, 98, 217, 266–67
Poilievre, Pierre, 221
points system, Canada, 23, 44, 72, 79, 236
politics: activism, 65, 123, 303n58; far-right, 17–18, 84, 86–87, 103, 168, 236, 255; of inclusion, imperial nostalgia and racial hierarchies in US, 255–58; Iranian Americans in, 55, 290n70; Iranian Canadians in, 77; Iranian Swedes in, 65, 235–36; leftists, 39, 59, 65, 158, 174, 235–36, 259; prisoners, 40, 50, 60, 101, 131, 218, 287n69, 300n132; of recognition, 8, 276, 308n23; Tirgan with, 219–27
Pompeo, Mike, 129

populations, 57, 234, 291n82; foreign-born, 42, 68; immigrants, 38, 42, 44, *47*, 68–69, 236
power, 8–10, 14, 15, 40, 88, 233; men and, 274–75; with multicultural frameworks in diaspora, 237–46; webs of, 16, 234, 237–38, 241, 253, 262, 269
pre-Islamic, 195, 296n49; history, 103–5, 244, 255, 276; influences on Iranian identity, 19–20, 254, 256; past, 20, 97, 104, 254, 258
*The Prince* (Machiavelli), 90
prison, Iranian: killings, 2, 218, 287n69, 300n132; political prisoners, 40, 50, 60, 101, 131, 218, 287n69, 300n132; torture, 39, 78, 101
"professional" (*herfeh-i*), 167
professionalism, 15, 31, 144, 156, 163–68, 241, 245
protests, 110, 265, 287n55, 303n58; anti-Iranian, 47–49, *48*, 52; "For Iran" protest festival, 221, 222–23; Freedom Sculpture as site of, 131–32, *133*; in Iran, 39, 219, 287n69; WLF, 74, 78, 132, 218, 220–22, 243, 265
Public Affairs Alliance of Iranian Americans (PAAIA), 238, 246, 294n2, 308n13
public performances, 8, 9, 143

Qajar dynasty (1789–1925), 98, 104, 195, *196*
quota system, immigration, 42, 43, 60
Quran, 287n55, 295n31

race, 14, 15, 45, 252; anxieties of representation, 170–74; Aryan racial identity, 104, 111, 254, 256, 257, 297n52; class and, 12, 16, 110, 112, 253, 270; religion, class and, 32, 33, 233, 235, 253–63, 272, 274
racial hierarchies, 104, 109, 134, 233, 255–58, 260
racialization, 12, 86, 257, 260; of class, 254, 286n48, 308n8; of Iranians, 104, 255, 261, 297n56; religion and, 254, 274

racism, 11, 14, 47, 65, 293n131; anti-Arab, 171, 172, 175, 254, 255, 256, 259; anti-Black, 256, 272, 273; anti-Muslim, 105, 164, 254–57, 294n161, 297n56; anti-racism, 111, 158, 173, 241, 258–60, 272–73; discrimination and, 64, 86, 174, 238, 257, 289n33, 302n42; nationalism and, 43, 272; scientific, 42, 43; white supremacy and, 256, 260

radio, 11; in Canada, 212; in Iran, 36–37; in Sweden, 12, 142, 149, 156–57, 162, 165, 173–74, 241, 244, 300n9; in US, 228

Rahimieh, Nasrin, 19–20, 292n123

Reagan, Ronald, 130

recognition, 16, 276, 308n23; Iranian identity and diaspora with representation and, 17, 18–21; misrecognition and, 3, 5, 8, 10, 17, 79, 94, 232, 237, 255, 269–71, 275

Refugee Act (1980), US, 43, 289n45

refugees, 41, 43, 71, 77; resettlement, 23, 57, 58, 68, 289n45; in Sweden, 23, 59–60, 62–63, 65, 67–69, 258–59

religion, 5, 8, 55, 103; class, race and, 32, 33, 233, 235, 253–63, 272, 274; freedom of, 65, 89–91, 106, 129, 130; Islam, 104, 164, 254–56, 287n55, 309n49; minorities, 7, 22, 36–37, 40, 59, 84–85, 163, 234; tolerance, 100, 121, 130, 295n20

representation, 5, 49, 194, 272; cultural, 3, 4, 8, 19, 21, 88, 143, 149, 152, 156, 195, 245, 255, 258, 268, 277; Iranian identity and diaspora with recognition and, 17, 18–21; of "Iranianness," 117, 118, 238; misrepresentation, 3, 8, 114, 175, 275, 276; racial anxieties of, 170–74

rights, 55, 65, 210, 219, 308n23; civil, 22, 42, 43, 55, 81, 256; equal, 81, 82, 112, 113; Indigenous groups, 85–86. *See also* human rights

Riksteatern (national touring theater), Sweden, 158, 169, 241, 243, 301n21; Chaharshanbeh Suri and, 166, 176, 271; with Eldfesten festival, 12–13, 136, 142,

148, 150–52, 162, 175, 177, 239, 250, 253; interculturalism produced by, 145–48

Rinkeby, Stockholm, 69, 160, 292n112

*Rinkebysvenska* (film), 310n14

riots, 36, 87

Roma people, 43

Roqe, 212, 213

Rosaldo, Renato, 131

Rostamalipour, Parviz, 300n132

"roving avengers" (*"gasht-i intiqam"*), 292n123

Rumbaut, Rubén, 286n36

*Ruznameh-ye Jashn-e Shahanshahi-e Iran* (The Newspaper of the Imperial Celebrations of Iran), 99

Ryerson University, Toronto, 69, 71. *See also* Toronto Metropolitan University

Sabet, Nushin, 132

Sadeghi, Sahar, 258

Saedinia, Arash, 296n46

Sami people, 45

sanctions: on Iran, 5, 7, 23, 35, 47, 77, 129, 287n70; "overcompliance," 293n131

San Francisco, California, 9, 22, 52, 294n2

Sarshar, Homa, 36–38, 53

SAVAK. *See* secret police

saving face (*aberu*), 155, 230, 308n3

Scarpa, Simone, 82

Schierup, Carl-Ulrik, 84

schools, 11, 75, 116, 238

scientific racism, 42, 43

Scotiabank Caribbean Carnival, 305n31

SD. *See* Sweden Democrats

Seattle City Hall, 9

secret police (SAVAK), 39, 101

segregation, 68, 287n55

"self-making," cultural citizenship and, 13, 14, 111, 178, 233

Selig, Dianne, 246

settler colonialism, 42, 260

sexual harassment, 210, 212, 214. *See also* #MeToo

sexuality, gender and, 274, 275
SFI. *See* Swedish for Immigrants
Shahbazi, Shapur, 296n37
Shahin (student leader) (pseudonym), 156, 170–73
*Shahnameh*, 98, 104, 105, 194
*Shahr-e Ghesseh* (City of Tales) (Mofid), 150–51, 301nn28–29
*Shahrvand* (newspaper), 75
*Shahs of Sunset* (TV series), 290n71, 308n10
*Shargh* (newspaper), 41
*shir-o-khorshid* (Lion and Sun) flag, 221–22, 265, *266*
Shiva (Tirgan volunteer), 206
Siosepol Bridge, *199*
Siu, Lok, 224
*Sizdeh Bedar* event, 114
skill level, education and, 64, 79
slavery, 100, 260, 294n10, 296n33
slogans, 18, 187, 195, 217, 218, 219, 222
Smith, Adam, 15
Smithsonian Institute, 89, 90, 93, 294n2
"social browning," 257, 258
social capital, 73, 268, 269, 270; arts and culture with, 32, 271; diasporic cultural and, 198–209; Farhang Foundation and, 118, 119, 250; networks as, 16, 217, 288n71; Tirgan and, 32, 183–84, 198–209, 214, 224–26
social inclusion, 8, 16, 145, 153
social media, *140*, 214, 276, 305n39; Instagram, 205, 220, 302n31; Tirgan, 205, 216, 218–20; Twitter, 129–30, 179, 210, 216, 247; YouTube, 142, 175, 292n123. *See also* Facebook
social mobility, 16, 56, 269, 288n71
social welfare, 73, 230, 231, 235
Soleimani, Qasem, 179
South Asian people, 42, 75, 76, 178, 254
Statistics Sweden, 291n107
Statue of Liberty, 120–21, *127*
Steele, Robert, 296n37, 296n40

stereotypes: negative, 2–3, 4, 55–56, 94, 124, 165, 235; terrorists, 5, 8, 55, 103, 113, 165, 235
stigmatization, 3, 9, 54, 103
Stockholm, Sweden, 3, 69, 157, 160, 292n110, 292n112; Farhang Förening, 136, 165–66, 168–69, 248–50; immigrants in, 23, 68, 236; Iranian diaspora and, 7, 21, 22, 23, 235–36; methodology, 27–28. *See also* Eldfesten Committee meetings; Eldfesten festival
Strass'Iran Festival, France, 7
stress tests, 184, 209, 214, 216, 223, 225
students, university, 35, 76, 156, 170–73, 217, 298n97; activists, 38–40, 47; Canada, 23, 41, 71, 73; Sweden, 41, 67; US, 22, 38, 41, 47, 56
subjectification, 14, 134, 178, 237
surveillance, 11, 14, 54, 113
"survival jobs," 79, 236
*Svenska Dagbladet* (newspaper), 163, 165
SVT. *See* Swedish national television
Sweden, 12, *61*, 287n55, 291n107, 300n8; anti-racism in, 258–60, 272–73; arriving to, 58–69; democracy and, 31, 156–62, 300n9; immigrants, 23, 45–46, 47, 62, 64, 68–69, 87, 235, 236; immigration, 45–46, 66, 83; intercultural exchange, 84, 146, 173; interculturalism and, 31, 84, 140–41, 143, 241–42; Iranian community-building in, 63–67; with Iranians in politics, 65, 235–36; Iranians today in, 67–69; Iranian Swedes, 14, 65, 88, 99, 235–36; multiculturalism in, 11, 60, 83, 241–42, 270; professionalism and, 167, 168, 241, 245; refugees in, 23, 59–60, 62–63, 65, 67–69, 258–59; transparency and, 31, 161–62, 168, 175–76, 241, 245, 251; university students, 41, 67; US, Canada and, 25–26; welfare state, 15, 45, 83–84. *See also* Riksteatern; Stockholm
Sweden Democrats (SD), 18, 63, 87, 168, 253, 259

Swedish Arts Council. *See* Kulturrådet
Swedish for Immigrants (SFI), 62
Swedish language, 11, 60, 62, 63, 83, 156
Swedish Model ("Middle Way"), 45, 83, 84
Swedish national television (SVT), 142, *142*, 244
Swedish Radio, 12, 142, 174, 300n9
Swedish TV, 12, 67, 142, *142*, 241, 244, 277, 301n16
symbolic capital, 16, 32, 183–84, 225–26, 268–71
symbolism, pre-Islamic, 105, 296n49
Syrians, 68, 176

ta'arof, gift giving and, 309n35
Tajikistan, 300n3
Taliban, 300n10
Taslimi, Susan, 58–60, 62, 67
Tavangar, Ardie, 119
TD Bank, 77, 304n14
teamwork, 123, 183, 189, 223, 245; challenges, 7, 113; diasporic cultural and social capital, 198–209; Tirgan and, 190–91, 195, 198, 201, 203–5, 209, 225, 232, 242–44
Tehrangeles, 52–56, 118, 124, 234
Tehranian, John, 257
Tehran Tea House, 1, 195, *196*
Tehranto, 71, 74–78, 181, 183, 192, 236, 244
terrorists, 13, 54, 78, 87; stereotypes, 5, 8, 55, 103, 113, 165, 235; threats, 94
Texas, 7, 49, 57
theater, 62, 67, 145, 146, 162, 173–74; Iranian, 58, 244; national, 11, 147, 176, 244; Persian-language, 65. *See also* Riksteatern
Thompson, Debra, 289n33
*300* (film), 5, *6*
Time's Up movement, 213
Tirgan, Canada: with Canada Mourns memorial, 179–83, 209–10, 217, 304n7; Canadian multicultural mosaic and, 185–90; the Canadian Way and, 184, 192, 198; constitution, 222, 225; cultural capital and, 183–84, 198–209, 226; with cultural citizenship, 224, 225, 226; "For Iran" protest festival, 221, 222–23; Freedom Sculpture and, 305n49; with gender equality, 215–16, 243; HC and, 190–91, 195, 198, 201, 209, 232, 239, 243–44; #MeToo and, 210–17, 226; with nonpartisanship, 32, 182, 184, 195, 216, 217–27, 242, 270, 307n97; with Nowruz event, 191, 210, 220–21, 223; political stance, 219–27; social capital and, 32, 183–84, 198–209, 214, 224–26; social media, 205, 216, 218–20; stress tests for, 184, 209, 214, 216, 223, 225; symbolic capital and, 32, 183–84, 225–26; teamwork and, 190–91, 195, 198, 201, 203–5, 209, 225, 232, 242–44; testing, 209–16; transparency and, 201–3, 216, 225, 242, 245; "Unity" press conference, 222; volunteers, 198, 201–9, *208*, 211, 214–16, 221, 225, 231, 232, 306n75
Tirgan Family, 32, 217, 218, 219; the Canadian Way and, 183, 243; emotional bonds of, 205–9, 225
Tirgan Festival, Toronto, *188*, *196*, *199*; with Arash the Archer, 192, *193*, 196–97, 305n39; artistic representation at, 194; artistic statement, 248; artistic themes, 196–98; authenticity and, 261–62; birth of, 186–87; branding, 198; corporate sponsorships and, 304n14, 305n31; Farhang Foundation and, 305n49; first, 7, 305n37; HC and, 189, 192, 194, 207, 242; "Message from Tirgan CEO," 305n48; as multiculturalism celebration, 191–98; naming, 191–93; spaces at, 195–96; volunteers, 1–2, 28, 33, 182–84, 189, 204, 207, 232, 242, 244, 245
*Tirgan Magazine*, 186–87, 191
TMU. *See* Toronto Metropolitan University
tolerance, 100–101, 110, 121, 130, 250, 295n20

Tomaj (community organizer), 164–66, 168, 303nn58–59
Toronto, Canada, 3, 79; Ashkenaz festival, 187; Canada Mourns memorial, 179–83, 209–10, 217, 304n7; Iranian diaspora and, 21, 22, 23, 236–37; "Little Persia," 293n129; Masala! Mehndi! Masti! Festival, 187, 305n31; methodology, 27–28; North York, 75–76, 76, 293n129; Ryerson University, 69, 71; Tehranto, 71, 74–78, 181, 183, 192, 236, 244; University of Toronto, 2, 74, 76, 179–80, 182. *See also* Tirgan Festival
Toronto Metropolitan University (TMU), 69, 71, 74
Toronto Pride, 77
torture, 39, 78, 101
transparency, 31, 159; Eldfesten Committee meetings with, 161–62, 168, 175–76, 241, 245, 251; Tirgan and, 201–3, 216, 225, 242, 245
Transportation Security Administration (TSA), 54, 113
Triadafilopoulos, Triadafilos, 287n51
Trudeau, Justin, 180
Trudeau, Pierre Elliott, 81, 82, 185–86
Trump, Donald, 18, 57–58, 129, 179, 287n70, 309n27
TSA. *See* Transportation Security Administration
Türkiye, 23, 41, 46, 60, 139, 147, 176
*Turkkiosken* (film), 310n14
TV, 29, 36, 146, 182, 308n10; journalists, 37, 53, 67; negative representations on, 4, 5, 49; Persian-language, 74; Swedish, 12, 67, 142, *142*, 241, 244, 277, 301n16
2500 Year Celebrations, 97, 98, 99, 101, 295n25
Twitter, 129–30, 179, 210, 216, 247

UCLA. *See* University of California, Los Angeles
Uganda, 46
Ukraine International Airlines Flight 752, downing of, 77, 80, 179–83, 216, 220, 222, 271, 293n144
undeserving, 15
unemployment: benefits, 45–46, 230; immigrants, 45–46, 64, 79, 87, 235; Iran, 23, 35, 39, 41, 72
United Kingdom, 41, 42, 297n56
United Nations, 23, 29, 43, 60, 100–101, 176
United Nations Committee on the Elimination of Racial Discrimination, 289n33
United States (US): American Community Survey, 57, 291nn82–83; arriving to, 46–58; Census, 42, 44, 57, 291n80; Chinese Exclusion Act, 42; Congress, 94, 290n70, 295n20; Constitution, 90, 109, 248; Declaration of Independence, 120, 130, 294n10; Department of State, 54, 90, 130; Executive Orders, 47, 57, 309n27; Founding Fathers, 90, 106, 109, 119, 121, 129, 248, 251; immigrant population, 42, *47*; immigration, 42, 43, 46, 72; imperial nostalgia, racial hierarchies and politics of inclusion in, 255–58; Iran and, 54, 90, 96, 179–80, 235, 256–57; Iranians today in, 56–58; Iranians with LPR status in, *51*; IRI and, 129–30, 180; as melting pot, 186, 304n20; Muslim Ban, 23–24, 57–58, 106, 110, 128–29, 235, 247, 257, 271; as "nation of immigrants," 85, 113, 135, 240, 267–68; neoliberal multiculturalism in, 31, 85, 111–13, 123, 132, 135, 239–40, 270; racial hierarchy in, 104, 109, 134, 233, 255–58, 260; refugees, 41, 43, 289n45; with sanctions against Iran, 287n70; Sweden, Canada and, 25–26; university students, 22, 38, 41, 47, 56. *See also* Los Angeles; New York
"Unity" press conference, Tirgan, 222
University of California, Los Angeles (UCLA), 52, 116

University of Southern California, 52, 116
University of Toronto, 2, 74, 76, 179–80, 182
U Thant, 101

Valanejad, Kurosh, 131–32
Vancouver, Canada, 23, 73, 74, 180, 181
Venmo, 293n131
violence, 5, 14, 54, 63, 214, 256; coercion, 82, 104; "Iranianness" and, 94; protests, 48, 287n69
Virginia, 22, 57
visibility, 16, 147, 184; hypervisibility, 4, 93; invisibility, 4–5, 93, 230, 273, 289n33
visible minorities, 44, 74, 289n33
volunteerism, 123, 199, 200, 239
volunteers, 29, 79, 238; Canada Mourns memorial, 182, 183; Eldfesten Committee meetings, 301n18; Eldfesten festival, 28, 157, 162, 173–74, 177, 242, 245; Farhang Förening, 169; Farhang Foundation, 117, 118, 244; Freedom Sculpture Committee, 119; HC, 187; Mehregan Festival of Autumn, 114; Nowruz festival, 298n97; Tirgan, 198, 201–9, *208*, 211, 214–16, 221, 225, 231, 232, 306n75; Tirgan Family, 243; Tirgan Festival, 1–2, 28, 33, 182–84, 189, 204, 207, 232, 242, 244, 245; training, 189, 239, 244; women, 274

War on Terror, 54
Washington, DC, 22, 39, 57, 89, 93, 294n2
Washington DC-Maryland-Virginia (DMV) area, 22, 57
*Washington Post* (newspaper), 109
wealth, 230, 247, 248, 253; freedom, dignity and, 132–35; philanthropy and, 231, 238–40, 262, 266, 298n100
Weinstein, Harvey, 213

Welcome Centre Immigration Services, Toronto, 79
welfare state, Sweden, 15, 45, 83–84
Westwood Nowruz Festival, LA, 114, *115*
whiteness, 15, 254–55, 258–60; discrimination and, 88, 110–11; *The Limits of Whiteness*, 256–57; racial hierarchies and, 104, 134, 233
white people, 4, 13, 57, 81, 110, 256. *See also* nonwhites
white supremacy, 256, 260
*Why Multiculturalism is Oppression*, 87
Williams, Pharrell, 108
WLF protests. *See* Women, Life, Freedom protests
women, 40, 57, 65, 132, 219, 274, 275; artists, 11–12, 14, 58–60, 62, 67; #MeToo, 210–17, 226, 243
Women, Life, Freedom (WLF) protests, 74, 78, 132, 218, 220–22, 243, 265
World War II, 42, 43
Wright, Matthew, 287n51

xenophobia, 86, 232, 276
Xenophon, 90, 98, 107, 127, 294n5

Yassaei, Mahshid, 211
Yonge Street, North York, 75, *76*
Yoshino, Kenji, 290n53
Yousefi, Pendar, 198
Yousefian, Bob, 55
YouTube, 142, 175, 292n123
Yuval-Davis, Nira, 10

*Zan-e-Ruz* (women's magazine), 36
Zerehi, Hassan, 75
Zerehi, Sima Sahar, 75
Zohreh (community organizer), 4–5, 33
Zoroastrianism, 95, 103, 164, 191, 234, 305n37

ABOUT THE AUTHOR

AMY MALEK is a sociocultural anthropologist specializing in the intersections of migration, citizenship, and culture. She is Associate Professor of Anthropology and American Studies at William & Mary.

www.ingramcontent.com/pod-product-compliance
Lightning Source LLC
Chambersburg PA
CBHW031138020426
42333CB00013B/431